D1562898

THE FATEFUL DISCOURSE
OF WORLDLY THINGS

The Fateful Discourse of Worldly Things

DAVID HALLIBURTON

Stanford University Press

Stanford, California 1997

Stanford University Press
Stanford, California

© 1997 by the Board of Trustees of the
Leland Stanford Junior University

Printed in the United States of America

CIP data are at the end of the book

Last date below indicates year of this printing:
06   05   04   03   02   01   00   99   98   97

For my family

Contents

THE FATEFUL DISCOURSE
OF WORLDLY THINGS

Beginning

The Fateful Discourse of Worldly Things began with the working title of Concrete Interpretation. A trial-run essay asked, "To what extent can the poetic thinking developed by Heidegger be complemented by a mode of interpretation that focuses on the relevance to literature of social, economic, and political concerns?" I had recently completed Poetic Thinking: An Approach to Heidegger, which traced that thinker's move beyond philosophy toward something between philosophy and poetry. Now it seemed time to address those other concerns, especially as much critical discourse was showing small regard for everyday human existence and action, for the facts of flesh and concrete experience.

Briefly stated, the aim of this first part of a planned two-volume study is to help reconstruct critical discourse, broadly defined, by exploring phenomena of the discursively mediated world, with emphasis on social, political, cultural, and what I call incorporate experience (discussed in Part IV). My project may be viewed as a grammar of the phenomena in that it deals with fundamental principles that underlie them. A companion volume, offering a rhetoric and a politics, will inquire into environment, memory, and acting, and into the relation of these to what we call learning. In this design I follow the lead of Kenneth Burke, who gave us *A Grammar of Motives* and then *A Rhetoric of Motives*.

My title comes from the French Renaissance poet Joachim du Bellay's *discours fatal des choses mondaines*, which Pater calls "that discourse about affairs which decides men's fates."[1] In French the first modifier points, like English *fatal*, to ending or cessation, but also to a culmination fateful in the sense of being full of moment, as in Dewey's concept of consummation, to which I will return in the pages that follow. Then there was the consideration that a discourse deciding fates, with possible overtones of predetermination, wasn't at all what I meant to take up. Thus I came to fateful, rather than fatal, discourse. As for the worldly things to be discussed, they are just that, the things of the everyday world as experienced and expressed.

Like Hannah Arendt in writing *The Human Condition*, and Kenneth Burke in writing *A Grammar of Motives* and *A Rhetoric of Motives*, I found in writing this portion of *The Fateful Discourse of Worldly Things* that matters of such scope, significance, and complexity led to far-ranging discussions longer than normal chapters. Admiring as I do almost everything in Arendt's and Burke's books, including their organization, I have organized my text into large parts with topical divisions into smaller parts. The idea of naming the large parts with gerunds derives from Dewey, who (as I explain more fully below) favors the ability of *-ing* words to suggest ongoing processes.

The present inquiry would follow Burke both in using all there is to use, and in adopting a variety of critical perspectives that are not quite anyone else's; which is a way of saying that Burke is a maverick. Mavericks as well are two other thinkers who have influenced this study, one conspicuously, the other subtly. The first is Charles Sanders Peirce, who, because he has so many kinds of good ideas, is all over my expository landscape. The other is Walter Benjamin, whom Arendt rightly credits with thinking poetically and crudely. Poetic thinking is what I believe Heidegger does, and is close in spirit to the thinking called crude. On this point Arendt (in *Men in Dark Times*) notes specific similarities between the two authors. Crude thinking, to use Bertolt Brecht's term for what he and Benjamin both did, brings theory to practice and involves the kind of worldly wisdom we find in "ordinary" language — for example, in proverbs.

If I say that using all there is to use really means using whatever makes a practical difference, I tip my pragmatist hand. But what, it may then be asked, is meant by that overdetermined adjective and its variants? Arthur O. Lovejoy believed he could distinguish no less than thirteen pragmatisms,[2] though a number of his distinctions are matters of terminology more than of substance.

For preliminary purposes William James, in his *Pragmatism* (1907), indicates pretty well what pragmatism, in a general sense, is all about: "The pragmatic method . . . is to try to interpret each notion by tracing its respective practical consequences. What difference would it practically make to anyone if this notion rather than that notion were true?" More than a predetermined technique or set of rules, pragmatism is "an attitude of orientation" that looks away from the formal categories of traditional metaphysics and epistemology "*towards last things, fruits, consequences, facts.*"[3]

The pragmatically oriented thinkers I draw upon most heavily are John Dewey, C. S. Peirce, William James, Justus Buchler, and George Herbert Mead. Kenneth Burke could be mentioned here as well to the extent that his "symbolic action" offers practical equipment for living. Much the same could be said of Emerson, whose thinking takes an increasingly pragmatic direction after his early idealist-humanist phase. Notwithstanding that Emerson criticism still stresses that phase, we find Emerson himself arguing for the primacy of action and the development of thought from action, rather than the other way around: "The preamble of thought, the transition through which it passes from the unconscious to the conscious, is action."[4]

My study happens to emerge during a pragmatist revival of sorts.[5] But it also happens that it does so in a context provided by European thinkers whose work in many instances I came to know earlier. Friedrich Nietzsche and Edmund Husserl are two cases in point. Jean-Paul Sartre and Maurice Merleau-Ponty are two others. All took my earlier thinking in a phenomenological direction, and the long-range effects will doubtless be apparent to the reader. The same reader will also note the influence in these pages of the broader hermeneutic tradition, which parallels the phenomenological tradition in so many ways. Here I must mention Martin Heidegger, Hans-Georg Gadamer, and Hannah Arendt, who have made the ideas of Greek and Roman antiquity accessible within the framework of the Western intellectual tradition.

Only much later did I come to realize the importance of the Italian rhetorical tradition, epitomized for my purposes by Giambattista Vico, in providing a corrective to Cartesian rationalism. Rationalism in a more general sense, as it shades into scientific thinking, produces in Alfred North Whitehead unifying concepts, such as concrescence, of which I make use. Jürgen Habermas's "communicative action," taking cues from Mead, Emile Durkheim, Husserl, and Talcott Parsons, *inter alia*, enters the discussion to show how science-based systems and social subsystems bid to take control of our everyday life-world (Husserl's *Lebenswelt*). From a different angle Stephen Toulmin both explains and demystifies systems and "the cult of systematicity," while Roland Barthes studies the quasi-religious authority invested in the modern phenomenon of the fashion system, and I draw upon these authors as well. Additionally, I discuss systems in both specific and general terms, and in relation to the educational scene.

My relation to all of these thinkers is so interwoven and complex that it is probably not helpful to spend the time it would take to unravel lines of descent and influences. It is easier to specify my debt in one important area, political philosophy, to which the orientation of the present inquiry has obliged me to pay increasing attention. Here I would mention first and foremost Hannah Arendt, to whose vision of humanity and polity I turn not only whenever I must but whenever I can; J. G. A. Pocock, who has demonstrated the importance of Machiavelli's reconstruction of civic republican discourse; and C. B. Macpherson, whose reading of Hobbes and Locke as founders of possessive individualism is from my perspective paradigmatic. As for Hobbes and Locke themselves, their roles in the present study are intended to be roughly proportionate to their roles in the history of Western thought. Feminists have recently brought attention to overlooked aspects of individualism. Among such feminists are Elizabeth Fox-Genovese and Gillian Brown, whose studies are complemented by scholars such as Carole Pateman and Melissa B. Butler. Steven Lukes's typology of seven major individualisms provides a useful background for these and other approaches.[6]

Part I of my study inquires into the phenomenon of Deweyan reconstruction and related developments in Western thought, drawing on methods and issues touched upon above. In the context of the present cultural moment, in which "theory" and "practice" tend to be valued in that order, I suggest that logically and actually practices precede theories, as both Dewey and Emerson propose. It is here that attention turns to the consequences of the rise of systems and systems discourse just noted, and to the interpretive methods of Sartre and René Girard, who are contrasted with Peirce, Buchler, and Kant, with particular reference to judgment and public communication. In the more explicitly political realm, the civil model developed by Hobbes and Locke, whose rationalism is conducive to system-making, is contrasted with Pater's efforts at imaginative reconstruction in *The Renaissance* and *Marius the Epicurean*, and with prophetic texts by Yeats in which he encounters both individualism and nature, finds neither to his liking, and proceeds to reconstruct the world in line with his own poetic system.

Part II takes its lead from the need to explain the model of the world of which I am making use. Among philosophers it is a need felt by the phenomenologically oriented, in particular, from Husserl to Sartre to Merleau-Ponty, and in social theory by Habermas and Niklas Luhmann, who both draw on but substantially modify Husserlian concepts, especially that of the life-world. Such thinkers have shown the relevance of questions along the lines of "What are the elements, aspects, principles, functions, and procedures of the social, political, economic, and cultural world, and how do they cohere? How, in short, is what we call the world constituted?" It is worth observing that Vico, in order to contest the Cartesian rush to analysis and dissection, had already asked many of the same questions.

Discussion of Husserl's foundational logic and Peirce's arguments for a triadic account of logic and being leads to consideration of world-making as consisting in the functions of *endowing, enabling*, and *entitling*. All of the terms have closely related senses. "Endow" signifies to provide, as with a bequest or gift, to invest with, to furnish. In the form of "endowment" this becomes "a gift, power, or other advantage with which a person is endowed by nature or fortune."[7] Drawing upon this nexus, endowing, in my usage, entails the provision of the basic "stuff" with which one is or has been supplied; that is, fundamental capacity or wherewithal. "Enabling" signifies "to authorize, sanction, empower" or "to supply with the requisite means or opportunities to an end or for an object." Enabling entails, in other words, whatever it takes to realize endowing. With "entitling," which derives from "right to possession," we enter the realm of "what ought to be, of what is just or right": "to give (a person or thing) a rightful claim to a possession, privilege, designation, mode of treatment, and so on." Entitling is then the process by which the preceding are adjudicated and assimilated into a larger context of perceived rightness or justice. This discussion is followed by consideration of political discourse, with emphasis on Jefferson in relation to slavery, Native Americans, the idea of measure in economic and sentimental spheres, and the construction of Manifest Destiny as reflected in texts by Walt Whitman and Robert Frost. Here as elsewhere (for example, in Part IV) I try to draw out the significance for my study of racial or ethnic issues.

Part III inquires into the "course" of discourse, starting with Cervantes, then moving on to the "discourse of reason" epitomized by Descartes, and the Platonic discursive practices in relation to the practices of such thinkers as Dewey, Emerson, Peirce, Rousseau, and Jefferson. An epochal consequence of Cartesian rationalism is the creation of *presentment*, a mode of representation wherein all things that exist in the world, insofar as they enter this mode, are reduced to the level of objectivity in relation to a perceiving, presenting subject. In this way the world becomes, to borrow Heidegger's phrase, a picture. Equally important in Cartesian practice is the analytical method, which proceeds by breaking phenomena down into supposedly minimal units, after which the philosopher has but to determine the mechanisms by which they operate. Notwithstanding his attempt to distance himself from the dangers of everyday living, Descartes in fact drew on it continually, as evidenced by his recourse to technological artifacts such as glass, and his use of "nonrational"

figurative language. The analytic method finds its most articulate early opponent in Vico, who proposes instead to trace, in ways that we now regard
as essentially historical, the means by which the world we experience came
about. Not only these terms but all means of communication come within the
purview of Peirce's triadic model of explanation, which distinguishes Firsts,
or qualities in themselves, from Seconds, or relations, and from Thirds, or
the consequences by which qualities are judged in relation to those consequences. Consequences are what Dewey terms "consummations," which are
most meaningful when what we generally speak of as experience takes the
shape of *an* experience, a shape acquired through interacting with the environment.

Again returning to the explicitly political, and to the origins of our terms
in antiquity, Plato conceives of only two kinds of discourse: the dialectical,
with its rationalist animus, and the dangerous, represented by the honeyed
muse of the poets. Plato ensures order not only by denouncing the latter but
by establishing his own form of measure, which consists in part in breaking
the polity into relatively small constitutive units. A similar idea appears in
Jefferson's call for organization into "little republics" or wards, small enough
for everyone to participate. The loss of such small-scale, local representative
units amounts to what Arendt calls the lost revolutionary tradition.

For Pater, order consists in large measure of the web wound through and
about us as natural creatures, tying us to cosmic processes, but constraining
our sense of freedom, and leading to a desire for renaissance and the sense of
new vitality that it brings. In *Marius the Epicurean* we see the case of someone
born too late for such a transformation. It is not surprising, then, that Pater
singles out in Rousseau a moment when the author sees himself as super-
annuated; but by this recognition he appreciates anew obligations and things,
which for the most part prove themselves to him affectively, not rationally as
in Descartes.

Regarding the title of the present study, it is suggested finally that a thing
may be any thing, from a material or "natural" entity or process to a human
conception or practice. In several languages a "thing" is defined as a gathering of persons, or the "things" with which they deal, and in English variously
signifies a matter of concern, a deed, an experience, or an expression.

Part IV deals with incorporating, the phenomenon of being "corporeal"
in a tangible world at once human and, for lack of a better term, natural. Assimilating Merleau-Ponty's idea of flesh as something more active, concrete,
and inclusive than body, I consider the consequences of Galileo's denaturing
of the world through the reduction of its primary physical qualities to secondary status. I go on to discuss how several modern authors—notably Hopkins,
Baudelaire, and Sartre—explore this phenomenon in their own anatomies,

and the manner in which Diderot's description of Rameau's nephew brings out the gestural worldliness of flesh. In our own period Rilke, one-time assistant to Rodin, explores the implications of sculpted figures in relation to their environment in general, and particularly in relation to the interplay between the environing air and the sculpture's surfaces. The ecphrastic tension between motion and immobility noted by virtually every writer in the "art object" tradition is taken up by Cernuda in his poem on Michelangelo's statue of David. Extending the same tradition, Rilke goes further, imagining with Rodin a work of art fairly modeled on the interaction of surface and air, and existing not only immediately but in a sense infinitely.

A contrast is drawn between Yeats's desire to escape nature, as in the Byzantium poems, and Hopkins, to whom nature is potentially regenerative; and between both poets and César Vallejo, for whom incorporate being embraces the artifacts made by human beings from the "materiality" of the earth, the nation of Peru from which he hails, all social and political practices, especially those that oppress the weak, and the earth itself. Vallejo's broadly conceived geopolitics is equally a geopoetics remarkable for its ability to bring things seemingly disparate into concrete interaction within a vision one can only call integrative.

Part V addresses the phenomena and modes of experience, especially as informed by Dewey's belief in the centrality of everyday doing and undergoing in relation to concrete environments. Experience is examined together with dialogue and dialectic, with particular reference to the dialectic of Hegel. Here it is argued that, whether in his theory of the interaction of quantity and quality in determining development, or in his comparison of Europe with the New World, Hegel, like Galileo and Descartes, and like the Plato disclosed by Gadamer, draws heavily on the lessons of everyday experience. Bertolt Brecht, who explicitly uses Hegel's concept of *Knotenpunkt*, or nodal point, works dialectical procedures into an experimental theater squarely aimed at social theatricality as a concrete experience. To deliver maximum effect, he creates a new genre, the *Lehrstück* (teaching play or didactic cantata), which is designed to be performed, one role after another, by the participants themselves (be they actors or members of workers' councils). The subsumption of participants becomes dangerous, however, when the force behind the process is, as here, authoritarian, for the principles to which the performers are obliged to submit are largely determined, at the time of Brecht's paradigmatic compositions in this genre, by his "hardline" political commitments.

This portion of the inquiry concludes with a kind of case study of representative experience, focusing on the ways in which the life of the Roman Lucretia is figured as the price that patriarchal leaders pay to found a non-tyrannical civil order. Machiavelli's largely antifeminine positions and strategies are compared to those of another Renaissance philosopher, Salutati, who makes some effort to approximate Lucretia's experience as Lucretia herself underwent it; this comparison is followed by discussions of her treatment at the hands of Shakespeare (who swings from convincing representation of her sacrifice from all sides of the matter, to set-piece descriptions that mainly serve to demonstrate his own poetic powers) and Chaucer, who sidesteps the issue of Lucretia's possible moral complicity that Shakespeare takes into account. In Christianizing Lucretia as he does, Chaucer looks back to the paradigmatic reader in that tradition, St. Augustine, who was the first to problematize Lucretia and to contrast her, to her disadvantage, with Christian female martyrs who died rather than surrender their honor. All of these authors deal in one way or another with the question of opportunity and occasion, as in Brutus's seizure of power at the instance of Lucretia's rape.

If the novel is the only fully "social" genre, as Arendt claims, a particular subgenre, the epistolary novel, is peculiarly effective in expressing experiential intensities. It does this in part by concentrating on personal experience at the moment when it gets expressed. Writers of epistolary fiction do not, however, present once-only narratives depicting a single series of events and feeling, but a reexperiencing of experiences already undergone, which by virtue of this fact are conducive to reflection. If this is especially the case in Richardson, it is also the case, though in a rather different way, in *The Sorrows of Young Werther*, which had the tragic and unforeseen consequence that young men all over Germany imitated the protagonist to the point not only of dressing like him but of killing themselves. Goethe hardly thought of Werther as a model, but Richardson thinks of his female protagonists as just that — as persons whose exemplarity is finally to become a moral force in society. Richardson represents both of his heroines, Pamela and Clarissa, as Lucretias pressed by male institutionalized power to serve its interest. Clarissa's case becomes tragic as the machinations of the offending male eventually go beyond the limits of what she can tolerate, even as through charity and other virtues she is herself becoming more godlike. Clarissa serves finally as an example of Mead's "social individual" who helps bring about a new social order in the process of disappearing from that very order, which for the most part continues in its established ways.

Let me close with a few remarks on the overall orientation of the pages that follow.

All experience, Peirce suggests, takes place in time conceived as sufficiently continuous to allow us to know and feel comprehendingly what is happening; otherwise there would be no way to tell that the event that is happening now is not the same event that happened a while ago; and there would be no place, for that matter, for *dis*continuity, which necessarily defines itself entirely in relation to continuity. The contrary office, the office of disconti- nuity, is discharged by Descartes, who sponsors the excessively exact, dualis- tic oppositions that are an anguish to the pragmatist's soul. Cartesian ratio- nalism would deny to a given sphere the possibility of interacting with any other given sphere. Hence the notion of a being that is extended in space and doesn't reason versus a being that is not extended in space and does reason. It is a matter of the analytical habit to which Vico offered an alternative by re- constructing in discourse the way things have come about historically, in the hope that through such reconstructing, edification would result. Not for Vico or the pragmatists the search for the exact and exacting commensurability be- tween, in Richard Rorty's phrase, philosophy and the mirror of nature.[8] That way lies the claim to infallibility that hovers in the background of system- atic doctrines and theories. Peirce identifies this attitude with the Ockhamites and contrasts it with his own "fallibilist" attitude, which considers that such settlement can be attained, if ever, only after a long effort at achieving more and better definiteness through the mediation of more and better conceptual approximations. Since I can neither improve upon nor adequately paraphrase Peirce's summary statement, I ask the reader's indulgence to quote it in full:

> Modern thought has been extravagantly Ockhamistic, owing to the acciden- tal circumstance that, at the revival of learning, the obscurantists, the fogeys, were adherents of Duns, of whom the politician Ockham was the typical opponent. But this had come about because, in those days of precise, if shal- low, thinking, the Scotistic doctrine had emerged triumphant from all the scholastic disputations, of which the reformers of learning had but the dim- mest idea. Get rid, thoughtful Reader, of the Ockhamistic prejudice of politi- cal partizenship [sic] that in thought, in being, and in development the in- definite is due to a degeneration from a primary state of perfect definiteness. The truth is rather on the side of the scholastic realists that the unsettled is the primal state, and that definiteness and determinateness are, in the large, approximations, developmentally, epistemologically, and metaphysically.[9]

The present text belongs, then, to the realist tradition, as thus defined.

In the hope that this study and its sequel will appeal not only to specialists in various fields but to readers with broad interests, I have focused as much as possible on primary texts; this means that in the case of Jefferson, let us say, I do not take on the enormous corpus of relevant scholarship, but have as- sumed that the reader will entertain broad arguments about his writings. Ac- cordingly, I have minimized notes, which with some exceptions are provided only for direct quotations, and by the same logic I employ wherever possible widely available texts. Unless otherwise indicated, translations are mine.

I should add that the overviews appearing at the beginning of each of the book's five parts are concise summaries of the main points in the pages that follow. If the brevity and condensation of these introductory efforts present a problem, the reader may wish to proceed directly to the main text.

Parts I and II revise and greatly expand upon, respectively, "Reconstructing Theory," *Comparative Criticism* 11, ed. E. S. Shaffer (1989), 71–95, and "Endowment, Enablement, and Entitlement: Toward a Theory of Constitution," in *Literature and the Question of Philosophy*, ed. Anthony J. Cascardi (Baltimore: Johns Hopkins University Press, 1987), 242–64. A very brief portion of Part II was published in *Virginia Woolf Miscellany* 30 (Spring 1988), 2–3, and appears here revised. "Dialectics of Experience: Brecht and the Theatre of Danger," in *Dialectic and Narrative*, ed. Thomas R. Flynn and Dalia Judovitz (Albany: State University of New York Press, 1989), 233–52, has been reduced in scope and assimilated to the argument of Part V. All of the remaining portions of Parts I, II, and V, which is to say most of them, and all of Parts III and IV appear here for the first time.

PART I

Reconstructing

1. Introductory Overview

Taking its point of departure from the pragmatist tradition and from political philosophy, Part I examines the theme of reconstructing, in a wide range of modes and texts. As here defined, reconstructing entails examining anew, from a broadly pragmatist perspective, the ways in which human beings act together to constitute a shared world.

Following a discussion of reconstructing tendencies in Dewey and James in the context of the current discursive marketplace, as well as changes in modes of production, especially those affecting education, I look for a grounding in what the dictionary tells us about practice and theory. Essentially, the polarities between these two concepts reflect particular changes in thinking and linguistic usage in the context of a more and more secularized and socially dynamic culture. The preliminary lesson I draw is that one can make a case for the overall primacy, in human affairs, of practice. Here Gadamer's reading of Aristotle is helpful, not least because he goes beyond the ambiguity in Aristotle's sense of practical philosophy by coming down on the side of practice rather than theory. I then suggest that the crude think-ing employed by Brecht and Benjamin works to the same end, which is why Benjamin can say that "crude thoughts . . . are nothing but the referral of theory to practice."

On the present critical scene, a certain sense of crisis hovers in the air, re-flecting at least in part a shift from the more or less traditional production of products to the contemporary production of productivity—what Lyotard calls "performativity." I suggest that with the rise to actual dominance of systems of all kinds, performativity shades into a pervasive "systematicity" (Toulmin's term for the quality epitomizing systems discourse) and "theo-rism" (my term for the contemporary overrating of theory). The ancient Greek *theor-ós*, originally signifying a spectator sent by a state to observe a sacred event or perform a sacred rite, cues the cultural prophecy of Barthes, who would demystify the virtual religiosity of the fashion system, or René Girard, who would reconstruct the origins of religion.

Dewey had already problematized theorism, or the overrating of theory, in concluding that the office of theory, in lagging behind science, had largely passed into hypothesis, which subsequently assumed a number of forms. As employed by Sartre, hypothesis creates a virtual history, whereas Girard em-ploys hypothesis to search for origins on a more scientific footing. Peircean hypothesis, by contrast, finds its worldliness in affect, in the way that infer-ence is signaled by nervous excitation. Such incorporate process is evinced in judgment. For the pragmatist, walking provides an instance by constituting a statement, as it were, of practical preferences: the walker judges one direc-tion to be preferable to another. To supplement this approach, I recall Kant's proposition that a judgment is not only something that *can* be communicated but something that *must* be communicated, and in public. Indeed, as the act of giving account, judgment is originally a political concept referring to the approval or censure with which Athenians reacted to their leaders. As I em-ploy the term here, communication is a means for achieving an end, which is neither stasis nor status but the final phase of an acting that is working toward consummation. The means-end relation issue in the present context is therefore generalized as: *interacting is the way (means) that the doing to be done (end) gets done (consummation).*

Before Dewey, Pater had undertaken a major reconstruction of his own, his *Renaissance* attesting that something momentously reconstructive is going on in history, in the cosmos, in one's very flesh. At the same time, I point out, the Renaissance relocation of artworks from public to private spaces fore-shadows the rise of individual consumption, which Pater legitimates on the view that *paideia* requires the development of individual sensibility.

For a wider perspective on the individual and individualism, I turn to the socioeconomic modeling of possessive individualism put forward by Macpherson. Focusing on Hobbes, we encounter the view that in language as in politics each worldly thing is one kind of thing, a material body, which is either in motion or motionless. A polity is then created additively, by the aggregation of bodies/individuals in support of some general representative. Discursive reason operates similarly, adding up or subtracting linguistic units or parts. Underlying the relation of parts both to each other and to a whole we discover the figure of synecdoche—the supreme political trope, since it conceives that one person, group, or class can stand as constituents of something larger even as the latter may stand for any and all constituents.

In the civil state reconstructed by Hobbes, man's worth is simply the price he can get from someone who would employ his labor. Whereas more traditional societies emphasized *quality*, *worth*, *use*, and *need*, the individualist order emphasizes *quantity*, *value*, *possession*, and *desire*. The acquisitiveness thus legitimized bespeaks the fear that the power now held by the individual will not be sufficient to secure him or her without the acquisition of more power. I conclude that for balance one should supplement the standard male and secular readings of both Hobbes and Locke by crediting the importance of the religious aspects in individualism, especially in Hobbes, and the extent to which both thinkers, when read from a feminist perspective, go some way toward restoring to Western political discourse the issues of gender in general and women's issues in particular.

In Yeats, who was challenged by the reconstructing and prophetic tendencies in Pater, a number of issues come together in ways relevant to the present study. It is to the same individualism that Yeats attributes modern selfishness and cultural disorder; he specifically blames Hobbes and Locke, the great modern revolutions, and the collective will represented in "certain great constructions" such as the British Empire. Yeats's antithetical and hierarchical disposition of time and art is evident in "Leda and the Swan," in which Leda is reconstructed as an enabling figure for the rebirth of history through sexual violence.

When Yeats imagines rebirth as a Second Coming, his paradigm seems to involve two types of discursive axes, one roughly natural, the other historical. But while the former appropriately turns through the seasons and cosmicity, the latter proves to be cyclical in much the same way that nature is. That Yeats's history remains naturalized may illustrate the manner in which, by identifying the civilized with the cyclical, poets reconstruct the world in Spenglerian terms.

Yeats's increasingly negative attitude toward humanity is illustrated by his play *Purgatory*, where purgatory becomes a space of time in which the principal character struggles to prevent regeneration: new birth would only mean perpetuating a marital misalliance symbolic of the present disorder of Irish culture.

Yeats's approach to reconstructing finally contrasts, I argue, with the approach taken by Pater. It is true that, like Yeats, Pater believes that the process of death and rebirth, having gone on countless times before, is cyclical; but Pater's attitude toward the future is one of relative serenity, whereas Yeats at times can barely conceal his rage at the passing of time. His is the dilemma of a man yearning to reconstruct the world on venerable principles but unable to find a satisfactory way of doing so. Notwithstanding his long involvement in public life, he does not, for example, articulate adequately the relation between the desired cultural new order and the state.

This contrasts with Pater's conception of rebirth, which is securely institutionalized, most notably in an imaginatively reconstructed church. I argue that the relative lack of any such foundation in Yeats helps to explain his valorization of individual sexual vitality as a response to the collective dissolution that is the fate of every age. I note that in the poem "Politics," a sexually laden text, the poet reassures himself of his virility by slyly proving that it is the girl standing nearby who commands his attention and not the political news. This playful poem exemplifies a feminized "rogue" element in Yeats, a deviation from a discursive system that would reconstruct in a manner too systematic for its own good.

2. "Reconstructing"

"Reconstruction," said John Dewey, "is a periodic need of life."[1] A quarter of a century later, after the First World War, he suggested, in *Reconstruction in Philosophy* (1920), that reconstructing the intellectual front was inevitable and laid out some directions to be taken. But after the experience of another war and another quarter century he forbore even to list all that remained to be done; it had become clear that thinkers would have to work a long time together before reconstruction could be realized. Reconstruction, both in its verb form and as a name for a historical phenomenon — the process of reassimilation of the Confederacy into the Union after the U.S. Civil War — illustrates a concept paradigmatic to Dewey and his fellow pragmatists, as well as to the Alfred North Whitehead of *Process and Reality* (1929): process becomes the revolutionary discovery of the age. The advantage of reconstructing, both as term and concept, is that it directs attention beyond mere process, which can become a fetish. Reconstructing is a continual re-collecting, re-examining, and re-building in which real doing gets done; in which there are genuine acts of achievement and times of closure, or, as Dewey would say, of consummation, which may then serve as bases for further reconstructing.

Dewey seems out of step in this age of high-speed rhetoric, when critical discourse is influenced by much the same quick packaging and recycling that drive other sectors of the market society. The pattern is conspicuous in the sector of society devoted to haute couture and its downpriced spinoffs, a sector whose practices Barthes unzips in *The Fashion System,* or in the collateral sector of musical production and consumption, where similar packaging and recycling loom large. In the confabulations of these sectors, each of which confusingly reflects the other, differentiae already marginal accelerate toward the infinitesimal, fashioning a feeling of variety that conceals combinatory mechanisms of remarkable poverty.

Now, ordinary redundancy is a fundamental dimension of discourse as of music, providing as it does a milieu from which communications, whether their mode is verbal or musical tonality, may emerge. By contrast, extraordinary redundancy, if one may term it so, is the qualitative state we experience when one audible blends echoically with another, the circumambience of Muzak being a case in point. It is to escape this contagion of sameness that the auditor-consumer submits, ironically, to ever new inoculations of the new, that is, to the familiar minimally modified. That even a condition such as this can yield notable art is demonstrated by Samuel Beckett, in whose corpus the discriminations of redundancy are wondrously (as Pater would say) fined down. According to the late actress Billie Whitelaw, a favorite of Beckett's, the creator of *Not I* was so attuned to the play's manic mouth that he would call for alterations in pauses so infinitesimal that no one else seemed able to perceive them.

The effect in question is far from being explained by mere absence of differences. The fashion system, for example, like all system discourse, has a warehouse of differentiae. The problem is that by coming onto the scene so rapidly and in such volume they blur into one another, each making its own attempt at being systematic and imperial—which is to say, its own way of being differently the same. In the postsecondary scene such ensembles have become, in Giles Gunn's words, "critical guilds" devoted to the "memorialization" of their founders and to the "colonization" of other areas of discourse.[2] It is all part of a game variously institutionalized by the educational credentialing system, by the weak market for jobs, and by the large number of outlets for critical discourse. It is equally a part of the game of heresy in which an individual or an ensemble compensates for feared sameness by positing it as a norm to be transgressed, the more theatrically as one secretly fears that the transgression may not turn out to count for much. But where anyone can play heretic who cannot play heresiarch, the glamor of the game wears thin: "In the currents of thought that have dominated us for a century, there is one tendency we must never forget: the fear of being regarded as naive or submissive, the desire to play at being the freest thinker—the most radical, etc. As long as you pander to this desire, you can make the modern intellectual say almost anything you like."[3]

In the discursive marketplace not ripeness but distinctiveness is all, and here again tempo enters in, for, given the competitive nature of the arena, each distinctiveness must be posited and represented, and the representations disseminated, as quickly as possible. The entire business is more like business than may be comfortable to admit. The hypostasis and speedy dissemination of distinctiveness really does call to mind Barthes's fashion system; contemporary commercial advertising; the fact that, within the academy as without, the locutions "buy" and "sell" have all but shouldered out "believe" and "persuade"; and the fact that the appeal of distinctiveness is not infrequently the mere appeal of newness. By contrast, William James, for all his innovating, claimed continuity with the past as much as difference from it. He gave *Pragmatism* (1907) the subtitle of *A New Name for Some Old Ways of Thinking*, dedicated the volume to the memory of J. S. Mill, and named as forerunners both Aristotle and Hume. It would not be difficult to show a similar pattern in the other pragmatists.

If the academy plays the role of mirror to society, which I think it mainly does, it should not be surprising that its mode of discursive production displays some or all of the same features as production elsewhere. The various ensembles derive much of their impetus, in any case, from a particular behavior associated with the postmodern, and one that it is no longer adequate to call mere productivity. For, unlike any before it that I know of, ours has been a society moving from the production of products to the production of productivity, then to the production, per se, of that performance for its own sake that Lyotard calls performativity. "If the performativity of the supposed social system is taken as the criterion of relevance (that is, when the perspective of systems theory is adopted), higher education becomes a subsystem of the social system, and the same performativity criterion is applied to each of these problems."[4] In education as in industry, performativity is increasingly institutionalized, as evidenced in the recent emergence of Total Quality Management (TQM) as a model for academic administration.

William James, recognizing the increasing importance of systems thinking, took his usual broad view:

> Human efforts are daily unifying the world more and more in definite systematic ways. We found postal, consular, commercial systems, all the parts

of which obey definite influences that propagate themselves within the system but not to facts outside of it. The result is innumerable little hangings-together of the world's parts within the larger hangings-together, little worlds, not only of discourse but of operation, within the larger universe. Each system exemplifies one type of grade of union, its parts being strong on that peculiar kind of relation, and the same part may figure in many different systems, as a man may hold various offices and belong to several clubs.[5]

Just such little hangings-together are the schools, movements, or groups of critics currently active on the academic scene, and such too are all the organizational units of the academy's administrative apparatus, not to mention its counterparts in business and industry. The problem for anyone who wishes to interpret or to intervene in these developments is how to shake these things up enough to sort them out. Thomas Jefferson's answer was the periodic revolution. William James's answer is to trace the activities and tendencies of any given hanging-together until you can extrapolate its consequences. If this was an outcome he believed in principle to be possible, he conceded that in practice it would be very hard to achieve. Dewey's answer is to take up Jefferson's proposal on a much more modest scale. In his introduction to *Reconstruction in Philosophy* (1948) he calls for "a Ministry of Disturbance, a regulated source of annoyance; a destroyer of routine; an underminer of complacency" (*MW* 12:263). Despite the novelty of the organizational trope, this is consonant with James's attitude toward theories: "Theories thus become instruments, not answers to enigmas, in which we can rest. We don't lie back upon them, we move forward, and, on occasion, make nature over again by their aid. Pragmatism unstiffens all our theories, limbers them up and sets each one at work."[6]

Doing what any of these voices call for is rendered difficult by the factors already adduced, and also because, under the influence of deconstruction in particular, the all-important question of means and ends can seem indefinitely deferrable. Initially, we may need to slow down and to step back, as Northrop Frye might say, the better to sort out from the discursive noise whatever there may be of discursive music, music's grayer name being message, intelligibility, communication. On the way lies the challenging task of examining extant discourses in their relations with one another, quite irrespective of whether the relations are presently explicit. Of principal concern is the relation between current debates in the humanities or social sciences and the discursive practices that may be gathered under the heading of systems discourse.

Skeptics may doubt that authors functioning as a self-absorbed elite have very much to do with faceless contributors to a discourse aimed at the masses. But the abstracting practices of the former are anything but opposed to the practices of the latter; indeed, abstraction appeals to the assimilative appetite of systems discourse, for which only concrete action is truly contestatory: movements against "systematicity" turn toward small-scale, participatory localism precisely because that is where such action seems most feasible.

Hegel would liken all the disparate bits of discourse to so many wheat straws lying on the ground, trivial one by one but adding up to a very definite stack when sufficiently accumulated; such adding-up, to be explored more fully in Part V, is what Hegel calls the nodal point (*Knotenpunkt*), the threshold at which a given quantum is qualitatively transformed.[7] To supplement this revolutionary script he considers the consequence of incremental, sheerly quantitative temperature change on the quality of water. Degree by degree, a decrease of temperature turns the aqueous medium for swimming into a frozen stratum for skating; while a like increase first turns the ice back into water, then turns the water into steam, which dissipates into nothing at all. The relevance of these narratives is that the bits of discourse too may eventually accumulate into something more significant than anything we now have. The end of the entire process might even prove to have been worked out *in* the process, an eventuality congenial to Dewey, who believed that the most stimulating thinking comes about in just this way. It may be through some such crisis—a transformation of quality arising through increments of quantity, as it were—that genuine reconstructing itself may come about.

Before this can happen we need to ask what it is that deserves to be reconstructed and how in particular theory relates to its streetwise in-law, practice.

3. Practice and Theory

As habitual or customary action, "practice" at the start of the sixteenth century bears already the important qualification, "action as distinguished from profession, theory, knowledge, etc." Like "theory" and "system" after it, "practice" soon branches into more "technical" spheres such as arts and crafts, then into business and the professions, and eventually applies to procedures in law courts (1623). Chronologically, "practice" succeeds "practic," which carries with it familiar meanings (e.g., "mode of action or operation") from Chaucer, among others. The gap between practice and theory is not a Renaissance development, however; the leading senses of "practic," while synonymous with "practice," already specify—and this as early as 1387—"practice as opposed to theory."

These meanings bespeak a practical need to sharpen distinctions concerning experience in a world not only increasingly secular but economically, politically, scientifically, and technologically dynamic to an unprecedented degree. If the realm of everyday activity had not been thus problematized, there would have been no occasion to specify distinctions for which it had never before been necessary to account.

Equally interesting are the distinctions specified by "theory," or a species of system; thus: "Systematic conception or statement of the principles of something; abstract knowledge, or the formulation of it" (1624). It may be surprising that this sense issues not from the philosopher's study but from the pen of Captain John Smith as he recalls his turbulent years in the Virginia colony. The systematic connection occurs as early as Hooker's *Ecclesiastical Polity*: "A conception or mental scheme of something to be done . . . a systematic statement of rules or principles to be followed" (1597).

Early seventeenth-century senses of sight or spectacle or mental view testify to affinities with the ancient Greek *theoria*, for viewing, contemplation, spectacle, or speculation, and to its religious origins. A *theorós* was a representative of a Greek *polis* who was sent to observe religious rites or to perform them. On the other hand, a *theor* was simply someone who traveled in order to see things. Eventually the specular relation that defines both roles became a hallmark of philosophy. This secularization, this movement away from the sacred observance to something more like worldly observation, is complemented in early Greek thought by the intertwining of theory and the more practical aspects of philosophy. *Epistēme, téchnē*, and even *theōría* itself all feed into the somewhat ambiguous phenomenon Gadamer translates as practical philosophy. In Aristotle's influential thinking each *hexis* or disposition — one toward the contemplative, the other toward the more practical pole — is deemed to be coequal, even though one, the disposition toward *theōría*, is thought to be somehow higher than the other. The elements of the paradox can be spelled out by syllogism, as follows. The orientation of *theōría* is toward immutable being and the orientation of practical philosophy toward mutable being; the former type of being is higher than the latter; therefore, theoretical philosophy is higher than practical philosophy. Nonetheless, Aristotle insists that "both dispositions of knowing and reason are something supreme. Practical reasonableness, phronesis, as well as theoretical reasonableness are 'bestnesses' [*aretai*]." Gadamer for his part concludes that "practice itself is the all-inclusive, distinctive characteristic of the human being. Thus, one must understand even theoretical activity as highest praxis."[8]

Differences in language and method aside, Brecht and Benjamin both finally emphasize what Gadamer emphasizes: in effect, ancient "practical philosophy" becomes the modern "crude thinking" (*das plumpe Denken*) named by Brecht, practiced by both Brecht and Benjamin, and described by Benjamin as "nothing but the referral of theory to practice." Such thinking shows a distinct family resemblance to the "prosaic wisdom" of the early Mikhail Bakhtin, who resisted all attempts to make the world and its interpretation systematic, grouping such attempts first under the term *theoretism*, then under the term *monologism*.[9]

I have brought these matters up to unstiffen our theories about theory and practice, and to suggest that at a minimum, practice rivals theory in importance. It will be further suggested in section 6 below that even Plato is more practically oriented than is commonly supposed.

The present argument, then, has followed a route from theory as observance to theory as observation, thence to *ethos* as the manner in which theory molds practical life. *Ethos* may now be considered in a further relevant aspect already implied in the sacral associations of *theorós* considered above. This aspect is prophecy.

4. Ethos and Prophecy

Dewey is typical of the tendency in pragmatism to underscore associations such as ethos and prophecy. In the *Ethics* of 1908 he observes, "The religious has always implied some relation of man's life to unseen powers or to the cosmos. The relation may be the social relation of kin or friend or companion, the political relation of subject to a sovereign, the cosmic relation of dependence, or that of seeking in the divine completer meaning or more perfect fulfillment for what is fragmentary and imperfect" (*MW* 5:182–83). The statement reveals the pragmatist concern with belief and conduct as they are intervolved in a universe no more the exclusive province of physics than of metaphysics. The intervolvement represented in Dewey's early call for "reconstruction in philosophy" may be even more to the point and is certainly more graphic. For the philosopher chooses to utter his call to a student organization with a religious orientation, explicitly tying reconstructing in philosophy to the controversy over the "higher criticism" that was then raging. Though the philosopher tells what will be and not what has been, Walter Benjamin would recognize in this occasion the performance of the storyteller's office, which is to balance the claims of news and wisdom—here, the news of the daily paper (to which Dewey pointedly refers) and the wisdom of the thinker thinking through aloud, in public, the larger meaning of this "intelligence from afar," to borrow Wordsworth's phrase.

René Girard's oeuvre reminds us that unresolved issues of a basic religious nature run through contemporary theoretical discourse like a seismic fault. At one extreme there is the influence of Heidegger's attempt to reconstruct the sacred as the holy, which can mean various things, including the epoch's lack of decision on the matter; that is, the epoch is "holy" in holding open a "space" that some *noumenon* may eventually come to "fill." A concern for the possibilities of religious revival may be seen to drive contemporary interest in

forgotten practices of female spirituality. At the same time one notes the persistence, over a wide spectrum of discourse, of an apocalyptic tenor of feeling
or thought, such as we find in much of Heidegger and some of Derrida. We
hear equally persistent rumblings over conflicting ways to contextualize and
in some sort evaluate the prophetic impulses, ideas, and ideals gathered under
the rubric of the American civil religion. And in Habermas's theory of communicative action, the force of binding validity claims turns out to be a sublimation of (here Durkheim's steps are audible) an originary sacred power.

Vatic offices may be filled in various ways. It has already been observed
that critical guilds try to memorialize their founders, who are themselves, or
through the notions others have of them, prophetic; and among guild members other prophetic ambitions may be expressed, if indeed the entire guild as
such is not already prophetic in orientation. Part of the process entails target-
ing a surrogate oracular site for a previously legitimized site, such as Delphi.
Lately Paris has served, as have Konstanz and New Haven, and in principle
there need be no end of such substitutions of the performative modes, each
highly individualized, that inhere in them. The overdetermination in which
these circumstances issue leaves it open as to which cenacle one ought to sup
in; but it may be worth remembering that an excess of "free choices" contributed to William James's "nervous breakdown." What has thereby evolved
is a sort of hysteresis, as Sartre calls the tendency of historical understanding to lag behind historical events: the hysteresis of a society yet sacralizing
in practice dimensions of existence long secularized in theory. I take this to
be one of the messages in the prophetic text Barthes calls *The Fashion System*. That Fashion is a false god does not make it any less a god-term, and
god-terms are sacralizing by definition. The Fashion text "constitutes a technique of opening the invisible, where one could almost rediscover, in secular
form, the sacred halo of divinatory texts." In a similar vein he suggests how
an analogy with something as sacralized as a liturgy can slide indistinguish-
ably into something as seemingly desacralized as a Fashion-serving theory:
"In their connoted aspect, weekend, spring, and the Riviera are 'scenes' in the
sense this would have in a liturgy, or better still, in a theory of fantasy; for, in
the end, it is a matter of absolute projections infinitely repeated and infinitely
evocative; the rhetorical activity of Fashion escapes time." [10]

Girard adds a dimension by filling another aspect of prophetic office,
which is the interpretation of Scripture. Thus, *Things Hidden Since the Foundation of the World* reexamines key biblical writings with a view toward reconstructing not only the role of sacrifice in the origin of religions generally,
but the destiny of a particular religion, nonviolent Christianity, in the modern world.

Suggestively, it is in 1595, squarely within the period of conceptual and linguistic negotiation between practice and theory, that the adjective *pro-phetic* appears. Deriving from medieval *prophecy*, the new modifier suggests a practical need to shift in directions at least potentially secular a capacity previously associated with strictly religious performance. One may surmise indeed that the overall turn toward secularization in the Renaissance is an enabling condition for the emergence of the vatic — this adjective having seen the light of day, in another remarkable coincidence of timing, only in 1594. The purport is after all to continue *mantikē* as best one can after its institutional foundations have been undermined. Although in the instance of 1594 that foundation is of course Judeo-Christian, the pattern as such has a familiar look; it is as if this Renaissance figure were to recapitulate the sojourn of the Neoplatonic prophets who were no longer organizational operatives (as in the days of the Delphic oracle) but relatively autonomous performers with new opportunities in roles molded long before.

5. From Deconstruction to Reconstructing

If Paul de Man is to be believed, deconstruction and what I call reconstructing are linked: "However negative it may sound, deconstruction implies the possibility of rebuilding."[11] Two problems immediately arise. One is that such rebuilding would necessarily be undertaken within the same system of infinite deferral of meaning, so that there could never be anything "new" to build with. Deconstruction, it seems to me, is more a matter of taking apart than of putting together, and to the extent that this is the case it continues the tradition of analysis and dissection. A second problem is the fact that for Peirce meanings, far from being indefinitely deferred, are arrived at all the time, just as beliefs are. Signs do signify, beliefs do get adopted. Derrida states: "The self-identity of the signified conceals itself unceasingly and is always on the move." But this is just what doesn't happen in Peirce. The signified in Peirce "does not 'conceal itself unceasingly,' but, on the contrary, produces itself progressively through the succession of signs or thoughts."[12] Where Derrida sees no closure at any time in the signifying chain, all kinds of closure occur in Peircean discourse, since otherwise there could be no new beginnings, that is, no further processes of signification.

Prophecy is as prophecy does. Which is another way of saying that the vatic office can be filled in various ways. Thus we find, on the one hand, a mode that Cornel West calls "progressive," which would include his own form of socially prophetic criticism, the feminist revisionism of Elaine Showalter, and Jim Merod's rethinking of the role of the critic in cultural politics. At the other end of the more or less political spectrum we find Allan Bloom's closing of the American mind, and Girard's cultural-anthropological investigation into the origins of religion. Derrida, who is not only prophetic but self-consciously so, presents a complex case requiring a closer examination than can be undertaken here. But we can consider the fact that deconstruction has tended to become preoccupied with its own real or putative distinctiveness. In contrast to the "progresssive" prophet, who is oppositional, the deconstructionst tends to be, or to enjoy appearing to be, transgressive. Opposition has of course its transgressive aspect, at least potentially. But opposition contests or subverts a recognizable other (in the case of left critics, it can be some version of reaction or just garden-variety liberalism) that opposes right back, as it were. Strictly speaking, transgression, by contrast, would violate "the bounds of legality or right . . . law, duty, or command" (late ME). These are the bounds of logocentrism, of course, but it is hard to violate bounds that Derrida himself has problematized in his reading of Peirce. Peirce is about as logocentric as you can get, and in just the way that Derrida would not wish him to be.

The main thing lacking in much transgressive discourse is something sacred enough to sin against. The violating gesture should be more sinful than eating too many sweets; breaking sumptuary laws would do, if our society had any worth mentioning. Which leaves transgressing for the sake of transgressing, on the assumption that whatever extreme proposition *can* be stated *should* be stated. But transgression for its own sake — like theory for its own sake — merely adds another layer to what has already been sedimented. In this connection let it be noted that transgression in the geological sense signifies "the spread of the sea over the land along a subsiding shore-line, producing an overlap by deposition of new strata upon old" (1882).

Excessive difference eventually passes into sameness, into a feeling that any position is as valid as any other. While such a view is defensible in the abstract, it is a pretty empty possibility. Ironically, one of the achievements of Derrida is to have strengthened possibility at the expense of probability. Under the animus of positivist science, the probable has enjoyed an alliance with the true, an alliance reinforced but also problematized by contemporary mathematical and logical systems, stochastic projections, and the like. Derrida challenges that alliance by proposing, for example, that Plato may be read as having in effect employed a certain word in a certain text whether or not it is actually to be found there. If space allowed I would argue that in practice Derrida often entertains the possible while proceeding on the basis of the probable. Later in the present discussion I will consider more concretely the relationship between possibility and probability in connection with a text by Yeats.

Derrida proves to be more useful when more concrete, as in a 1983 lecture on the state of the university. Here the traditional philosophical theme of the principle of reason leads to the examination of institutional practices.

It is not a matter simply of questions that one *formulates* while submitting oneself, as I am doing here, to the principle of reason, but also of preparing oneself thereby to transform the modes of writing, approaches to pedagogy, the procedures of academic exchange, the relation to languages, to other disciplines, to the institution in general, to its inside and its outside. . . . There is a double gesture here, a double postulation: to ensure professional competence and the most serious tradition of the university even while going as far as possible, theoretically and practically, in the most directly underground thinking about the abyss beneath the university.[13]

Through the abyss Derrida tropes the vaguely menacing implications of such academic practices as are co-opted by "multinational military-industrial complexes or techno-economic networks, or rather international technomilitary networks that are apparently multi- or trans-national in form."[14] The indissoluble relation of concrete to abstract is reconfirmed by the present inseparability of scientific research, technology, and the fundamental questions conventionally called philosophical: "One can no longer distinguish between technology on the one hand and theory, science and rationality on the other. . . . We can no longer—and this is finally what Heidegger calls on us to think through—we can no longer dissociate the principle of reason from the very idea of technology in the realm of their modernity."[15] From this it is unclear how far the called-for underground thinking can go toward a concrete problematizing of research; the term "gesture" bespeaks a degree of uncertainty underlined by "as far as possible." In any case the relevance of theory remains in force for Derrida even as it remains in question for Girard, a divergence that reveals the latter to be much closer than the former to the Deweyan position. At the same time, even while anticipating the Girardian preference for hypothesis over theory, Dewey anticipates the intervolvement of theory and practice, of the concrete and the abstract, attested to by Derrida. In considering the nature of modern "academic" research, moreover, Dewey offers something more than a gesture: "Scientific inquiry has raised activities, materials, tools, of the type once regarded as practical (in a low utilitarian sense) into itself; it has incorporated them into its own being. . . . Theory in formal statement also is as yet far behind theory in scientific practice. Theory in fact— that is, in the conduct of scientific inquiry—has lost ultimacy. Theories have passed into hypotheses" (*MW* 12:276).

Several points suggest themselves. When Dewey concludes that theory and practice proceed at different rates he is uttering a generality whose sources are evidently empirical: it was the case that then-contemporary science had assimilated practice into its inquiries at a pace faster than philosophy's ability to theorize that practice. This observation may be compared, to come to the second point, with the relation between inquiries and ends, a relation that

Dewey specifies in the following way: "The only situation in which knowing is fully stimulated is one in which the end is developed in the process of inquiry and testing" (*MW* 12:164). One can draw from this the inference that an end you happen to start out with won't necessarily be the one you conclude with. The processual character of the inquiry and the testing, in other words, are only the enabling conditions for attaining one's ends; and the same may be said of the processual character of assimilated practices, the difference being that end and process converge in a fully stimulated knowing while theory and practice, their counterparts in the previous formulation, do not.

Third, the philosopher, when he is not downplaying theory, endeavors to make it as active and practical as possible: "Theory is the cross-section of the given state of action in order to know the conduct that should be; practice is the realization of the idea thus gained; it is theory in action" (*EW* 3:109). Subsequently he makes it clear that everything comes down to consequence in the realm of experience: "An ounce of experience is better than a ton of theory simply because it is only in experience that any theory has vital and verifiable significance. An experience, a very humble experience, is capable of generating and carrying any amount of theory (or intellectual content), but a theory apart from experience cannot be definitely grasped even as theory" (*MW* 9:151). These remarks weave together three crucial assumptions about the preeminence of experience, Dewey's equivalent of what I have been calling practice: 1) only by experience can theory be tested; 2) experience is more generative than theory; 3) it is only through experience that theory can even be understood. Here Dewey anticipates, if in different terms, Wittgenstein's emphasis on experience in the *Philosophical Investigations*; the American thinker would have understood very well the problem of determining what is common to a variety of instances — that is, their susceptibility to theoretical reduction, such as the experience of willingly being guided on a playing field while blindfolded, of being led somewhere unwillingly, of being guided by a partner in a dance, of being taken for a walk, of following someone in conversation, or of following a path in the woods. To put it "mundanely," Dewey and Wittgenstein both reject the tacit philosophical disdain for worldly things, whose compelling claims form both the climax of the *Tractatus* and the structure of assumptions characterizing Dewey's thought overall.

6. Teaching, Learning, and Training

To this day the relevance of Dewey's turn to art as consummatory mode of experience, both in human terms and in relation to a redefined nature, is not well understood. The same applies to his recourse to technology and science, also redefined. Dewey was convinced that everything we use in pursuing every inquiry is essentially, in a broad sense, instrumental, and is therefore, again in a broad sense, a tool. After calling his method "instrumentalism" and then "experimentalism," he finally settled on "technology," thinking that this would indicate the pragmatic manner in which experimental, scientific inquiry actually works its way to consummation. Even Dewey's vision of education, with its emphasis on child-centered learning, is not particularly well understood, and the discussion that follows will attempt in a necessarily limited way to rectify that situation.[16]

The most institutionalized form of Dewey's educational approach is of course the Laboratory School of the University of Chicago, in the activities of which he was practically and deeply engaged. "Activities" is an indispensable key; for "the true centre of correlation of the school subjects is not science, nor literature, nor history, nor geography, but the child's own social activities" (*EW* 5:89). The way to learn history is not to stare at texts but to relive experiences: to reconstruct.

This means something very different, however, from the Collingwood "idea of history," which, impressive as it is in its own right, is a theory of historiography grounded in sympathetic identification with past lives through self-conscious mentation. For Dewey, by contrast, "the primary basis of education is in the child's powers at work along the same general constructive lines as those which have brought civilization into being" (*EW* 5:89–90). If "history" becomes "civilization" in the second passage, it is because history is too often overintellectualized and detached from concrete socioeconomic contexts, whereas "civilization" embraces precisely these even as it foregrounds the material institutions of the social order and its technologies as these help weave the fabric of everyday collective being.

It would be difficult to overestimate the importance of a reorientation toward educational practices — toward what and how learners learn and teachers teach. With such a statement the I. A. Richards of *Practical Criticism* would presumably concur, as would Robert Penn Warren and Cleanth Brooks, whose joint productions did so much to put New Criticism in the classroom where, at least on the secondary level of education, it remains to this day, reduced as its visibility may be. At present few scholars perceive a need for such a reorientation: the Derridean overture noted above, commendable as in many ways it is, represents a mere inching toward an involvement frontal enough and serious enough to reinvest the term "pragmatic" with its proper patrimony. But this is just what is needed, as occasional articles in publications like the *Times Higher Education Supplement* or the *Chronicle of Higher Education* remind us. Overall, the academy clings to abstract knowledge-based criteria as remote from questions of concrete practice as much musical theory is from music in performance. "Knowledge" may serve when we want to designate an entity, but "learning," "teaching," and "training" do a rather better job of suggesting *activities*. Fittingly, all these verbal nouns serve equally as participles or modifiers, which makes it harder to narrow or reify them as "knowledge" has been narrowed and reified. It is for this reason that I have entitled this part of my study *Reconstructing* rather than *Reconstruction*, and why I follow the same practice in the other parts as well.

To learn civilization (if you will), the first order of business is not to survey abstract principles. It is to engage in direct saying and doing: "Consequently the beginning is made with the child's expressive activities in dealing with the fundamental social materials — housing (carpentry), clothing (sewing), food (cooking). These *direct* modes of expression at once require the derived modes of expression, which bring out more distinctly the factors of social communication — speech, reading, drawing, moulding, modelling, etc." (*EW* 5:229-30). Theory in Dewey's usage is redolent of *theōría* in the old sense of the specular that is speculative because it will not or cannot act in the everyday world. Thus isolated, it may stockpile abstractions, but it can never put us in touch with the concrete processes that *are* that experience. The abstract knowledge of the specular curriculum is hardly better off, as suggested by the following passage in which "theory" may be substituted for the words in quotation marks with no loss of meaning:

> To take either "science" on one hand, or "history and literature" on the other, as the basis of correlation is psychologically to attempt the impossible task of getting a synthesis in terms of knowledge, when only action really unifies, and sociologically, it abstracts either *materials* or else *results*, neglecting, or relegating to a subsidiary position, the *process* which unites and explains both materials and outcome. (*EW* 5:230)

We have far to go before the implications of such a statement can be reconstructively applied. To examine the present state of theories about teaching, for example, is to confront rapidly recycled ideas with little to recommend them even in their original form: the redundancy in this genre is redolent of system discourse at its noisiest. And, if anything, the state of theories about learning is worse. "Learning theory" has become as much of a misnomer as "information theory." In fact information theory, as far as I can see, lacks a theory of information: even as its users issue protocols for transmitting it without really knowing what it is, learning or "developmental" theories categorize putative stages of development without sufficiently demonstrating why or how the stages occur. The problem is that exponents have been led on by a desire for a chartable sequence of growth stages analogous to those put forward by Lawrence Kohlberg in moral development and Jane Loevinger in ego development, a desire that has lured even so respectable a theorist as

Habermas. Such models are rarely if ever tested by hands-on practice. Dewey himself criticized the inadequacies of the specular aspects of classical Greek thinking without perhaps realizing the extent to which they were practical:

> The Greeks saw human intellectual efforts as directed not primarily at attaining assurance of some fact, but at reducing the extent to which human beings are left at the mercy of events that just happen, of fortune or *tuche*. What reduced human vulnerability to such events is intelligent foresight and control, which when organized into a teachable body of precise and universally applicable explanations constitutes *techne* or *episteme*.[17]

Aristotle believes in a fundamental disposition which, if properly inculcated, is intellectually enabling. Through the learned habituation that is *ethos* the learner's *praxis* is induced to enlargement, adjustment, and ethical refinement. *Praxis* thus conceived is consequent upon the training of *hexis*. Gadamer remarks that according to Aristotle "we are capable of cultivating in ourselves a constant disposition (*hexis*), so to speak, which enables us to obey our reason, the logos. This capacity too is human nature. Aristotle explicitly emphasizes that it is, when he characterizes the realm of *praxis* and *ethos*, which takes shape in habituation and habit, as specifically human."[18] If trained disposition is worldly for Aristotle, it is hardly less so for Plato, despite the common assumption that the latter places too much emphasis on mentation. Indeed, Gadamer notes, "Plato's entire *Republic* may be viewed as a program of training, leading not only, and not even primarily, to insight into what the good is, but to an inculcated disposition (*hexis, ethos*) to hold to the good in practice."[19]

By way of qualification, the merely habitual, if it is not subjected to judgment and reflection, can become a problem in its own right — one of those things "out there" in the world of contingency to which we are daily exposed. Habits become controlling, Dewey warns, and "unless we become aware of what they accomplish, and pass judgment upon the worth of the result, we do not control them" (*MW* 9:34–35). Some of the requisites for passing judgment will be taken up in section 8 below.

Although Dewey sometimes distinguishes education from training, at other times he seems to use the terms interchangeably. Moreover, in a variety of texts (for instance, *How We Think*) "training" is the key word; and in a major essay of 1908 he states that "one of the main offices of education is the training of mind." (*MW* 4:181). But if we follow Richard Rorty's lead in letting Dewey converse with Wittgenstein, the latter will suggest that there is something to be said for approaching educating in terms of training. An active participant in the Austrian school-reform movement, Wittgenstein, after six long years of teaching young village children, had learned to appreciate the importance of training: *Abrichtung* and its variants, signifying "training," are the terms he uses in the *Investigations* where almost any other author could be expected to use "education" or *Bildung*. This term has training, in any case, as one of its senses. Wittgenstein's schoolroom experience may also help to explain the opening scene of the *Investigations*, where a saint-to-be explains how, as a young learner, he came to understand words; or the preoccupation throughout the book with games. Somewhere along the line Wittgenstein had learned what Dewey, his nearest American counterpart, was to conclude: "To learn to be human involves learning how to play by rules. There are many early instances of this in the miniature games we play from peek-a-boo to knocking down towers of blocks. But the supreme game of course is language; it is the game of games, the one which opens up the avenues to all the rest of the culture's activities through education." [20]

A recent study (Baker and Hacker) of the *Philosophical Investigations* distinguishes between training and teaching, the former enjoying an enabling relation to the latter. That is, training needs to occur so that teaching can occur, a relation, I hasten to add, that does not reduce the efficacy of either gerund. Teaching, for Wittgenstein, facilitates explanations, which account for what goes on "within" a given language game without connecting this with the "outside" world of normal "reality." As higher-order operations, explanations, in being taught, "presuppose considerable knowledge (with us, acquired through drill and training) in order to get a grip. One can, by means of explanations, extend the nascent network of the learner's language, but only if it is there to be extended." [21]

Kenneth Burke, every bit as practical in his theories as Wittgenstein or Dewey, taught a course using a book on philosophies of education. To his surprise, when attention turned to the question of pedagogical practice raised by the various theories, the participants concluded that guided discussion, as employed by the Socratic dialogues, was the preferred model. In the same text Burke goes on to define the office of teaching in a manner broad enough to encompass the range of activities presently under consideration:

> Under "teach," besides the obvious main function of formal education, would fall in generally the institutionalized purveying of information (as with journalism). . . . Speculations in "pure theory" would seem best classifiable under this head; and here would fall those rare but necessary moments in which some few members of a society pause to examine critically the very assumptions or presuppositions on which that society is based. . . . Teaching has an implied function of government insofar as it inculcates values and attitudes that lead to corresponding modes of conduct. [22]

7. Systems

The questions raised in this section are germane for at least two reasons. First, there is a tendency toward the systematic in theory as such. Theory attempts to explain attributes of system functions such as equilibration, self-regulation, and autonomy. And at the same time actually existing systems, as in artificial-intelligence operations, make use of theories to maintain symmetry, equilibrium, and coherence. To say no more than this is already to have begun a little organon on systems, the social, economic, political, and cultural nexus in which so much of contemporary discourse is inextricably situated. Only by addressing this situation can the noise that presently surrounds and confounds us become articulate. What then is system?

In its first general senses, falling within the above-named period of negotiation between practice and theory, a *system* is a connected set of things forming a unity, a whole composed of parts, and the like (1638), a notion that through Locke spreads into physics, then into biology, and through Lyell into various scientific and technical applications. Well into the Enlightenment the term can signify any "formal definite or established scheme or method," building on the notion of a "comprehensive body of doctrines, conclusions, speculations, or theses" (1656). At the turn of the seventeenth century "system," like "theory," learns to stand without an article as "orderly arrangement or method; systematic form or order."

Such definitions as well as common usage take for granted that a system is constituted of units, that the units are susceptible to analysis, and that, when analyzed or "broken down," they can be reassembled into unity. The fuller implications of this analytic method will be taken up in Part III, "Discoursing." Here it suffices to observe that the more rational the system and the less complex the units that need to be managed, the greater the overall calculability and efficiency. In this way an epistemological and organizational model that is in fact highly specialized has spread into general use, whether in the practices and self-representations of contemporary systems in science and technology, business and industry, the media, education, or the proliferating discourses of systems. Perhaps the clearest message one gets from the latter is that systems are as overdetermined in fact as they are underdetermined in theory. The present discussion will in any case look into critical aspects of such overdetermination.

Systems were long thought of as sets of organized relations sustaining their own structures and united as parts within a whole. With Ludwig von Bertalanffy, attention turned to the means by which biological systems maintain equilibrium, rather by analogy with self-regulating feedback mechanisms, such as thermostats. In sociology Talcott Parsons's systems discourse emphasized that systems must adapt and operate in environments that are themselves complex and in flux; that is, they must learn to maintain their identities by maintaining their boundaries. Parsons's approach directly influenced the social theories and methodologies of Jürgen Habermas and Niklas Luhmann, though eventually the former took a formal-pragmatic path toward "communicative action" while the latter pursued a neo-evolutionary functionalism. Hermann Broch went further, and in a more positivist direction, in arguing for the primacy of cognition over art and the grounding not only of cognitive science but all formal systems in worldly experience. That the same experiential grounding underlies even the most abstract moments of Hegelian system-making will be argued in Part V. Of more immediate interest here is that Habermas, Luhmann, and Broch also employ as a point of departure the concept of the life-world. According to Husserl the *Lebenswelt* is the immediately given and common realm of concrete everyday experience. Ordinarily it is not something one talks and thinks about; it becomes something to talk and think about because of the ways in which it changes under that influence of Galilean science which is a focus of the present study. In remarking above on systems, Lyotard inquires into the effect of systems on social modes of performance and institutionalization that are aspects of the life-world. Habermas takes the further step of connecting this with our themes of possessive individualism:

> To the degree that the economic system subjects the life-forms of private households and the life conduct of consumers and employees to its imperatives, consumerism and possessive individualism, motives of performance, and competition gain the force to shape behavior. . . . When stripped of their ideological veils, the imperatives of autonomous subsystems make their way into the lifeworld from the outside — like colonial masters coming into a tribal society — and force a process of assimilation upon it.[23]

At the center of Stephen Toulmin's critique of systems is "the philosophical cult of systematicity" and its belief that conceptual change can be explained, not empirically and pragmatically, but by appeal to purely logical principles. On the contrary, he argues, "the intellectual content of any rational activity forms neither a single logical system, nor a temporal sequence of such systems. Rather it is an intellectual enterprise whose 'rationality' lies in the procedures governing its historical development and evolution."[24] Frege and Collingwood, failing to address the concretely historical aspects of change while at the same time assuming the primacy of rationality, cannot cope with the changes in question; and if the philosophers fall short, it is hardly surprising that those less professionally focused do the same. Thus Toulmin generalizes, "Whenever rational questions arise about conceptual change on the fundamental level, anyone who accepts these 'systematic' assumptions will be unable to tackle them."[25]

Toulmin deals with changes wrought in concepts, Lukács with changes wrought in production. But Lukács anticipates Toulmin in denying the system's own assumptions about itself, and by looking instead at the principle its practices obey. In accordance with the nature of the modern market society, this is "the principle of rationalization based on what can be calculated." What can be calculated then depends upon the analytic method, which, in minimizing quality, complexity, and history, emerges as sheer mechanism. In Lukács's words:

> The mechanical analysis of work-processes denotes a break with the organic, irrational and qualitatively determined unity of the product. Rationalisation in the sense of being able to predict with ever greater precision all the results to be achieved is only to be acquired by the exact breakdown of every complex into its elements and the study of the special laws governing production. Accordingly it must declare war on the organic manufacture of whole products based on the traditional amalgam of empirical experiences of work: rationalisation is unthinkable without specialisation.[26]

To get a feel for the things Lukács is investigating one could do worse than reread Adam Smith's famous description, in *The Wealth of Nations* (1776), of the eighteen separate operations required in the manufacture of pins, a description presenting the worker as a mechanized instrument in a mechanized system.

> As labour is progressively rationalised and mechanised his lack of will is reinforced by the way in which his activity becomes less and less active and more and more *contemplative*. The contemplative stance adopted towards a process mechanically conforming to fixed laws and enacted independently of man's consciousness and impervious to human intervention, i.e. a perfectly closed system, must likewise transform the basic categories of man's immediate attitude to the world; it reduces space and time to a common denominator and degrades time to the dimension of space.[27]

Since Lukács wrote the above, we have seen the accelerating development of an unprecedented complexity of organization with unprecedented flexibility and resourcefulness. The prevalence of such systems on every level of contemporary collective life hardly needs to be insisted upon. The issue arises in the present context because so many things combine in this "age of systems" to increase the distance between theories and practices. The abstracting tendency in theory—in itself, paradoxically, one of its great attractions—conduces to a supposition of autonomy vis-à-vis system discourse that the facts of the case do not justify. And the more autonomous theoreticians believe themselves to be, the more difficult it becomes to recognize for what they are the discursive practices that not only define the available store of information but determine its distribution to users. This is not to suggest that there is no "other" to system discourse, no alternative or contestatory voices. It is to suggest the possibility that such voices have yet to generate tropes or terminologies that system discourse cannot assimilate. It is fundamental to its unprecedented complexity, flexibility, and resourcefulness that it soaks up almost anything, and that the more it ingests the more complex and flexible and resourceful it is: contestatory words themselves become a resource. There nonetheless remains the possibility that other modes of discourse from other voices may already be invalidating the tentative generalization I have just made. Beyond the range of things such a generalization can cover at a given time there are other things that the next, more inclusive, and hence more accurate generalization will be in a better position to embrace.

I refer to developments on the "margins" of mainstream discourse, whether that discourse takes the form of scholarship or "popular culture" representations in the media. Especially conspicuous on those margins, and arguably more audible than ever, are members of racial or ethnic minorities, feminists, and gays and lesbians, who testify to pressures and oppressions not limited to but certainly including the types of degradation to which Lukács attests.

8. Judging

As promised above, attention now turns to the question of judging, which should not, I think, be overintellectualized. Judging is neither cerebral or transcendental; it is, like training in Wittgenstein, a practical matter all around. Peirce makes it clear that even something as esoteric-sounding as "hypothetic inference" entails corporeal perception in the most everyday sense of the term. The process goes something like this: faced with a situation in which any number of predicates might be attached to a given subject, one feels "a peculiar sensation belonging to the fact of thinking that each of these predicates inheres in the subject." Following this preliminary phase, the mode of judging that is hypothetic inference effects

> a single feeling of greater intensity, that belonging to the act of thinking the hypothetic conclusion. Now, when our nervous system is excited in a complicated way, there being a relation between the elements of the excitation, the result is a single harmonious disturbance which I call an emotion. Thus, the various sounds made by the instruments of an orchestra strike upon the ear, and the result is a peculiar musical emotion, quite distinct from the sounds themselves. This emotion is essentially the same thing as an hypothetic inference, and every hypothetic inference involves the formation of such an emotion. (2.643)

The philosopher is concerned to recover in inference the worldliness that abstract reasoning ignores. He asks: When you draw a hypothetic inference, what do you actually feel in the flesh? The interrogation of experience here reveals reason to be physiology as much as it is mentation. To put it another way, Peircean reason, unafraid of experience, offers a perceptual judgment all the more semiotic for being, in a sense of the term developed in Part IV, incorporate. Judging thus conceived does not follow experience but is itself experiential, even as judging does not follow perception but is itself perceptual.

In general a social act, judging is specifically an act of communication. Indeed, logic itself is "rooted in the social principle" (2.654), which, far from being an abstraction, is an everyday worldly activity operating through signs. Science, to put the matter as practically as possible, is particular scientists communicating with one another:

> The considerable numbers of the workers, and the singleness of heart with which . . . they cast their whole being into the service of science lead, of course, to their unreserved discussions with one another, to each being fully informed about the work of his neighbour, and availing himself of that neighbour's results; and thus in storming the stronghold of truth one mounts upon the shoulders of another who has to ordinary apprehension failed, but has in truth succeeded by virtue of the lessons of his failure. This is the veritable essence of science. It is in the memory of these concrete living gests that we gain the speaking portraiture of true science in all her life and beauty. (7.51)

By contrast, humanists for the most part work in an isolation that, by reinforcing already existing tendencies toward the specular, helps to perpetuate individual detachment. There are fortunate exceptions to the rule. One thinks of Dewey and Bentley, or of Deleuze and Guattari, and there are such organized learning communities as the Centre d'Etudes des Communications de Masse or the various groups Raymond Williams touches upon in his book *Communications*.

The judgments that all such undertakings habitually make, by whatever name, presuppose the concept of a *sensus communis*, signifying a faculty specifically shared among a plurality of acting persons: in the words of Kant, "the idea of a *public* sense, i.e., a critical faculty which in its reflective act takes account (*a priori*) of the mode of representation of everyone else, in order, *as it were*, to weight its judgment with the collective reason of mankind."[28]

Where learning is a prime concern, the crucial activity in judging is communicating, a theme that will be taken up at greater length in Part III. Though in all such situations the communicating will be human at a minimum, it need not be exclusively so; for, Justus Buchler suggests, nature too enjoys the capacity for intelligible utterance: "The ocean communicates its vastness; history and the history of one's own time communicate in the sense that they transmit symbols for proceptive assimilation. . . . The historian, the scientist generally speaking, interrogates nature (to use Kant's great metaphor) for what it *can* communicate."[29]

Although for Buchler communication is a mode of production, he suggests not that every judgment is a product but that "every product is a judgment. A judgment is a pronouncement: every product is a commentary on the proceiver's words as well as a faint image of the proceptive direction" (47). A proceiver is any individual viewed with respect to the interplay of that individual's "activities and dimensions" as they take this or that direction. "The term is designed to suggest a moving union of seeking and receiving, of forward propulsion and patient absorption" (4). In judgment so understood emphasis thus falls on the "ultimate function, status, and direction of human concretizations," or productive experience (48) — in short, on the realm of ends brought to issue early in the argument, and specifically insofar as that realm *becomes* the judging activity that bears on it.

Walking somewhere is an *active* judgment because the walker is making a choice of direction or goal. By contrast, *assertive* judgment is the kind that philosophers perform when they put forward a proposition in terms of truth or certainty. Different again is the *exhibitive* judgment produced through art, which "does not call primarily or at all for interpretation in terms of truth or falsity, nor for interpretation in terms of expediency or rightness in the pattern of conduct" (52). While Buchler adopts the perspective of the audience, it is also proper to look at the work of art from the standpoint of the artist. In so doing, one would observe, I think, that a good deal of active judgment is going on, or even that the artist's judgment is active per se, and possibly assertive as well, in order to be exhibitive in its emergence for and assimilation by the audience.

The importance of that emergence and that assimilation cannot be overemphasized, and for a reason that Kant, arguably the first explorer of judgment among the moderns, understands. The reason is that a judgment, to merit the name, must not only be communicable, it must actually *be* communicated. Inasmuch as communication requires community, the question of judgment becomes a concretely shared, experiential, and political question: "We may safely state that the external power which deprives man of the freedom to communicate his thoughts *publicly* also takes away his freedom to *think*, the only treasure left to us in our civic life and through which alone there may be a remedy against all evils of the present state of affairs."[30] Anyone on the lookout for idealist bias would expect the logic to run: If you can't think you can't speak. Remarkably, Kant says the reverse: If you can't speak you can't think; from which it equally follows that you can't judge if you can't

thetic criticism the first step towards seeing one's object as it really is, is to know one's own impression as it really is, to discriminate it, to realise it distinctly" (*R* xix). Possibly Pater accepts Arnold's premise about the need for independent, nonpartisan perception, however idealistic the premise may be; at the same time, in a less moralistic and more "scientific" vein, he recognizes the indissoluble interrelation of a thing and the experience of that thing. To realize for one's self is not to realize something selfish, it is to enable the fulfillment of the thing through one's agency; and it is after all the worldly thing itself that gets realized.

Pater's approach to realization does not stop with the impression but begins with it, and endeavors "to define beauty, not in the most abstract but in the most concrete terms possible" (*R* xix). Pater can therefore posit the reciprocity of the thing and the experience of the thing: "The esthetic critic, then, regards all the objects with which he has to do, all works of art, and the fairer forms of nature and human life, as powers or forces producing pleasurable sensations, each of a more or less peculiar or unique kind" (*R* xx). So much has been made of the sensations that the powers tend to get overlooked. Pater does not make that mistake, though he shares responsibility for it insofar as he sometimes dwells on the role of sensations, impressions, and the like. He makes these elaborations, however, because he sees them as educatively enabling: "Our education becomes complete in proportion as our susceptibility to these impressions increases in depth and variety" (*R* xx). The influence of both Arnold and Sainte-Beuve is apparent in this conception of the critic's educative responsibility, a responsibility that, while it necessarily has its private side, quite as necessarily requires the performance of a public role. Pater is writing, after all, for an audience, and this theme could hardly be a more public one. The closer he gets to it, moreover, the more it becomes necessary to distinguish between instances of isolated esthetic production and the greater instance of the cultural epoch he has chosen to study.

> The various forms of intellectual activity which together make up the culture of an age, move for the most part from different starting-points and by unconnected roads . . . of the producers themselves, each group is solitary, gaining what advantage or disadvantage there may be in intellectual isolation. . . . There come, however, from time to time, eras of more favourable conditions, in which the thoughts of men draw nearer together than is their wont, and the many interests of the intellectual world combine in one complete type of general culture. (*R* xxiii–xxiv)

In situating *Marius the Epicurean* (1885) Pater selects as another paradigmatic instance of integrated intellectual interests the time of Marcus Aurelius. Having done so, the challenge is to discover and delineate the active principle or "virtue" characterizing the individual, Marius, as a viaticum for experiencing the epoch's culture. Pater must somehow communicate in Marius the correlative of Wordsworthian virtue, "that strange, mystical sense of a life in natural things, and of man's life as a part of nature, drawing strength and colour and character from local influences, from the hills and streams, and from natural sights and sounds" (*R* xxii). That Pater is thinking in just these terms becomes clear in his description of the "sense of conscious powers external to ourselves" that has become a habit in Marius:

> The old-fashioned, partly puritanic awe, the power of which Wordsworth noted and valued so highly in a northern peasantry, had its counterpart in the feeling of the Roman lad, as he passed the spot, "touched of heaven," where the lightning had struck dead an aged labourer in the field: an upright stone, still with mouldering garlands about it, marked the place. He brought to that system of symbolic usages, and they in turn developed in him further, a great seriousness — an impressibility to the sacredness of time, or life and its events, and the circumstances of family fellowship; of such gifts to men as fire, water, the earth, from labour on which they live, really understood by him as gifts — a sense of religious responsibility in the reception of time.[32]

The endowment Pater calls "impressibility" anticipates the perceptual registers organized into an esthetic by the Impressionists; and the idea of impression may be implicit in the "Conclusion" of *The Renaissance*, with its emphasis on the sensuous experience of the moment. But impressibility is more than that, it is the very capacity for receptiveness to worldly things of every species and shape, from the history wrought in nature to the nature wrought in history. The awe Pater re-collects from Wordsworth is not, as might have been expected, nature as an ensemble of "objects or phenomena . . . of the earth itself, as contrasted with those of human civilization" (1662). The awe is in human beings engaged in their occupations, participating in a civilization not the less human for being based in natural cultivation, and within the constraints of their time and condition, makers of history. Which is to say that it is, as it were, in their nature, as something around them that is somehow also in themselves. Further, Pater, like Wordsworth, has an eye for nature-become-history: it is nature in the shape of lightning that kills the aged laborer in the field and it is nature in the shape of an upright stone that marks the spot; but the lightning and the stone, marking the existence of the man and of the spot in a space that is equally a spot in time, are by this marking historicized.

Far from operating in isolation, Marius's impressibility is oriented toward a specifically communal commemoration. For Pater reconstructs a more inclusive cultural space than is molded on the individual as such. Much as the domestic affects depicted by Wordsworth are enabled and nurtured by the centripetal power of both the nuclear and the extended family, which feels virtue as something embodied in household and earth, so are they enabled and nurtured for Marius in home and filial piety. Thus the religion of Numa is first of all a set of practices encompassed within the family circle: "The day of the 'little' or private *Ambarvalia* was come, to be celebrated by a single family for the welfare of all belonging to it, as the great college of the Arval Brothers officiated at Rome in the interest of the whole state" (*ME* 5).

Only on the basis of such continuity in experience can there develop those cultural patterns that give the stamp of typicality to a particular time. And it is only because such continuity enables recollecting and reconstructing that the critic can discern the overarching virtue in a culture or, on a smaller scale, the coherence that characterizes, for example, a school of painting. When Pater singles out the followers of Giorgione as constituting such a school, he indicates in effect a distinctive, more or less modern mode of worldly rendering directly relevant to the question of the individual in relation to the social, a relation to be taken up at length in the final pages of this study. This is the practice of detaching painted images from the fixity of the wall, of making them movable by mounting them in transportable frames. Paintings created in this way meet one of Pater's principal criteria of value, namely, educative power:

> He frames them by the hand of some skilful carver, so that people may move them readily and take with them where they go, as one might a poem in manuscript, or a musical instrument, to be used, at will, as a means of self-education, stimulus or solace, coming like an animated present, from one's cabinet, to enrich the air as with some choice aroma, and, like persons, live with us, for a day or a lifetime. (*R* 111)

This removal from public spaces to private ones, enabling the consumption of the enframed images in conditions of relative intimacy, is one among several features prepared for by the kinship of early capitalism and Protestantism, connected with the rise of possessive individualism, and reaching its first full expression in Hobbes and Locke, to whom I will turn below. The painter who helped make this possible lives for posterity as "the inventor of *genre*, of those easily movable pictures which serve neither for uses of devotion, nor of allegorical or historic teaching—little groups of real men and women, amid congruous furniture or landscape—morsels of actual life, conversation or music or play, but refined upon or idealised, till they come to seem like glimpses of life from afar" (*R* 110–11). So distance remains after all; yet the one at issue here is just the one that the individual user of a work of art does not want closed. For precisely this quality of the ideal presents the individual with a possibly better world. It is not for nothing that Pater finds in Christianity an interanimation of the "spiritual" and the "physical." Through stained glass and statues, through organ tones and spoken words, the cathedral, church, or chapel puts the believer in temporary proximity to something more than daily doings. In any event, the "freeing" of the artwork for individual possession is an enabling condition for that consumption of worldly things as esthetic objects that comes to characterize modern individualism. This consumption is particularly well suited to the theory and practice of the individualism whose paradigmatic mode is possession.

The legitimation of this consumption occurs in Pater's treatment of the Cyrenaic tendencies of Marius, whose guiding light is an ideal of teaching and training enabled by a capacity for reception:

> With this view he would demand culture, *paideia*, as the Cyrenaics said, or, in other words, a wide, a completed, education — an education partly negative, as ascertaining the true limits of man's capacities, but for the most part positive, and directed especially to the expansion and refinement of the power of reception; of those powers, above all, which are immediately relative to fleeting phenomena, the powers of emotion and sense. (*ME* 104)

The setting for the educational exercise is the individual sensorium and sensibility, the inwardness of which is a correlative of the type of private space that comes about in the Renaissance as artists, under patronage, create works to be owned by private individuals and displayed in venues owned by those individuals. Inward delectation is already a value in the New Cyrenaicism, where Pater explains that Marius's pensiveness exists "quite independently of the general habits of that pensive age" (*ME* 104). The pensive individual savors the sequestered moment of solitude, a moment endowed with a susceptibility to being recollected and hence reconstructed. As a temporal economy, this "state of reminiscence" is a kind of pre-living of posterity:

> Amid his eager grasping at the sensation, the consciousness, of the present, he had come to see that, after all, the main point of economy in the conduct of the present, was the question: — How will it look to me, at what shall I value it, this day next year? — that in any given day or month one's main concern was its impression for the memory. (*ME* 104)

Such posterity-in-reminiscence is for those who experience the moment alone. The solipsist tendency in Pater, while not always manifest, is strong: "We are never to get beyond the walls of the closely shut cell of one's personality." When Marius credits the help he has received from others, it is because this facilitated his own "pleasurable apprehension of art, of nature, or of life" (*ME* 109).

It is not that Pater's protagonist is selfish, it is just that he is that highly recognizable creature we see in modern fiction as well as in modern history:

the individual. Pater's vision is impressively and impressionistically a vision of the individual in historical epochs—the Roman Empire, the Renaissance, the Victorian present—each of which turns out to be, beneath their varied vestments, an age of individualism.

10. *Individuals and Individualism*

The prevalence of individualism in this our modern age is a commonplace, and the individual as term and concept is a vested interest of our culture. But there is no obvious consensus as to when individualism began nor is there much clarity over its essential attributes. It has been argued that even so early a figure as Boccacio moved in the direction of individualism: "Boccacian sovereignty is always rooted in the excessive self-centeredness of the Boccacian individual. This individual is the prototype for the Machiavellian and the Hobbesian conception of man, which radically transformed the relation of individual and community in the West."[33] But in exploring the claims for the emergence in the twelfth century of a proto-modern sense of individuality, Caroline Walker Bynum sounds a cautionary note. This is a time in which various new types of group and social role-playing are emerging simultaneously and competitively. Further, in the then prevailing studies of dialectic the individual as *individuum* did not signify a self exclusive or unique, a being possessed of infinite potential for discrete development. On the contrary, citizens of twelfth-century groups, classes, and polities "regarded the discovery of *homo interior*, or *se ipsum*, as the discovery within oneself of human nature made in the image of God—an *imago Dei* that is the same for all human beings."[34] Feeling and thinking take their direction from, and hence are disposed toward, deity; in the religious callings and orders wherein selves, conceived as instances of a universality divinely designed, converge in concrete modes of social organization, the same processes of direction and disposition may be discerned.

In this as in yet more traditional societies, a binding commonality enables the articulation of offices, functions, and responsibilities, now in cooperative modes, now in competitive ones. Doubtless the rationale of differentiation prevailing in societies takes for granted the individuation of the person as a kind of ontological and epistemological datum: by the *principium individuationis*, no one entity occupies the selfsame space occupied by another such, nor exists in another's selfsame time. Individuation does not become individuality in the social, political, economic, and cultural senses of the term until the assumptions and practices of the modern market society have become second nature. Stated a little differently, persons in earlier, nonindividualist societies have particular names and identities but they do not make a virtue of their alienation as individuals from other alienated individuals.

Societies of the earlier type, based largely on inherited status, bound by sets of time-honored traditions, and resistant to the rationalizing that is a part of the "human nature" noted above, differ profoundly from simple market societies and possessive market societies. In a more status-oriented traditional society, as Macpherson points out, work is authoritatively allocated, the process of allocation being enforced by tradition, which is to say by custom, or by positive law, or by both.[35] Further, allocations are essentially fixed, and rewards are conferred along lines determined by a dominant stratum of community consensus. While land may be worked privately, private ownership is a kind of concession, on the understanding that in the long run obligations to a community, to a superior personage, or to the state take precedence. Finally, the entire work force of such a society is tied either to the will of superiors, to allocated performances, or to land.

No such authoritative allocation occurs in the simple market society, which permits its members to work where opportunity offers. Though contracts are authoritatively defined and enforced, there is no authoritatively allocated system of rewards. All members of this society follow a rationale of individual benefit and seek the most they can get from the utilization of their skills, energies, and goods. And finally, they possess land or some other resource from which to earn their living.

Individuality is far more prominent in the simple market society than in a status society. In the absence of traditional modes of collective authorization, individuals become their own authorities to the extent of attempting to exploit their opportunities as they see fit, and close connections to the working life of the society as a whole weaken. Labor performed in this society results in products exchanged one for the other. That is, labor is not exchanged in itself, as in the fully competitive or possessive market society, but only in the form of objects produced. The direct exchange of labor means that someone converts more of another's power than the other converts of his: the differential of this surplus is the very reason for exchanging labor at all. But in the simple market society, "If there are some men who want more than they have, who want to increase the amount of satisfactions they enjoy, they can do so by exerting more energy or skill and so producing more and getting more in exchange. But in doing so they are still not converting more of the powers of others to their use than others are converting of theirs."[36]

In a possessive market society, of the type that took shape in England in the seventeenth century, the same characteristics may be found that are found in the simple market society. There also appears a matrix of additional features, not all of which are exclusive to this type of society, but all of which are exclusive to it when combined. These are: that some individuals are better endowed (whether with resources, energies, or skills); that all individuals want more than they have; that all own land or other resources, which are alienable; and especially important, that the capacity to labor is the property of the individual and is alienable. The importance of being the owner of one's self consists in the fact that it enables the defining not only of power itself, but of the entitlements or rights that exist in relation to power. In Macpherson's words,

> the original seventeenth-century individualism contained the central difficulty, which lay in its possessive quality. Its possessive quality is found in its conception of the individual as essentially the proprietor of his own person or capacities, owing nothing to society for them. The individual was seen neither as a moral whole, nor as part of a larger social whole, but as owner of himself. . . . Society becomes a lot of free equal individuals related to each other as proprietors of their own capacities and of what they have acquired by their exercise. Society consists of relations of exchange between proprietors.[37]

To compete successfully in such a society is, as noted above, to convert to your use more of another's similar power than the other converts of yours. Without this differential there would be, for example, no capitalism and no classes. To benefit from this differential, the entrepreneur expends capital in competition with other entrepreneurs, necessitating, in order to gain or to keep an edge, greater efficiency in modes of production. This means expending more capital for more efficiency, the higher efficiency permitting increased population needing to sell its labor. Unable to produce independently, these individuals who own themselves as labor and labor themselves as owned cannot command a wage equal to the wage they would earn if they produced from their own capital or land. When the owner of land or capital then pays them less, he can keep the difference which falls to him because the extra he does not offer in wages remains in his possession.

Resentment over unequal allocations of rewards reflects the tension between a supposed inherent equality among individuals and the actual inequality of the market system. "A market society generates class differentiation in effective rights and rationality, yet requires for its justification a postulate of equal natural rights and rationality."[38] In this system of theorizing, the paradigm instance of the sovereign individual is the professionally oriented individual who is "the author." The advent of the concept of the author "constitutes the privileged moment of individualization in the history of ideas, knowledge, literature, philosophy, and the sciences. Even today, when we reconstruct the history of a concept, literary genre, or school of philosophy, such categories seem relatively weak, secondary, and superimposed scansions in comparison with the solid and fundamental unit of the author and the work."[39]

As author, Hobbes makes it clear that his views on discourse are indissociable from his vision of the presocial "natural condition," in which "the life of man is solitary, poore, nasty, brutish, and short."[40] Here strife reigns supreme, and discourse fits this deplorable state by being deplorably ambiguous and lacking any mark of hierarchy: the same words might mean this or they might mean that.

Figurative usages endanger understanding and judgment. Metaphor confuses, according to Hobbes, because it belongs to a world naturally rather than socially constituted, a world whose occupants claim identical rights in being possessed of identical acquisitiveness. Metaphor permits meaning to be transferred irresponsibly from one discursive locus to another. To overcome this condition, reason makes discourse good that it may be better. Ordinary words — words not yet made perspicuous — are no better than metaphor; they are entities of a realm in which no one knows how to reckon — and only by reckoning can words be made clear and discourse rational. To reckon is to add up by a rational accounting the value of all words, and all their combinations, according to exact definitions: words are units of signifying convenience, like coins, which carry an assigned value translatable into "real" worldly things; meaning is something you exchange.

For Hobbes, reckoning and number belong to the concrete realm of worldly things to which discourse itself belongs. The prospéct of pure intelligibility that opens before him discloses its continuity with science simply because it is indissociable from number:

> So that without words, there is no possibility of reckoning of Number; much less of Magnitudes, of Swiftnesse, of Force, and other things, the reckoning whereof are necessary to the being, or well-being, of man-kind. . . . So that in the right Definition of Names, lyes the first use of Speech, which is the acquisition of Science. (*L* 104–6)

This belief in the primacy of words suggests the degree to which Hobbes remains to one side of a disposition in modern thought, from Leibniz on, toward systems of numerical, ultimately machinable, notation. He belongs wholeheartedly, nonetheless, to the party of science, seeing in Galilean *scientia* a privileged source of well-nigh apodictic certainty. In Galileo, to whom Hobbes pays a memorable visit, the very constitution of worldly things is revealed. The world is seen to be so many bodies moving, though it is not until his journey homeward that Hobbes, on horseback, receives the full gospel of inertia: now motion takes dominion everywhere, is not merely the medium of intellection but the very ground of the intelligible, the one and only universal and the *mathesis* of the mundane.

Philosophy has a venerable peripatetic tradition. In Hobbes's own time Descartes weaves motifs of movement throughout his discourse. Rousseau will later hold forth on the reveries made possible by the promenade; while Montaigne, meditating on the passage of worldly things, can write: "The world is but a perennial movement. All things in it are in constant motion— the earth, the rocks of the Caucasus, the pyramids of Egypt—both with the common motion and with their own. Stability itself is nothing but a more languid motion. . . . I do not portray being: I portray passing."[41] Montaigne reconstructs a post-Copernican experience. The sometime mayor of Bordeaux never saw with his own eyes the oscillations of the earth or the pyramids of Egypt. Nor in our everyday sense of perception did Copernicus observe them; rather, he proved their actuality by their necessity. With this access to the invisible, which in itself never comes to sight but exists in a mode of virtuality, commonplaces about mutability both gain and lose force. They gain because through the new perception they acquire a certain added resonance. They lose because somehow that very resonance exceeds what the received wisdom is prepared to give. So Montaigne takes the course of re-constructing, which requires collecting and memorializing, weaving into his discourse the same kinds of commonplaces, proverbs, or maxims that were to be a perpetual endowment for Benjamin and Brecht and their "crude thinking."

Hobbes's reconstructing is as radical in its own way as Galileo's or Plato's, for in Hobbes all things are shown to be finally only one sort of thing, bodies, and the one thing they do (rest being merely the temporary absence of motion) is move. It is the fate of all such bodies, when they are human, to possess some power and to want more, the greatest power being the collective power attained when many bodies allow some single body to represent them. Put a little differently, numerous individuals build a commonwealth by adding themselves up to a total of one. The same principle applies to any activity entailing discourse of reason:

> When a man *Reasoneth*, he does nothing else but conceive a summe totall, from *Addition* of parcels; or conceive a Remainder, from *Subtraction* of one summe from another: which (if it be done by Words,) is conceiving of the consequence of the names of all the parts, to the name of the other part, to the name of the whole; or from the names of the whole and one part, to the name of the other part. . . .
>
> [The process of adding up to a sum total, or of subtracting from the same, applies not only to numbers but to all manner of things that can be added together, and taken one out of another.] For as Arithmeticians teach to adde and subtract in *numbers*. . . . Writers of Politiques, adde together *Pactions*,

to find mens *duties*; and Lawyers, *Lawes* and *facts*, to find what is *right* and *wrong* in the actions of private men. In summe, in what matter soever there is place for *addition* and *subtraction*, there also is place for *Reason*; and where these have no place, there *Reason* has nothing at all to do. (*L* 110–11)

Whatever the adding together adds up to, it is a given that all the parts are alike as to power and desire. The relation here employed is that of synecdoche, the supreme political figure, entailing representation in the sense of standing for, as, for example, a class of society, or a group within a class, or an individual delegated by some collectivity, may stand for some larger corporate entity, itself representative in terms of the class, group, or individual. *Leviathan* is such adding together of numerous persons as will compact them into governance by a smaller number bound by that very adding together.

The secret of synecdoche, to take a cue from Kenneth Burke, is the principle of convertibility.[42] If whole can be figured as part, part as whole, the power in the relation can be concentrated, in principle, now in the one, now in the other. What particularly attracts Hobbes is the process of representation in which the concentration of power in a simple part (a single individual) takes its authority from the many persons represented in that concentration by virtue of their having combined themselves — added themselves up — to a "sum" embodied in a single sovereign. Convertibility thus consists in a practical reversibility, the first tenet of which is that each single part, or single "author" of the sovereign's total "authority," is essentially like any other. This obviously applies equally to the sovereign, so that the process in which the many endowed the one with the power to represent them can be reversed; free to reconstruct, they may envision and enable an alternative polity more in keeping both with their altering desire for power and with their altering actual power. Hence the elasticity of the Hobbesian vision, for the same argument that can be used to support one or another species of arbitrary, authoritarian, or centralized power, as in a monarchy, can be used to support, as in a commonwealth, a more balanced, distributive, and popularly representative power. The power required to overcome the natural condition of combativeness persists as long as individuals would enlarge their own power at the expense of others. Such power can come into being only with the constitution of a civil state, and only with such constitution do justice and propriety begin, including the condition of being owned or the fact of owning, or the right to such owning; a particular character or individuality; and rightness or conformity with rule or principle.

Finally, I would remark that little if any notice has been taken of the relation between theorism — the proliferation of untested theoretical strategies and models — and individualism. As theories spin off in directions and ways

other worldly things — or (to foreground agency) it is the place where actors exchange such things by means of negotiation. Though the discursive dimension of buying and selling tends to be downplayed by political economists, it should be observed that the marketplace is a talking place, and a scene in a drama. On its stage actors inhabit for a time a privileged realm of concentrated engagement. It is a world of its own, paradoxically, to the extent that there always exists another, encompassing world with which it is never identical but of which it is always synecdochically a part. A market is a world, not *the* world. The sense of being related in this way to something greater throws into relief what is particular about this place and its processes; for example, that other places are communal but no other is communal in just this way.

The concentration to which I allude is to an important extent a reflection of scale, which in the early model tends to be relatively small, so that there exist a great many markets, an overall view of which is hard to come by; whereas in the modern market system an overview is a more feasible objective because activities are consolidated into fewer, larger venues. To say that the old market is the right size for conversation is to say that it is the wrong size for commerce, a Renaissance development in which the concept of buying and selling commodities as such soon gives rise to the process of doing so on a large scale between regions and countries, a change suggesting among other things the increasing importance of the nation-state.

To go to market is to negotiate prices, and all prices are in modern parlance representations. But what and how they represent changes drastically as you move from the exchange of things for money in order to get more things, to the "capitalist" model in which things are acquired for money in order to acquire more money. Anyone familiar with Marx will recall his discussion, in *Capital*, of the difference between C-M-C, or selling a commodity to obtain another commodity, and M-C-M, or buying a commodity in order to obtain more money. If price obviously enters both types of transaction, it does so in very different ways. Now, price in the earlier model is as much a representation as price in the Hobbesian or Marxist model. The early term *worth* in Old English signifies what a thing is in relation to what one is willing to pay for it. By the Middle Ages, the foundation already entailed in the earlier term is specified: "the relative value of a thing in respect of its qualities or of the estimation in which it is held." Though here again we must question the insertion of value, the definition properly identifies the foundation as the *qualitative* basis on which the quantum of price is determined. Price may be quantitative, but different approaches to quantity entail different relations to quality.

Consider the approach of Hobbes, who substitutes for the customary conception of the market a synecdoche of society as a whole: the marketplace is simply a particular setting in which occurs the general practice of buying and selling at a price. But even more to the point, what is quantified in price undergoes a fateful—one might say, more precisely, a revolutionary—transformation. In a stroke worth passes into value (still confusingly called worth); value is disclosed as price; and price is the value determined, not for the things a human being needs or wants, but *for that human being*: "The *value*, or WORTH of a man, is as of all other things, his Price; that is to say, so much as would be given for the use of his Power; and therefore is not absolute; but a thing dependent on the need and judgment of another" (*L* 152–53). The allusion to worth may mean that Hobbes just isn't ready to divorce his discourse from concepts he is helping to subvert. The allusion could also be strategic: to speak of worth as if it were synonymous with value eases the transition from the latter to the former. The direction of the discourse, in any case, is clearly from the old to the new, from worth to value, understood as price. "Man" as generic human being is no longer a complex of concrete qualities, but is judged to be a simple quantum—the price of his power for labor. To be sure, pricing always involves redefinition or reduction. A marketed vegetable is endowed with qualities of which the price is a representation in one set of terms of something that otherwise exists in another; if this is not a reduction, it is certainly a simplification, even an impoverishment. For, compared to all that could be said in words about the thing, its price "says" relatively little, though what it says in the practical contexts of buying and selling can be definitive.

Hobbes revolutionizes by extending this process to human beings. In a stroke human quality and multiplicity are reduced to functioning in the same way as the objects we call commodities, the Renaissance neologism for articles of trade. Ironically, writers of the Renaissance felt that they had rediscovered precisely the fact that human beings are variously constituted, that they do many different kinds of acts and exist in a wondrous range of modes and realms, ontological, economic, social, intellectual, psychological, cultural, and spiritual. Hobbes will have none of it because the systematic thinking he helped pioneer will have none of it. That the consequences of Hobbes's radical reconstructing are far-reaching may be shown by contrasting feature by feature the market model obtaining before *Leviathan* and the one Hobbes sets as already supplanting it. Features emphasized in the more traditional market society may be specified as *quality, worth, difference, use,* and *need.* Features emphasized in the modern commercial model may be specified as *quantity, value, possession,* and *desire.* In the former model the quality of each different thing is the worth to be exchanged for whatever use is indicated by need. In the latter the value of any object is its equivalence to another object desired in the interest of possession. According to the former model, to rework a suggestion made above, *a market is in a world.* According to the latter, *the world is a market.*

Painting with broad strokes, as has been necessary here, does not allow for the type of adjustments in emphasis or in detail that alone would satisfy the interests of exhaustiveness. Even to aim at the latter one would have to consider the extent to which elements of desire and possessiveness may already figure in the earlier societal model, or the extent to which need and use continue from it into the later, commercial model. Nonetheless, there is as significant a difference between the role and nature of these last two features as there is between any of the other features. What Hobbes seems in this regard to have intuited Marx spells out in explicit terms. When need and use predominate, we sell in order to buy: C-M-C; when desire and possession predominate, we buy in order to sell: M-C-M.

> The repetition or renewal of the act of selling in order to buy is kept within bounds by the very object it aims at, namely, consumption or the satisfaction of definite wants, an aim that lies altogether outside the sphere of circulation. But when we buy in order to sell, we, on the contrary, begin and end with the same thing, money, exchange value; and thereby the movement becomes interminable. . . . The circulation of money as capital is . . . an end in itself, for the expansion of value takes place only within this constantly renewed movement. The circulation of capital has therefore no limits.[45]

Hobbes's historical moment enables him to locate this infinite disposition as an inherent characteristic of the species that is equally a metaphysics of desire. It is, in other words, precisely by virtue of what is peculiar about social and economic developments in late-Renaissance England that Hobbes can universalize: "So that in the first place, I put for a generall inclination of all mankind, a perpetuall and restlesse desire of Power after power, that ceaseth onely in Death . . . but because [man] cannot assure the power and means to live well, which he hath present, without the acquisition of more" (*L* 161).

This is not of course the whole story, as Hobbes here attempts no explanation for the crucial anterior condition, which is that of insecurity. Why insecurity? Because in a state of nature some persons possess more power than others. "*Naturall Power*, is the eminence of the Faculties of Body, or Mind: as extraordinary Strength, Forme, Prudence, Arts, Eloquence, Liberality, Nobility" (*L* 150). Except for fortune, or chance, such natural endowment is the exclusive means by which to acquire what Hobbes calls in the same place instrumental (that is, sociopolitical) power; and instrumental power is simply the means by which "to acquire more: as Riches, Reputation, Friends and the secret working of God, which men call Good Luck. For the nature of Power, is in this point, like to Fame, increasing as it proceeds; or like the motion of heavy bodies, which the further they go, make still the more hast" (*L* 150). The problem is that being endowed with any of these powers puts one immediately into opposition with others similarly endowed, so that, ex-

relative novelty of Hobbes's egalitarian move. What finally resolves the matter is convention in the form of law: "In Common-wealths, this controversie is decided by the Civill Law: and for the most part, (but not alwayes) the sentence is in favour of the Father; because for the most part Common-wealths have been erected by the Fathers, not by the Mothers of families" (*L* 253). It seems surprising that again the woman fares so much better than in prior philosophical discourse on the same subject. In a patriarchal society, conferring dominion on the male is to be expected. But it is clear that Hobbes is not endorsing it as necessary in principle. His comments are more descriptive than prescriptive: it is just the case historically that men have usually been the founders of civil states, but in principle it could have been otherwise.

> But the question lyeth now in the state of meer Nature; where are supposed no lawes of Matrimony; no lawes for the Education of Children; but the Law of Nature, and the natural inclination of the Sexes, one to another, and to their children. In this condition of meer Nature, either the Parents between themselves dispose of the dominion over the Child by Contract; or do not dispose thereof at all. If they dispose thereof, the right passeth according to the Contract. (*L* 254)

Amazons illustrate the universality of contracts. Desiring issue, they contract with the men of neighboring states to produce offspring, sending all the male babies off with their fathers "so that the dominion of the Females was in the Mother" (*L* 254). Pateman clarifies the extent of female power: "By nature, a mother is a lord who can do as she wills with her infant. If she decides to 'breed him,' the condition on which she does so . . . is that 'being grown to full age he become not her enemy.' That is to say, the infant must contract to obey her. The mother's political right over her child originates in contract, and gives her absolute power." [56]

Three other considerations remain to be taken up, two of which relate directly to women's will. First, only the mother of a child knows who the father is, and since she is free to identify him or not to identify him, she has dominion over the child. The second consideration turns on the principle that every individual is by nature bound to preserve her own life. If the mother chooses to preserve the life of her child, the child "is therefore obliged to obey her, rather than any other; and by consequence the Dominion over it is hers" (*L* 254). By the same logic, if the woman exposes the child and some other person elects to raise it, dominion passes to that person.

Finally, in the state of nature, where a kind of spontaneous contract reigns in the absence of that higher form of contract which is civil law, the relation of female and male is egalitarian precisely because it is, and just insofar as it is, contractual: "If the Mother be the Fathers subject, the Child, is in the Fathers power: and if the Father be the Mothers subject, (as when a Soveraign Queen marrieth one of her subjects,) the Child is subject to the Mother; because the Father also is her subject" (*L* 254). We note: contract does not make the genders in principle equal; rather, because they are in principle equal they can contract.

If we then ask, in conclusion, what all this has to do with reconstructing the assumptions of individualist ideology, liberal contract theory, and the market system, the answer is everything. A society grounded in contract is, to look first at the negative side, not a society of immemorial custom, filial piety, and Adam Smith's fellow-feeling. It is a society in which every one makes a deal. I split the pronoun to throw into relief the singular and individual basis on which contractual obligation depends. Whatever generic features it may display, every contract has an indefeasible uniqueness: it is this arrangement here and now that I as an individual make with you as an individual.

Locke, for his part, goes some way toward enfranchising women, at least to the extent that he justified a freedom of choice far from normative in his day. Radically, he denies that Adam's dominion over Eve amounts to an unquestioned authorization to govern. God declared Eve subject to Adam as her punishment, and no more, in consequence of which God's words on Eve's punishment will "import no more but that Subjection they should ordinarily be in to their Husbands."[57] The qualification has the same force as those we have seen in Hobbes. Locke attempts a *reductio ad absurdum* by asking whether the marriage of Queen Elizabeth or Queen Mary to one of their subjects would have meant their monarch's subjection to him.

He objects to arbitrary male dominion which, if allowed, abuses the freedom to contract, whether exercised by a man or by a woman. By way of a further *reductio* he asks rhetorically, "what will become of *Paternal Power* in that part of the World where one Woman hath more than one husband at a time? Or in those parts of *America* where, when the Husband and Wife part . . . the Children are all left to the Mother?" (*L* 1.65).

Locke refutes Sir Robert Filmer, spokesman for patriarchy, by noting how the latter reduces the biblical commandment to "honor thy father," rather than "honor thy father and mother." Locke turns to Scripture for a number of passages supporting his critique and points out that when God conferred dominion in Genesis 1:28 he did not omit the conjunction, but specifically conferred dominion upon Adam and Eve alike. Gathering together Locke's somewhat incidental remarks on women in other writings, Melissa A. Butler underlines Locke's crucial belief in female rationality. Without the ability to reason, even as a man reasons, a woman would not be free to contract, to manage her own property, and to behave prudently in the conduct of conjugal life—or in the instance of divorce, the right to which was one of his most controversial innovations. Locke believed that girls and boys alike could be guided by his *Thoughts on Education*; he even suggests a certain crossing of gender in the opposite educational direction by recommending dancing lessons for males as well as females. Finally, he openly admired the preaching of the Quaker Rebecca Coller, recommended that she keep it up, and generalized that "Women, indeed, had the honour first to publish the resurrection of the Lord of Love; why not again the resurrection of the Spirit of Love?"[58]

All of which goes some way, at least, toward reconstructing from scattered passages the role of gender, and more especially the role of women, in Hobbes and Locke. It does not follow, however, that these authors should be assimilated to worldviews that their historical situation could not have allowed them to foretell. My purpose is not to claim a radical revision of either thinker, but to show how radical in their own way they already were. As Elizabeth Fox-Genovese remarks, "They did not repudiate the political and social necessity for the subordination of women, but they justified it on new grounds and, in so doing, opened the way to subsequent notions of female individualism and equality."[59]

It should also be said that in so doing they were in their own way systematic. They aim to order, connect, classify, adjudicate, and articulate all that they see as inhering in the whole of polity. More than most of their predecessors, with the partial exception of Francis Bacon, they subscribe to the goals of prediction and control that have become normative for modern science. But these are hard goals to achieve. In particular, to systematize a worldview placing special emphasis on the individual requires the most careful monitoring of the parts being systematized. The most graphic instance of a solution to the problem may be Jeremy Bentham's Panopticon, so designed as to give the centrally positioned keeper maximum surveillance of the prisoners. The Panopticon is the will of the penal system architecturalized. But it hardly addresses the difficult issues facing a political philosopher who wants to be truly systematic. Locke especially would reject any apparatus denying freedom of choice to the social agent.

No more than any other human constructions or reconstructions are systems able to secure the autonomy of their operations. More precisely, it is doubtful that any imaginable system would have the capacity for the comprehensive monitoring and surveillance that it would take to prevent all destabilizing irregularity and deviance. Any system is tense with the struggle of its own parts—subjects, actors, call them what you will—in all their unruly complexity, and this is even more vividly the case when, as in Hobbes and Locke, the phenomena they are trying to systematize are largely determined by the acts of discrete individuals.

All of this supposed imperfection, when viewed from another angle, turns into qualities on which we usually set a high value, including flexibility, freedom, and individuality. There is also the element, and it is a crucial one, of chance, which has a way of interrupting and overriding, and in a given context can be decisive. In his reconstruction of Aristotelian assumptions, Machiavelli makes a connection between chance (*caso*) and fortune (*fortuna*), envisaging the latter grammatically as a *she* and metaphorically as "a rapid torrent."[60] Because in Machiavelli this disruptive woman is highly active, he must resist her with all the discursive means at his disposal. Paradoxically, of course, in the very process of doing this he is making room for her in the role of a central "otherness" against which to rally masculine counterforce. That she has stirred much scholarly controversy attests at once to her ambiguity and Machiavelli's ambivalence.

I believe the same applies, *mutatis mutandis*, in the contract theorists, and especially in Locke, who doesn't know quite what to do with women, but, in granting them a portion of equality, at least does something besides ignore them. More than Hobbes, Locke provides a representational space in which the phenomenon of the female, along with the aleatory, can emerge not as capable of activity but as actually active. She fills, in effect, the role of the rogue element in contemporary systems theory—the chancy, unpredictable something or other the system doesn't know what to do with but in a way can't do without. And here lies a danger for the rogue female, who may be regarded, by whatever (male) authority holds most power, as just the dose the system needs to get over the very disorder that she represents. In direct contrast to Kafka's Hunger Artist, who never finds anything he wants to consume, systems never find anything else.

Turning from prose to poetry, and from political to what might be called symbolic philosophy, we find in W. B. Yeats a great figure greatly involved with issues very similar to the ones we have been considering. In his approach to what he calls "great constructions" Yeats reveals a disposition to resist or problematize the worldview of the contract theorists. He cannot accept the privileging of the individual and market mechanisms, nor can he accept the manner in which Hobbes in particular reduces worldly being to materiality and motion. At the same time Yeats, like both Hobbes and Locke, reveals a disposition toward a more or less theoretical reconstruction of the civil order, and is even inclined to be systematic in the process of carrying out that reconstruction.

15. *Certain Great Constructions*

In an essay demonstrating knowledge of the intellectual revolution of Hobbes and Locke, the Industrial Revolution, and the British Empire, Yeats observes, "It is customary to praise English empirical genius, English sense of reality, and yet throughout the eighteenth century when her Indian Empire was founded England lived for certain great constructions that were true only in relation to the will."[61]

To Yeats the proximate cause of the historical and natural world envisaged by Hobbes and Locke lay in the hegemony of individualist ideology spread by a democratization of the masses, a democratization that must lead to their exploitation: "I thought 'After the individualist, demagogic movement, founded by Hobbes and popularised by the Encyclopaedists and the French Revolution, we have a soil so exhausted that it cannot grow that crop again for centuries.' Then I thought 'Nothing is now possible but some movement or birth from above, preceded by some violent annunciation'" (*CW* 1:655). Here as in other texts, Yeats's reconstructive conception operates as an idea and as a birth, or more precisely a rebirth. The process is complex. In the first place, it is recollective: the poet reimagines moments that were, moreover, already recollective, for he is looking back at junctures in which he represents himself in the act of even then looking back to prior historical times. In the second place, the recollection of a previously imagined possibility, the possibility of a movement or birth from above, indicates as it were the dispositional direction of the vision, itself a movement from past through present to future. Third, by virtue of being self-begotten (to recall one of the poet's conceits), this discourse becomes the author's re-constructing of his own conception of re-creation. Fourth, such discourse can claim the status of a seeding or generative text, constituting as it does a matrix from which the future will be seen to come forth. Fifth, the agonistic relation always in evidence when Yeats talks about time consists here partly in the annunciative violence, which must be destructive in order to be creative, and partly in the otherness through which the poet confronts himself: the "I" in *A Vision* proceeds by citing an other who, as an oracle of annunciation, is the poet himself in another time and place. Finally, in reconstructing the condition of possibility for an epochal rebirth, the text already suggests the mythic dimension of which "Leda and the Swan" will serve here as representative text.

The antitheses in this poem are so characteristic of Yeats as scarcely to require remarking, but their specific nature warrants comment, as does their interrelationship with hierarchy, which figures in Yeats with comparable prominence. The text represents as antithetical, hence fatefully intervolved, the realms of the divine and the human, of the male and the female, of the natural and the historical, and finally of power and knowledge. What is antithetical is at the same time hierarchical. Everything on the "swan" side of the list is understood to be somehow superior or transcendental: the natural or cosmic is higher than the human or historical, the male is stronger than the female, and so on, which is to say that there is radical inequality between the two depicted beings with regard to the ways in which they are endowed, enabled, and entitled (see Part II below). Leda embodies the creatural, for, notwithstanding her archetypal nature, she is mortal in contrast to the divine Zeus. Zeus, moreover, is endowed with the capacity of universal creativity, and in the agon of the poem relates to his victim much as spirit relates to body or man relates to woman in the dominant traditions of Western discourse. Leda is an enabling figure whose submission to cosmic-divine power is a *sine qua non* of the procreation in question. Without her flesh, the spirit in the swan could not engender the history signified:

> A shudder in the loins engenders there
> The broken wall, the burning roof and tower
> And Agamemnon dead.
>   Being so caught up,
> So mastered by the brute blood of the air,
> Did she put on his knowledge with his power
> Before the indifferent beak could let her drop?
>   (*CW* 214–15)

To perform sexually, on a "lower" ontic level, the flesh of nature must be put on, raising the ironic possibility that the carnal act has eventuated in something "higher," a supposed condition of knowledge. This is ironic, first, because the locution may echo St. Paul commanding the corruptible to put on incorruption, as Leo Spitzer suggests; and second, because it echoes Locke's notion, in *The Second Treatise of Government*, that you can divest yourself of natural liberty only by putting on the bonds of civil society—the irony compounded by the likelihood that Locke is already fiddling the Pauline overtones. Irony of such density, polarized between apocalyptic foresight and political theory, seems only fitting in a poet of Yeats's complexity and range.

The text is more provocative on the question of entitling, which is where considerations of legitimacy enter in, questions of what ought to be or determinations of wherein justice or injustice lies. It is not accidental that the poem ends with a question, "Did she put on his knowledge with his power / Before the indifferent beak could let her drop?" The question, in the manner of a Burkean terministic screen, tends to deflect attention away from concern for the victim of the violence, who is already discursively subdued by being reduced from particularity to the level of "a mass-word referring to body as a substance, a substance subject to molding by a superhuman force."[62] Plainly put, one wonders whether Leda gets as much commiseration as she is entitled to as a defenseless mortal woman violently used by an omnipotent immortal male. Spitzer hears empathy in the first question, "How can those terrified vague fingers push / The feathered glory from her loosening thighs?" It may also be that she is warming to the experience of coupling with a god, in which case commiseration is not in order. But Spitzer is certainly right in applying the term "objective" to the concluding question about knowledge and power: according to the objective-subjective dichotomy Yeats was wont to employ, the poem's final interrogation occurs at the opposite pole from the "subjective" realm, as exemplified in Leda's experience of the rape.

Yet more plainly, Leda may be seen as a sacrificial figure in the long line of "expendable" females epitomized by Lucretia, who will be treated in Part V, on experiencing. On this reading, the text would reconstruct an economics in which destiny is achieved by violence at the expense of the female victim. In Yeats it is not always the fate of such a victim to suffer in silence, as "Michael Robartes and the Dancer" attests, but even in that poem the male attempts an assault on the woman who seeks only the knowledge, the "thought" as Robartes calls it, to which she believes that her enabling, educative program entitles her:

> *He.* Opinion is not worth a rush;
> In this altar-piece the knight,
> Who grips his long spear so to push
> That dragon through the fading light,
> Loved the lady; and it's plain
> The half-dead dragon was her thought,
> That every morning rose again
> And dug its claws and shrieked and fought.
> (*CW* 175)

It seems inevitable that the figures in the described work of art should be identified as Saint George and the Dragon; in any case, Robartes's recourse to so high a subject lends a tone of mock epic with which his later pedantic appeal to the Latin text is notably in tune. Thus ironized, Robartes's highfalutin discourse enables the reader to see in him a spokesman for (male) order and system over against the woman who stands for "roguish" independence.

Robartes would change history by appeal to nature. He believes that what is of the flesh is right because natural, that it is the dancer's destiny to be a "natural" rather than an intellectual woman, and that he can only free her from the latter identity by drawing on discursive authorities that she may lack the means to contest. The dancer for her part sees formal education ("college" and "school") as enabling, and it is precisely because Robartes basically agrees that he refutes her desire for learning, insisting instead on the primacy of fleshly endowment, in which he shows an interest befitting both a suitor and a student of theology (he will later invoke both the Eucharist and the Incarnation), not to mention a sexist:

> While Michael Angelo's Sistine roof,
> His "Morning" and his "Night" disclose
> How sinew that has been pulled tight,

> Or it may be loosened in repose,
> Can rule by supernatural right
> Yet be but sinew.

If fleshly endowment as sinew is thus its own entitlement, it is by the same stroke empowered: by right it rules, and there is no elevated point of view from which, as at the end of "Leda and the Swan," to problematize the consequence of so much exercised power. The consequence, where Robartes is concerned, is access to flesh; the rendered scene is precoital. In lieu of sexual climax it offers the knight's discursive violence against the woman's thought, which she calls "My wretched dragon." Moving in for the rhetorical kill, he does obeisance to women on the condition that they sacrifice their claim to formal education.

> *He.* I have principles to prove me right.
>   It follows from this Latin text
>   That blest souls are not composite,
>   And that all beautiful women may
>   Live in uncomposite blessedness,
>   And leads us to the like—if they
>   Will banish every thought, unless
>   The lineaments that please their view
>   When the long looking-glass is full,
>   Even from the foot-sole think it too.

When She replies, in the poem's last line, "They say such different things at school," she has at least the solace of not putting on his knowledge with his power because she is not after all putting on his power. Irony stands off irony: Robartes strikes at the dragon of a feminine and at least potentially feminist thought with the strength of instituted learning, in the form of his Latin text, only to be met with—instituted learning, in the form of school. Stepping back from the poem the better to observe its shape, we see a discursive axis of antitheses in which nature—sinew, body, lineaments, foot-sole—endeavors to overpower history—opinion, thought, college, school. In effect, "Leda and the Swan," some three years later, will then "gyre" the agon, hypostatizing nature, expressed in incarnation, animality, coitus, and sexual generation, as the supreme power to whose costly dispensations history must subscribe; indeed, its dispensations *are* history.

16. Discursive Axis

The concept of a discursive axis, from the root sense of that around which something rotates or revolves (1619), is enriched, where Yeats is concerned, by the idea of "a geometrical line, by the revolution of a superficies about which globes, cylinders, cones, etc., are conceived to be generated" (1571). One such axis is what Yeats, weaving a passage from Swift into Vico's *New Science* (1725; 1740), calls "the eternal circuit": "I suggest to the Cellars and Garrets that though history is too short to change either the idea of progress or the eternal circuit into scientific fact, the eternal circuit may best suit our preoccupation with the soul's salvation, our individualism, our solitude. Besides we love antiquity, and that other idea — progress — the sole religious myth of modern man, is only two hundred years old" (*E* 355). It is within the eternal circuit, presumably, that the movement or birth from above will destroy the existing order of individualist demagoguery — in, again, the matrix of Hobbes, the Encyclopedia, and the French Revolution — to create in its place the results of an all-transforming revolution. Or so this discursive axis runs.

Yeats's main task may well be, by perpetual reconstructing, to articulate a coherent vision of his epochal situation. It is a task at once historical and natural. It is historical because it involves human individuals and communities perceiving, feeling, and acting. And it is natural because all such perception, feeling, and action requires — now as material or mediation, now as both — the entities and forces of what we somewhat misleadingly call the physical universe, cosmos, or nature, which is precisely, of course, a nature historicized, discursive: even the idea of a pure nature is reconstructed from worldly givens, a thing of words.

The intertwining of the historical and the natural, thus understood, is the more elusive as the stuff of history is the more involved with the stuff of nature. "Thus, the history of man is an adventure of nature, not only because man is a material organism with material needs, but also because worked matter, as an exteriorisation of interiority, produces man, who produces or uses this worked matter in so far as he is forced to re-interiorise the exteriority of his product." [63] Traversing this field of the *practico-inert*, Sartre seeks to discover a dialectical intelligibility, on the basis of which the world can cease to be that darkened realm which is Hobbes's natural world. Yeats seeks for such intelligibility in the book of nature as read in terms at once personal and (theoretically) universal. He offers a coherent view of the ways in which Lockean reason combines with technological development (in the sphere of the practico-inert) to transform both the everyday world and its paradisal archetype; the danger is always that, with his will to systematize, his view will become, as it were, only too coherent:

> I can see in a sort of nightmare vision the "primary qualities" torn from the side of Locke, Johnson's ponderous body bent above the letter to Lord Chesterfield, some obscure person somewhere inventing the spinning-jenny, upon his face the look of benevolence kept by painters and engravers, from

the middle of the eighteenth century to the time of the Prince Consort, for
such as he, or, to simplify the tale —

> Locke sank into a swoon;
> The Garden died;
> God took the spinning-jenny
> Out of his side.

(E 359)

The fateful separation of primary from secondary qualities is scarcely original
with Locke; Hobbes had already assimilated it into his design for a civil state,
having learned the distinction from Galileo, whose epochal discourse on this
issue will be discussed in Part IV below. In any event it is Locke who epitomizes to Yeats this radical inversion by which the dispensation of worldly
things as concrete qualities and familiar powers, known from time immemorial, is itself dispensed with.

Primary or original qualities, says Locke, "are utterly inseparable from
the body," and may be found in "solidity, extension, figure, motion or rest,
or numbers." The more familiar features of worldly things, "qualities which
in truth are nothing in the objects themselves but powers to produce various
sensations in us by their primary qualities, i.e. by the bulk, figure, texture,
and motion of their insensible parts, as colours, sounds, tastes, &c." are cor-
respondingly reduced, as in Galileo, to the status of secondary phenomena
(L 1.46).

In a bold strategy, Locke extends this discursive axis right into the realm
of things supernatural, arguing that a piece of manna gives us ideas of its
figure when stationary and of its motion when moved, but that other ideas
are merely, as it were, aspects of ordinary experience: "And yet men are hardly
to be brought to think that sweetness and whiteness are not really in manna,
which are but the effects of the operations of manna, by the motion, size,
and figure of its particles, on the eyes and palate, as the pain and sickness
caused by manna are confessedly nothing but the effects of its operations on
the stomach and guts, by the size, motion, and figure of its insensible parts"
(L 1.115–16).

Whether or not Yeats had passages such as this in mind, they are the *kind*
of thing that prepossesses him even when, as in the present text, he is following mainstream historiography; for in tracing modern social, political,
and economic developments to Hobbes and Locke, Yeats takes for granted
the direct connections that historians have drawn between the increasingly
mechanistic and systematic philosophies of the seventeenth century and the
civic and technological innovations of the periods that followed. For a symbol of the latter, Yeats could have chosen Sir Richard Arkwright's water-frame
spinning machine (1769) or Samuel Crompton's spinning mule (circa 1779);

choosing instead the spinning-jenny (patented 1769) of James Hargreaves has two advantages.[64] A hand-driven invention simulating the motions of hand-spinners, the spinning-jenny forms a link between a more traditional manual stage of labor and the era of heavier, machine-tool industry. Second, there is more poetic punch in the very name, which passes immediately into the Yeatsian axis of revolving, winding, and gyring. That such a link can only be forged at great expense is made clear by the contiguity between the creation of the jenny and the death of the Garden.

Within the symbolism of Yeats's natural-historical system, expense or sacrifice, often by means of violence against women, is positively productive. We are back again to those constructions true only in relation to the will, however fantastic or forced they seem, or are; if one such construction is, explicitly, as Yeats suggests, the portion of the British Empire founded in India, another is, implicitly, the portion founded in Eire. It is part of the colonized's costly knowledge that imperialism requires a whole pharmacy of abstractions: "But who does not serve these abstractions? Without them corporate life would be impossible." At which point the poet introduces, by analogy, a homelier and more traditional technology: "They are as serviceable as those leaf-like shapes of tin that mould the ornament for the apple-pie, and we give them belief, service, devotion" (*E&I* 400–401). While this may seem far from Byzantine beauty or the spinning-jenny, the statement turns on the same discursive axis, plays a part in the same grand temporal and spatial dynamic.

In Yeats's visionary economy Locke's very devolution of the world is the price the epoch pays for the new order that science and system "beget," but ironically that price is a profitable exaction:

> And of all these [abstractions] the most comprehensive, the most useful, was invented by Locke when he separated the primary and the secondary qualities; and from that day to this the conception of a physical world without colour, sound, taste, tangibility, though indicted by Berkeley as Burke was to indict Warren Hastings fifty years later . . . has remained the assumption of science, the groundwork of every text-book. It worked, and the mechanical inventions of the next age, its symbols that seemed its confirmation, worked even better. (*E&I* 400–401)

If Yeats can then identify the assumption with dialectical materialism, he can as easily revolve around to a more positive dispensation, foretelling a time when assumptions such as this will constitute an apocalyptic new system more radically reconstructive than the *scienza nuova* of Vico, who already saw in Descartes the danger that humanistic discourse would be subjected to too much systematicity. In this connection Yeats predicts, "We may meet again, not the old simple celebration of life tuned to the highest pitch, neither Homer nor the Greek dramatists, something more deliberate than that, more systematised, more external, more self-conscious, as must be a second coming, Plato's Republic, not the Siege of Troy" (*E* 374). Yeats's fateful choice of a radically reconstructive paradigm is part of the systematizing process, a way of making history cyclical in the way that nature is. But this is a debatable move. Although we speak, to be sure, of "economic cycles," the term is an analogical derivation from the root sense of periodicity, which is another sort of thing altogether, as is the later, more common signification of a pattern of happenings or entities within a succession of equal periods (1662). If this were the way that business cycles work everyone would know in advance how long they would last and we would not need economists or stockbrokers. Nor does Yeats mean "cycles" in the loose sense of a round or period or course; his is rather a hermetically sealed schema of the high numerological exactitude and obsessive structuring typical in occult practices. A poetry of process thus understood is in one phase constructive or generative, in another destructive or degenerative, in yet another reconstructive or regenerative. And it is always, or tries always to be, systematic.

This triad of phases draws on the natural processes of the cosmos. "The fundamental form of process," says Northrop Frye, "is cyclical movement, the alternation of success and decline, effort and repose, life and death which is the rhythm of process." But he is closer to the specific Yeatsian instance in noting how "Poets, like critics, have generally been Spenglerians, in the sense that in poetry, as in Spengler, civilized life is frequently assimilated to the organic cycle of growth, maturity, decline, death, and rebirth in another individual form."[65] What this comes to in Yeats, who indeed counts Spengler as an influence, is a certain tendency, in all the rigor about systematic symmetries, toward mortification—rigor as *rigor mortis*, if you like. One reason may be that a process known in advance, or a process of constant reconstruction and revolution, can begin to look like a stasis. Delving further, we might surmise that such an outcome is a risk the poet runs as soon as he decides, thinking rather like a scientist, that prediction and control are of the essence. This is presumably part of what leads Frye to find nihilism in Yeats's system, but I find something more like a fatalism owing to a naturalization of history subordinating action to motion.

It is no accident that in his handling of Leda and the swan Yeats shows a minimum of interest in the volitional and a maximum of interest in the mechanical: "Did she put on his knowledge with his power / Before the indifferent beak could let her drop?" revolves, where Jove is concerned, around that "could," which subordinates him, even as it subordinates his victim, to what is automatic in the procreative process. Beyond a certain point flesh is compelled to its consummations, which is one of the reasons there is an aura of inevitability in scenes like these. Another reason for mortification is that in a strictly cyclical system the antipodes can come to seem versions of one another, so that, where organic existence is concerned, life becomes a phase of death and death a phase of life. This can be, in a way, a comfort: after death there will inevitably be new life, as promised in certain Judeo-Christian myths. But Yeats often seems attuned to the negative in natality; the regenerative process may yield a sense, as in the sonnet's last lines, of indifference. "Before the indifferent beak could let her drop" highlights the pertinent adjective, importantly assisted by the article; where one might have expected another "his," reinforcing the idea that the power exerted is somehow the possession of the god, "the" suggests something nearer the reverse, that the power did the possessing, that the possessing has passed, and that there is no need to attribute a gender to, no need even to humanize, the beak that can no longer grasp.

17. Purgatorial Regeneration

In *Purgatory* regeneration is literally the fate worse than death. The play is a fable of three generations, those of the Boy, the Old Man, and the Old Man's Father, with the Old Man as the protagonist and murderer. The only way to interrupt the predestined cycle of transgression initiated by his mother is for the old man to kill his son even as he has killed his father.

> I killed that lad because had he grown up
> He would have struck a woman's fancy,
> Begot, and passed pollution on.
>
> (P 205)

Yeats' character, if not Yeats, conflates regeneration with degeneration; as the poet explains, in a statement after the premiere of the play in 1938:

> In my play, a spirit suffers because of its share, when alive, in the destruction of an honoured house; that destruction is taking place all over Ireland today. Sometimes it is the result of poverty, but more often because a new individualistic generation has lost interest in the ancient sanctities. I know of old houses, old pictures, old furniture that have been sold without apparent regret. In some few cases a house has been destroyed by a *mesaillance* [sic]. I have founded my play on this exceptional case, partly because of my interest in certain problems of eugenics, partly because it enables me to depict more vividly than would otherwise be possible the tragedy of the house.[66]

Fifteen years after "Leda and the Swan," Yeats is as concerned as ever with the social, cultural, and political consequences of the liberal individualism espoused by Hobbes, Locke, and their heirs. Had he tried for verisimilitude in his handling of these consequences, he would have composed a different play, probably offering more in the way of realistic situations. By focusing on an exceptional case he paradoxically makes the representation, in one way, more individual: the case in hand is not the typical case; all the same it is paradigmatic insofar as it performs the historical score in a natural key. Regeneration mediates degeneration, as a woman representing the honor of the house married beneath her class, violating the principle of hierarchy and the sanctity of custom, and passing something like a familial curse on to her son, now an old man. By this act a historical datum becomes a natural one, destined and destining, and the only way to take nature out of the picture, finally, is to interrupt the natal process itself. To state the problem another way, nature needs a scene in which to appear and the Old Man would deny it that scene.

The poet has created a difficult case. He who lives for process cannot let process die, for in a strictly cyclical system cycles can never end, or — what comes to the same thing — they keep ending all the time, as they must in order to begin again. It is a rough beast, self-reconstructing perpetually. The moment the Old Man has ceased to explain himself the axis starts revolving in its new/old way:

> Twice a murderer and all for nothing,
> And she must animate that dead night
> Not once but many times!
>
> (*P* 205)

Jacques Le Goff has traced the emergence of a Purgatory in the period of rapid economic and social change beginning in the eleventh century and extending into the Industrial Revolution, in a close parallel to the period of 1050 to the present spelled out in Yeats's *A Vision* (1925; 1937). Yeats writes, "Since the rebirth of the secular intellect in the eleventh century, faculty has been separating from faculty, poetry from music, the worshipper from the worshipped, but all have remained within a common fading circle — Christendom — and so within the human soul" (*V* 293). Such a rebirth entails a "nascent individualism," a leading factor in the formation of what we typically call humanism (when we are looking at movements) and the Renaissance (when we are looking at periodization). According to a growing number of scholars in religious history, political theory, and literary studies, these names do begin to make a certain sense by the twelfth century, with its emphasis on the citizen versus the (monarchical) subject, the identifiable versus the anonymous author, and the centrality of a discrete autonomous self. "Purgatory became an annex of the earth and extended the time of life and of memory. . . . Though the new solidarity between the living and the dead . . . strengthened family, corporate, and fraternal ties, Purgatory, caught up in a personalization of spiritual life, actually fostered individualism."[67]

This long-term, large-scale reconstructing of relations is seen to be coterminous with social memory. Purgatory is not only a place but a process by means of which the future is formed from an ever-lengthening past; the longer the aristocratic family recollects and reconstructs itself the more it is assured of remaining aristocratic—the more memorable as it is the more sacred, the more sacred as it is the more ancient. Eventually you reach the stage where each marital alliance or act of generation serves to increase familial substance (or, when that is degenerate, as in the play by Yeats, to do the opposite). The latter case being by Yeats' own admission the exception, the process is effectively developmental, and what develops, eventually, is the institution of the individual, not merely some abstracted schema of disparate persons but their concrete convergence, organized and operating in the interest of all that is possessive and individual.

If Purgatory aims through the individual to prolong the family, *Purgatory* aims through the individual to stop it. The Old Man would insure that his ancestral house, having known degeneration, will never know regeneration. To this extent history, the human act, imposes its power on nature, but only on nature's terms. The remedy for the mother's historical act of marrying beneath her station is to guarantee that there will be no more renaissance because there will be no more mother.

To the old man who is Yeats, daimonic systematizer of cosmos and culture, renaissance is for those who are willing to put on the power that comes with the knowledge of "science," exemplified by psychical and eugenic research, as well as by occult symbolic systems. If all these "sciences" present their own difficulties, the first is sufficiently dangerous, and the second more dangerous still. It is then the more regrettable that Yeats, when the mood was upon him, could advance their claims at the expense, for the duration of the mood, of the relative benignity of the occult systems. Looking forward to a renaissance that will be a new age of action, he states:

> Yet we must hold to what we have that the next civilisation may be born, not from a virgin's womb, nor a womb without a body, not from a void, but of our own rich experience. These gifts must return, not in the mediumistic sleep, dreaming or dreamless, but when we are wide awake. Eugenical and psychical research are the revolutionary movements with that element of novelty and sensation which sooner or later stir men to action. (*E* 437)

These movements can be conceived of as revolutionary because what they define themselves as knowing and what they therefore have power over is nature as well as culture; but this is once more to approach the problems of the historical moment in nature's terms, and not those of history.

18. Reconstructing and History

For Yeats, reconstructing entails the recollecting and reworking of any-thing and everything, and since the poet typically functions in a cyclical symbolic system, a given theme or motif may return at any time. This makes for a highly complex interweaving, some elements of which look like alea-tory rogues, but whatever they are, they provide occasional relief from the insistency of Yeats's systems. To complicate matters, the very fact that Yeats is so antithetically inclined leads to the almost dialectical necessity of such counter-systematic elements.

Turning again to "Under Ben Bulben," we read:

> Many times man lives and dies
> Between his two eternities,
> That of race and that of soul.
>   (*CW* 325, ll. 1315)

Here is the cyclical system humming again, and the antithetical tensions, but there is a jarring note as well. "Race" can signify the Irish people whose causes the public and private Yeats endeavored to champion, but also, more ques-tionably, a privileged genetic stock. The reader who misses the pertinence of the poet's comments on eugenics from the same period must face the impli-cations of Yeats's advice to future Irish poets to

> Scorn the sort now growing up
> All out of shape from toe to top,
> Their unremembering hearts and heads
> Base-born products of base beds.
>   (*CW* 327, ll. 70–73)

In his recourse to race and a corresponding notion of purity, Yeats would in effect bind history to nature. How one is natally endowed becomes a des-tiny more determining than what one becomes; this is one of the ideas that Yeats shares with more radical ideologists of the political right. The idealiza-tions in the apostrophe to Irish poets may then constitute all the knowledge they need in order to reconstruct their racial, natural, national culture—a knowledge, one notes, with little institutionalization other than its own dis-cursive expression. By contrast, Pater's Marius finds an enabling institution in the early church, finds the liminal existence that enables him to dwell for a time on the edge of a dispensation that only his successors will fully know:

> Revelation, vision, the discovery of a vision, the *seeing* of a perfect humanity, in a perfect world—through all his alternations of mind, by some dominant instinct, determined by the original necessities of his own nature and char-acter, he had always set that above the *having*, or even the *doing*, of anything.

For, such vision, if received with due attitude on his part, was, in reality, the *being* something, and as such was surely a pleasant offering or sacrifice to whatever gods there might be, observant of him. (*ME* 327)

The relative serenity of Pater's perspective on history and nature contrasts with the bitterly cold eye for which Yeats will call below. Marius can accept his own destiny even while foreseeing the existential expense: "He had delivered his brother, after the manner he had sometimes vaguely anticipated as a kind of distinction in his destiny; though indeed always with wistful calculation as to what it might cost him" (*ME* 323–24). To the passing individual the community comes with compensations; it does not rescue him from isolation, for he has never felt more a part of the community, but it enacts the verity of his vision, the kind of indemnification that comes only when passage into posterity carries some sort of institutional guarantee: "It was the same people who, in the gray, austere evening of that day, took up his remains, and buried them secretly, with their accustomed prayers; but with joy also, holding his death, according to their generous view in this matter, to have been of the nature of a martyrdom; and martyrdom, as the church had always said, a kind of sacrament with plenary grace" (*ME* 331).

Compare this with the passing at the end of "Under Ben Bulben," as the poet's individual, reconstructive animus tries to salvage something from the once-vital institutions of church and community:

> Under bare Ben Bulben's head
> In Drumcliff churchyard Yeats is laid,
> An ancestor was rector there
> Long years ago; a church stands near
> By the road an ancient Cross.
> No marble, no conventional phrase,
> On limestone quarried near the spot
> By his command these words are cut:
>> Cast a cold eye
>> On life, on death.
>> Horseman, pass by!
> (*CW* 327–28, ll. 84–94)

Feeling put upon by age and change, Yeats elevates the vital element into the necessity of a sexual ideal countering that other necessity which is the unwinding of the thread of life that every age undergoes at the hands of another. Here is, as it were, the good news. The bad news is the fact that in Yeats's historical system the Irish have come to suffer the same fate as the Greeks, ruined as they are not by "All Asiatic vague immensities" ("The Statues," *CW* 337, l. 12) but by the centrifugal forces of modern civilization.

In a sense it hardly matters whether the news is good or bad, since if bad in one way it is good in another, and vice versa. Thus, if news of destruction is obviously bad in the short term, the same news is good in the long run because "A brief parting from those dear / Is the worst man has to fear" (*CW* 325, ll. 19–20). Destroying is precisely the condition of possibility for reconstructing. But there is the further problem that in order to become what they are capable of becoming the Irish must undergo immersion in the destructive element. The closing stanza of "The Statues" states the problem.

> We Irish, born into that ancient sect
> But thrown upon this filthy modern tide
> And by its formless spawning fury wrecked,
> Climb to our proper dark, that we may trace
> The lineaments of a plummet-measured face.
>   (*CW* 337, ll. 28–32)

The seemingly contradictory characterization of the place of trial and endeavor as both dark and proper makes perfect poetic sense. The place is dark because those who must go to it do not know what will happen there. The place is, for the Irish, fitting because they are deemed to be unique. Similar to other races, yes: any culture or nationality undergoes trials, faces the unknown. Each undergoes and faces in its own way, however, and as the consummation of a vast complex of concrete circumstances, traditions, capacities, constraints—the list could be extended indefinitely, and it would still be for Yeats a distinctively Irish list.

What we are talking about, when we talk about reconstructing and the rest, is a new beginning. Understanding this, Yeats would give his readers to understand that no matter how grand or pure an ideal may be, it may be, in origin, just the opposite. If our dark place is a sufficiently forbidding version of such an antithesis, the place of origin disclosed at the end of "The Circus Animals' Desertion" comes across as an even more repellent one.

> Those masterful images because complete
> Grew in pure mind but out of what began?
> A mound of refuse or the sweepings of a street,
> Old kettles, old bottles, and a broken can,
> Old iron, old bones, old rags, that raving slut
> Who keeps the till. Now that my ladder's gone,
> I must lie down where all the ladders start,
> In the foul rag-and-bone shop of the heart.
>   (*CW* 347–48, ll. 33–40)

The last of the major late poems, "Politics," being a single sentence, preceded by another single sentence, must be quoted in its entirety:

> How can I, that girl standing there,
> My attention fix

On Roman or on Russian
Or on Spanish politics,
Yet here's a travelled man that knows
What he talks about,
And there's a politician
That has read and thought,
And maybe what they say is true
Of war and war's alarms,
But O that I were young again
And held her in my arms!
        (*CW* 348, ll. 1–12)

Following his own lead on the literal versus rhetorical reading of Yeats, de Man would read the stated question as rhetorical: "With that girl standing there, how can I attend to politics?" The "answer" is of course that he can't. The deconstructionist could then engage the poet as sparring partner, substituting for the rhetorical question a possible literal one. But to guard against the eventuality that this will turn out to be a merely formal possibility, prudence would reconstruct a context that is, as Vico might say, copious. Discovered patterns of recurrence, especially in a system-oriented writer like Yeats, will tend to aggregate toward interpretive probabilities without prejudicing their possible counterparts. The hermeneutic maxim would be: before reading transgressively, read reconstructively.

In the context that is Yeats's canon the question in "Politics" cannot but relate in general to the poet's sexual politics and in particular to the issue of the author's age and virility. The text is an inversion of Lovelace's argument to Lucasta, with Yeats saying that war or politics become secondary in the circumstance he depicts, since the poet is after all virile, though old. Against this we may place at least two possible "literal" meanings. One of these runs, "How is it that I, an old man, can attend to politics when that girl is standing there?" Read thus, as an exercise in the genre of the complaint, the text would question the speaker's virility as pointedly as the "rhetorical" reading affirms it. A second "literal" meaning runs, along the lines of de Man's substitute question about the Yeatsian dancer and dance, "By what means could I attend to politics, not to the girl?" In this mode of entreaty, the poet makes a show of seeking help, but he only needs this kind of help because his virility is foremost — because the girl is on his mind, not politics.

The centrality of sexual desire in Yeats's symbolic system is too well known to require documenting here, and much the same may be said of his concern, as he ages, to affirm his own sexual capacities. To a degree, sexuality has a life of its own, and can find expression in ways that seem too unbuttoned to be constrained within the system. Such is the case with the banter of "Michael Robartes and the Dancer" and it is the case *mutatis mutandis* with "Politics." In recursively assimilating the drift of the ending of "Western Wind" — "Christ, if my love were in my arms / And I in my bed again!" — the poem foregrounds the primacy of sexual desire over politics in the usual sense of statecraft, warfare, and the like, refusing almost casually to take the latter seriously.

Given Yeats's reconstructive placement of "Under Ben Bulben" at the beginning and "Politics" at the end of this sequence of late poems, we see that the animus behind the playfulness of the latter is antithetical. After the speaker in "Under Ben Bulben" effectively inters himself, "Politics" suggests a movement in the opposite direction, insisting that the old boy still has life in him. Indeed, the life the old boy has in him as poet *is*, at this point, this poem. In its sparely stated way, the text can even be read as suggestive of resurrection, or at least of vital persistence, as in the first poem of the sequence life goes, while in the final one it flourishes. At the same time, in the speaker of the latter poem there is more than a little of the Jovean swan, as he too is compelled by the urgencies of desire. For both males, erotic passion practically if temporarily suspends the claims of the nonsexual realm of human existence — which precisely requires such passion to get the other realm going and keep it going.

Finally, "Politics" connects back through the Yeatsian system by virtue of the very playfulness referred to, already figuring in the system as permissible roguery or deviation. Of course it is possible that the poem has no such role, in which case we have to believe that just here, at the climax of the poet's sequential reconstruction, he dissolves all relation to commitments elaborated throughout the canon: a considerable burden for a one-sentence text. But this is to misunderstand that the seeming irrelevance of the text *is* its way of being relevant to the Yeatsian system as a whole. Like the aleatory element roaming through the discourse of systems theory, or like the fool in the royal court, "Politics" brings things back to earth. It is a trickster text wearing as its title a mask its lines peel away. Producing an intercalary space of time, it offers a moment of relief, a duration in which we don't have to think about the weighty system, the genius of which consists in its ability thus to lighten itself while remaining essentially intact.

PART II

Constituting

1. Introductory Overview

Part I inquired into reconstructing, in a variety of modes, what we term the "world." The purpose of Part II of this study is to inquire into the nature of the latter by considering its particular ways of being and doing. In phenomenological language, the issue is the "constitution" of the world: What is it a world "of" and "how" is it a world?

The world is, in Kenneth Burke's terms, a scene, understood as a motivational ground for experience and belonging with the family of "stance" terms that have to do with place or placement. These include *destiny*, *system*, and *constitution*, each a key term in the pages that follow.

Although my approach is not primarily phenomenological, I follow Husserl's lead into constitution in the first, more general sense of the term, indicating all that goes into the composition or construction of the "ordinary" life-world. Here the point of departure is what Husserl calls a "foundational relation," differing from most if not all other types of relation. Founding occurs when there is no Y without X because X is a condition of possibility for the existence of Y. Thus, Y is founded by X; or, X founds Y. I postpone for the moment the relation of this to the Peircean model of constitution. Consideration of foundational relations makes it possible to discern the constitutive function that I call *cofoundational*.

The cofounding offices I propose are *endowing*, *enabling*, and *entitling*. *Endowing* indicates wherewithal, and *enabling* is the process of helping the wherewithal to realize its possibilities, while *entitling* indicates the area of rights, oughtness, the juridical. As regards discourse, for example, human beings are normally endowed with the capacity to use language and this capacity is developed through training. The capacity is thereby seen to be enabling. The question of entitling enters under the aspect of justness or right. In the case of a feral child such as Kaspar Hauser, native endowment has not been enabled, and this we deem wrong. Someone born into the world is presupposed to have the natal equipment and possibilities that are normal for the species. But these remain mere possibilities unless this endowment is enabled, by training and acculturation, into a state of well-being, a subject to which surprisingly little attention has been given. By contrast the literature of impairment, in which well-being is interrupted or rendered inoperative, is large. A leading example is Calderón's Segismundo, who, normally endowed, is entitled to an education and to princely power but is deprived of his birthright by his father. To which Virginia Woolf replies with a discourse of illness as enabling; by virtue of interrupting routine life the ailing person's eyes are opened to previously undisclosed areas of experience.

Endowing, enabling, and entitling are operative, it seems, in any polity. For the U.S. Constitution to be effective, political representatives and government functionaries facilitate the legislation and regulations the Constitution makes possible and the process is adjudicated by properly vested authorities. If the Constitution is here an endowing process, legislation is the enabling office, and adjudicating the entitling office.

In a related document, the Declaration of Independence, a key assumption is that liberty is at once endowing and entitling; it is a wherewithal and a right extending indefinitely, a sort of "social destiny" that serves as a justification both for revolution and for expansion. Equally indefinite, and constitutive, is the "pursuit of happiness," which Tocqueville views as an "ardent and restless passion" driving settlers endlessly westward. Jefferson, for his part, largely locates the driving force in the nexus of credit and debt that came with the financial revolution of the late seventeenth century, and that could be controlled, he reasoned, only by the application of, if you will, moral measure and governmental measures. We find such measure in his concern for size and scale in esthetic design, in the moral calculus he devises for judging human behavior, and in his insistence that every "man" is entitled to a portion of earth as his endowment. The political correlate of such small-scale land allotments is, for him, the ward, the small-scale representative unit into which he believed that American counties should be subdivided. Only thus constituted would the polity be capable of maximizing political participation by the citizenry.

If land is constitutive for the well-being of the polity, the extension of sovereignty over terrain lying mainly to the west seems logical enough, and eventually earned the name of Manifest Destiny. A persistent problem for the expansionist Jefferson, however, was how to acquire these vast lands without decimating the populations that occupied them. This problem is first viewed, in my discussion, in the context of Jefferson's overall approach to American Indians, and then in comparison with Whitman's approach to the same or similar issues in a series of poems on American Indians. "Osceola," for example, portrays the Seminole leader's last moments as he gathers his wife and others around him. Though all is left fairly mysterious, Whitman is confident that, as he later remarks, Osceola "literally died of a broken heart." On the actual circumstances of the Indians' striking decrease in numbers Whitman has little if anything to say, despite the knowledge he had acquired while working in the Bureau of Indian Affairs.

I compare Whitman's treatment of Indians in this group of poems with the passage on "the hounded slave" in *Song of Myself*, where the speaker identifies with practically everything, including "the murderous buckshot and the bullets." Less interested in the encountered suffering than in his own self-realization in one or another identity, the poet peoples the world with others that he entitled by that process to identify with him, the better to assimilate them as being inherently, "democratically," equal to himself in his representativeness.

Since Whitman, the poet who has spoken most forcefully on the constitutive function of a national destiny is Robert Frost, and the occasion of his doing so was the inauguration of President Kennedy. On the threshold of a "new Augustan age," the bard tells how the American people were endowed by, in effect, possessing the entire transcontinental land mass even before coming into formal possession of it; and it was this gratuitous endowment of the land that gave the colonists the wherewithal with which to complete their escape from prior possession by another country, Great Britain. But the enabling process wherein the endowment comes to them is curiously passive—a business not of assertion but of merely ceasing to withhold oneself from destiny. The "many deeds of war" required along the way are confined to half a line. Of those who previously occupied the land, and of their relation to the deeds of war, there is no mention; while in their possession, the poet explains, the land was, after all, "unstoried, artless, unenhanced." He does specify the gender of the land, however, and inevitably it is female, another variation on the virgin-land theme, suggesting that it was a "natural" thing to take possession of her at whatever cost. I conclude that the process the poet depicts mystifies to the extent that it is not contextual, aggressive, motivated, or historical but autotelic, immanent, passive, gratuitous, and natural.

2. Cofounding

"Scene," in the sense noted above, tends to converge with Dewey's concept of "environment," embracing everything from immediate surroundings to the larger historical world, indeed the entire cosmos. Locke understands the scene in relation to which ideas come about as a realm of external things, which we imagine to be supported from below, as from a substratum going by the name of "substance." In Spinoza we find a species of universal scene that is not merely a motivational but an ontological ground; to speak of worldly things is to speak of beings *sub specie aeternitatis* because only something that vast can serve as context for our experienced world.[1]

Scene as substance, as motivational ground for human experience, comes from Burke's "Stance family," whose members "all derive from a concept of place, or placement."

> In the Indo-Germanic languages the root for this family is *stá*, to stand (Sanskrit, *stha*). And out of it there has developed this essential family, comprising such members as: consist, constancy, constitution, contrast, destiny, ecstasy, existence, hypostatize, obstacle, stage, state, status, statute, stead, subsist, and system. In German, an important member of the Stance family is *stellen*, to place, a root that figures in *Vorstellung*, a philosopher's and a psychologist's word for representation, conception, idea, image.[2]

The list calls attention to some of the key words in the discussion that follows: constitution, destiny, state, and representation. Constitution as the "making" of the world forms the principal interest of Part II, with destiny running throughout my discourse as a correlate of its cousins from the "fate" family.

Of the several senses of "constitution," the most general, from 1601, is "the way in which anything is constituted or made up; make, frame, composition" deriving from a narrower application to the physical conditions, such as the health of the body (1553); this consideration will be taken up below in connection with the phenomenon of well-being. In less than a decade the general sense comes to specify the way in which a state is composed or organized (1610). After the English Civil War, and the debates over political, social, economic, and religious issues, constitution is systematized as the corpus of principles by which a body politic, including the nation-state, is constituted (1735). None of this would have been possible without Hobbes, who nominalizes the verb form by stating that "before constitution of Sovereign Power all men had right to all things" (1651).

The discussion that follows, as already suggested, does not conform to a phenomenological model as such. Rather, it contests the tradition of analytic decomposition that Vico was perhaps the first to demystify.[3] But, as investigators as different as Habermas and Luhmann implicitly attest, Husserl remains an important point of departure. In the course of investigating formal logic, Husserl discovered a type of relation that is not accommodated by many conceptual models in Western theoretical discourse, such as causality, sequence, or organicism.[4] The relation in question he calls "foundational," and may be approached, in a preliminary way, through negation. The foundational relation is not causal; neither of its members exists because the other brings it about. It is not sequential — that is, it does not presuppose temporality as successiveness: neither member antedates the other. It is not organic, there being no parturition or growth. Neither is it spatial, there being no way to assign it to a location through the fixing of coordinates. Founding occurs when X is the condition of possibility of Y. In a foundational relation there can be no Y without X. Therefore Y may be said to be founded by X; or, X founds Y.

To extend this preliminary view we need also to consider a phenomenon standing in close proximity to the first, but differing from it in crucial respects. Peirce points the way. As with Husserl, the aim is the construction of a more rigorous logic, but the realm of application would extend far beyond logic into the entire realm of worldly things. The key concepts in Peirce are the ideas of Firstness, Secondness, and Thirdness. Firstness is the mode of being that is what it is without regard to any other. Secondness is the mode of being that is what it is with regard to another but not to a third. Thirdness is the mode of being that is what it is by virtue of relating a Second to a First. By way of illustration Peirce asks his readers to imagine themselves

> to be seated alone at night in the basket of a balloon, far above the earth, calmly enjoying the absolute calm and stillness. Suddenly the piercing shriek of a steam-whistle breaks upon you, and continues for a good while. The impression of stillness was an idea of Firstness, a quality of feeling. The piercing whistle does not allow you to think or do anything but suffer. So that too is absolutely simple. Another Firstness. But the breaking of the silence by the noise was an experience. (1.330)

Experience, it must be said, is in Peircean terms a Second. It is "the sphere of effort and resistance" and of the "long arm of the law" you feel when the sheriff constrainingly places his hand on your shoulder.

The laws themselves, however, are Thirds, possessing the power of lawfulness as such, that power of the general which alone gives sense to and enlarges the particular. If Secondness indicates the sheriff or the long arm of the law in its executive office, Thirdness is the court, or law in its judicial office. Drop a pencil and there will be brute action, resistance in the friction of the body against the air as it descends, and in the striking, bouncing, and settling of the pencil on the floor: Secondness. But the falling as such is determined by Thirdness, specifically, the law of gravity. This is why a sign may be thought of as in general a kind of law, for it brings about a relation whose lawfulness, habit, or general rule comes to be only in the being of that relation.

Despite his distaste for Hegel, Peirce admitted at one point that he was working out a version of Hegelian thought, and his theory follows similar "progressive" lines, with Thirdness or lawfulness implicitly taking the lead. Thirdness has a temporal function in a way that Firstness and Secondness do not; without Thirdness, Firstness and Secondness would be unable to connect. It is the office of Thirds, by bringing the other constituents into relation with one another and itself, to make those relations efficient, hence meaningful, hence proleptic of something better. This ameliorative aspect bespeaks the philosopher's commitment to a knowledge that keeps growing until the foreseeable moment when, enough time and effort having been exerted, all reasonable persons will reach agreement on whatever it was that irritated them into a quest for relief. This commitment helps to explain the hierarchical aspect of the Peircean dynamic, in which Firsts have the power to realize the potential in Seconds, which for their part must content themselves with trafficking in reactions, resistances, and the like, while Firsts must content themselves with whatever basic wherewithal or "stuff" there must be in order for Seconds so to traffic.

What I call *cofoundational* offices differ importantly from the model, significant in its own right, which has just been described. A cofounding relation privileges no function or office, and there is no leading up from one to another, as in the movement from First through Seconds to Thirds. Heidegger in a way comes closer to a cofounding relation in his conception of the artist, artwork, and audience as constitutive matrix, or in his later conception of the fourfold world, consisting of the earth, the heavens, mortals, and immortals or gods. In my terms, though not in Heidegger's, this model is cofoundational insofar as it privileges no member of a relation, as is arguably the case in Peirce. The fourfold constituents instantiate something like the "experiential togetherness" or "concrescence" described by Whitehead: "There is a togetherness of the component elements in individual experience. This 'togetherness' has that special peculiar meaning of 'togetherness in experience.' It is a togetherness of its own kind, explicable by reference to nothing else." [5] Searching for ultimate meanings in the world of things, Whitehead finds his answer in creativity, understood as the production in the world of genuine novelty—the irruption of an "actual occasion" or an "entity" unlike any other. In such an occasion, there are unique ways in which various things, beings, or entities come together and are therefore concrescent. "Thus the 'production of novel togetherness' is the ultimate notion embodied in the term 'concrescence.'" [6] Although Whitehead would not recognize the language, what he describes comes about as close as the Heideggerian conception to approximating what I term cofoundational relations. The salient question, in any case, is what follows from or may be added to all this in a way that helps to elucidate the constitution of the world. The question may be answered, in at least a preliminary way, by reference to the cofoundational relations of *endowing*, *enabling*, and *entitling*, to which we may now turn.

3. *Endowing, Enabling, Entitling*

Endowing, enabling, and entitling are performative and connective, and each is so in its particular way.

A way is a bearing, which carries the venerable sense, as in *Hamlet*, of the manner in which one carries oneself. It is, again, Burke's directional substance, the derivation of a motivational ground or "way" in which to head, a tendency to take, or a movement to make, in the sense of a discrete motion, as well as its collective permutation in the form of a (social) movement: an equivalent, then, for the term "disposition" described above. This family of offices comes into increasing prominence in the epoch with which the present study is concerned, an epoch constitutive of so much that passes for second nature, such as the concept and practice of the political constitution itself, not to mention "the development from status to contract, alienation of property, the growth of the monetary rationale, [and] revolutionary innovations in the means of transportation and communication." [7] One must add to these the innovation of the modern political revolution, systematic individualism in the possessive mode, and advanced technology.

Endowing, enabling, and entitling are readily approached as and through discourse. A crucial criterion of being human is the capacity to use and understand language. In most instances the basic endowment is adequate: at birth, most human beings are prepared to develop along lines normal for the species; that this is so shows both the extent and the limits of such founding. It shows the extent because, without this "given," other functions cannot be performed—the function, say, of interpreting a text. It shows the limits because a founding relationship—here, the endowment of the basic capacity to learn linguistic functions—does not guarantee that cofounding will occur. In the present case it does not guarantee, specifically, the existence of enabling conditions, nor can it correct its own deficiencies. The capacity for such correction, which is to say the capacity to enable, requires interaction with the entire network of prevailing practices insofar as these bear upon the learning of the relevant linguistic functions.

Without the capacity afforded by endowing, no cofounding can occur, hence no enabling; without the latter, the possibilities constituted by the former remain unfulfilled; and without both, no basis exists for entitling. Cofounding most visibly characterizes what we call the world, by which we usually mean the human world: the entire nexus of particular worldly things and practices in particular historical circumstances, including arrangements for the support of daily life, the maintenance of institutions, and the securing of cultural continuity through social and cultural organization. These make our medium of living, or environment — both the field of action and the acts within it.

We find the office of endowing, for example, in Plato, for whom the world as we know it could not be without that other, higher one, the realm of the Ideas, which transcends it, and which it imperfectly reflects. The former endows the latter; the latter is endowed by the former. In *The Question Concerning Technology* Heidegger tries another, related angle. The issue is a reversal Plato makes in the basic concept of an idea.

> For *eidos*, in the common speech, meant the outward aspect [*Ansicht*] that a visible thing offers to the physical eye. Plato exacts of this word, however, something utterly extraordinary: that it name what precisely is not and never will be perceivable with physical eyes. But even this is by no means the full extent of what is extraordinary here. For *idea* names not only the nonsensuous aspect of what is physically visible. Aspect (*idea*) names and is, also, that which constitutes the essence in the audible, the tastable, the tactile, in everything that is in any way accessible.[8]

This concept of idea depends upon endowing. There must be in the phenomenon that on the basis of which we experience any or all of its aspects. Because the orange is constituted as it is we can have an idea of its rondure, say; we could experience no such aspect, or any other, were it not endowed with those aspects. The Platonic treatment of the everyday concept is daringly straightforward: he just turns it around. His theory of constitution is such that there must be, as the condition of an orange or any other worldly thing, another world beyond it, a conception hierarchical through and through in that the idea on the empyrean plane is forever "above" any embodiments of it on the earthly plane. Negatively, the relation of the former to the latter is neither foundational nor cofoundational, as is the case with the ancient fourfold of causality as elucidated by Heidegger, whose explanatory key is the concept of co-responsibility, a concept with more than a passing affinity with cofoundation. *Causa materialis, formalis, finalis*, and *efficiens*, according to the argument, alter beyond recognition the Greek *aition* from which they derive. For *aition* does not mean causing or bringing about, but responsibility. The silver of which a chalice is made, the *hyle* or material, is said to be co-responsible for the chalice. To the silver the chalice is indebted for its appearing as this particular configuration and not some other, such as a ring: "Thus the sacrificial vessel is at the same time indebted to the aspect [*eidos*] of chaliceness."[9] Here *eidos* signifies aspect, in the traditional sense that Plato reversed. What accounts for the sacrificial character of the chalice is neither the stuff it is made of nor the aspect singly, nor even their relation. What accounts for this character is the debt of that relation to the governing *telos*, as what determines the boundary of the thing. The stuff would not emerge in the aspect of chalice were it not for this responsible or enabling guidance.

In the world as fourfold, what is called co-responsibility in the previous passage reappears as a kind of reciprocity among equals that is essentially cofoundational, as figured in the dancing, playing, and mirroring of all the realms together. Indeed, there is so much togetherness or concrescence that fourfold slides, as it were, toward a onefold, as a more intervolving way of expressing the essence of the world: "This appropriating mirror-play of the simple onefold of earth and sky, divinities and mortals, we call the world. . . . The united four are already strangled in their essential nature when we think of them only as separate realities, which are to be grounded in and explained by one another."[10]

With these preliminaries accomplished, it is time to consider more closely the nature and relations of the offices of entitling, enabling, and endowing, mentioned here in a different order to underline that they do not follow one another in any necessary sequence, except for purposes of exposition. For the same reason, the nominal form will appear indifferently as the verbal-noun equivalent, that is, endowing.

Endowing may be thought of as, again, wherewithal, enabling as the process of capacitating the former, entitling as the degree of rightness entailed in that process and wherewithal. The endowing that is birth is, in an obvious sense, the most fundamental of all. For this reason Arendt, countering Heidegger's being-toward-death, affirms the significance of natality, which, paradigmatic to the human being's historicity as a creature of birth, is first and foremost the process of worldly beginning. To emphasize the latter, however, is not merely to counter Heidegger; the shift from mortality to natality is a real shift in attitude, emphasis, and mood. The shift does not entail "naturalizing" the process so much as historicizing it, or rather, recognizing in it the fact that it is historical by definition. As born, every human being possesses the wherewithal of such vital capacities and powers as gradually—in the mode of gender, race, ethnicity, class, national identity, or acculturation—will come to enable. That is, natality as such remains at the level of the condition of possibility unless it is trained up in the world and educated—in short, enabled. Other human beings already endowed and enabled must draw the newborn into the realm of other worldly things, into the course of these and of their discourse; which is simply to say that society judges this creature to be entitled to be by virtue of the way in which it is creatural: what we mean when we speak of birthright. This right means also, and centrally, that the endowed creature is entitled to general well-being together with the right to have a voice and to participate in a community. Although there is a long tradition of treatises on "happiness," it seems fair to say that Western philosophy (Hume being a rare exception) has paid the phenomenon of well-being less attention than it deserves. Speaking generally, *bien-être, bienestar, Wohlsein, well-being* converge in the sense of overall health or welfare, a condition that may also embrace happiness or comfort, or the felicity associated with prosperity; thus, "the state of being or doing well in life; happy, healthy, or prosperous conditions; moral and physical welfare" (1613).

One can hear in these words an echo at least of the Greek *eudaimonia*, especially as it appears in Plato's *Laws*, where the best life is the most pleasant, as well as in the *Republic*, where Socrates follows the *via negativa* of defectiveness to show that a healthy condition is prerequisite to any capacity or function. Most of us probably assume that ordinary well-being goes along with ordinary being-well, and leave it at that. Not so the inhabitants of More's *Utopia*, who make the ordinary seem extraordinary by attending to it. Never tempted to take normal endowment for granted, they revel in their well-being, which is expressed as two kinds of pleasure, one of which "fills the whole organism with a conscious sense of enjoyment," exemplified by eating and drinking, sexual intercourse, scratching where it itches or rubbing where it hurts, and listening to music. The Utopians equally enjoy the pleasure that

> arises from the calm and regular functioning of the body—that is, from a state of health undisturbed by any minor ailments. In the absence of mental discomfort, this gives one a good feeling, even without the help of external pleasures. Of course, it's less ostentatious and forces itself less violently on one's attention than the crude delights of eating and drinking, but even so it's often considered the greatest pleasure in life. Practically everyone in Utopia would agree that it's a very important one, because it's the basis of all the others.[11]

In the New World that Tocqueville describes, well-being, as the foundation of "the good life," had come to signify possessions that were expressive of the individual owner, whose consumption of which became conspicuous in the ironic discourse of Thorstein Veblen. Devoting an entire chapter to the subject, Tocqueville proposes that social equality, enabled by the breakup of hereditary endowments, creates among have-nots an insatiable appetite for the best facsimile of such possessions that they can get. So pervasive is this appetite that he can generalize, "The taste for well-being is the prominent and indelible feature of democratic times." [12]

This taste, which Tocqueville also calls love or desire, is an appetite incapable, in true Hobbesian style, of being satisfied; for what is desired are just those worldly things of which everyone who desires them already knows there can never be enough. Persons equally entitled but not equally enabled — so runs this paradoxical democratic script — will rarely if ever achieve the parity or superiority they seek; always some differentiae exist, like the insignia of rank in prerevolutionary days, signifying the excess of endowment enjoyed by those higher in the hierarchy. Hence the ratio: "The desire of equality always becomes more insatiable in proportion as equality is more complete." [13]

An analogy with passion is no more out of place in connection with such desire than in connection with democracy, in which Tocqueville discerns an affectivity so intense that any religious development that might in theory endanger it

> would in the end be destroyed by it; and if it attempted to wean men entirely from the contemplation of the good things of this world in order to devote their faculties exclusively to the thought of another, it may be foreseen that the minds of men would at length escape its grasp, to plunge into the exclusive enjoyment of present and material pleasures.[14]

Possibly Tocqueville is defining well-being more narrowly than necessary; his worldly things are little more than earthly riches. Later in the century Pater will move in a different direction, elevating well-being to a higher plane that might even be called spiritual, and essentializing it in the same temporal phenomenon, the moment, that infuses the "Conclusion" of his *Renaissance* (see "Beginning," n. 1), to which we may now return. Specifically at issue is Leonardo da Vinci's "happy moment" of creative culmination,

> that moment of *bien-être*, which to imaginative men is the moment of invention. On this he waits with a perfect patience; other moments are but a preparation, or after-taste of it. Few men distinguish between them as jealously as he. Hence, so many flaws even in the choicest work. But for Leonardo the distinction is absolute, and, in the moment of *bien-être*, the alchemy complete: the idea is stricken into colour and imagery: a cloudy mysticism is refined to a subdued and graceful mystery, and painting pleases the eye while it satisfies the soul. (*R* 89)

Though few of us are Leonardo, all persons in their own way experience — in kind if not in degree — the alchemy described, and all must sometime watch as ideas that have come to them are struck into whatever is the counterpart, in their circumstance, of color and imagery. And, like the painter, it may well seem that they are not "doing" anything, that a movement simply occurs that carries them along with it. A feeling for this autonomous-seeming animus, of which our knowledge comes after its initiative and never before, stands behind one of Alain's aphorisms on fate: "We do not know how to begin anything, not even when it comes to stretching out our arms; nobody begins by giving an order to his nerves or his muscles, the movement begins by itself; our business is to follow it along and complete it as best we can."[15]

The creatural endowing presupposed in well-being would be nothing if not enabled by the nurture to which all are entitled. Other human beings, previously endowed and enabled, must draw those in the stage of mere endowment, the newborn, into their proper entitlement by enabling them to become in essential ways what their predecessors have become. Endowment makes possible such enabling as is necessary to realize the entitlement of having a language and therefore a voice and a membership in a community.

4. Impairing

But endowment may be incomplete, or enablement may be delayed or suspended, or the entitlement to enabling endowment may go unrecognized. Witness Pedro Calderón de la Barca's *Life Is a Dream*, in which King Basilio, warned that his son Segismundo is a danger to the state and if properly enabled will usurp the throne, deprives him of his liberty. It is Basilio's way of preventing the enabling of endowment to which Segismundo is entitled by a legitimacy more fundamental than any mere right of blood. When, in the person of a mediator sympathetic to the prince, the world steals in after all, interest shifts from the question of what is and was to the question of what ought to be: not to the relation between endowing and enabling, but to the relation between that nexus and entitlement. Being born is taken normally as the right to come into one's own and into belonging. A legitimate prince should be taught to speak so as to command and contract. It is the might for which his legitimacy calls — what he is entitled to. But the degree to which he can be enabled while imprisoned falls short of what he must possess to compete with those already possessed of all that their enabled station confers. Only when enablingly endowed to a comparable degree can the prince wield might for right, which is why so much of the play concerns the distance between entitling on the one hand and the nexus of enabling and endowing on the other. Calderón's is a memorable attempt to vivify the concrete dilemma of a politi-

cal actor so constrained by unjust power as to be denied his most basic rights; the dilemma of a particular human being who is thus delayed in the timely enabling of his endowment. The first dilemma seems a matter of history, the latter one of nature, but this is a nature wholly social: the constraint that keeps the prince from recognition and reciprocity implements the policy of the monarch to preserve his authority by wielding the full power of the state.

The consequences of depriving human beings of what they need if they are to attain their endowed entitling have figured in many major texts. One thinks of Gregor Samsa's metamorphosis into an insect in the Kafka tale, or of the struggle between the condition of the "brute" and a higher human condition in Frank Norris. Then there is Georg Trakl's reopening of the case of Kaspar Hauser, the mysterious youth who claims that he has been imprisoned in a hole, and who is taken in by a nobleman in the conviction that the lad is entitled to develop—that is, enable—the capacities with which he has been endowed. The birthright he lacks is both less and more than that of the other prisoner we have seen. It is less in that he has no claim to a particular social or political status. It is more in that his role is merely (in the conjoint senses of "absolutely" and "only") that of a human being. More or less normally endowed, Hauser has a language of sorts, but he is not very good at using it, and cannot tell his proper story; he must first be enabled as a functioning member in his "new" society, which would mean the acquisition of its languages and codes. Once he had these Kaspar could be enabled to develop in any number of ways. But he doesn't develop, and the mystery surrounding him (the uncertainty concerning his origins, for example) remains dark. Is the fatal blow that fells him administered by his own hand, in despair of ever belonging to society, or by the hand of a person supposing him to be the heir of some hated court? Trakl leaves the questions open and raises new questions:

> Ernsthaft war sein Wohnen im Schatten des Baums
> Und rein sein Antlitz.
> Gott sprach eine sanfte Flamme zu seinem Herzen:
> O Mensch!
>
> Stille fand sein Schritt die Stadt am Abend;
> Die dunkle Klage seines Munds:
> Ich will ein Reiter werden.[16]

> Solemn was his dwelling in the shadow of the tree
> And pure his countenance.
> God spoke a tender flame into his heart:
> O man!
>
> Silent his footstep found the city in the night;
> The dark lament of his mouth:
> I want to be a horseman.

Purity of countenance implies the absence of taint or corruption suitable to one not yet entirely of this world. It is perhaps to make Kaspar more worldly that God speaks into him forcefully if ambiguously. A flame, with overtones of deity as breath or *pneuma*, performs an enabling function if it heats to action or otherwise inspires; such a beneficent interpretation appears to be supported by the fact that the flame is tender. But a flame is capable of harming or destroying. As ambiguous as this nexus is, Kaspar does come away from it linguistically enabled though sorrowful, since the desire he expresses is already forlorn.

> Ihm aber folgte Busch und Tier,
> Haus und Dämmergarten weisser Menschen
> Und sein Mörder suchte nach ihm.
>
> Frühling und Sommer and schön der Herbst
> Des Gerechten, sein leiser Schritt
> Auf den dunklen Zimmern Traumender hin.
> Nachts blieb er mit seinem Stern allein;
>
> Sah, dass Schnee fiel in Kahles Gezweig
> Und im dämmernden Hausflur den Schatten des Mörders.
>
> Silbern sank des Ungebornen Haupt hin.

> But bush and animal pursued him,
> House and twilight garden of pale men
> And his murderer sought after him.
>
> Spring and summer and beautiful the fall
> Of the righteous one, his faint step
> Along beside the dreamers' dark room.
> At night he stayed alone with his star;
>
> Saw snow fall through frigid branch
> And in the darkening hall the shadow of the murderer.
>
> Silver sank the head of the unborn down.

Before endowing has properly begun, murder dis-endows: the desire expressed cannot be enabled, hence "dark lament." Stranger to shared worldly things and their discourse, Kaspar must die still unborn. To be capable of such discourse he would have had to have been enabled more, by proper nurturing or training. For only after this has occurred does creatural endowment come into its own.

Dewey is thinking of similar processes when he states, "The three factors of educative development are (a) the native structure of our bodily organs and their functional activities, (b) the uses to which the activities of these organs are put under the influence of other persons; (c) their direct interaction with the environment" (*MW* 9:119–20). Factor (a) embraces the office of endow-

ment and its functions and (b) their enablement, extending into (c) as the scene of their operation. The wherewithal of endowment, in other words, is not some static substratum on which the other offices draw, but is rather, by virtue of being cofoundational with its counterparts, as susceptible to their influence as it is reciprocal with their functions.

When wherewithal is impaired, as by injury or illness, the norm of everyday well-being, by contrast, may suddenly loom large. We are all at once so much *less* that we immediately perceive how much *more* we were before. Reflecting the breakdowns in life, the moments of loss and deficiency, the literature of impairment has become as large as the philosophical discourse of well-being has remained small. Greek antiquity portrays the rockbound sufferings of Prometheus exposed to the attacks of hungry birds, the wound of Philoctetes resulting in expulsion from society, the self-blinding of Oedipus. The Bible records the large-scale affliction of plagues or, as in the case of Job, the small-scale affliction of boils. Conversely, the New Testament tells of impairment reversed:

> The rhythmic return in the Hebraic scripture to a scene of wounding here becomes instead a rhythmic return to a scene of healing, a scene that occupies the same fixed and central locus in the strategies of belief: epilepsy, disease, and pain are eliminated (Matthew 4:23), a paralytic walks (9:4; 8:5), a man's withered hand becomes whole (12:9), a dumb man speaks (12:22), a dead child is restored to life (Luke 8:41–56; Mark 5:22–43).[17]

The suffering that is part illness and other types of impairing is redeemed in a measure, and in certain contexts justified, by its enabling function. Without the afflictions just depicted, there would be no cure, any more than there would be, in the same dispensation, ultimate salvation without the requisite fall. Thus Montaigne can justify the use of pain in the educative process: "Now practice at enduring work is practice at enduring pain: *Work hardens one against pain* [Cicero]. The boy must be broken into pain and harshness of exercises, to build him up against the pain and harshness of dislocation, colic, cauterization, and the dungeon, and torture."[18]

To this must be added Virginia Woolf's remarkable discourse on the enabling power of being impaired. She begins with a peroration whose syntax makes it difficult to abbreviate:

> Considering how common illness is, how tremendous the spiritual change that it brings, how astonishing, when the lights of health go down, the undiscovered countries that are then disclosed, what wastes and deserts of the soul a slight attack of influenza brings to view, what precipices and lawns sprinkled with bright flowers a little rise in temperature reveals, what ancient and obdurate oaks are uprooted in us by the act of sickness, how we go down into

the pit of death and feel the waters of annihilation close above our heads and wake thinking to find ourselves in the presence of the angels and the harpies when we have a tooth out and come to the surface in the dentist's arm-chair and confuse his "Rinse the mouth—rinse the mouth" with the greeting of the Deity stooping from the floor of Heaven to welcome us—when we think of this, as we are so frequently forced to think of it, it becomes strange indeed that illness has not taken its place with love and battle and jealousy among the prime themes of literature.[19]

For Woolf illness is not something from which to seek relief, it *is* that relief: "How tremendous the spiritual change that it brings, how astonishing . . . the undiscovered countries that are then disclosed." Woolf is suggesting the *felix culpa* implications by listing the enabling possibilities not otherwise available, to compensate for deprivation, suffering, or loss, and even to transcend them.

To emphasize the flesh, as a genuine exploration of illness requires, is in Woolf's view to go against the grain of literary tradition, which she sees as mentalist: "Literature does its best to maintain that its concern is with the mind; that the body is a sheet of plain glass through which the soul looks straight and clear." (W 16). Woolf understands that she is playing a dangerous game so far as the usual standards are concerned, for flesh unbound by illness is liminal, transgressive. In the anarchy of illness, boundaries between beings begin to dissolve; the world is dangerously, or wonderfully, one.

In Woolf's account, a key enabling factor is, as in Proust, the change of perspective entailed in adjusting to being impaired. Thus she finds herself "helter-skelter with the dead leaves on the lawn, irresponsible and disinterested and able, perhaps for the first time in years, to look round, to look up—to look, for example, at the sky" (W 18). When it stops serving merely "as a background for man . . . the sky is discovered to be something so different from this that really it is a little shocking" (W 18). The new entitling thus enabled is nothing less than recovered worldly plenitude. Under this new-old dispensation one is able to experience in words what normative well-being bars: "In illness words seem to possess a mystic quality. We grasp what is beyond their surface meaning . . . and then, if at last we grasp the meaning, it is all the richer for having come to us sensually first, by way of the palate and the nostrils, like some queer odour" (W 21).

There is a special wonder too in the intercalary time this enabling passage opens into, a time out of time that is anything, however, but otherworldly. Consider the gruelling regimen that Woolf underwent when as a teenager she was rushed about from place to place and duty to duty for fear that time to herself would conduce to mental illness. From this disenabling rush, the onset of fleshly impairment provides a relief almost desperately desired. Reading a family history, Woolf, now woman and wife, observes of the author: "So Hare,

too, takes his time; the charm steals upon us imperceptibly; by degrees we become almost one of the family, yet not quite." And later: "There seems no end to the space and the leisure of those early Victorian days" (W 23). This is no longer the *recherche du temps perdu* but its virtual *récupération*.

Leisure: how bourgeois. But the concept is not in principle classbound, nor should it be so taken here. In its first, medieval sense it signifies "opportunity afforded by unoccupied time," before shifting to "time allowed before it is too late." Even if one does not accept Josef Pieper's thesis that leisure is the very basis of culture, one should accept where Woolf is concerned the connotations of relief, repose, transition, and liminality (with a flavor even of Lawrencian lapsing-out).

The "almost" and the "seems" hint to us, on the other hand, that the midsummer night's dream is coming to an end, that a sort of curing is under way. One can even touch the place where the rhapsody begins to wear thin, to wear into something like normality: it is the final, long paragraph, which contains the ominous statement that "The law is on the side of the normal," the state of being in which much madness is no longer divinest sense. And now at last the advent of suffering, strangely missing heretofore, as this essay by one woman turns into a short story about another, a Lady Waterford, who, like the essayist, has artistic talent, worries over "her father's house," and has to keep busy all day. She is not a genuine artist, however, she is "nothing but a sketcher" (W 24), and what she sketches is her patriarch, her Perceval, who, like his knightly counterpart in *The Waves*, one day falls while horseback riding and never comes home.

Just here the story breaks off: "and never could Sir John Leslie forget . . . how the curtain, heavy, mid-Victorian plush perhaps, was all crushed together where she had grasped it in her agony" (W 24). So manifest is the grief of Lady Waterford that Woolf needs only a single strong detail to communicate it. If she does not go on to portray the full process of mourning, this lack, while certainly related to her own struggle with grieving, reflects a more general problem. Aware of everything traditional that it has lost — aware, with the War, of the fragility of civilization itself — the culture of modernity is aggrieved, but hard put to deal with its grief. The old ceremonies no longer work, and new ones are wanting. Traditionally, mourning is an enabling process through which the dead are released from life as the living are released back to it. To fail to mourn is to hold on to the dead, it is to incorporate death into life, as *In Memoriam* risks doing, a melancholy prospect casting shadows not only over some of Woolf's writings but over a goodly number of other modernist works as well.

On the brighter side, the moves Woolf makes manage at least a small success, and arguably a large one. For the purport of the curious turn to the

Waterfords is to disconnect illness from mortality and causality while associating it with the aleatory: the lady's lord, enjoying a general well-being, perishes in an accident. Collaterally, Woolf evidently unburdens herself of some *ressentiment* by the implicit parallel between Lady Waterford and herself, also a woman left deserted by death in the family. And finally Woolf affirms the discursive immortality of her Victorian counterpart, already hypostatized by the historian Hare.

On leaving a text like Woolf's, most of us are likely to return to an everyday world in which we are not significantly impaired; or, more positively, in which achieved enabling is the norm. It is normative too that enabling becomes a stage in a series of stages that together build up the world. By way of example, a language learner who turns into a writer becomes an enabler in turn, training the community to a new level of realization: "Language [*langage*] has a function analogous to the language [*langue*] of a new writer who, at first, is not understood, but who little by little becomes understandable by teaching people to understand him. His gestures seem to point in non-existent directions; then, little by little, some notions begin to find for themselves a potential [*virtuel*] home in these gestures."[20] So to function is to enlarge the range of entitlement and, at the same time, to enable its realization. Enlarging and enabling entitlement in such a manner alters taste, the importance of which was recognized by the Spanish philosopher Baltasar Gracián.[21] His *gusto* is, in my terminology, a component of creatural endowment. *Gusto* indicates the innate but trainable capacity to distinguish one flavor from another, to discriminate between this bouquet and that one, and so on. The function of training, which he calls by the more usual name of education, is to enlarge the range of entitlements: to establish new experiences as susceptible of positive judgment, as meeting criteria of correctness and good upbringing. Training at the same time enables all this by teaching the learner how to make proper distinctions and discriminations, thus transforming the creatural endowment into proper worldliness.

In no political thinker do entitling, enabling, and endowing figure more prominently than in Hobbes. The "artificial" animal who is man is a trope for the one kind of entity, body, and the one kind of function, motion: body capable of motion is the central creatural endowment. Now, so long as bodies and their motions remain at their original stage, which Hobbes calls nature, they keep moving in their own interest, there being no disposition toward another. In this stage to be or to have is to be or have more. The state of eternal war that this amounts to is justified by the First Law of Nature, "*That every man, ought to endeavour Peace, so farre as he has hope of obtaining it; and when he cannot obtain it, that he may seek, and use, all helps; and advantages*

of Warre" (*L* 190). The conception of the first law holds out the obligation Hobbes would invoke. Parties are entitled to war only on the condition that peace is unobtainable. This is an important qualification. If the philosopher can devise a theory enabling entitlement to peace, no party can claim it is entitled to war. Hobbes's theory will manage, of course, to do just that. But let us take a closer look at the First Law of Nature.

The deontological "ought" entitles every actor to do what he can to obtain peace, such doing being precisely the enabling acts that could effect peace. The vague "hope" evidently embraces the range of these possible acts, the anticipation of their result, and the situations in which they are performed. By recognizing that some people have more advantages than others, Hobbes proposes a secondary endowment modeled on the creatural. For just as the creatural gives one such-and-such capacities primordially, so may such-and-such capacities be conferred at a later stage. This is no invention of Hobbes. He is simply attending to a phenomenon that many other thinkers had noticed. But the function of modeling marks a significant difference. The stored-up capacities, whether inherited or acquired, resemble creatural endowment, but do not come to the same thing. The secondary phenomenon is something to which one is entitled because society has enabled one to possess it, and not because it manifested itself primordially as a necessary condition of worldly being. This is to say that the phenomenon in question is, for all practical purposes, a worldly endowment.

Contract, or covenant, enables the entitling quantum called price. Transcendence of the warring state and supersession of the civil occurs when equals agree to binding obligations, such as the delegating of authority from many persons to one person. Delegation of authority to a sovereign, as a way of endowing, is marked by reciprocity, in contrast to the unilateral nature of its creatural counterpart: "And because the Multitude naturally is not *One*, but *Many*; they cannot be understood for one; but many Authors, of every thing their Representative saith, or doth in their name; Every man giving their common Representer, Authority from himself in particular; and owning all the actions the Representer doth, in case they gave him Authority without stint" (*L* 220–21).

In giving up their natural right to act only in their own interest, those who covenant realize their entitlement to "propriety"—the "ownness" of a thing, including the right to alienate it for a price; in a word, property. The highest name for entitling in this system, which defines what is right as that which is contracted for, is justice. Taking rare recourse to the Schools, Hobbes borrows the definition of justice as "*the constant Will of giving to every man his own. And therefore where there is no Own, that is, no Propriety, there is no Injus-*

tice; and where there is no coercive Power erected, that is, where there is no Common-wealth, there is no Propriety; all men having Right to all things" (*L* 202).

The Leviathan state enables the entitlement of well-being, language, and membership in a community. The communal resides in the commonwealth as such, which guarantees that the weal shall be common, the mode of guarantee being the contract, which relies on words. As we have seen, words work, in the Hobbesian theory, by forming chains of reasoning that lead to consequences; meaning is that which names add up to, or can be reduced to by subtraction. Hence the ease with which Hobbes turns reason into reckoning. He holds nonetheless to the enabling primacy of language: "So that without words, there is no possibility of reckoning of Numbers, much lesse of Magnitudes, of Swiftnesse, of Force, and other things, the reckonings whereof are necessary to the being, or well-being of man-kind" (*L* 104). This makes linguistic capacity as such a creatural endowment, on the basis of which words, and then numbers, are learned. This does not mean that well-being can be equated with value or price. It means that well-being is the enabled entitlement of full participation in the price-structure system. It is the very being of the individual as possessor of entities, including himself, whose ultimate social expression is price.

That endowing, enabling, and entitling appear in a major work of political philosophy is far from accidental. The theory of constitution I am describing is palpably political, taking that term in a broad sense. By way of further demonstration, each function of the manifold corresponds to the functions of government sketchily drawn by Montesquieu in his discussion of democracy as an ideal type, and implemented in the Constitution of the United States. Through the Constitution and the other laws it passes, the legislative power confers a worldly endowment; for without such legislation no constitutional democracy would exist. Enabling, for its part, falls to the executive branch. Through administrative enforcement, statutes and regulations are put into effect to carry out in detail the general legislative intent. Finally, the office of entitling is assigned to the judiciary. Endowment having been enabled, courts then adjudicate, deciding which parties to adversarial proceedings have the more just or most just claim.

5. Constituting Political Discourse

For a political discourse in which threefold constitution is crucial and demonstrable, consider the declaration, "We hold these truths to be self-evident: that all men are created equal; that they are endowed by their creator with inherent and inalienable rights . . ."[22] Not all the functions are set forth in this

sentence of the Declaration of Independence, there being a chiasmus between what might be called the expository structure and the interest structure. The expository structure is the sequence of words as it unfolds. The interest structure is the case the authors want to plead. As the interest structure proceeds from assumptions, the expository structure proceeds toward suasion.

The expository structure approaches endowing through self-evidence, a concept at once rhetorical and epistemological. Following Common Sense philosophy, epitomized by the Scottish Enlightenment's Thomas Reid, the Declaration implicitly assumes that there is a better, because more natural, way of knowing a moral truth. Jay Fliegelman explains, "Reid's self-evident truths were intuitively known by a communitarian rather than individualistic or subjective epistemology."[23] By virtue of such directly communicated rightness, the community of readers finds it all the more natural to state the case of universal equality, which feeds immediately into the crucial statement on endowment of rights. It is all the more natural in that the ulterior origin of the endowing is God. Enabling, for its part, consists not so much in the rights that are specified as in the *possession* of the rights, which is cannily couched in negative terms. The privative adjective reflects the assumption that it is *right* to possess them *because* we possess them, in consequence of which they cannot be alienated. "Rights" can then appear at the end of the clause as the culminative entitling that is the ultimate aim, in this discursive situation, of the authors' worldly interests.

The interest structure as such begins where the clause ends, with entitling. Now the aim is to elevate rights to primacy without appearing to do so, which means that the clause reinforces the general drift of the document: above all, the claim of entitled independence must be argued convincingly; otherwise the authors are lawbreakers and their actions are illegitimate. How do we come to be entitled? By being divinely founded. Had the authors made the expository and the interest structures coincide, the statement would not lead, as it presently does, with the strong suit of self-evidence and divine endowment. Leading with entitlement would put that function up for immediate scrutiny, following which the claim of endowment could appear gratuitous.

The second sentence of the Declaration asserts that among these rights are life, liberty, and the pursuit of happiness. The position of liberty next to life, like that of the pursuit of happiness next to liberty, may be meant to suggest how each office relates to the one it follows or succeeds. Then again the arrangement could be sequential, moving from basal condition to function and concluding with the prospect of realization. Or the sequence could be construed as leading from the least to the most problematic conditions—from the fact of being in existence to the relative indeterminacy of mere prospect. Each reading is compatible with the view that life, liberty, and the pursuit of

happiness more or less correspond with the offices of, respectively, endowing, enabling, and entitling. Less technically, only alive and free could you act to achieve your desire.

The situation looks somewhat different when one considers the implications of the word that "the pursuit of happiness" replaces. Jefferson was not so idealistic as to forget that the pursuit of property makes many people happy. If Jefferson is in fact taking the possession of "property" for granted, then the substitution is not without a euphemistic function. But of course it is much more, for the substitution is transcendental at the same time, suggesting that, even as happiness is indefinable, its pursuit may be infinite. Like the democratic concept of "the people," the pursuit of happiness draws on the ideological fund that speaks of the American state and character as protean, energetic, expansive, inexhaustible, and free.

In the second place, offering property as a basic entitlement could make it seem a kind of bottom-line endowment, as if to admit that property was what those other ringing words, life and liberty, reduce to in practice. Jefferson's substitution offers a different kind of ultimacy, and a vaguer one, the sheer ineffability of which accounts for much of its power.

The situation is of course more complicated than that, for all three rights are entitlings made possible by endowing. Having proferred the "self-evident" truth that all men are created equal, the text intensifies the originary magic by specifying the creator as the source of the endowed entitlings, the better to lend the entire discourse an aura of the divinely destined. This is not to sacralize the secular purport of these opening remarks or of the document as a whole. For, Jefferson insists, "Man was destined for society. His morality therefore was to be formed to this object. He was endowed with a sense of right & wrong merely relative to this. This sense is as much a part of his nature as the sense of hearing, seeing, feeling; it is the true foundation of morality" (J 901).

6. Social Destiny

The passive phrasing, paralleling "endowed by their creator," lends a quality of irresistibility to social destiny: "was destined," "was to be formed," "was endowed." This scarcely makes a story line with a fully temporizing essence—of, say, the Genesis type, "In the beginning God formed his morality"—but the proposition that *is* put forward, that "his morality therefore was to be formed to this object," is effective in its own way. First, the conjunction sounds a necessitarian note, as if to say that whatever follows derives irresistibly from its antecedents; then the peculiar locution "was to be formed" establishes as its equally peculiar corollary the moment of creative

endowment, or rather an imagined, intercalary space of time just before that moment when, as by a sort of advance hindsight, future morality is suddenly seen as already formed; finally, the process unfurls despite the fact that God is not actually shown to perform an enabling act. Once man was destined for society, the apposite morality followed as a matter of course. All of which adds up to a fateful discourse unusual in the degree to which it wrestles explicitly with the phenomenon of fate, or destiny, as such.

To underline that the endowed sense of right and wrong is worldly in a sensory way Jefferson assimilates the moral to the perceptual and physiological with the observation that "The moral sense, or conscience, is as much a part of man as his leg or arm. It is given to all human beings in a stronger or weaker degree" (J 901). No less perceptual is the reason to which Jefferson, in good Enlightenment fashion, abundantly appeals, for reason is ultimately worldly because practical. Reason is aligned with science and experimentation, not to mention everyday life: "Reason and persuasion are the only practicable instruments" (J 286). Further, reason and free enquiry are "the only effectual agents against error. Give a loose to them, they will support the true religion, by bringing every false one to their tribunal, to the test of their investigation" (J 285). "Enquiry," "tribunal," "test," and "investigation" harken back to the Baconian nexus of experience and experiment even as it looks forward to the reworking of that nexus in the American pragmatist tradition. With Bacon and the pragmatists Jefferson accepts as axiomatic that experiential process is equally moral process. His correspondent is answerable, we note, not for the *rational* correctness of the decision he makes but for its uprightness, its *moral* justness. Such a decision falls within the domain of what pragmatists from Peirce to Buchler call *judgment*, a conspicuous term in the Jefferson vocabulary as well. When reading the Pseudo-Evangelists, Jefferson's correspondent is advised, "you are to judge their pretensions by your own reason, & not by the reason of those ecclesiastics" (J 904).

Jefferson is cognizant too, again with the pragmatists, of the crucial role of habit in the everyday world, a concept correlative, as we shall see, with his advice on regular exercise. In traveling, even mature men "learn new habits which cannot be gratified when they return home," while their youthful counterparts acquire "a habit of idleness." Jefferson adds, a little portentously perhaps, "These observations are founded in experience" (J 904).

Since everything in the letter *is* so founded, if its recipient will but take it all to heart, morally sound habits will come about as surely as soundness of limbs comes about; for the sense of right and wrong with which we are endowed is as much a part of being human as a leg or an arm and, like them, it gains strength through exercise. Such moralizing exercise is quintessentially social, inasmuch as what one exercises *with* is the experience of one's fellows.

"State a moral case to a ploughman & a professor. The former will decide it as well, & often better than the latter, because he has not been led astray by artificial rules" (J 902). While the forensic point is that professional expertise enjoys no privilege in moral matters, Jefferson is appealing fundamentally to that enabling education in life which is untutored everyday experience, an education he aligns with common sense over against the narrow reason of professional expertise: "This sense is submitted indeed in some degree to the guidance of reason; but it is a small stock which is required for this: even a less one than what we call common sense" (J 902).

Social destiny is thus seen to be, in a broad sense, both moral and democratic. Not otherwise could a thousand ordinary men judge as well as a man of science, or a ploughman better than a professor. But contributions to moral education come from a more elite quarter as well: "In this branch therefore read good books because they will encourage as well as direct your feelings. The writings of Sterne particularly form the best course of morality that ever was written" (J 902).

Looking to a master of literary sentiment for moral coursework is consistent with Jefferson's appreciation of judgments made by his thousand men or his ploughman. Such egalitarian preferences as he held are rigorously reasoned; his affecting the common man is no affectation. Many years later, he demonstrates as wide a range of appreciativeness as ever, as he decides for the essential equality of two unlikely bedfellows. The issue is "the simple and the sublime" (J 1451) in literary style, and the premise is that he likes them—there is no other way to put it—equally. Had he praised Thomas Paine, democrat supreme, for his achievements in the simple style, and left it at that, one could have concluded that he is merely favoring a political brother. Instead, he applauds so grand an aristocrat as Lord Bolingbroke for the latter's achievement in the complementary, sublime style.

Jefferson presumably admires Sterne's handling of the "social affections," as Shaftesbury called the inclinations conducing to social order. Sterne, Richard Steele, and Henry Mackenzie "attempt to universalize Shaftesbury's 'natural Affections,' to expand the ranks of the innately virtuous and good-natured to include merchants, minor clergymen, the minor gentry, technocrats, and writers. These strategies do not subvert, radically undermine, or fundamentally realign the hereditary bases of wealth and power but seek to expand them."[24] The evident validity of such an account does not, however, extend to the American instance, or at any rate to Jefferson's elucidation of it, as witnessed by the fact that Jefferson not only does not discriminate between the ordinary citizen and the professional in their capacity for moral judgment, but undercuts any special claims for the latter. In Jeffersonian discourse affections that are natural must be rooted in the nature that everyone shares;

to hold otherwise is more than a contradiction in sense, it is a repudiation of experience. The difference between the British and the American social landscape could be further demonstrated by imagining Sterne or the other writers saying what Jefferson says of the ploughman or, unlikelier still, of the American aborigine. Moralizing, in *Notes on the State of Virginia*, Jefferson affirms that the "affections" of the Indians "comprehend his other connections, weakening, as with us, from circle to circle, as they recede from the center: that his friendships are strong and faithful to the uttermost extremity: that his sensibility is keen, even the warriors weeping most bitterly on the loss of their children . . . that his capacity and activity of mind is equal to ours in the same situation" (J 185).

Destiny is social, and morality informs social destiny. To be moral is to habituate oneself—in a kind of self-enabling exercise equally useful to society—to being grateful, generous, charitable, humane, true, just, and the like. A matter of flesh as well as of mind or spirit, a performance of the senses and the limbs, morality is finally the course laid out by the best discourse, which, encouraging feelings, enables the entitling of what we call virtue.

7. Constituting Liberty

Liberty, like freedom, is a notoriously difficult concept to define positively, as a power or capacity in itself rather than as the absence of something of such capacity. Thus to Renaissance ways of thinking liberty signifies "exemption or release from captivity, bondage or slavery"; closer to home it signifies "freedom from arbitrary, despotic, or autocratic rule or control" (1484). In the Victorian era J. S. Mill still finds it easier to specify what limits liberty—what is liable to dis-enable it, if you will—than to stipulate what it is. But if one looks at liberty more affirmatively, as capacity or potentiality, its enabling function, as posited, for instance, in the Declaration, is readily discerned. Now we get the "faculty or power to do as one likes" or "free opportunity or scope *to* do something; hence, leave, permission." In representative remarks on liberty published in the American colonies between 1747 and 1775, liberty oscillates between the poles of something one is entitled to and something one can be deprived of, the source of potential deprivation being social constraints, in particular those of law:

> For political liberty, as opposed to the theoretical liberty that existed in a state of nature, was traditionally known to be "a natural power of doing or not doing whatever we have a mind" [sic] so long as that doing was "consistent with the rules of virtue and the established laws of the society to which we belong. . . ." Liberty, that is, was the capacity to exercise "natural rights" within limits set not by mere will or desire of men in power but by non-

arbitrary law — law enacted by legislatures containing within them the proper balance of forces.[25]

The negative "other" of liberty becomes in Jefferson's text the problem of security: "That to secure these rights, Governments are instituted among Men, deriving their just powers from the consent of the governed." That is, although the rights are not defined by negation, they are subject to tyrannical government, corruption, parties, and so on. Security enables. To be endowed with a right is not to exercise that right unless one has the capacity to do so, a clear assumption behind the physiology of exercise in Jefferson's text on social destiny; and one will not enjoy that capacity unless an office is performed in such a way that nothing can interfere with the capacity in question. If this way of putting the matter casts a new shadow of negativity, it is because of the element of repulsion and resistance that seems necessary to the concept of security. Security is security-from, complementing "negative" liberty, or freedom-from.

Equally complementary but more affirmative are the divinely endowed "natural" rights to life, liberty, and the pursuit of happiness — natural, in the period's way of thinking, *because* divinely endowed — and the natural law. The positive, positing character of such law consists precisely in its institutionality, and has not a single aspect but a conjoint one: security can enable endowed rights because institutions enable security.

That the concatenation does not end there is already implied in the derivation of just powers from the consent of the governed, in view of which we may equally say that the governed enable the institutions to enable the security that enables rights. At the same time one recognizes in the three crucial terms of the derivative clause at least a hint of the operation of the correlative offices. For if "consent" is the term denoting the enabling act performed by the governed, "powers" indicates the wherewithal or endowing function, leaving it to the modifier "just" to indicate that the powers so derived are those to which the securing institutions are by that very process entitled.

When attention shifts to an eventuality of epochal proportions, the screw of the Declaration's discourse gets a fateful turn: "that whenever any form of government becomes destructive of these ends, it is the right of the people to alter or to abolish it, & to institute new government, laying it's [sic] foundation on such principles, & organizing it's powers in such form, as to them shall seem most likely to effect their safety & happiness" (J 19). Here two points are in order. The first is that liberty goes far beyond the consent that the governed are free to give. In the scenario drawn by the statement, the most negative of institutional prospects comes about as the very government instituted by the enabling consent of the governed eliminates their security, taking away rights as if it owned them when in fact the rights are borrowed. But the principle of inherent natural rights already posited instantly legitimates the liberty to consent to new institutions. On such entitling there is scarcely any limit, including limit of time; it is the very principle of world-making, its privileged temporality being secured by divine endowment against anything that does have a limit, such as an administration or a regime, a parliament, or a king. The paradox of its temporality is that, far from being transhistorical, as the preceding statement may have seemed to imply, it is historical precisely in its way of transcending, in the manner of "general nature," particular historical circumstances. The just powers here derive not from the consent of the governed but from that of the governor: infinite being infinitely entitles, securing rights that cannot be alienated because any alienation is fated to occur within definite time limits.

The purport of the statement about the right to abolish and begin anew is to justify revolution. But the seed of such justification was planted the moment the consent of the governed was made the immediate, and God the mediate, origin of governmental institutions. Like the Lord, the governed giveth and the governed taketh away, thereby, or so it seems, securing happiness and security itself, now termed "safety." But caution: on what principles are the foundations of the new government to be laid, and in what form are its powers to be organized? On such principles and forms "as to them shall seem most likely to effect their safety and happiness." A strain of Stoicism may be detected here, but if in that case the attitude looks back to classical tradition, it looks forward in the regard it shows for the probabilistic ("most likely"). As if to make the prospect more problematic still, even this can be determined only by appearance ("seem"), and further, both probability and seeming are engaged only from the perspective of the governed; there is something somehow daunting, capable of stirring heroism or arousing anxiety, in the conception of "the people" standing alone, sole destroyers and sole creators of whatever social order they are destining the world to see.

The note one hears in the last words and phrases is in fact sounded for the first time in the document when the third of the great constitutive offices, entitling, is expressed as the pursuit of happiness.

8. The Pursuit of Happiness

Locke states the importance of the idea of happiness with characteristic bluntness: "If it be further asked, what it is moves desire? I answer, happiness, and that alone. 'Happiness' and 'misery' are the names of two extremes, the utmost bounds whereof we know not; it is what 'eye hath not seen, ear hath not heard, nor hath it entered into the heart of man to conceive.'"[26] Desire and pursuit go well together. To desire something that would make one happy no more guarantees that one will obtain it than pursuit guarantees that one will catch up to whatever is being pursued.

Happiness being elusive, it seems fitting that pursuit is the term Jefferson chooses to associate with it. Pursuit is desire in motion, and, like the right to life and the right to liberty, is in principle illimitable. Pursuit entails Viconian *conatus*—volition, effort, endeavor—which, when oriented toward happiness, may take various paths and run various dangers; there may even be as much enjoyment in the pursuit as in the consequences. Bacon, a favorite of Jefferson's, speaks of the pleasure experienced in process for the sake of process, deriving from the aspect of human endowment he terms "the affection which is natural in man towards variety and proceeding." He continues, "so as it is well said, *Vita sine proposito languida et vaga est* [life without an object to pursue is a languid and tiresome thing]."[27] Pleasure in proceeding can become its own end when desire creates conditions that deny the possibility of its satisfaction, which is the case with the Ohio settlers who, in Tocqueville's account, shift to Illinois in pursuit of a happiness no more to be found in the spaces they are entering than in the ones they have left. Indeed, a restless pleasure in proceeding appears to a visitor to the new republic to characterize the nation as a whole: "America is a land of wonders, in which everything is in constant motion and every change seems an improvement," in which the fluctuations of wealth produce "a perpetual feverish agitation, which admirably invigorates their exertions and keeps them, so to speak, above the ordinary level of humanity. The whole life of an American is passed like a game of chance, a revolutionary crisis, or a battle."[28]

If on the other hand we look at entitling from the standpoint of happiness, an issue arises of such importance that it is hard to explain the relative lack of attention it receives. The issue is who shall be the primary beneficiaries of the civic order that endowing, enabling, and entitling will have made possible? The statement requires the future tense; the issue, in Jefferson's view, had not been addressed adequately in the past, and a truly virtuous state cannot exist until the issue is addressed. Looking ahead, one must decide what measures to take, once the beneficiaries have been identified, in order to assure their political, social, religious, and cultural well-being. Before this can be explored here, however, it will be necessary to consider, as Jefferson himself did, its relation to another crucial matter involving the future, namely, the nexus of debt and credit.

The situation of the American state in this regard reflected the experience of politicians and writers who had wrangled over a British society more and more driven by dangerous credit-debt ratios, rampant speculation, and the proliferation of discursive constructs surrounding the shift from tan-

gible specie to the abstraction of paper money, whose fictitious character was
known to be as arbitrary as its value was unstable. Beginning in the 1690s
(the Bank of England was founded in 1694), the National Debt became a preoccupation and quick profit an obsession, at least among those South Sea
Company directors (and others of a speculative bent) whose manipulations
strained an economic order overly reliant on confidence, opinion, and hope,
of which credit was a most expressive synonym. Pocock concludes that "the
ancient faculty of experience" took on the new form of "credit, or opinion,"
an equivalence suited to market actors who "must constantly translate their
evaluations of the public good into actions of investment and speculation, so
that political behavior is based upon opinion concerning a future rather than
memory of a past." [29]

Hume puts his finger on the relevant when he declares: "This avidity
alone, of acquiring goods and possessions for ourselves and our nearest
friends, is insatiable, perpetual, universal, and directly destructive of society." [30] Some of Tocqueville's sharpest pronouncements on Americans aim
at this quintessentially Hobbesian desire. When Tocqueville lashes out at the
love of well-being in the narrow materialist sense he is reacting to the same
desire and with a similar uneasiness.

Given the issues at stake, the discourse surrounding the British financial
revolution set off in the late seventeenth century could not have been anything
but fateful. The dangers facing those who gambled in the marketplace were
epitomized by the discursive figure of a woman of easy virtue or by tropes
of disease. A decade after the onset of the American Revolution, Jefferson
adopts the trope of disease to figure the danger to the new American nation
posed by excessive credit. The problem of how to pay off the United States'
large debt to the Crown of France, and its obligations to French officers who
had fought beside the colonists, was particularly acute for a state that had entitled itself into being before it could be sure that it was endowed with enough
political and economic wherewithal to survive, let alone prosper. The practice of speculation, which Jefferson despised, directly endangered the value of
American federal paper. After confidence in that paper had been restored, he
feared that European speculation in the United States' domestic debt would
threaten not only the financial stability and the prestige of the nation but its
citizens' moral fiber: "I own it to be my opinion that good will arise from the
destruction of our credit. I see nothing else which can restrain our disposition
to luxury, and the loss of those manners which alone can preserve republican
government" (J 844). [31] Decried by moralists, luxury signified luxuriance, in
the sense of "superabundant growth or development; exuberance," with the
last example in the OED appearing the year after the founding of the Bank of
England. [32] Luxury flourished as a morally weighted term in the half-century

following the Glorious Revolution, an era in which the earlier sense of luxury as "choice or costly" goods broadened to include "sumptuous and exquisite food or surroundings" (1704), or "refined and intense enjoyment" (1715). To comprehend the revulsion of many writers, including Jefferson, one recalls that the sense of lasciviousness still reverberated in this noun and its cognates. In any case the excess of desire signified by "luxury" violated Jefferson's sense of reasonable measure or scale.

9. Measure

The danger Jefferson sees derives from a kind of distended temporality, a protraction of obligation beyond the limits of reason as embodied in custom, as that was understood before the financial revolution. Like a medical ailment, the contracting of long-term debt disenables wherewithal. To restore social and economic well-being it is necessary to observe measure and measuring, in the broad sense of both terms, whether in the mode of scale, size, degree, or proportion. This is the case whether the issue is something as modest as a bookplate, which must be "of a proper size" (J 858) — or something as imposing as a statue of George Washington, which elicits an argument one must quote at some length as it weaves together in a single discursive texture strands not only of esthetic interest but of economic, moral, and political import as well.[33] Jefferson entreats the Virginia delegates in Congress to consider themselves "in some measure bound to patronize" the sculptor Houdon by hiring him to create an equestrian statue of the general; the degree to which they are bound is thought to be proportional to the extent that Jefferson has represented Virginia in securing the interest of that artist. The latter will have an advantage over others, the argument goes, to the extent that "he will have seen General Washington, have taken his measures in every part." Moreover, Houdon already possesses "the house, the furnaces, & all the apparatus" for a statue of Louis XV, so that engaging anyone else entails the additional expense of furnishing its equivalent. This apparatus being "immense," "the price of the work . . . will be much greater than Congress is aware of, probably," whereupon Jefferson starts spelling out the esthetic and moral measuring that supports the recommendations he is making:

> And as far as I have seen, the smaller they are, the more agreeable. The smallest yet made is infinitely above the size of life, and they all appear outrée and monstrous. That of Louis XV. is probably the best in the world, and it is the smallest here. . . . A statue is not made, like a mountain, to be seen at a great distance. To perceive those minuter circumstances which constitute its beauty you must be near it, and, in that case, it should be so little above the size of the life, as to appear actually of that size from your point of view. I should not

therefore fear to propose that the one intended by Congress should be considerably smaller than any of those to be seen here; as I think it will be more
beautiful, and also cheaper. (J 813–14)

The criterion of scale applies equally to real property, of which it is unjust
that an excessive amount should belong to a few, as in France, with its unequal division of land between a relative handful of aristocrats and a myriad
of more or less impoverished commoners. Jefferson concludes that "legislators cannot invent too many devices for subdividing property, only taking
care to let their subdivisions go hand in hand with the natural affections of
the human mind" (J 841). These are the same affections displayed in Sterne's
A Sentimental Journey, and the writings of Sterne, we recall, form for Jefferson the best course of morality that ever was written. It seems fitting, then,
that the incident that excites the American visitor shares the general lineaments of the incidents in Sterne's novel about an English visitor to the same
country. Walking from Fontainebleau, Jefferson falls in with a poor woman
obliged to support her two children, despite being breadless and often unemployed. Jefferson concludes the interview, in the manner of Sterne's Yorick,
by letting money express his affective endowment:

> As we had walked together near a mile and she had so far served me as a guide,
> I gave her, on parting, 24 sous. She burst into tears of a gratitude which I could
> perceive was unfeigned because she was unable to utter a word. She had prob-
> ably never before received so great an aid. This little *attendrissement*, with the
> solitude of my walk, led me into a train of reflections on that unequal division
> of property which occasions the numberless instances of wretchedness which
> I had observed in this country and is to be observed all over Europe. (J 841)

Giving money to someone in need is only one of the elements connecting
this incident to Sterne and illustrating Jefferson's moral calculus. In Jefferson
as in Sterne, a consequence of the gift is weeping. Then there is the knack for
reading attitudes: Jefferson can perceive that the woman's tears are unfeigned
because she cannot speak, a statement that is less a description than an interpretation of causality, not to mention character.[34] Yorick is forever doing
the same, a case in point occurring in Versailles, a setting similar to the one
in Jefferson's text, when Yorick explains how, by scrutinizing a duke's face, he
will "observe what character is written in it; take notice in which posture he
stands to hear you—mark the turns and expressions of his body and limbs."[35]
Economic suffering entitles Yorick to perform a benevolent act that at the
same time gratifies his sensibility, which expresses itself in tears. By having
Yorick slip to the pretty young *fille de chambre* a larger than usual piece of
currency, Sterne demonstrates that Yorick's benevolent disposition is not to
be measured by any narrowly economic criteria. The narrative then contra-

dicts the impression, as Yorick places a definite value on his behavior: "My advice, my dear, would not have been worth a pin to you, said I, if I had not given this along with it: but now, when you see the crown, you'll remember it — so don't, my dear, lay it out in ribbands" (S 65).

The texts by Sterne and Jefferson contrast with one another in several ways. First, Yorick's effusive expressions are enabling acts, putting him in the intensely sentimental mode that pleases both himself and the maid. Yorick gives as gratuitously as possible, as Sterne plays up transactions in which sensibility is expressed and intensified in the act of giving for no apparent cause. By contrast, Jefferson, while obviously moved by his experience, is by Yorick's measure less expressive, and he justifies his giving by interpreting the woman's relation to him as that of guide to visitor, so that the money becomes a payment or a reward. In the second place, Jefferson makes no mention of any other financial matters, such as another purpose he might have for the money, whereas Yorick can be quite explicit in his details: "I had a parcel of crowns in my hand to pay for Shakespear; and as she had let go the purse intirely, I put a single one in . . . and returned it to her" (S 65). Which is to say, both that his generosity "costs" him, and that his sentimental temperature, as he puts it, is such that the expenditure hurt him no more than the expenditure of tears that typically accompanies his giving. Third, Jefferson shows a sense of the implicit historical and social context — "She had probably never before received so great an aid" — generally missing in Sterne; had such a thought occurred to the protagonist he would have been far more effusive about it, and would certainly have moralized it as much as possible. Fourth, in Jefferson's text only the woman weeps, while in Sterne's anyone might weep at almost any time. Finally, Sterne has more concern for the prepolitical person, so to speak, than has Jefferson. Yorick confesses: "I feel some little principles within me, which incline me to be merciful towards this poor blighted part of my species, who have neither size or strength to get on in the world — I cannot bear to see one of them trod upon" (S 60).

If Yorick is attending-from the economic status of the trod-upon, he is attending-to the potential that that status possesses for affective and moral expression. "Poor" is at once an economic indicator and the characterization of a more abstractly pitiable condition, the abstractness appearing as well in the subsumption of the poor person into a faceless "part" in an even vaguer "species." Yorick's moral measuring turns quantitative when he attributes the condition of the part to an amount of endowment insufficient to be enabling: with too little size or strength, one does not get on in the world. Yorick doesn't see that the condition of the poor part is social, political, and systemic, or that "compleasance" has concrete motives and implications. Manners such as his "enable people to get along," recalling Hume's defense of politeness and gallantry as modes of expression essential in monarchical states in which "the people 'must turn their attention upward, to court the good graces and favour of the great,' and to be prosperous a man must 'render himself *agreeable*, by his wit, complaisance, or civility.'"[36] Hume thus understands the enabling that is complaisant from both sides of the relation—from the side of the one who must please because lower in status and from the side of the one who must be pleased because higher in status.

Though genuinely moved by the plight of the destitute woman, and though inclined with Sterne to associate charity with virtue, the heart of the matter, for Jefferson, lies elsewhere than in the expression of Shaftesburyan sensibility. It lies in the political arrangements from which the woman's condition derives, and more particularly, as noted above, in the fact that, even as untold numbers of fellow citizens live at or near the level of subsistence, a relative handful of proprietors are endowed with vast estates, with up to 200 domestic servants. By Jefferson's moral measure they are wrong not only for disregarding the needs of impoverished populations eager to work, but for failing to recognize their fundamental right as human beings to a material if minimal endowment.

The only way of enabling such an entitling is by endowing through economic redistribution. This Jefferson calls for, though not unconditionally; for if his proposal is radical it is not revolutionary, there being a "natural" constraint on how much of the property can be alienated, even to enable the alleviation of intense suffering: "I am conscious that an equal division of property is impracticable, but the consequences of this enormous inequality producing so much misery to the bulk of mankind, legislators cannot invent too many devices for subdividing property, only taking care to let their subdivisions go hand in hand with the natural affections of the human mind" (J 841). Guided by this proviso, the measures to be taken are not only properly politic to the state or citizenry, they are then properly moral as well. Dividing legacies equally among descendants "is a politic measure and a practicable one" (J 841) because justly measured by established entitlement, which is what the concept of natural affections here comes down to.

The scene in which Jefferson takes his stand is finally that of the endowing earth itself. As substratum the earth is literally what lies under—the wherewithal to which we are entitled by natural right. In Jefferson's language, such right is grounded in the originary giving from God so as to render illegitimate even the enabling laws of the state when those laws disregard that grounding. "Whenever there are in any country uncultivated lands and unemployed poor, it is clear that the laws of property have been so far extended as to violate natural right. The earth is given as a common stock for man to labor and live on" (J 841–42). While earth furnishes the scene of worldly things and human discourse, it does so in a more than human way, for earth as a cosmic term—like sun, moon, or star—opens to the widest of contexts with the earliest of origins, that of creation itself. Even a deist like Jefferson traces terrestrial endowing to a Creator. Earth and land are correlative and overlapping but not synonymous terms. The surface of the planet being largely water, earth includes land but is not limited to land. Nevertheless Jefferson uses the terms more or less interchangeably, depending upon the perspective, and also perhaps for the sake of variety. What the sense of "the earth" provides that the sense of "the land" does not is, then, something of a poetic aura, suggesting the chthonic foundation or endowment underlying institutions, which could not exist were there not earth "beneath" the land on which all things are constructed.

The question of being entitled to land is to a considerable extent a question of scale: "It is not too soon to provide by every possible means that as few as possible shall be without a little portion of land. The small landholders are the most precious part of a state" (J 842) as they constitute, ideally, that sovereign people by whose sole authority constitutions themselves may be changed. These are the citizens who will congregate in small social units, or wards, assembling as occasion warrants to decide their own destiny in public proceedings. So to believe is already, implicitly, to invoke once more a measure of temporality, for when one speaks of landholders one speaks of them now, existing, on earth. Jefferson is getting to the most basic of basics: these citizens are the living. The living, however, die; while the earth rolls on through the infinite reaches of cosmic time, the existence of the landholders reaches its term, which is temporally small as their holdings in land are small topographically, and new earthly laborers rise up to take their place in the drama of social destiny.

In a letter to James Madison in 1789, the scene shifts from the earth to a more explicitly discursive ground: "I set out on this ground which I suppose to be self evident, *'that the earth belongs in usufruct to the living'*; that the dead have neither powers nor rights over it" (J 959). Possession is scaled to the length of a generation: "Then no man can by *natural right* oblige the land he occupied, or the persons who succeed him in that occupation, to the payment of debts contracted by him. For if he could, he might during his own life, eat up the usufruct of the lands for several generations to come, and then the lands would belong to the dead, and not to the living" (J 959–60).

An individual may in fact be bound in such a way that successors are obligated for the credit he drew on, hence for its cancellation by repayment. But the same should not apply, Jefferson argues, to a generation. The question becomes how to measure a generation. Showing his mathematical propensity, Jefferson maneuvers among statistics, including life expectancy and average

age of an ideal-case society, and concludes that "19. years is the term beyond which neither the representatives of a nation, nor even the whole nation itself assembled can validly extend a debt" (J 961). His tolerance of change makes him welcome a little rebellion now and then, or "a law of limited duration" (J 963) that, in effect, has change written into it: at the end of that period, just as everything in law is liable to amendment through new legislation, so everything in the society is liable to amendment, through other modes of adaptation or alteration. This becomes relevant for the concept of the pursuit of happiness insofar as pursuit presupposes precisely such a capacity, without which one would not be flexible enough to change as circumstances change; capacity resembles pursuit, moreover, in denoting not performance but potentiality or expectation. Happiness may then be seen as such secured adaptation or alteration as becomes, for a given generation, the norm. Finally, the short course to which laws are thus limited is the temporal correlate of the limitations posited for the war (number of citizens, size of landholdings, etc.), a topic Jefferson raises anew by a *via negativa* that sounds almost despairing. In reading it, one should bear in mind that he was writing in France, less than two months after the start of the French Revolution; the concept of the hundred as a minimal unit of political representation does not enter the correspondence until 1810, and is refined into the idea of a ward only in 1814. "The people cannot assemble themselves; their representation is unequal and vicious. Various checks are exposed to every legislative proposition. Factions get possession of the public councils. Bribery corrupts them. Personal interests lead them astray from the general interests of their constituents" (J 963). In a word, the body politic is subject, as ever in the discourse of civic humanism, to corruption. Jefferson makes specific reference to that condition on a number of occasions, and the attitude he expresses reflects the concerns traditional to that discourse, in particular a concern to ensure that the endowments to which a republic is entitled are responsibly enabled.

With the appearance of this phenomenon, this danger not merely to the stability of the state but to the very essence of the body politic, we enter further into important considerations of which the *via negativa* above furnished a foretaste. These considerations are negative for the same reason that they are important: they endanger, threaten, intimidate, interrupt, undermine, deprive, constrain, oppose, reduce, interfere with, harm, afflict, damage, infect, or otherwise affect adversely, even to the extent of eliminating, whatever worldly things they inhere in or bear upon. Amounting to anything and everything that can or does go wrong, they are the mighty host of impairments, of disentitlings and disenablings and disendowings to which both in principle and in fact the realm of worldly things is ever prone, and are here brought together in the concept of declension.

10. *Some Versions of Declension*

In his *Notes on the State of Virginia* Jefferson seems to suggest that declension is all but inevitable as he predicts "a time, and that not a distant one,
when corruption in this, as in the country from which we derive our origin,
will have seized the heads of government, and be spread by them through
the body of the people; when they will purchase the voices of the people,
and make them pay the price" (J 246). Jefferson is admonishing more than
predicting; for legislators, being on your guard against corruption is better
than not being on guard. Here is a discourse, then, not of predestination but
of fatefulness, a counsel of wisdom more than a publishing of news. Working from the assumption that every worldly thing has its way of going wrong
suggests that what is wrong in the present case is a constitutive imbalance
wherein certain members of the body politic arrogate to themselves goods
and powers to which they are not entitled.

Such an imbalance could be thought of in neoclassical terms as disproportion, which is basically how Jefferson thinks of it when he argues for the
virtue of a state wherein a majority of citizens are landholding agricultur-
ists; for, "generally speaking, the proportion which the aggregate of the other
classes of citizens bears in any state to that of its husbandmen, is the proportion of its unsound to its healthy parts, and is a good-enough barometer
whereby to measure its degree of corruption" (J 291). Turning the rhetorical
screw, Jefferson concludes by elaborating on the traditional trope of corruption as disease: "The mobs of great cities add just so much to the support
of pure government, as sores do to the strength of the human body. It is the
manners and spirit of a people which preserve a republic in vigour" (J 291).

Jefferson is not naive enough to suppose that such manners and such a
spirit are guaranteed to survive, for all of these passages suppose that people
are susceptible to declension. This was a relatively new presupposition. "Prior
to the modern age and the rise of society, this danger [of corruption] used
to arise from the public realm, from the tendency of public power to expand and to trespass upon private interests." With the accelerated economic
growth and privatization exemplified by the British developments previously
discussed, "the dangers of corruption and perversion were much more likely
to arise from private interests than from public power."[37] When Jefferson
states above that personal interests lead them astray from the general interests
of their constituencies, he is speaking of course of the elected representatives
of the people. But, as we have seen, he also warns of the danger that corruption may spread throughout the entire body politic, a body consisting chiefly,
in proportional terms, of the popular electorate. Such corruption becomes
possible, in principle, from the moment that the people are endowed with
political power: only those who possess power can misuse it. Equally impor-

tant is the fact that the people are seen as an aggregate of private individuals, a fact that permits the little republic of the ward system to show its usefulness once more. Republican theory and institutions endow members of the public with powers to which they are entitled specifically as private individuals. But usually individuals act as persons with interests, and more is needed if the well-being of the state is to be assured. That is the capacity of these same persons to participate in the public realm, not as discrete individuals but as active members of a sovereign body politic, that is, as citizens. This, again, is what the ward is meant to provide: only if there exist such scaled-down versions of the public realm, proportionate in their entitling powers and responsibilities to their venue, can the people participate fully in government.

The body politic is social destiny incorporate, liable to the disenabling synonymous with the decline of civic virtue. Playing out the logic of this venerable corporeal trope, political discourse figures such going-wrong as a disease manifesting itself now as contagion, now as infection, now as poison, all of which can kill unless a cure is found. With tropes come dangers, and here the danger is a particular reductiveness, by which I mean taking the phenomenon in question too narrowly, as though it supplied merely the frame for higher functions. A similar risk attends the use of "endowment" as a sort of deposit to be drawn upon, as would legitimately be the case if the issue were the setting up of, say, a financial trust. On the contrary, endowing is no more or less "fundamental" than its correlates, each of which requires being both responsible to and responsible for the others.

The concept of the body politic should also be viewed from a constitutive point of view as a made thing or artificial person, a legal fiction first appearing in 1461, and broadening by 1532–33 into our sense of "the body politic" as "the nation in its corporate character; the state." Such a body is not a mere collection but a cohesive gathering, and the same holds for the body of lawmakers who enable the entitling capacities with which the people are endowed. It is this body that Jefferson identifies as the source of civic disenablement: "The people cannot assemble themselves; their representation is unequal and vicious. Various checks are opposed to every legislative proposition" (J 963).

Within the juridical sphere, in the broadest sense of the term, all of our constitutive offices may be seen to operate. When democratic legislators enact laws they *endow*, providing the wherewithal of governance; by definition the latter does not exist without being so endowed. *Enabling* consists in the effecting of law by application, enforcement; it is the long arm of the law in the form of the district attorney, say, who puts into action what the lawmakers supply. The action of judging the laws themselves, of reviewing and ruling upon them, then falls to the office of *entitling*, filled by juridical constituents of the legal system.

In practice, and according to Jefferson in theory as well, one office has a

way of being more equal than the others: "All the powers of government, legislative, executive, and judiciary, result to the legislative body. . . . The judiciary
and executive members were left dependant [sic] on the legislative, for their
subsistence in office, and some of them for their continuance in it" (J 245–46).
Jefferson concludes that this excess capacity, as it were, leads legislators to do
things they are not entitled to do: "They have accordingly, in many instances,
decided rights which should have been left to judiciary controversy" (J 246).
He seems undisturbed, however, by this undertow of deviation in which he
allows himself to be carried along; and as far as the views of the members of
the present assembly are concerned, these "are perfectly upright. When they
are led out of their regular province, it is by art in others, and inadvertence in
themselves" (J 246).

In the same passage Jefferson describes the spread of declension through
the body of the people. If such a pathology is not necessarily fatal, it is fateful
both in Pope's sense of "prophetic of destiny" (1715–20) and in Coleridge's
sense of "fraught with destiny" (1800); corruption can be foreseen because it
is one of the eventualities worldly beings face.

In a letter Jefferson expresses both personal and general concerns in the
face of declensions in legal education, which trained prospective attorneys in
Whig political principles until Toryism made such inroads that "nearly all the
young brood of lawyers now are of that hue" (J 1514). The cure for such an
ailment is a different kind of educative enabling. Here his breeding trope can
be misleading in a way that Jefferson's alternative "nursery" is not. Educators
do not endow their students with capacities with which they are already endowed. The question is not one (as it will be in Yeats) of eugenics. Educators
work with what learners bring, helping them to realize the capacities they
already have. The cure for the ailment of Toryism is a different educational
policy and practice, one that will forestall political degeneracy by tutoring
new generations of learners in political principles: "If we are true and vigilant
in our trust, within a dozen or twenty years a majority of our own legislature
will be from one school, and many disciples will have carried its doctrines
home with them to their several States, and will have leavened thus the whole
mass" (J 1514).

On a more personal note, the elderly statesman returns to the issue of
debt, now a pressing problem as Jefferson the private citizen confronts the
loss of wherewithal, his Monticello property; and this moreover in a context
of national affliction: "But the long succession of years of stunted crops, of reduced prices, the general prostration of the farming business, under levies for
the support of manufactures, &c., with the calamitous fluctuations of value
in our paper medium, have kept agriculture in a state of abject depression"

(J 1514). Despite a *"coup de grace"* (J 1514) requiring increased payment on a debt that was sapping income while family obligations were draining capital, Jefferson still could have managed were it not for the nationwide trends described above. Nothing stands in the way of further decline but a claimed entitlement:

> Reflecting on these things, the practice occurred to me, of selling, on fair valuation, and by way of lottery, often resorted to before the Revolution to effect large sales, and still in constant usage in every State for individual as well as corporation purposes. If it is permitted in my case, my lands here alone, with the mills, &c., will pay every thing and leave me Monticello and a farm free. (J 1515)

Unfortunately, Jefferson does not contemplate the freeing of the slaves on whose labor he relied in the hope of paying off his debts; the human price paid for the freedom of Monticello and a farm is not the less clear for being passed over in silence.[38] The emancipation in which Jefferson believed remained an ideal, something to be postponed until his slaves had ensured his own financial freedom. During the postponement, which proved to be lifelong, Jefferson behaved like many another slaveowner, buying, selling, and breeding human beings, and ordering punishment by lash when he deemed it necessary. For stealing nails, he has a man "severely flogged in the presence of his old companions, and committed to jail."[39]

Jefferson's plan to free the nation of slavery through expatriation may be read as a grotesque parody of Hobbes's definition of a man as his price. "The estimated value of the new-born infant is so low, (say twelve dollars and fifty cents,) that it would probably be yielded by the owner gratis," which would reduce to $37.5 millions the $600 millions he sets as the "estimated value" of the total slave property, "leaving only the expense of nourishment while with the mother, and of transportation" (J 1485). Such calculation leaves little room for moral imagination, notwithstanding that it required such imagination for him to see in emancipation a right to which all slaves were inherently entitled.

One of the more chilling moments in the text comes near the end, as he tries to balance constitutional and human scruples: "I am aware that this subject involves some constitutional scruples. But a liberal construction, justified by the object, may go far, and an amendment of the constitution, the whole length necessary. The separation of infants from their mothers, too, would produce some scruples of humanity. But this would be straining at a gnat, and swallowing a camel" (J 1487).

As the statesman-author finds himself reduced by economic pressures to the role of petitioner, a feeling of fatality broods over his discourse; he sounds death-infected, and is certainly death-haunted: "If refused, I must sell everything here, perhaps considerably in Bedford, move thither with my family, where I have not even a log hut to put my head into, and whether ground for burial, will depend on the depredations which, under the form of sales, shall have been committed on my property" (J 1515).

A degree of consolation is still to be had in contemplating the past state of happiness enabled by democratic fraternity, expressed in terms that are intimately personal while carrying institutional implications: "The friendship which has subsisted between us, now half a century, and the harmony of our political principles and pursuits, have been sources of constant happiness to me through that long period" (J 151). The perspective of this 1826 letter to Madison then widens to the institutional, and at the same time toward the limits of existence and the *ultrum horum*, the final hour of earthly being (J 1515): "And if I remove beyond the reach of attention to the University, or beyond the bourne of life itself, as I soon must, it is a comfort to leave that institution under your care" (J 1515). The circularity in the thinking, from institution to the limits of existence and back to the institution, typifies the author's constant sense of the connectedness of things. At its widest the perspective is cosmic, as the spectacle of American government is seen from a planetary point of view; in offering this perspective, Jefferson typically moves beyond the personal to the general level as he takes a last look at happiness: "If ever the earth has beheld a system of administration conducted with a single and steadfast eye to the general interest and happiness of those committed to it . . . it is that to which our lives have been devoted. To myself you have been a pillar of support through life. Take care of me when dead, and be assured that I shall leave with you my last affections" (J 1515). "Take care of me when dead" is about as far from the formal language of testament and valediction as one can imagine. Jefferson took care of the latter, largely legal business, of course. But there remains the caretaking that is in the hands of the living who alone can perform the offices of memory and mourning. These are similar but not the same. What mourning is or does will be a concern in the discussion to follow. What Jefferson is presently concerned about is memory, the faculty through whose vigilance even the impairment that is death itself may be at least in a measure overcome. Memory keeps open the way through mortality, given the cofounding of life and death, not only with each other, but with worldliness as such. Hannah Arendt writes:

> The birth and death of human beings are not simple natural occurrences, but are related to a world into which single individuals, unique, unexchangeable, and unrepeatable entities, appear and from which they depart. Birth and death presuppose a world which is not in constant movement, but whose durability and relative permanence make appearance and disappearance pos-

sible, which existed before any one individual appeared into it and will survive his eventual departure.[40]

Jefferson's plea for care is not an appeal to another world, but an appeal for continuation into the posterity of which he is writing. That he is unique, unexchangeable, and unrepeatable is the paradoxical expression of his creatural equality with everyone else. Now all this distinctiveness can continue beyond impairment only when granted the portion of discursiveness to which it is entitled. Take care of me when dead, Jefferson says; he might as well have said, Tell my story. "The chief characteristic of this specifically human life, whose appearance and disappearance constitute worldly events, is that it is itself always full of events which ultimately can be told as a story, establish a biography."[41]

A course of life is entitled, through enabling discourse, to the dignity of having mattered. To take care of the friend is to honor his right to be still in the world that otherwise goes on without him; to be *still*, to be left in peace, free from oblivion; to *be* still, to participate in posterity through the remembrance the story uniquely enables.

11. *When Destiny Is Manifest*

The social destiny conceived by Jefferson entails self-realization, development, and, when the scene is geopolitical, expansion. A decade after the Declaration, independence is being declared anew by individual settlers who, itching for land, add up to a formidable colonizing power. Like Tocqueville, Jefferson attributes the expansive impulses of his fellow citizens to an almost existential restlessness: "The present population of the inhabited parts of the U.S. is of about 10. to the square mile; & experience has shown us, that wherever we reach that the inhabitants become uneasy, as too much compressed, and go off in great numbers to search for vacant country" (J 589). He does not raise the issue of the settlers' entitlement—it is almost as if possessive individual desire were justification in itself. As his use of the term "experience" suggests, his stance is less a matter of reasoned conviction than that of perceived actuality, to which he testifies, moreover, with the conviction of the eyewitness:

> We have seen lately a single person go & decide on a settlement in Kentucky, many hundred miles from any white inhabitant, remove thither with his family and a few neighbors, & though perpetually harassed by the Indians, that settlement in the course of 10 years has acquired 30.000 inhabitants, it's [sic] numbers are increasing while we are writing, and the state of which it formerly made a part has offered it independance [sic]. (J 590)

Though lacking Timothy Dwight's evangelical strain, Jefferson shares in the latter's conflation of expansion, civic virtue, commerce, and education; in his *Greenfield Hill*, composed in the year following the Jefferson text above, Dwight declares that

> Towns, cities, fanes, shall lift their towery pride;
> The village bloom, on every streamlets side;
> Proud Commerce' mole the western surges lave . . .
> Where marshes teem'd with death, shall meads unfold;
> Untrodden cliffs resign their stores of gold
> And new-born Oxfords cheer the evening skies . . .[42]

This type of vision first took the form of a British empire of land and sea within whose vast boundaries, according to Benjamin Franklin and a co-author, writing in 1760, commerce would increase with increasing population. Eleven years later, H. H. Brackenridge and Philip Freneau sounded what would become a familiar note by predicting how the new dominion would stretch to the shores of the Pacific. By 1784 the conception of manifest destiny exists in all but name as Thomas Hutchins describes the westward march that he hopes will result not only in a transcontinental endowment but in the subordination to an American imperium encompassing the entire globe.[43]

While not disposed to such grandiloquence, Jefferson believed that the newborn nation could and must expand. The breeding trope in the following passage expresses the collateral belief that such growth is naturally entitled and endowed with its own drive: "Our confederacy must be viewed as the nest from which all America, North & South, is to be peopled" (J 844). Unlike many other writers of expansionist discourse, Jefferson carried a responsibility to bring it about, which helps to explain why he is sometimes more strategic than visionary in his thinking about it. To William H. Harrison he spells out a detailed plan to inveigle Indian occupants of coveted land into the very indebtedness that he deemed an affliction when the republic or Thomas Jefferson had to resort to it: "We shall push our trading uses, and be glad to see the good and influential individuals among them run in debt, because we observe that when these debts get beyond what the individual can pay, they become willing to lop them off by a cession of lands . . . and they will in time either incorporate with us as citizens of the United States, or remove beyond the Mississippi" (J 1118). Entitling entails a degree of reciprocity. Notwithstanding the irresistible power of his government, Jefferson enables the compensations conducive to the Indians' own happiness, as he sees it. This may be done by attracting them to cultivation of land and to weaving, an adaptation that will have the additional advantage of revealing to them that all their forests are after all "useless to them" (J 1118). Nor does he seek profit: in contrast with private trading posts, which must show gains in the account books, those supported by the government should only break even. On the other hand, disendowing the native inhabitants by dispossessing them of their lands seems not to weigh on his conscience, and the same may be said of something greatly worse, their decimation: "The Cahokias extinct, we are entitled to the country by our paramount sovereignty. . . . The Kaskaskia being reduced to a few families, I presume we may purchase their whole country for what would place every individual of them at his ease, and be a small price to us" (J 1119). Jefferson's basic problem is differential entitling, enabling, and endowing, and it is complex. Jefferson takes for granted that the native inhabitants have rights, capacities, and possessions; he effectively assumes, at the same time, that as political actors the Indians are molded on the same Lockean model that so profoundly influenced the authors of the Constitution — Jefferson pronounces Locke, Bacon, and Newton to be the three greatest men who ever lived. In Locke's *Second Treatise* we read:

> Though the Earth, and all inferior Creatures be common to all Men, yet every Man has a *Property* in his own *Person*. This no Body has any Right to but himself. The Labour of his Body, and *Work* of his Hands, we may say, are properly his. Whatsoever then he removes out of the State that Nature hath provided, and left it in, he hath mixed his *Labour* with, and joyned to it something that is his own, and thereby makes it his *Property*.[44]

Regarding our three offices, "man" is thus entitled to such endowment as is enabled by his labor, a concept extending to any human activity through which any worldly thing comes into possession or use. Far from excluding the practices of hunting and gathering peoples, Locke grounds his ideology in just such practices, arguing that the deer belongs to the Indian who labored to kill it even as acorns and apples belong to those who labor to pick them up.

The situation becomes more difficult, where Indians are concerned, when the property in question is land. "But the *chief matter of Property* being now not the Fruits of the Earth, and the Beasts that subsist on it, but the Earth it self; as that which takes in and carries with it all the rest: I think it is plain, that *Property* in that too is acquired as the former. *As much Land* as a Man Tills, Plants, Improves, Cultivates, and can use the Product of, so much is his *Property*."[45] The hunting and gathering peoples, with whom the president deals in his 1806 letter to the Cherokee chiefs, cannot by this reasoning claim ownership of the land on which they subsist. They possess it nonetheless by virtue of occupancy and the implied right of inheritance, though that right has not been recorded in the statutory mode of positive law to which Jefferson desires the Indians to accustom themselves. Thus, a native who has accepted the compensation of a smallish enclosed plot for cultivation will welcome protection as the only way of guaranteeing to his survivors their familial entitlements:

"When a man has enclosed and improved his farm, builds a good house on it and raised plentiful stocks of animals, he will wish when he dies that these things shall go to his wife and children, whom he loves more than he does his other relations. . . . You will, therefore, find it necessary to establish laws for this" (J 561).

Natives thus settled have obviously given up the practice of warfare, a theme that is rarely far from Jefferson's thoughts, even when writing to these his "children" in his most patriarchal vein. Fighting the Indians in order to possess the land they already possess is the hard way to manifest the destiny that is the American state. Treating with them is the easier way, and the more equitable. Jefferson regards natives as fellow human beings endowed like their white counterparts with reason; this being the case, it appears that they are as entitled to just treatment under law, once they accept its rule, as are citizens of the United States. To facilitate the transition from natural right to entitling by positive law, Jefferson invokes the mediating trope of the family as imagined origin of polity. If the people of the Indian nations can come to accept the notion of an englobing family administered by a benevolent patriarch, they will be more accepting of the compensations with which the United States will endow them. It helps, one supposes, that members of Indian tribes are at the same time members of families, and that they are equally members of nations, and not only in the familiar sense, from 1650, of aboriginal tribes, but also in a larger sense that Jefferson seems to adopt in certain key places: "My friends and children, we are descended from the old nations which live beyond the great water, but we and our forefathers have been so long here that we seem like you to have grown out of this land. We consider ourselves no longer of the old Nations beyond the great water, but as united in one family with our red brethren here" (J 564). Here is the first sense of "nation," from 1300, signifying an aggregate of persons bound together by commonalities such as shared language, history, and race, and usually situated in a delimited space. This is not, however, what the new family amounts to, but what it departs from. Wanting to know more about his native children, once Spain had departed from the scene, the President "sent our beloved man, Captain Lewis, one of my own family, to . . . get acquainted with all the Indian nations in the neighborhood" (J 546). Here "nation" applies narrowly to the native constituency and not, as in the case of the new nation-family, to the unifying fact of mutual extended occupancy, an idea much enhanced, to the Enlightenment way of thinking, by shared natural origins: "we seem like you to have grown out of the land" (J 564). Tacitly drawing strength from the traditional association, in western political discourse, of the provenance of society and state from the primal family, this new crucible of world-making accommodates both concepts of nation. Though members of a nation in the colonial sense, the Indians are also, and to more purpose, a nation in the first sense. The recognition comes in Jefferson's 1803 letter to the Choctaws: "Our seventeen States compose a great and growing nation. Their children are as the leaves of the trees, which the winds are spreading over the forest. But we are just also. We take from no nation what belongs to it" (J 558). Such a generality is persuasive if and only if it envisages the Indian body politic in a similarly general way, i.e., as a nation among others in the first, broad sense of the term. There is no point in asserting that the government respects the rights of every nation unless, in making such a claim, it is addressing such a nation. The discourse thus implicitly endows both longtime occupants of the land with the same corporate character.

A crucial differential, on the other hand, is the discrepancy in size and disposition between the U.S. and the Indian populations. Immediately after the "no-nation" statement, the motif of the nation whose children spread like wind-borne leaves issues in the observation that "our growing numbers make us always willing to buy lands from our red brethren, when they are willing to sell" (J 558). The disproportion in numbers and their accelerating rate are the enabling factors that destine geographical expansion and make Indian acquiescence inevitable. "Within 40 years the whole territory will be peopled at the existing rate. . . . The present occupiers will just have force enough to repress & restrain the emigrations to a certain degree of consistence" (J 589–90).

If Americans lacking land are entitled thereby to take possession of more, the corollary is that the present occupiers have too much. The notion of a natural due measure or proportion in the amount of property one owns is a Lockean creation as well: "*God has given us all things richly*, 1 Tim. vi.17. is the Voice of Reason confirmed by Inspiration. But how far has he given it us? *To enjoy. . . .* Whatever is beyond this, is more than his share, and belongs to others."[46] Vacant lands accordingly invite expanding populations to take possession of them, notwithstanding that such vacancy sometimes exhibits Indian occupancy as a conspicuous feature. Another important corollary, also from Locke, is that intrinsic value must give way to improved value. An endowment of land left untouched, which is to say unworked, must be worth less than the same land enabled by being worked: only productive land yields profit.

For the American colonial as rebel, sovereignty proved a fateful theme: "In the last analysis," says Bernard Bailyn, "it was over this issue that the Revolution was fought."[47] The fateful discourse of the Constitution, with its creative compromises, resolved the question by deciding first that sovereignty rests ultimately with the people, that overdetermined corporate person of Lockean tradition, whose supreme power over the otherwise sovereign legislature makes the latter's power representative only, by delegation; and next that by prudential forethought all such delegated powers must be distributed among separate, distinct, but coresponsible units of government.

Its polysemous nature can make sovereignty appear one thing from one angle and another from another. Thus its power as such may be equated with endowing, its modes of operation with enabling, its justness with entitling. This is to see the facets one at a time, however, and not in their synchrony. Sovereignty is power, efficacy, justness all at once: *entitling, that is enabled and endowed; enabling, that is entitled and endowed; endowing, that is entitled and enabled.*

> Endowed with the faculties and the rights of men, breathing an ardent love of liberty and independence, and occupying a country which left them no desire but to be undisturbed, the stream of overflowing population from other regions directed itself on these shores; . . . now reduced within limits too narrow for the hunter's state, humanity enjoins us to teach them agriculture and the domestic arts; to encourage them to that industry which alone can enable them to maintain their place in existence, and to prepare them in time for that state of society, which to bodily comforts adds the improvement in mind and morals. (J 520)

The office performed in the first sentence corresponds with endowing as described in the present study; the faculties perform enabling functions; and the rights are entitlements. Jefferson's concern with the latter recurs in the statement that "humanity enjoins us to teach them," while the concluding words address the process of enabling commensurate with such enjoining. Finally, industry is to perform an enabling in the absence of which their endowment is in danger of the ultimate impairment, which is the dissolution of being itself.

To the extent that any one concept underlies the tendencies and patterns thus portrayed, it is the concept of manifest destiny. As it proceeds, discussion broadens to consider ways in which the ideological implications of the texts entail or are entailed by issues that go beyond the more national aspects of the discourse in question. Which is just a way of saying that the question of manifest destiny is inseparable from the question of human destiny as such.

12. *Destiny According to the Poets*

Manifest destiny found its first major poet in Walt Whitman and its most recent one in Robert Frost. The Jeffersonian Democrat who edited the Brooklyn *Eagle* applauded the policies of fellow Jacksonian Democrat James Polk, thanks to whose presidential policies the United States annexed Texas in 1845, acquired Oregon in 1846, and in the same year launched an unnecessary war with Mexico. Whitman wanted to go even further, having convinced himself that Cuba and Canada should also be encompassed within the expansion of the American state. Some of the poet's most characteristic work is accordingly expansionist as well as expansive: in "Years of the Modern" (1865/1881) he says of "average man,"

> His daring foot is on land and sea everywhere, he colonizes the Pacific, the
>   archipelagoes,
> With the steamship, the electric telegraph, the newspaper, the wholesale
>   engines of war,
> With these and the world-spreading factories he interlinks all geography,
>   all lands . . .[48]

In these lines, technology, which Whitman tends to foreground when in this mood, gets off to a rather American start. Jefferson himself is the first lexical authority for "steamship" (1790), while American inventors like Robert Fulton and Robert Fitch were celebrated for their pioneering work in steam-driven vessels. When the poet specifies *electric telegraph* he recognizes its difference from the telegraph per se, which from the late eighteenth century signified any device for transmitting audible or visual signals, and tacitly invokes Samuel F. B. Morse, the American inventor and painter, who has been credited with key developments leading to the electric telegraph, and who devised the Morse code just five years before the first version of this Whitman text. No such native claims may be made, by contrast, for the newspaper, the engine of war, or factories, which are international. Whitman's international or ecumenical inclinations are easily traced in other expansive or expansionist texts, such as "A Broadway Pageant," where "the tann'd Japanee" and "the murky night-morning of wonder and fable inscrutable" (2: 515.34–36) suggest at least a residual racism.

Greater difficulties loom when the poet faces the more urgent problem of African Americans dispossessed of the entitlements, enablements, and endowments possessed by their white masters. The short poem featuring an African American, "Ethiopia Saluting the Colors," which Whitman composed half a dozen years after the Civil War,[49] bears witness to his struggle to come to poetic terms with the still dispossessed state of the black populace as a whole:

> Who are you dusky woman, so ancient hardly human,
> With your woolly-white and turban'd head, and bare bony feet?
> Why rising by the roadside here, do you the colors greet?
>   (3:631, 1–3)

These lines, like most of those that follow, show the poet regressing to the studied rhyming and structure that had channeled his early creative energies

into verse of remarkable conventionality. Here Whitman adopts the venerable device of an encounter between an itinerant speaker and a mysterious
figure through whose agency certain themes may be broached. The interrogative strategy of the opening and the closing stanzas evidently aims at a note of
sublimity, open-ended questions on high matters being traditional with that
mode. No Edmund Burke is required to explain that obscurity and darkness
are sources of sublimity as well, whereas one recognizes the grotesque, a mix-
ture bordering on the sublime and also on the comedic, in the details of the
"bare bony feet" and the animalistic overtones of "hardly human."

As a palliative to the racist tinge, the latter attribute is more or less metonymically linked to the woman's age, the absence of a comma between
"ancient" and "hardly human" creating a run-on effect of virtual merger, as
though the extent of her years somehow accounts for her approximation to
animality. The woman who is "Ethiopia" greets the colors to much the same
semiological purpose as the photograph, described by Roland Barthes, in
which a black soldier of colonial origin salutes the French tricolor to signify
"that France is a great Empire, that all her sons, without any colour discrimination, faithfully serve under the flag, and that there is no better answer to
the detractors of an alleged colonialism than the zeal shown by this Negro in
serving his so-called oppressors."[50] What Whitman's nineteenth-century icon
signifies in a similar way is black gratitude for the war that abolished slavery
in the United States, and African-American devotion to the flag as symbol of
the triumphant Union cause. But while the colors are coming closer to Ethiopia, her awkwardly symbolic name works to the opposite effect, distancing
her from the no less symbolic colors by forcing attention onto her area of origin rather than the country to which, the Confederacy having ceased to exist,
she now belongs. This is entirely consistent with the lines of stanza three:

> *Me master years a hundred since from my parents sunder'd,*
> *A little child, they caught me as the savage beast is caught,*
> *Then hither me across the sea the cruel slaver brought.*
>
> (3:362, 7–9)

Awkward in a different way, struggling to render the patterns of speech the
woman has acquired in the American South, these lines must be judged a
partial failure at best. Her speech is not the speech of any recorded dialect of
which this reader is aware, and Whitman was too keen a student of language
to suppose that the likes of "sunder'd" or "savage beast" would be taken for
genuine dialect terms. Moreover, dialect is largely a matter of idiom, phrase-
ology, vocabulary and diction, not of syntactical deviance from the standard
tongue of reference; yet it is precisely such deviance that Ethiopia's utterances foreground: "Me master years a hundred since from my parents sun-

der'd." Such alienating effects enhance the exotic flavor introduced by the name Ethiopia, exposing a less attractive side of the poet's cosmopolitanism. Changes in punctuation should also be taken into account. The 1871 text offers, for example, "Me, master, years a hundred, since from my parents sunder'd" (3:632, 7) which has too much formal balance and thereby lessens the "primal" aura engendered by the more obscure final version, and also makes the woman's statement into an apostrophe to the speaker who, as master, falls into the slaver's role.

Reduced to silence for the rest of the poem, Ethiopia functions gesturally: "Her high-borne turban'd head she wags, and rolls her darkling eye, / And courtesies to the regiments, the guidons moving by" (3:632, 11–12). The one detail that holds attention to the woman's past suffering is "high-borne," meaning "of noble birth" but also "carried or sustained," which is all the more fitting in that, despite her age and condition, she keeps at her activities all day long. The activities themselves approach pantomime, the effect of which is to reinforce both her otherness and the poet's specular relation to that otherness. The modifier he selects for her eye, "darkling," helps to preserve her mystery. Finally, attentive to detail, the poet changes the original text's "curtsy," which was current usage, to "courtesies," whose courtly origins may be meant to invest Ethiopia with the mystique of superior social status.

The poet asks:

> What is it fateful woman, so blear, hardly human?
> Why wag your head with turban bound, yellow, red and green?
> Are the things so strange and marvelous you see or have seen?
> (3:632, 13–15)

If there is something unsettling in this figure, it is partly because of the earlier statement that she is hardly human, and partly because of her obscurity, which may be illusory as well as opaque: "blear" suggests an almost ominous quality to her fatefulness. Betsy Erkilla notes: "The black woman's 'hardly human' figure is 'blear'—something indistinct, dim, and out of focus in Whitman's vision of America. She is a 'fateful woman' whose liberation and rising are part of the world's fated march toward the democratic future, but in her fatefulness, she is also a figure of fate, a possibly ominous presence who will affect the country's destiny in uncertain ways." [51]

The question of the ultimate destiny of "emancipated" African Americans and the manifest destiny exemplified in the "removal" of Native Americans to inferior land allotments come together for Whitman in the late 1850s as he confronts the nightmares into which expansionist dreams could metamorphose. U.S. acquisition of the island of Cuba, of tracts in Central America, and of the American Southwest entailed the expansion, he now saw, of our

most "peculiar institution." As editor of the Brooklyn *Daily Times* he therefore turned away from the expansionist policies of President Polk and anything else that could lead to another adventure such as the Mexican War.

If some twenty years later another adventure prompted a contradictory
posture, this may be explained in part by the fact that the 1876 battle at Little
Big Horn did not seem to be connected to the slavery question, which had
for so long concerned the poet. Annexation of lands by the federal state must
never entitle former slave-owners to regain that ownership, or so his reasoning appears to run when the extension of the peculiar institution into new
states was still an active possibility. But taking possession of lands possessed
by native populations, the purpose finally served by cavalry deployments in
areas such as the Dakota Territory, never becomes a comparable concern to
the poet. Only when distance in time permits him to look back at the fate of
American Indians does he begin to perceive the suffering in their being in all
ways impaired. But in his rendering of an event that had transpired as recently
as the Custer fiasco, white participants loom so large on the discursive canvas
that there is barely room for the Indians. Just two of the twenty-six lines of
"From Far Dakota's Cañons" contain specific references to them, and only in
the second of these do the Indians even begin to come alive. The centerpiece
of the poem is the tableaulike immolation of Custer:

> Thou of the tawny flowing hair in battle,
> I erewhile saw, with erect head, pressing ever in front, bearing a bright sword
> in thy hand,
> Now ending well in death the splendid fever of thy deeds
>
> (3:654, 18–20)

The first poem in which Whitman attempts a closer look at things Indian
is "Red Jacket (from Aloft)," a kind of pastoral elegy for the Iroquois leader
who acknowledged the sovereignty of the United States and threw tribal support behind the nation in the War of 1812. Occasioned by the reburial of Red
Jacket's bones and the erection of a monument to him in Buffalo City in 1884,
the text reveals the bard in his most "official" public mode:

> Upon this scene, this show,
> Yielded to-day by fashion, learning, wealth,
> (Nor in caprice alone—some grains of deepest meaning,)
> Haply, aloft (who knows?) from distant sky-clouds' blended shapes,
> As some old tree, or rock or cliff, thrill'd with its soul,
> Product of Nature's sun, stars, earth direct—a towering human form,
> In hunting-shirt of film, arm'd with the rifle, a half-ironical smile curving
> its phantom lips,
> Like one of Ossian's ghosts looks down.
>
> (3:711–12, 1–8)

As in the Custer poem, Whitman, trying to tell the story while it is still fresh, produces a discourse static and specular, in the manner of those once-popular *tableaux vivants* in which silent performers froze themselves in the attitudes of personages from celebrated historical scenes.

Likening Red Jacket to one of Ossian's ghosts assimilates the chief to foreign literary tradition. Whitman may be thinking that Ossian is a suitable resource because James Macpherson's influential poems in Scots English involve ancient Gaelic materials; so Whitman in his way is reconstructing too. A second point is that Whitman in *Specimen Days* recalls "a real Ossianic night," stormy, swift, and weirdly silent, a night he might equally have called sublime (to mention another tradition). The Anglo-American literary phenomenon that "Ossian" became is thus assimilated to nature in the form of the American landscape and in the form of the American Indian, who in popular representations had largely become a feature of that landscape.[52] Whitman could claim that in this reconstruction he had the natives' best interests at heart. But reconstructing is as reconstructing does, and what Whitman does here is uncomfortably close to the practices of the "friends of the Indians," a group of vocal whites who, in the last twenty years of the nineteenth century, were willing to override all opposition from native tribes in an effort to transform bad Indians into good Americans.[53]

"Yonnondio," the second of Whitman's Indian poems, written two years before the U.S. Army's massacre of Indian men, women, and children at Wounded Knee in 1890, is a more earnest attempt to engage the fate of the country's native population. It is marred, however, by evasiveness. The poem teases itself into elaborating its own entitlement, lodged in the Iroquois name and word, meaning "lament for the aborigines" (3:716), that is inscribed above the text:

> A song, a poem of itself — the word itself a dirge,
> Amid the wilds, the rocks, the storm and wintry night,
> To me such misty, strange tableaux the syllables calling up
> (3:716, 1–3)

While storm and wintry night register a note of activity, they mainly provide, with the wilds and rocks, the conditions for another tableau, the effect of which more nearly resembles the mysterious vagueness of "Red Jacket" and "Ethiopia Saluting the Colors" than the lightning flash of the Custer poem. The true poetic interest is in the invocation of the entitling name that introduces the central vision:

> Yonnondio — I see, far in the west or north, a limitless ravine, with plains
> and mountains dark,

> I see swarms of stalwart chieftains, medicine-men, and warriors,
> As flitting by like clouds of ghosts, they pass and are gone in the twilight
>   (3:716, 4-6)

Such a landscape contains enough vastness and obscurity to be characterized as sublime, an effect that the sonorous name Yonnondio enhances; as mellifluous as Poe's Ulalume, it is even more unlike any familiar English term ("Ulalume" having cognates in the semantically relevant "ullulate" family), and may be taken as another touch of the exotic. The centrality of the vision thus introduced consists in its rendering of the disappearance of the lamented aborigines, or rather in its partial rendering: the poet is silent in these texts about the specific historical causes of their afflictions, and this is directly related to the silence of the Indians themselves. Yonnondio does not speak, it is the poet who speaks, and what he speaks is every word in the poem, including "Yonnondio." Yonnondio does not so much as utter his own name, which has been taken over by the speaker in the text. The latter can, the former cannot, be silent when he wishes. This silencing of the native's voice, together with the appropriation of his euphonic name, far from being original with Whitman, had become a matter of convention. When stoicism is indicated the American is mute or close to it; fuller utterance is then valorized as being eloquent or poetic, aboriginal names for persons and places being particularly prized.[54]

The evasion cannot be attributed to ignorance. As early as 1846 Whitman published an essay entitled "Indian Life and Customs," and he later recorded memorable moments with Native Americans during his wartime service in the federal Indian Bureau in Washington, D.C. As an informed journalist he would have known of the epochal Removal Bill of 1830, which entitled the government to expropriate native endowment, in the form of Southeastern lands, in exchange for much less desirable spaces west of the Mississippi River. Press reports of Andrew Jackson's campaigns against the Creeks seized the public imagination and smoothed the general's way to the White House. Journalists would later tell how, as president, Jackson defied Chief Justice Marshall's decision favoring Cherokee land entitlements, the fateful result of which was the Trail of Tears, a harrowing march that killed off nearly one-quarter of the participants. Finally, the Indian poems were composed during or shortly after much public debate over additional ways to entitle and enable the expropriation of aboriginal endowment. Congressional efforts to force land ownership in severalty culminated in the Dawes Act of 1887, the purport of which was to entitle whites, by less direct means than forced evacuation, to turn still more Indians into ghosts: the legislation, adopted in the same year as "Yonnondio" was written, mandated the breaking up of reservations into individual allotments as a way of ultimately breaking down tribal territorial integrity.[55]

Here is some at least of the history that appears to have informed the poet more than the poem. The Indians of "Yonnondio" are not so much historical persons as they are features of landscape, "flitting," like insects, into oblivion.

> (Race of the woods, the landscapes free, and the falls!
> No picture, poem, statement, passing them to the future:)
> Yonnondio! Yonnondio! — unlimn'd they disappear
>
> (3:717, 7–9)

The two parenthetic lines carry the expressive burden of the poem: the Indians are disappearing and there is no record to tell their fate. What is curious is that "Yonnondio" appears to be just such a record, to which the only plausible reply is that the force of the emphasis of the line is not on the lack of picture, poem, or statement but on the fact that, though these exist, they do not project the vanished race into posterity. An intriguing *peripeteia* immediately follows:

> To-day gives place, and faces — the cities, farms, factories fade;
> A muffled sonorous sound, a wailing word is borne through the air for a
>   moment,
> Then blank and gone and still, and utterly lost.
>
> (3:717, 10–12)

It is hard to imagine a more abrupt reversal than the one that occurs when, by a kind of chiasmus, the civilization of the dispossessor disappears as well. The problem is that in 1888 it is hardly factual to suggest that the aborigines are now no more, and it is hardly responsible to weep for their passing rather than look to the greatly impaired condition of the actual survivors. Someone credited like Whitman with an ecumenical imagination might be expected to have avoided both errors. At the time Whitman was writing, those survivors, as indicated above, occupied a foreground of public discourse. In evading the living to lament the vanished, Whitman's text, already holding so much under erasure, virtually voids that existence, insuring that nothing will interfere with the poem's salving nostalgia.

The muted and muting sound near the end of the poem manages to be obscure without becoming sublime and without transcending an inherent contradiction. For, while the only antecedent for the sound is "Yonnondio," signifying "lament for the aborigines," it is borne through the air in relation to the fading of *non*-aboriginal existence. This apocalyptic moment, so strangely muffled, derives much of its quality from indeterminacy, which is a polite way of noting how much the poet fails to deliver. His text is peculiarly empty in the center; it treats of the fateful course of two civilizations, of two apocalypses, really, without even a suggestion as to the agents or agency effecting the disappearance. In E. M. Forster's terms, the poet tells a story without a plot. " 'The king died and then the queen died,' is a story. 'The king died, and then the queen died of grief' is a plot."[56] Whitman's story line, in other words, is "The Indian civilization disappeared and then the white American civilization disappeared too." But it is a strange story because, to the extent that Indians were sacrificed as a civilization, it was mainly the white American civilization that carried out the sacrifice. Nor does the text provide a way of determining why apocalypse one inspires a thrice-sounded cry while apocalypse two inspires a muffled sound that lasts but a moment. In the second disappearance, is the poet trying to enable what the Indians are entitled to by being dispossessed, namely, retributive justice *for the dispossessers*? The poem that follows, while it raises less vexing questions, also needs explaining.

Like "Red-Jacket" and "From Far Dakota's Cañons," Whitman's last Indian poem, "Osceola," takes its departure from a concrete historical event, in this case the death in captivity of the young Seminole leader whose name is transliterated as Asi-Yahola and anglicized as Osceola.

> When his hour of death had come,
> He slowly rais'd himself from the bed on the floor,
> Drew on his war-dress, shirt, leggings, and girdled the belt around his waist.
> Call'd for vermilion paint (his looking-glass was held before him,)
> Painted half his face and neck, his wrists, and back-hands.
>
> (3:743, 1–5)

One notes the high incidence, which will continue throughout the text, of oddly convincing details: the slowness of the rising, the holding of the looking-glass, the particular paint and mode of application. According to his note at the head of the text, Whitman was drawing on firsthand information supplied by a U.S. Marine shortly after Osceola's death in captivity at Fort Moultrie, South Carolina, in 1838. In the note the poet identifies Osceola, perhaps without realizing the pun in the second modifier, as "a young, brave, leading Seminole in the Florida war of that time — was surrender'd to our troops, imprison'd and literally died of 'a broken heart' in Fort Moultrie. He sicken'd of his confinement — the doctor and officers made every allowance and kindness possible for him, then the close" (3:743). A few months later Whitman offered a different provenance: "The poem is given almost word for word out of conversations I have had with Catlin: Catlin, the great Indian man." Calling attention to the Catlin print, Whitman observes, "That is from life: a fine spectacle he makes, too! But Osceola was like a great many of the niggers — like Douglass — in being of mixed blood, having a dash of white, not pure Indian." It is hard to decide whether this racial condition is meant to make Osceola more appealing or less so, though the analogy with Douglass as "nigger" suggests the latter; nor do Whitman's further ramblings in the same general direction add light. In any event he recalls how, loafing about the Brooklyn Navy Yard, "I learned that he literally died of a broken heart — died of the confinement, imprisonment."[57]

How much the poet got from these sources is a matter of conjecture. At a minimum, he probably did learn something from George Catlin, who was finishing his portrait of Osceola shortly before the Indian leader died. That Whitman knew of Osceola's various impairments appears likely in view of the similarity between his text and the text of the attending physician, whose well-publicized account may have been one of the items that he "pieced" together to make the poem. The following columns cite passages from the report that correlate with passages in the poem:[58]

Report	Poem
. . . [H]e rose up in his bed, which was on the floor, and put on his shirt, his leggings. . . . He then called for his red paint, and his looking-glass, which was held before him, when he deliberately painted one-half of his face, his neck, and throat — his wrists — the backs of his hands. . . . His knife he then placed in its sheath, under his belt. . . . [H]e laid [*sic*] down a few minutes to recover strength sufficient, when he rose up as before, and with most benignant and pleasing smiles, extended his hand to me and to all the officers and chiefs . . . he made a signal for them to lower him down upon his bed . . . and he then slowly drew from his war-belt his scalping knife, . . . and a moment later smiled away his last breath, without a struggle or a groan.	He slowly rais'd himself from the bed on the floor, Drew on his war-dress, shirt, leggings . . . Call'd for vermilion paint (his looking-glass was held before him,) Painted half his face and neck, his wrists, and back-hands. Put the scalp-knife carefully in his belt Rose again, half sitting, smiled, gave in silence his extended hand to each and all, Sank faintly to the floor (tightly grasping the tomahawk handle,) Fix'd his look of wife and little children — the last And here a line in memory of his name and death.

The doctor's firsthand report, together with whatever else the Marine or the painter may have contributed, issues in a sense of felt experience lacking in the other Indian pieces. The poem seems to enable a remembrance grounded in concrete circumstance. "Osceola" looks, in other words, to be a picture, poem, or statement "passing the Indian to the future."

According to Whitman's diagnosis, as noted above, Osceola died of a broken heart. In fact, he contracted malaria during his many months in the swamp. While he was sitting for Catlin's portrait the army surgeon diagnosed tonsillitis as well. Whether the poet possessed this information may be less important than his evident belief that Indians could not survive in any sort of confinement. The belief could be put to contrasting uses. Sympathizers could use it to resist attempts to force natives into reservations, because this would ultimately destroy them, while antagonists could draw inverse conclusions from the same premise: since confinement would ultimately destroy them (and since they were incorrigible anyway), they might as well be eliminated outright.

To understand the Osceola behind "Osceola" it will be necessary to review a few established facts about him that bear upon our reading of the poem. Asi-Yaholo was of a Creek branch who, like others of his nation, combined with the few aboriginal Seminoles who had not been driven from their lands, and with others, including runaway slaves, to form a kind of second-wave people who came to be called by the same name as members of the aboriginal population. The young warrior, who rose swiftly to prominence, was widely acknowledged by his enemies to be a determined and resourceful opponent. When he was finally captured despite his flag of truce, he became an appealing figure in the eyes of many whites, who objected to the unscrupulous tactics employed against him and other natives.

If Whitman's Osceola, by contrast, is transformed into the very picture of resignation, several reasons may be adduced. First, his health, as we have seen, had been ruined. Second, the fact that he had been more than once ready to parley, and was captured while actually doing so, suggests a willingness to acquiesce in what looked to be an inescapable fate; numerous tribes had already succumbed, at the time of Osceola's struggles, to pressure from advancing white populations. A third consideration opens into characterological features: Osceola was consistently described as pleasant and gentlemanly. Though hardly explanatory in themselves, such traits may help to explain the graciousness with which he brought strangers and enemies together for his final moments. The seemliness of Osceola's manners, from the white perspective, is more fully explained by the ease with which they assimilated him to Eurocentric, even classical norms. One eyewitness observes a Grecian nose that "would be perfectly Phidian but that it becomes slightly arched." Another saw "black and piercing" eyes that "were full of dark fire, but when in repose they were softer than the soft eye of woman. His mouth, when relieved by a smile, wore an expression of great sweetness; — and his lips were chiseled with the accuracy of sculpture." [59]

Our final consideration has equally to do with assimilation, as Whitman's poem confers on his Indian subject the type of Last-Moment scene so characteristic of the Christian culture of the time; the sorrow-laden but edifying process in which the dying person resigns himself to fate blends with a general aura of repose and reconciliation. Anger over being tricked into capture and the shame of submission all have disappeared. The poet's sympathy with this process of sublimation (if that is what it is) greatly intensifies the poignancy of the tableau.

By virtue of this essentially enabling process an acceptable degree of assimilation is the more readily achieved. It is exemplified in the cult of the

Ghost Dance, which was taking on a new life, ironically, just around the time Whitman was writing the poem. The Ghost Dance had originated some twenty years earlier with a native revivalist movement in northern California. Around 1887 a Paiute medicine man, having experienced a kind of spiritual death and having borne witness to a joyous afterlife in which the old ways of his people had been resumed, was commanded by God to "go back and tell his people they must be good and love one another, have no quarrelling and live in peace with the whites . . . if they faithfully obeyed his instructions they would at last be reunited with their friends in the other world."[60] When the still unpacified Sioux threw themselves into Ghost Dance activities, white overreaction culminated, near the end of the year in which Whitman began writing his poem, in the massacre at Wounded Knee.

A similar process of sublimation may be hypothesized where Whitman himself is concerned. Here the too-easy poise and equanimity the poet exhibited before the world comes once more into consideration. Whitman seemed "ostentatiously mild" after being fired from his Washington post in Indian affairs because *Leaves of Grass* offended the new secretary of the interior.[61] It is then not hard to imagine that this longtime student of the Indians, partly recollecting and partly repressing old memories as he looked at once to his own and his country's past and posterity, could identify with another hero who was comparably poised and mild as he approached his end.

In his last moments, according to the record, Osceola brings as much history as possible into the scene around him: "Although he could not speak he signified by signs that he wished me to send for the chiefs and the officers of the past, whom I called." On Osceola's request both of his wives then enter the picture, bringing in the items of war-dress described in the poem. More telling than the poet's omission of the second wife is the omission of the chiefs and army officers, whose presence alone bodies forth the historical context of the scene and testifies to the purposiveness of Osceola's acts. Without them there is nothing to look at but the impaired individual. In other respects Osceola is enabled beyond his actual capacities, for in the poem he lowers himself whereas in fact he was so weak that he asked to be helped back into his bed. Depicting him as not requiring help reinforces the image of a man acting self-reliantly, like a good Emersonian. By thus excluding the larger social world, the world whose representatives Osceola himself brought into the scene of assimilation and apotheosis, the poem can center on the companionate couple, whose marriage of true love sorts well with the patriarchal piety here implied: well may such sensibility surrender to a broken heart. But this obscures the historical facts. The explanation of the Seminole's fate is his dis-enabling and dis-entitling by false imprisonment, compounded by the dis-endowment of disease. Here is impairment writ large but hardly seen.

Even at the height of his powers, the vision that can make Whitman great is apt to abandon him.

> A man's body at auction,
> (For before the war I often go to the slave-mart and watch the sale,)
> I help the auctioneer, the sloven does not half know his business.
>
> (1:128, 95–97)

The implications of teaching the auctioneer his business are, so to speak, both horizontal and vertical. Horizontal: the slave embodies moral and ontic indifference and could be exchanged for any other body as easily as the poet exchanges himself for the auctioneer. Vertical: the poet alone can elect to be an object on the horizontal level, such as the auctioneer, and thus be the equivalent of any other object on the same level, such as the slave. Looked at socially, verticality is a hierarchy in which the poet occupies the apex of endowing, enabling, and entitling, the auctioneer the next position beneath him, and the slave, proportionately impaired, the lowest position of all. This is the meaning, for him, of freedom — but only in the abstract; concretely, his vision is disenabling, exposing the abstraction, in which the poet's actual unfreedom is reified, as a failure of moral vision. The problem lies in a poetic rapture not disconnected from an impulse to assault, an impulse so to force one's self on an other that the meaning of the other *for* the other is sacrificed for the thrill of feeling *oneself* thereby expressed. At which point, this somewhat skewed dialectic having served its purpose, and the rapture having passed, the forcer, now as indifferent as Zeus in Yeats's "Leda and the Swan," can let the other drop.

"Song of Myself" generally resists the poet's inclination, where racial others are concerned, to operate manipulatively, as though the beings in question were interchangeable. Thus the episode of the runaway slave, who is ministered to in the speaker's home: "And brought water and fill'd a tub for his sweated body and bruis'd feet, / And gave him a room that enter'd from my own, and gave him some coarse clean clothes" (1:12, 193–94). The runaway slave is the first in a series of male figures whose flesh is exposed to the poet's admiring attention, and the appearance of the 28 young men bathing by the shore (section 11) extends the metonymic sequence on to the butcher-boy and more beguilingly to the blacksmiths: "From the cinder-strew'd threshold I follow their movements, / The lithe sheer of their waists plays even with their massive arms" (221–22). The sequence culminates with the return of dark glamor in the form of the black teamster:

> His blue shirt exposes his ample neck and breast and loosens over his hip-band
> His glance is calm and commanding, he tosses the slouch of his hat away
>   from his forehead,

The sun falls on his crispy hair and mustache, falls on the black of his polish'd
  and perfect limbs.

I behold the picturesque giant and love him, and I do not stop there,
I go with the team also.

In me the caresser of life wherever moving, backward as well as forward
    sluing,
To niches aside and junior bending, not a person or object missing,
Absorbing all to myself and for this song.

(1:14, 227-34)

If we look back at the concluding scene of "Osceola," the assimilative function of the present scene becomes more apparent. The poet arrays the figures for what proves to be a climactic assimilation of the most radical kind: in the interest of his song the "I" literally takes individual inward possession of every worldly thing in reach. In retrospect, the episode with the runaway slave can be seen to serve a similar purpose; the difference is that what becomes radical assimilation in the form of absorption there assumes the more "domestic" form of taking the man into the home, where his contiguity (his room is entered from the speaker's room) opens either fraternal or erotic possibilities, or both.

The figure of the slave returns in section 33, where the self-transforming first-person posits what needs to be seen as a disturbing equivalence:

The hounded slave that flags in the race, leans by the fence, blowing, cover'd
    with sweat,
The twinges that sting like needles his legs and neck, the murderous buckshot
    and the bullets,
All these I feel or am.

(1:51, 835-37)

Here is a power entitling itself to enable itself to endow itself through, in, as any worldly thing it desires. The same characterization, it should be said, applies to other moments of metamorphosis in which the "I" passes into an other, such moments having a metonymic counterpart in the catalogues, which run rapidly through changing identities. But the process of metamorphosis looks less innocent if one takes the trouble to experience through empathy the suffering of the slave, to whom the difference between being the slave and being the buckshot and the bullets is all the difference in the world. But "All these I feel or am" tells a story of in-difference that exposes that other impairment, the dis-enabling of moral vision, which is the price the poet pays for the "right" to such an affective relation ("feel") or identification ("am"). No longer a concrete moral equal, the other is posited as a randomly encountered instance equivalent to other instances randomly encountered. In this mode poetic expressiveness is the generation of objects for a subject in whose adaptable nature freedom, equality, and fraternity are increasingly liable to mutation. The narcissist strain in Whitman is self-realizing and self-regarding even when it identifies with some other person or entity, for, inasmuch as the originary never entirely abandons itself to becoming other, it is forever populating the world with itself.

The self-absorption characteristic of such narcissism "prevents one from understanding what belongs within the domain of the self and self-gratification and what belongs outside it. Thus narcissism is an obsession with " 'what this person, that event means to me.' This question about the personal relevance of other people and outside act is posed so repetitively that a clear perception of those persons and events in themselves is obscured."[62] Confusion between the private and the public spheres is another way of stating the process of peopling the world with oneself. Just because the difference between the public and the private spheres has become in-difference, every "I" I image is an image of my "I."

Compare the following from the "Héautontimorouménos" of Baudelaire:

> Je suis la plaie et le couteau!
> Je suis le soufflet et la joue!
> Je suis les membres et la roue,
> Et la victime et le bourreau.[63]

> I am the wound and the knife!
> I am the slap and the cheek.
> I am the limbs and the wheel,
> Both the victim and the executioner.

Baudelaire creates a double vision in the specifically ocular sense of the term: he brings into being and bears witness to simultaneous versions of himself. The conjunction here conjoins a two-for-one, co-foundational dynamic; for the "I" is both the source of production and its specular consumption. The poet desires nothing so much as to watch himself being created by himself, or, to paraphrase Sartre, he feigns spontaneity and appears to abandon himself to impulse in order to surprise himself as the object of his own gaze, to which he will suddenly appear as an other.[64] Endower of his own world, the poet is autonomous and autotelic, a perfect monad.

Whitman peoples the world with himself more kinetically, thrusting himself out into, through, and as whatever he encounters—a process with an element of the polymorphous as it implicates the participant in any coupling, and an element of the perverse as it entails watching himself do so. If this helps to make the poet more public in his identifications, these retain enough of a private core to insure that the boundary line between the two spheres is being thoroughly transgressed, a transgression made the more daring by a publicity coup at once onomastic and ocular: the "I" identifies himself as the historical concretum Walt Whitman in order to incorporate himself, to the extent that this can occur discursively, in his own text, affixing to the published text a portrait of himself as the visual-iconic counterpart of that very incorporating.

Neither poet is finally satisfied, though Baudelaire is more explicit about the fact; indeed, the lack of satisfaction is part of his poetic program, aimed as it is at an infinitude to which he alone is entitled, as the one who through his discourse uniquely enables the corresponding endowment. Whitman's lack of satisfaction derives from the pursuit of what either fails to turn out to be what he desired, or what turns out to be just that, triggering a new try not without its own whiff of infinity. The desire of Narcissus can never achieve expression in genuine coupling, which is genuine only when the other is genuinely other. And there is quite as much double binding when the essential either/or extrapolates into the equally essential both/and: "This isn't what I wanted / I want more of the same." On such a reading, the first-person of a poem like "Spontaneous Me" can enable himself for either climax, which is to say for both, by the very process of being spontaneous. Spontaneity is a strategy for catching each difference before it is experienced as the same. And a disenabling strategy it is. The poet believes himself entitled to identify with other worldly things in their equality with himself—the democratic clause in the program. But in every spontaneous identification the desired identity, once possessed, must immediately be replaced for fear that it merely represents its equivalence with any other; which is to say that the meaning a given thing has for the deserving persona inheres in its status as object for a subject. If a thing is concrete and unique, an object is its reductive recension. Bringing worldly things before itself as their source of value and utility, the subject levels their differences into such objectifications as it posits for them, all such objectifications resembling one another more than they resemble any real worldly thing.

The age of Whitman was the age of Andrew Jackson: an age of political, social, and economic policies geared to practices and technologies that were themselves undergoing incessant adaptation and proliferation; and an age of competition growing ever more competitive, of systems growing ever more systematic. The rationale of possessive individualism at the heart of a society so organized plays an entitling role: the same rights enjoyed by that society as a general principle shall be enjoyed by the individual. Such individualization of the laissez-faire policy so essential to the liberal democratic state guarantees that no one will prevent you from adopting new roles, or packing up and moving on when the spirit moves you, or feeling or doing or being whatever you want to feel or do or be; to look at the riskier side of the entitling, it is therefore to be everything potentially but nothing in particular.

In Whitman's conception, it has been argued, individualism "integrated the radical democratic concept of a free society with its connotations of laissez-faire, inalienable rights, and its distrust of centralized political power, with the transcendentalist-Unitarian concept of individual self-determination and self-perfectibility." [65] In the American state, as interpreted on individualist lines, equality is an entitled condition of social possibility enabling concrete attainments by persons similarly endowed and entitled. What equivalence entitles and enables, by contrast, is interchange; it functions most efficiently not in the town or ward meeting, where custom and mutual respect provide a necessary measure of civic order, but in the impersonal mechanisms of the self-regulating marketplace, where worth is value and value is price. The democratic idealization of fraternity may be explained at least in part as a compensation for this reductive recension of equality and equivalence, and as an attempt to ease the pain of fragmentation, which is a common experience in a society requiring incessant adjustments inimical to any sense of continuity.

Fraternity plays such a role in the poetry of Whitman. But genuine fraternity presupposes concrete equality, a concept Whitman is more comfortable with in the abstract. Genuine freedom for the other requires the recognition of difference, not the demonstration of an in-difference that not only transforms itself at will into anyone or anything, but tries to make the process look easy. The only freedom here is the freedom of the individualist whose entitlements, enablements, and endowments are without limits, which is another way of saying that he embodies *in* himself *for* himself power, freedom, and equality. Power: he has the wherewithal to actualize potential. Freedom: he is entitled to the exercise of such power. Equality: he is on the level of all other beings (the tautology is essential) who are endowed, enabled, and entitled to like degree. All of this is explicitly expressed in the self-transformation acted out in the poem. What the process entails but does not explicitly express is the constraint that destines the other to negation and sacrifice. Here impoverishment is so extreme that it hardly takes any words to formulate: the other is the one who is not free to transform himself; who is not free to transform himself because he has not the power; who has not the power to transform himself because he is not equal.

The poet is entitled not only to be the slave but the auctioneer and the bullet or buckshot that diminish the slave's endowment. The slave is entitled to be the slave.

Whitman does not appear to see any contradiction between his opposition to slavery and what amounts to his discursive impairment of African Americans. Of the like impairment of American Indians, he seems equally unaware, despite his experience of them when he worked in the Bureau of Indian Affairs.

The illusion created by the presentation of both minorities in what is at first glance a positive light, a presentation that is probably well-meaning in its own way, helps cover over the political disillusionment Whitman began to feel at least as early as the Mexican War years, which promoted second thoughts about militarization. The disillusionment grew with the closing of the West, the danger that slavery would spread into newly opened territories, the Civil War, and the troubling aftermath of that war. The disillusionment can be heard in "Facing West from California," in which a movement of perspective carries the first-person from the shores of the title over the waves to originary Asia, then brings him back to those shores, there to face what has failed to come about:

> Now I face home again, very pleas'd and joyous,
> (But where is what I started for so long ago?
> And why is it yet unfound?)
>
> (2:361, 9–11)

This is written in 1860, before the breakout of the tragic conflict that will become a paradigmatic experience of the nation. Erkilla notes, "Whitman is poised for the flight into spiritual seas that became his characteristic renunciatory gesture as America's political failure became increasingly apparent in the post-Civil war period." [66]

Nearly a quarter-century passes before Whitman begins the series of Indian poems in which his spiritual flight assumes the form, as we have seen, of sentiment, nostalgia, and mystification. Perhaps the single saving feature of this renunciatory phase is that his sympathies are directed at last where they are due if not overdue. But even this consolation fails to offset the anomaly of the poet's lamentation, which disregards the causes and circumstances of the destroyed peoples as the price he is willing to pay for the bitter savor of his own melancholy.

The course that Robert Frost pursues in "For John F. Kennedy His Inauguration" and "The Gift Outright," the most public of his public poems, is in certain important respects different from Jefferson's and Whitman's and in certain important respects the same. One of the respects in which Frost's course is different is that he does not express disillusion over the destiny that is manifest, or the loss of Jeffersonian measure. Indeed, for more years than Whitman was a doubter, Frost was a believer. One of the respects in which the course Frost follows is the same is to be found in the now concealing, now revealing interplay of entitling, endowing, and enabling; the later poet even displays the same tendency to screen concrete history through sentiment, nostalgia, and mystification. If the third president had been standing beside the poet instead of the thirty-fifth, he would have comprehended perfectly the drift of the discourse the poet composed for the latter's inauguration.

In "John F. Kennedy His Inauguration," Frost, taking for granted that the discovery of the New World constituted a fundamental endowment, features the enabling that brought America to power:

> Colonial had been the thing to be
> As long as the great issue was to see
> What country'd be the one to dominate
> By character, by tongue, by native trait,
> The new world Christopher Columbus found.
> The French, the Spanish, and the Dutch were downed
> And counted out. Heroic deeds were done.
> Elizabeth the First and England won.[67]

In the poet's vision American destiny carries, as an aspect of its enabled and enabling capacities, an entitlement over whatever counts as other, a *noblesse oblige* democratized, such that others — Frost names them "races" — fall within an area of educative and fiduciary responsibility peculiarly our own.

> We see how seriously the races swarm
> In their attempts at sovereignty and form.
> They are our wards we think to some extent
> For the time being and with consent,
> To teach them how Democracy is meant.
>   (34-38)

What the poet entitles the swarming races to, then, is a political lesson about democratic principles in the highest, most universal form — as the capitalization of "Democracy" appears to imply. But the incorrigibly witty Frost may be enlisting no less than three senses of the noun: the one, already noted, meaning just what Madison said was meant in 1801, namely, the governmental order reposing ultimate political power in the people as a whole; the second, meaning "the people, or the main portion of them, making up the population of the United States; the nation so made up" (*DAE* 3. 1816); and finally, "the principles of the Democratic party in the United States" (*DAE* 2. 1814), the one definition of the three that is strictly an Americanism. It would be sly, of course, and a little outrageous, to weave this last sense into the others; but Frost is sly, and a little outrageous. The issue, one must admit, is not perfectly decidable. Frost salts other poems with capitalized words. But in the present text "Democracy" gives way later to the lower case:

> There was the book of profile tales declaring
> For the emboldened politicians daring
> To break with the followers when in the wrong,
> A healthy independence of the throne,
> A democratic form of right divine
> To rule first answerable to high design.
>   (60-65)

In celebrating the hour of investiture, the preliminary history in rhyme at the same time inaugurates in the derivative sense of marking the beginning of a new period or space of time:

> It makes the prophet in us all presage
> The glory of a next Augustan age
> Of a power leading from its strength and pride,
> Of young ambition eager to be tried,
> Firm in our free beliefs without dismay,
> In any game the nations want to play.
> A golden age of poetry and power
> Of which this noonday's the beginning hour.
>
> (70–77)

To be properly Augustan, the glory the poem would enable, at least in imagination, would be consonant with refinements in taste, a classical propriety in discourse, and protocols for excellence in every other cultural sphere. Such at least are the sorts of things we mean when speaking of an Augustan age of the arts. In the present text, however, the terms employed are pretty distinctly political, with "power" leading the way for "young ambition" in its eagerness to play "in any game the nations want to play." Which is to say, not that esthetic considerations have been put aside, but that the Augustan age being inaugurated is an age of rising political power in which, because of the type of alliance illustrated here, poetry and power will both be seen to flourish: the conjunction between those two nouns is to be taken seriously.

By contrast to this political prospect-poem, in "The Gift Outright" the poet strives to explain more broadly how the American people have been endowed, how it is they were enabled to come into full possession of that endowment, and how it was that they were entitled to do so.

The Gift Outright

> The land was ours before we were the land's.
> She was our land more than a hundred years
> Before we were her people. She was ours
> In Massachusetts, in Virginia,
> But we were England's, still colonials,
> Possessing what we still were unpossessed by,
> Possessed by what we now no more possessed.
> Something we were withholding made us weak
> Until we found out that it was ourselves
> We were withholding from our land of living,
> And forthwith found salvation in surrender.
> Such as we were we gave ourselves outright
> (The deed of gift was many deeds of war)
> To the land vaguely realizing westward,

> But still unstoried, artless, unenhanced,
> Such as she was, such as she would become.

The trope of the gift becomes the more resonant the more one thinks of it in relation to the state's relation to deity. When the Declaration of Independence speaks of rights deriving from the Creator, it attends-from these as things given not merely in the sense of stipulations but literally granted, proffered, conferred.

The idea of gratuitousness characterizes some of the longest-surviving ideas about the ways in which worldly things are ordered by divinity; thus the foregrounding of grace as God's free favor, or as the bestowal of a "free gift" (Rom. 5.15), a concept shading toward benediction as the grant of a divine gift, which on one apostolic account embraces such enabling capacities as "the gifts of healing," "prophecy," and "the interpretation of tongues" (1 Cor. 12.9–10). Mediating between this background and the intellectual environment of the American Founders, Locke focuses on the originary grant that occurs in the first book of the Bible. On the authority of Genesis 1.28, he argues, "God gave [Adam] not Private Dominion over the Interior Creatures, but right in common with all Mankind."[68] Such giving is thus seen both as endowing—providing the possessor with the wherewithal of worldly power—and as entitling—establishing such provision as a right. Indeed, the very title of the chapter, "Of Adam's Title to Sovereignty," displays the origin of the entitling and empowerment in the act of such giving.

What distinguishes the gift from that in the Frost poem is just that in the poem it is outright, which first means entire and unconditional, and later indicates the finality of finishing something at once and altogether, as in selling or killing outright (1623 and 1603 respectively). The pertinence of the latter sense, which carries over the absoluteness in the former, grows more apparent as one attends-to the hidden history that enabled the dominion to be a thing that Frost, like Whitman, could celebrate and exalt.

A gift outright is understood to be a conferral without constraint and gratuitous: a free bestowing. Some two centuries before "The Gift Outright," the concept of the free gift as applied to property, of whatever type, enabled the colonists to revive a principle denying to the Crown what it saw as manifest entitlements, such as tax collection and the acquisition of colonial property. The Stamp Act Congress of 1765 declared "That ALL *supplies to the crown*, being free gifts of the people, it is *unreasonable, and inconsistent . . .* for the people of *Great Britain* to grant to his Majesty *the property of the colonies.*" That is, the colonial endowment having already been drawn upon by the colonists' own free giving, the people of Great Britain, even if the endowment were theirs, which it was not, could never be entitled to do the same; and, absent endowing and entitling, enabling is absent as well. Two years later, a leading colonial pamphleteer, forcefully appealing to settled precepts in Coke's *Institutes*, concludes that "aids, tallages, tasks, taxes and subsidies, etc." were invariably "gifts and grants" by the people of their own property and were, in short, "gifts of the people to the crown."[69]

"The land was ours before we were the land's." This bond of land and people, the *we*, is paradigmatic in the social destiny of the democratic state, envisaged here in the most general terms. To go back "more than a hundred years" is to find the franchise, for example, typically limited to adult male persons holding substantial freehold property of specified values, testifying to the venerable principle that the landed have uniquely privileged stakes in society.[70] It should also be observed that the *land* in the ringing opening lines is an American coinage from six years prior to the Declaration and means the United States when the term is employed in high or ceremonious fashion, as in this *land of liberty* (DAE 2a).

If the land belongs to the possessive pronoun specified in the opening line, that pronoun belongs to the people as first person plural, an obvious correlate of the "we" of the preamble: "We see how seriously the races swarm / In their attempts at sovereignty and form." The races being distantly other as they swarm before our specular and superior presence, we remain people-in-the-abstract entitled to be endowed with the land by our own enabling, which meant, where "necessary," the expropriation of land occupied by its original inhabitants. In other words: as inhabitants or occupants, we were entitled to possess the land, such possession being an enabling process, as shown above; and by so doing, our endowment was a fact before the land became identified with the sovereignty of the new nation, which then possessed us insofar as we belonged to it as citizens.

The ensuing lines elaborate the nature of the gift as it existed more than a century ago, concluding with the statement,

> But we were England's, still colonials,
> Possessing what we still were unpossessed by,
> Possessed by what we now no more possessed.
>
> (5–7)

While this says what was said before—that we possessed the land as inhabitants before the land-become-nation possessed us—it adds the corollary that, being still colonials, we were at the same time in the possession of the mother country despite the fact that the opposite had come to be the case—that we no longer belonged to the identity that had been ours precisely because we were already assuming a new one.

The poem notably omits other instances of endowing, enabling, and entitling, such as those named in the preliminary history; perhaps most notably, at no time do American Indians appear: they are present neither in the latter's description of the new world found by Columbus (even though depictions of the explorer among natives have had a long existence) nor in the shorter poem's rendering of manifest destiny.

> Something we were withholding made us weak
> Until we found out that it was ourselves
> We were withholding from our land of living,
> And forthwith found salvation in surrender.
>
> (8–11)

From this angle, enabling consists in the process by which the people become aware of what they already possess and thus the more possess it. In a moment of recognition their entitlement comes on like a light, with the self-evidence of truths in Adam Smith or the Declaration. Such truths need not be argued; to the extent that they are ever explained they explain themselves — as by an act of faith, they are suddenly just known for what they are. During the poet's childhood knowledge so based came to be termed *fideism*, a conative position that may well inform the peculiar piety here evoked. But the moment of revelation invites comparison as well with the critical juncture in American conversion narratives, when the most sovereign of powers exacts a saving submission — what Frost aptly calls salvation in surrender. In sum, for the people, being-enabled means: the moment they are illumined by their destiny, when suddenly they know that it is they themselves who must be surrendered, they are given outright to the land, which is to say, possessed of it. On reflection this proves to be every bit the paradox it seems to be at first glance, as the protracted myriad acts of westward expansion, acts that were manifestly deeds of conquest, are collapsed into an instant version of the opposite.

> Such as we were we gave ourselves outright
> (The deed of gift was many deeds of war)
> To the land vaguely realizing westward
> But still unstoried, artless, unenhanced,
> Such as she was, such as she would become.
>
> (12–16)

Our land of living, land being taken in both the general sense and the special American sense noted above, provides a scene for symbolic action; but in fact there is precious little acting to be observed where the people are concerned. Their doing consists in surrendering, whereupon, in another reversal, the land shifts from being the scene to being the agent, for it is the land, not the people, which goes vaguely realizing westward. Curious terms. Frost runs a risk, by using this adverb, of reminding the reader how vague is the present text, a function, to be sure, of expressing a more or less exalted vision, but a function as well of unexplained reticence, or uncertainty, or confusion, or all three. Frost is depicting an immensely fateful historical process extending through a time of changes as momentous as they were numerous, in view of which it is not surprising that the term "vague," applied to statements, came into being amid the turbulence of the Renaissance (1548), while the sense of imprecision in language and imprecision in ideas or knowledge both came into being (in 1690 and 1704 respectively) through Locke's contribution to the groundbreaking Augustan debates, discussed above, that spiraled around trade, credit, land, and other economic and political questions of high moment. Frost's modifier for "realizing" occurs in another text about epochal events, Gibbon's *The Decline and Fall of the Roman Empire* (1781). *Prima facie*, the definition of "realize" coming closest to Frost's usage is "to turn out (well or ill) when sold" (1884), though a modifier bearing more on profit or loss would be more fitting than the poet's "vaguely." Such a gloss means either that the poem is more economically oriented than is otherwise apparent; or that "vaguely realizing" piggybacks on selling: a market society so saturates discourse with economic overtones that they may be heard even when they are residual or marginal to the issue at hand.

The story does not end there, however, for the colonists, in the process of inventing a nation, reinvented "realize," producing two related transitives that relate in turn to Frost. For John Adams in 1776, to realize is "To pass through or have actual experience of" (*DAE* 1), and George Washington employs the term in the same sense in 1791; while in some revolutionary correspondence from ten years earlier, to realize means "To conceive of as being real; to apprehend or understand clearly" (*DAE* 2), being regarded by both *OED* and *DAE* as "chiefly American."

Such innovations testify to the gaps that developed between the perspectives of British citizens who stayed home and the perspectives of those who went to found a new country. By neologizing, the latter tried to express their sense that the reality they partly found and partly fashioned was different from anything they had encountered before. The British, for their part, would have none of these new predicates, especially the second one; *DAE* devotes a separate section to the derisory treatment it received by Britons. The significance of this word first recorded in the year of the Declaration by the man who would become the second U.S. president, and echoed after the Revolution by the first president, consists, then, in the feeling of great innovation in the realm of worldly things, of a difference in their fateful course that must be marked in discourse *about* it. The consequent innovation in language registers a preoccupation with experience as such, a preoccupation by no means exclusive to Americans, but one that nonetheless characterizes an enduring strain in American culture into and beyond the period of the new republic. Thus in 1806 we find the coinage "a realizing sense" for "a sense of actuality, reality, or familiarity" (*DAE* 2).

Any depiction of experience is necessarily selective, bound as it is to leave out of consideration much that could have been included only at the expense of altering the nature of the depiction. But the problem in Frost's text is that he leaves out too much that is essential, even as Whitman does. Frost has assimilated the notion, pervasive in political discourse of the century in which he was born, that white settlers first found the western lands they were destined to develop. That these lands were long occupied by aboriginal peoples had never really figured significantly, since it had fallen out of the historical account, and it is these peoples, accordingly, who are so conspicuously missing from both of Frost's poems: these are they who left the land unstoried, artless, and unenhanced. It is consistent with such a conception that the land be feminized: "She was our land . . . / Such as she was, such as she would become." The land as female is land in the state of nature, the earth-mother who is nothing but the possibility of becoming a male possession. The sexual note comes closest to being sounded explicitly in the climax of outright giving when "the people," unable to hold back, spontaneously surrender; one could hardly conceive a more revealing substitute for the unimagined Indian absence than this imagined female presence.

That absence and that presence do not possess in the way the people do. Female and Indian do not give themselves, outright or otherwise; they must be taken, as taken they were. These are the others of a poem proclaiming the hegemony of the same, those others united with the poet not in respect of any personal or Whitmanesque identification, but through his identification with the new order of the ages that is the poem's manifest monument.

The poet writes from loyalty to the party returning to political power and from an even longer loyalty to the American polity, as well as to its "people," but in a version of the reductive recension, such that concrete hegemonic representatives are represented as an abstract "democratic" collectivity.

> There exist duties and obligations that arise from personal and local loyalties, and from past commitments to a cause. . . . There are obligations which are entirely backward-looking and which would not be explained and defended by any clear form of practical reasoning: debts of honour, either to persons or to groups and to societies who have had a certain weight and influence in one's life. The obligation might be more sensitively seen not as the repayment of a debt, but as the acknowledgment, much later, of a gift and of a contribution.[71]

This seems a fair description of the enabling motivational scene in terms of which the poetic is entitled to endow an implicit vision of the future from the received endowment of an explicit vision of the past: to give or give anew what has already been given. Such an aim is entirely justified as an expression of gratitude the absence of which can be powerfully enabling, as Shakespeare demonstrates in the fateful discourse of *King Lear*. Stuart Hampshire discusses this, writing, "Not to feel gratitude towards the past is, within most conceptions of the good, a disabling defect, a kind of inhumanity; and a grateful disposition is a virtue, a form of generosity of feeling and the contrary of meanness and envy, the passions that surely destroy life and pleasure."[72]

The problem, where Frost is concerned, is that because his conception of the people is as exclusionary as his conception of manifest destiny, the enabling he represents, this process by which people come into entitled endowment in an explicit past for the sake of an implicit future, forgets too much that history should oblige us to remember. In contrast to such history, the process the poet depicts is autotelic, immanent, passive, gratuitous, natural. *Autotelic*: the people never oppose nor support any other body of persons, but proceed to their fate as by entelechy—Aristotle would recognize the scenario. *Immanent*: the discovery that the people are the agents of what is fated to be derived, not from any transcendental source or endower, as Jefferson would have it, but from a dawning-within—the enabling process is a self-endowing. *Passive*: the people neither act nor interact, there being no other with whom to relate; to enable the possession of their entitled endowment, they have only to cease withholding themselves. *Gratuitous*: the entire enabling, entitling, endowing process is a "free," because unconditional, bestowal, the people themselves being both the givers and the given. *Natural*: it is not a people's history that is realizing, but the land's, a process that is as much a phase of unexamined nature as the act of sexual possession the poem implicitly analogizes.

By the way in which it says what it does say, the poem gainsays the worldly facticity which, if given, would amount to the previous list turned inside out; would amount to: a myriad of motives and capacities of transcendence; pervasive activity; causes and occasions; and the centrality of human as well as "natural" beings.

The manner in which the poem says what it does is basically the manner of the manifesto, offering in verse of genuine distinction a vision continuous with the vision of manifest destiny that came to the journalist John O'Sullivan in July of 1846. What the journalist foretells, the poet, having borne witness, retells. "Manifesto" enters the language, as it happens, precisely two hundred years before that date, when the New England divine Nathaniel Ward wishes that states would tell their people "beforehand" what they need to know. The term then expands to any public declaration, including those by individuals, that are revelatory not only of the future but of the past as well. Exploiting this expansion of sense, the individual poet proclaims the public salvation achieved in the past, paradoxically, by a foreseen futurity (in the guise of the land) realizing what must be from what must have been.

So to manifest a destiny is, in the endowing, enabling, entitling narrative, to temporize its essence: whatever has come to pass is mere playing out, the generating of inevitable statements from immutable paradigms.

Consequences follow. To retell the story of the gift outright is equally to forget the *they* and remember the *we*; it is to fix all manner of unforeseen free deeds into fate foreknown. Rewritten in light of these, the course of empire is no longer our surrender to ourselves, it is their surrender to us. In sum, this alternative retelling, which seeks to remember what has been forgotten in texts such as Frost's, then runs: *The land was theirs and we took possession of it because possessed to do so.*

To rewrite in this way is hardly to produce a better piece of poetic discourse. It is to question the endowing and enabling to which the discourse in question entitles itself. It is to make manifest how the poet's words can come, like Whitman's, like any writer's, to constitute a fateful discourse of worldly things.

PART III

Discoursing

1. Introductory Overview

Part I addressed the issue of discursive reconstructing. Part II, investigating the constitution of the world, explored the operation of the three constitutive modes: endowing, enabling, and entitling. Part III inquires into the question, What is the representational mode called discourse, which is said to be "of" or "about" things, and how does it work?

Discourse is considered first under the aspect of the modifier "fateful," together with other members of the "fate" family, including *fatum*, "fatal," and "destiny." Here the crucial text is Du Bellay's "ce discours fatal des choses mondaines," which Pater renders as "that discourse about affairs which decides men's fate." Because this translation seems to imply more predetermination than is warranted, I adopt and expand upon the term "fateful." Turning to representation as such, we find in Descartes a framework of paradigmatic significance for the modern age. In Heidegger's words, "The fact that whatever is comes into being in and through representedness transforms the age in which this occurs into a new age," the age of the world picture. In such representation, or *presentment* — to introduce my term for it — the world becomes preeminently an object for a representing subject. This process of abstraction diminishes the plenitude of worldly things.

Looking more closely at the Cartesian discourse of reason, we find an origin in John Dee, who marks a historical watershed by foregrounding a new sense of what counts as a constitutive unit. "Unit" as "unity" had heretofore signified the quality or state of coherence or togetherness. But henceforth "unit" signifies a single quantum, numberable and discrete. The philosopher/scientist has now but to locate the mechanisms that explain how the units operate; and this explanation Descartes finds, not surprisingly, in mechanism itself, as represented by the clock, by physiology, and by the automaton.

In examining his own origin, Descartes encounters in himself the likeness of God Himself, a proof of which is that the philosopher bears the mark of the divine craftsman. Such borrowing from the realm of worldly fabrication illustrates Descartes's great debt to the worldly things he would fain put behind him, or alter to fit his needs. Consider, for example, fire and glass. Descartes's interest in fire is prompted by its capacity to make light, a capacity it shares with heavenly bodies, which are associated honorifically with the discourse of reason. Glass serves Descartes preeminently in the form of the magnifying lens designed to isolate things for research.

In his struggle between doubt and certainty, what finally reassures the thinker that his existence is more than illusion is not so much *ratio*, I suggest, as it is experience and memory. The power of reconstructing on the basis of things known from an anterior time, though left implicit, is never entirely in doubt. Santayana, equating thinking with discourse, wonders whether Descartes isn't in fact mainly interested in "the play of terms in discourse itself." Vico attacks the Cartesian or analytic method more frontally, as incapable neither of dealing in the world with what is already there in its multiplicity and concreteness, nor of interpreting these things of the world. Where Descartes relies on *ratio* Vico relies on *ingenium*, creative "mother wit," which inquires into the way things are brought into being in an experienced world: by its knowledge of the way things are made "the mind makes the thing, because in knowing it puts together the elements of that thing." Vico stresses interrogation, context, and concreteness in a temporality not determined by religious doctrine; in this sense he historicizes.

Nietzsche complements this orientation with his interpretation of human being as *fatum*, which, originally signifying utterance, reminds us that such being is discursive through and through. Emphasizing the actual production of utterance through the mouth, Nietzsche affirms speech as a kind of innate power of inscription even as he affirms that the world, existing without unity or purpose, is justifiable only in esthetic terms. It remains for Peirce, to whom my discussion then turns, to inquire rigorously into signification and the entire realm of communications considered in relation to human consciousness. To Peirce the latter is no more and no less than the knowledge of what is in our own minds, and since this is the same kind of knowledge that words have, he concludes that there is no essential difference between human and discursive being.

What enables this conclusion, I argue, is something closer to Vico's imagination, which operates in historical time, as attested by the work of the Peircean scientist. Communicating with one another, investigators develop methods with the certainty that in the future "a destined center," or agreed-upon truth, will ultimately be arrived at. Science thus defined, and Peirce's self-declared theism, go hand in hand since in either role the thinker or the scientist must meet the pragmatic test, the test of conduct, which in his case, as in Dewey's, means participating actively in creation, conceived as ongoing process.

To Dewey discourse is communication, which he conceives to be "the most wonderful of things," foreshadowing Heidegger's veneration of the work of words, especially in poetic modes. Dewey's conception of communication is naturalistic, however, in the sense that he is more concerned with the "material" world and "the live creature." But Dewey and Heidegger are alike, it seems to me, in believing in the world-making power of words and the social nature of that making, as well as the capacity of discourse to disclose existence and meaning. Overall, we could say that Heidegger focuses on the nature of being, Dewey on the being of nature. It should be understood that Dewey's nature is a relation of interactive togetherness; for only as things interact do they have consequences, and consequences are what "enter finally into human action and destiny." Dewey seeks in this way "a more adequate discourse" than that of analysis: more adequate in that, instead of ordering things and breaking things down, it narrates and describes.

On Platonist grounds, which Dewey examined, such a discourse must be regarded as not only *in*adequate but dangerous, like the discourse of the "honeyed muse" who jeopardizes law and order, which is inseparable in turn from the issue of scale and measure noted above. Here Jefferson is again illustrative and deserves, I suggest, a closer look. Desiring that individual voices in the polity be heard, Jefferson proposed, as we have seen, to divide states into counties and counties into wards, or "little republics." What Arendt calls the lost treasure of revolutionary tradition consists of these formations and their counterparts, such as the French revolutionary societies of the 1790s and the soviets of the Russian Revolution. All of these failed to survive, Arendt explains, in part because even revolutionaries fear radical change. Believing that a tradition is best preserved in cultural memory by poets, she invokes René Char, who worried that in returning to normal life after the German Occupation he would lose the opportunity to perform the emancipatory deeds that he enjoyed in the Resistance. For with action came "involuntary self-discourse," a kind of acting out of the self in behalf of collective interest.

A similar self-discourse appears in Emerson, who spoke in a way that made his personal words a form of public action. For Emerson the genius of poetry, as of political eloquence, exists in every human being but finds ready expression in venues such as the *bethel*, where relatively small numbers gather. Located in such small-scale organizations, the spirit that is nature in worldly form becomes so internalized in the members that "the work will be done with concert, though no man spoke."

Emerson assumes that the nature of a discourse is determined by its author; but what might be called daily discourse has no author in this sense. The story of daily life is, as it were, written by the characters who live both as its producers and its protagonists, and becomes fully significant only after the lives have been lived. In his approach to that collectivizing of life stories which is cultural memory, Pater is inclined to speak in terms of fate and necessity, but also in terms of freedom. In modern life, he suggests, the need for "the sense of freedom" is constrained by "a magic web woven through and through us," connecting us with everything else in the cosmos; the freedom thus exercised is limited and is also, like other things in Pater, ephemeral.

In *Marius the Epicurean* Pater discoursed of a world in which the protagonist, having been born too late for it, is in a sense already deceased. Not surprisingly, in reading Rousseau's *Confessions*, Pater is drawn to passages in which Rousseau, having also looked upon himself as already dead, sets new store by the worldly things around him and his obligation to them and to himself. As introspective as Descartes, whom he had studied, Rousseau also sought certainty, though from a different point of departure. If Descartes cannot doubt that he thinks, Rousseau cannot doubt that he feels. At the same time he laments the lack of fraternity, viewed in possessive as well as affective terms; but, following Arendt, I counter by recalling that fraternity in early Greek antiquity is essentially discursive and political: "In discourse the political importance of friendship, and the humanness peculiar to it, were made manifest."

2. The Course of Discourse

The constituting of discourse in its varied offices may be approached, at least in a preliminary way, through its relation to the overarching theme of fatefulness. Since "fateful" as a modifier precedes "discourse" in my title, and suggests how discourse is here conceived, we may well begin with the "fate" family of terms.

Fatum, fate, fateful, fatal, fatality, destine, predestine, destination, destiny: the discursive range of the "fate" and "destiny" families is broad as it is enduring. The naming of fateful agency or power informs the mythic discourse of the Greek *Moira* as well as of the Roman *Fata* or *Parcae*. In the myth of Er, as Plato relates it, a fateful binding power exerts itself through crucial actions human beings take. *Beowulf* discourses of destiny in the form of the *weird*, a term later applied to the lot of a particular person rather than to supernatural agency; Chaucer, Shakespeare, and Milton still speak of fate as a synonym for *weird* in this sense. With the early fifteenth century the overtone of the eternal diminishes until "fate" signifies worldly destruction or ruin. Three and a half centuries will pass before "fate" comes to mean, as it seems mainly to mean today, ultimate determination or destiny.

Discourse is "of" things, it is "about them," as we say, and so "belongs" to them, as they to it. This reciprocity and interplay will be considered here largely through discursive formations from the Renaissance to the twentieth century. In defending the merits of his native tongue Joaquim Du Bellay upholds the power of discourse to figure the textures of worldly things. The dead languages, thought Du Bellay, are truly fit for burying; only a living language could open to a national community its proper fateful course. The living language "must be for him the medium of what he calls, in one of his great phrases, *le discours fatal des choses mondaines*—that discourse about affairs which decides men's fates" (*R*, 130). It has been said that Pater mistranslates here. According to a modern editor, *discours* means only *cours*, course; but when Pater remarks that the prefix *dis* contributes "an idea of space, of dispersion," he grazes something else that Du Bellay and his language—and others in the Renaissance—have already caught. This is the fact that human life is discursive through and through and that discourse itself is distinctly a course—a kind of running. The *dis* of *discours* reaffirms the space and dispersion that is already a course, which is ever going somewhere. As the first sense of "discourse," now obsolete, the *OED* offers "onward course; process or succession of time, events, actions, etc." (1612), this having been preceded by the Renaissance sense of "understanding, thought or reason, or the faculty thereof," and succeeded by the sense of "a narration" and of "an oral or written treatment of a subject at some length."

The coursing of lives fatefully discursive is crucial to Cervantes's "The Colloquy of the Dogs." Cipión confirms Berganza's amazement over his fellow canine's ability to speak, and his own to understand. Even more remarkable "is that, not only do we speak, but we speak discursively, as if we were capable of reason [*con discurso como fuerámos capaces de razón*], being as we are so lacking in it that the difference between a brute animal and a man is that the man is a rational animal, the brute, irrational."[1] This presupposes a distinction between those beings who merely speak and those who speak, in the Renaissance phrase, discourse of reason. Discourse as the medium of reason, in the broadest sense of the term, is the endowment that makes the colloquy of the dogs miraculous.

Turning the course of the conversation to his own experience, Berganza states that "in the discourse of my life" (*en el discurso de mi vida*) he has heard tell of "great prerogatives" possessed by dogs, including something approaching "understanding, capable of discourse" (*entendimiento, capaz de discurso*).[2] Berganza rings a further variation on the interplay between "course" and "discourse" when he alludes to students coursing (*cursaban*) through the university; and finally, Cipión later calls the course of life itself "*el discurso.*"[3]

We may now delve further into the discursive world of the Renaissance as exemplified by a paradigmatic text for the theme of discourse in general and for the theme of the discourse of reason in particular. This text is *The Discourse on Method* of Descartes, which, together with the same author's *Meditations*, opens up for discussion a variety of considerations crucial to the present study.

3. Discourse of Reason

As early as the third paragraph Descartes indicates that his discourse of reason is to be understood as a mode of expression broadly imaginative and specifically narrative: "I . . . am presenting this work only as a history or, if you prefer, a fable in which, among certain examples worthy of imitation, you will perhaps also find many others that it would be right not to follow; and so I hope it will be useful for some without being harmful to any, and that everyone will be grateful to me for my frankness."[4] The statement places the *Discourse* within the French moralist tradition and in its contemporary context. For, even as Cartesian metaphysics met resistance in learned circles, "a more 'popular' appropriation of Cartesian thought crystallized amid the urbane intelligentsia of wealthy bourgeois and disenfranchised nobility, who enthusiastically discussed Descartes's ideas in the salon world."[5] As a storyteller Descartes can dramatize his quest for certainty, giving his readership glimpses of the fallibility and frailty he must heroically overcome. In the *Discourse* there is indeed much the same confessional strain as we find in Rousseau, who is forever admitting his insufficiencies, especially his leaky memory.

That the discourse is merely a history or a fable is a way of saying that rational method, as the essence of that discourse, does not depend on the worldliness represented in those two genres. As the means by which reason reaches ultimate truth, method is to essence as accidence is to narrative, which in one form (fable) is admittedly fictitious and in the other (history) is only ostensibly true.

Discourse as such is liable to a double delinquency. On the one hand, the author does not seek words to express with exactitude what he thinks since, on principle, no words could. On the other hand, as an occupant of the realm of worldly things, he relies on words. Can mind express itself in language if discourse impedes the very functioning of mind? The answer must be no.

Even high types of discourse exhibit their shortcomings, though the author veils his disappointments in a politesse that is almost too guarded. The dangerous siren in the tenth book of *The Republic* is the mother of Descartes's "best poets," defined as "those with the most pleasing conceits and the ability to express them with the most embellishment and sweetness" (*OP* 114). Philosophy for its part is not, in a sense, poetic enough. But in order to be poetic enough it must avoid being poetic in the usual way. The latter is for Descartes little more than a modestly heightened form of ordinary language. Relying on images, it must turn to the corporeality inherent in them, or in which they inhere. Poetry belongs to nature more than to reason. "I valued oratory and was fond of poetry; but I thought both were the gifts of the mind rather than fruits of study. Those with the strongest reasoning and the most skill at ordering their thoughts so as to make them clear and intelligible are always the most persuasive, even if they speak only low Breton and have never learned rhetoric" (*PW* 1:114).

The discourse that is poetry, with its pleasing embellishment and sweetness, cannot please *ratio*, or better, can only please it. It cannot serve as the clear and distinct (which is to say the objective and abstract) pole of the subjective, the "I think, therefore I am." The overriding importance of the subject-object polarity as such is complete and determinative. Distinctive of modern philosophical discourse in the rationalist tradition, and of other modes of discourse predicated on the same polarity, its acts of representation, or of *presentment*, as they might more accurately be called, characterize the age of the world picture.

4. Presentment

Heidegger writes: "The fact that whatever is comes into being in and through representedness transforms the age in which this occurs into a new age. . . . The world picture does not change from an earlier medieval one into a modern one, but rather the fact that the world becomes picture at all is what distinguishes the essence of the modern age [*der Neuzeit*]."[6] This type of representedness is to be distinguished from the early Greek model, which requires an apprehension peculiarly immediate by modern standards, though the foundation for world-picturing is already laid by Plato in postulating the primacy of *eidos*, as aspect or view. "In distinction from Greek apprehending, modern representing [*Vorstellen*] means to bring what is present at hand [*das Vor-handene*] before oneself as something standing over against, to relate it to the one representing it, and to force it back into this relationship to oneself as the normative realm."[7] In Cartesian terms, it is of course the subject who represents, as it is the object that is represented—and in such a way, further-more, that the world *is* only as the aggregate of such objects.

Such representation may be termed *presentment*, both as a way of distin-guishing this from other modes of representation and as a way of more nearly specifying the basis of the distinction. Presentment in the *OED* signifies "all the modifications of consciousness directly involved in the knowing or being aware of an object in a single moment of thought." This gets it about right, it seems to me, if only one recognizes such knowing as a general pattern with its own, specifically modern historicity and rhetoric.

In presentment the world becomes the type of object we call a picture and the one who views the picture becomes the type of subject traditionally termed *subiectum*—ironically, since this development ruptures tradition. It is indeed a fateful break.

> The interweaving of these two events, which for the modern age is decisive — that the world is transformed into picture and man into *subiectum*—throws light at the same time on the grounding event of modern history, an event that at first glance seems almost absurd. Namely, the more extensively and the more effectually the world stands at man's disposal as conquered, and the more objectively the object appears, all the more subjectively, i.e., the more importantely, does the *subiectum* rise up, and all the more impetuously, too, do observation of and teaching about the world change into a doctrine of man, into anthropology. It is no wonder that humanism first arises where the world becomes picture.[8]

The same development is a condition of possibility for the phenomenon of individualism, while at the same time, and again ironically, it is a condition of possibility for transcending individualism precisely through the mediation of the subject. As Heidegger observes: "Only where man is essentially already subject does there exist the possibility of his slipping into the aberration of subjectivism in the sense of individualism. But also, only where man *remains* subject does the positive struggle against individualism and for the commu-nity as the sphere of those goals that govern all achievement and usefulness have any meaning."[9] Presentment admits into being nothing that is not con-ferred on the object in relation to the subject; if the subject does not bring to the relation what occurs in another (nonobjectifying or nonsubjectifying) mode of experience, what thus occurs is excluded. By such omission the object is, so long as the subject maintains the relation, effectively reduced. Poetic discourse, for its part, can yet remain itself insofar as it does not enter the relation — a stance that could be called denial, or resistance, except that it isn't really a stance; it is just what poetry does, or is.

The threat is from a worldview so calculating and systematic as to require that poetry, as object, appear to a subject as solely its being for, its relation to, that subject. To the extent that such a view becomes pervasive, it may be said that poetic discourse changes in the age of the world picture.

In its compensatory phase presentment shifts attention from the damage it does to worldly things to a sort of indemnity for that damage. Having reduced the plenitude and array of worldly things to their representational value as objects for a subject, presentment offers, by way of compensation for this loss, a gesture of valuation.

> Where anything that is has become the object of presentment, it first incurs in a certain manner a loss of Being. This loss is adequately perceived, if but vaguely and unclearly, and is compensated for with corresponding swiftness through the fact that we impart value to the object and to that which is interpreted as object, and that we take the measure of whatever is, solely in keeping with the criterion of value, and make of values themselves the goal of all activity. . . . Value is the objectification of needs as goals.[10]

The perspectivism that thus comes into position derives at least in part from rationalizing and systematizing tendencies by no means exclusive to science and technology. Indeed, a telling instance takes us back to a pictorial experiment by Brunellesco, the architect often called Brunelleschi, in fifteenth-century Florence. In order to paint a picture of one church, the artist had to step back into a church opposite. His admirer Antonio Manetti explains:

> Thus, to prevent the spectator from falling into error in choosing his viewpoint, Filippo made a hole in the picture at that point in the view of the church of S. Giovanni which is directly opposite to the eye of the spectator, who might be standing in the central portal of S. Maria del Fiore in order to paint the scene. . . . Filippo had the beholder put his eye against the reverse side where the hole was large, and while he shaded his eye with his one hand, with the other he was told to hold a flat mirror on the far side in such a way that the painting was reflected in it. The distance from the mirror to the hand near the eye had to be in a given proportion to the distance between the point where Filippo stood in painting his picture and the church of San Giovanni.[11]

The strategy by which the artist thus represents the targeted worldly thing, the church, as it emerges for him as positioned spectator, constitutes a mode of presentment. By fixing the requisite point of view for all spectators to come, the artist has constructed a world picture in little, a representation fulfilling those desiderata of prediction and control that are central to systems and sciences. A complete derealization, however, it is not. On the contrary, it is not only possible to recover, as it were, a pre-presentment world, a world of everyday experience; it is necessary to do so. The burden of my argument in the present discussion is both that presentment alters everyday experience and that everyday experience persists nonetheless.

Descartes likewise draws the assumptions and practices of the everyday world he ostensibly transcends through his systematizing rationalism. Thus his putative disregard for the rules of rhetoric finds its counterpart in regard for the rules of the ordinary world. But how does he know, in a world with many kinds of discourse, which rules should govern him? He will follow the ones "commonly accepted in practice by the most sensible of those with whom I should have to live" (*PW* 1:122).

The world that Descartes acknowledges by his practices is the same one identified in the equivalences arrived at previously. It is that of the present: here, now, is where one lives, and the norms that obtain here and now are the ones to be obeyed. It is perfectly consistent with this assumption that in the same section he dispenses the maxims he worked out as the moral equivalent of his steps in logic. For the old maxims cannot be relied on any more than the old morals: hence "I formed a provisional moral code" (*PW* 1:122). Descartes does not attend to this assumption. No more does he attend to his reliance on that world and its "old" discursive modes. His acknowledgment of it is inversely proportional to the debts he owes it. For, to a considerable extent, Cartesian metaphysics derives from medieval authorities, themselves informed by canonical authorities of antiquity, of whom Descartes most frequently names Aristotle. So that the two worlds, the rejected old and the accepted new, are not easily separated. What is critically new is not this world as such but the Cartesian view of it in presentment, and the distinctive ways in which Descartes creates and justifies that view.

5. Discoursing of Things

In the *Discourse on Method* Descartes famously divided worldly things into those that are extended and those that think; thus the problem of the thing stands at the center of the thinking. Yet the thing receives much less explicit attention than does the performer of thinking. The thing shares the fate of thinking overall, which never undergoes the type of scrutiny applied to that species of it called doubt. The primary notion of thing from which Descartes attends is the notion of *res extensa*, the world as an ensemble of objectivities for the subjectivity inscribed in the discourse. But in fact the life Descartes lives every day is discursive through and through in familiar and, as it were, prescientific ways. In his contemporary travels he takes part in conversations; in his travels into the past he takes part in the virtual conversation which is reading, becoming the author of a philosophical discourse that is in some ways hardly less confessional than Rousseau's discourse of 1781–88, to which I will turn below. The curious fact remains that this authorial type of thing, this type that thinks, should be conceived by the discourse of reason as, somehow, other than the other things in the world, hence as true substance.

6. The Danger of Romance

As the passage in the *Discourse* unfolds, it becomes more evident that the complaint against travel is one of a series of reflections on excess. With the concluding statement in the passage we come to a particularly excessive excess represented by a kind of discourse antithetical to the discourse of reason:

> Moreover, fables make us imagine many events as possible when they are not. And even the most accurate histories, while not altering or exaggerating the importance of matters to make them worthy of being read, at any rate almost always omit the baser and less notable events; as a result, the other events appear in a false light, and those who regulate their conduct by examples drawn from these works are liable to fall into the excesses of the knights-errant in our tales of chivalry, and conceive plans beyond their powers. (*PW* 1:114)

The equivalence here can be expressed as the ratio "Excess is to ignorance as fictive discourse (including written historical discourse) is to extravagance." It would be equally valid the other way round—"Ignorance is to fictive discourse as excess is to extravagance"—and this has the advantage of exhibiting the tautology. Excess thus amounts to extravagance as fiction amounts to ignorance as becoming ignorant of the present amounts to becoming a stranger to—that is, ignorant of—your own country. Such discourse is more attitude than argument, more discourse, if you like, than reason. Descartes finds no amusement in the adventures of romance; his preoccupation with errancy is as earnest and straitlaced as Cervantes's is playful and unbuttoned, and it is so because the philosopher takes in a spirit of gravity a premise offered in a spirit of levity. Discourses of the wrong kind can lure you from the path of reason and righteousness, and not merely those that are explicitly fictional; by not being faithful enough to truth, divinely ordained and clear to the eye of reason, even histories lead one astray.

Once the thinker completes the course of study that began in his childhood, he concludes that it did not escape the danger of romance. In a kind of negative epiphany there stands revealed the utter falsity of things he has been taught. Not truth but "example and custom" (*PW* 1:116) had been his guide. Now his guide, led in turn by the light of natural reason, must be himself. To take this recourse he must in some sort distance himself from the realm of worldly things; therefore "I resolved one day to undertake studies within myself too and to use all the powers of my mind in choosing the paths I should follow" (*PW* 1:116). Accordingly, he seeks a scene of retirement remote from the ordinary world. Yet the withdrawal he effects is importantly on the world's terms:

> At that time I was in Germany, where I had been called by the wars that had not yet ended there. While I was returning to the army from the coronation of the Emperor, the onset of winter detained me in quarters where . . . I stayed all day shut up alone in a stove-heated room, where I was completely free to converse with myself about my own thoughts. Among the first that occurred to me was the thought that there is not usually so much perfection in works composed of several parts and produced by various different craftsmen as in the works of one man. Thus we see that buildings undertaken and completed by a single architect are usually more attractive and better planned than those which several have tried to patch up by adapting old walls built for different purposes. (*PW* 1:116)

Notwithstanding his bias against fictive discourse, Descartes himself employs various literary strategies, including metonymy. The contiguity can hardly be missed: "the Emperor" and "I" appear together in the same sentence. This association having been implied, Descartes draws the already implied parallel between solo architect and solo thinker as a transition to the next parallel and the next contiguity: "And to speak of human affairs, I believe that if Sparta was at one time very flourishing, this was not because each of its laws in particular was good . . . but because they were devised by a single man and hence all tended to the same end" (*PW* 1:117). "Single man" signifies Lycurgus, by tradition the founder of the Spartan constitution, even as it entails the single man who is I. Descartes then draws the enabling parallel: "And so I thought that since the science contained in books . . . is compounded and amassed little by little from the opinions of many different persons, it never comes as close to the truth as the simple reasoning which a man of good sense naturally makes concerning whatever he comes across" (*PW* 1:117). The metonymic chain *Emperor-Descartes-Lycurgus-Descartes* thus obligates the reader not only to respect the parallelisms but to comprehend the powerful political authorities as discursive figures one must "go through" in order to arrive at the authority who is the author of *Discourse on Method*.

While the discursive formations of the "book of the world" are supposed to rule, decisive power belongs to the text of the ruling self, which is to say the ruling solitary mind. In this Descartes seems to follow his predecessor Montaigne, who was the first after St. Augustine to concentrate on himself (even as Rousseau, while claiming himself to be the first ever to do so, was the first after Descartes). But Descartes and Montaigne relate to things in different ways. Descartes is so fully mind that flesh can but be a humble associate, not the sort of companion you would take along by choice. Cartesian discourse knows nothing of Montaigne's desire for a closer union that is actually a re-union between "body and soul": "We must order the soul not to draw aside and entertain itself apart. . . . but to rally to the body, embrace it, cherish it, assist it, control it, advise it, set it right and bring it back when it goes astray; in short, to marry it and be a husband to it, so that their actions may appear not different and contrary, but harmonious and uniform." [12]

Montaigne accepts flesh in terms familiar to us from Christian tradition, to which we may also attribute the masculinization of the soul, which is clearly the dominant partner. Yet Montaigne would transcend what Descartes would reinforce; ever reconstructing, Montaigne would overcome the Cartesian schism in order to reunite the partners in a condition like the condition originally ordained. Descartes for his part wants, in this context, all the disunion he can get: the Cartesian body is a vehicle for mind.

7. Unit Analysis

If the philosopher is to create a discourse of reason, he must develop analytical procedures that challenge the primacy of worldly things as given. Analysis, entering English usage thirty years after the *Discourse* as "the resolution of anything complex into its simple elements," underlines the important assumption that elementary units or parts — here called elements — constitute the foundation of any phenomenon, and that the nature of any phenomenon can be exposed by disassembling and reassembling this foundation. In 1570 John Dee goes out of his way to explain, in the first printed use of the term, the transition from unity to unit: "Note the word, Vnit, to express the Greke Monas, and not Vnitie: as all commonly, till now, vsed." "Till now": Dee grasps the historical significance of the change by which the world, so long a theme of contemplation, becomes an object of analysis and calculation. A dramatically altered and altering assumption about the constitution of worldly things here comes to the fore. Unity denotes quality entailing togetherness, in the manner of Whitehead's concrescence, while unit signifies any single *quantum* of a *totum*. A unit is equally the primary constituent of the procedure that approaches an existing complex entity by reducing that entity to the parts which, being "simple," are most easily apprehended and managed.

Where a unity exists there is a qualitative condition of harmony and gathering, which is why in early usage the term was employed in connection with deity and the combining that forms a church or a state. The unit, however, specifies not a qualitative state but a means of measure. It is, as Dee recognized, essentially mathematical, as another passage affirms: "Number, we define, to be, a certayne Mathematicall Summe, of Vnits. And, an Vnit, is that thing Mathematicall, Indiuisible, by participation of some likeness of whose property, any thing, which is in deed, or is counted One, may reasonably be called One." [13] In early usage a "whole" indicates what is sound or unharmed, and, in late Middle English, what is full or complete. The linking of soundness to completeness may derive from the idea of perfection, which came to mean the consummate and superlative, the very best; but this meaning stems from the earlier belief that perfection characterizes the state of being that is simply and entirely all that it can be. Anything sound—not impaired or defective—attains perfection when it comes into its own as itself, a thing among but not identical with other things—the process Hopkins envisages when he speaks of selving. A world of things thus perfected is a created world in the traditional sense. Its being is that of *ens creatum*, which is the work of God, the uncreated, *ens perfectissimum*.

The later, still current sense of "unit" is "something made up of parts in combination or mutual connexion; a complex unity or system" (1697). Something made up is something composed, and the distinction between what is composed and what is not lies at the heart of the Cartesian discourse of mentation. Mentation itself is unextended and noncomposite. It is what cannot be taken apart, whereas body is divisible. Conversely, bodies combine to form wholes, which are the complex unity of the simples that the bodies already are. For Descartes composition is among the more self-evident of givens, and wholly accessible to rational analysis. Once analysis achieves hegemony, it is the fate of things to be de-composed, which helps to explain analogies between mentation, on the one hand, and the process of tearing down and erecting buildings, on the other. "Admittedly, we never see people pulling down all the houses of a city for the sole purpose of rebuilding them in a different style to make the streets more attractive; but we do see many individuals having their houses pulled down in order to rebuild them, some even being forced to do so when the houses are in danger of falling down and their foundations are insecure" (*PW* 1:117). Sometimes, as here, the course of the *Discourse* is explicitly the course of shared worldy experience, although the author alters the being he borrows. For the force of the analogy lies not in the cited architectural particulars, but in the shift from these to what is collateral to them in the discourse of reason. Descartes's architecture is an abstract architectonic; in a convergence of senses that emerge within fifty years following the publication of the *Discourse*, the latter term signifies what pertains to anything constructed, or constructive, and enjoying control through superintendence (1678).

In departing from what it derives from, the Cartesian architectonic, assimilated into the discourse of reason, reveals the same rationality as the architectonic of Dee. The human form that Dee takes as his point of departure is from start to finish geometrical, as in Leonardo's celebrated drawing of a man so placed as to illustrate the symmetry of the square and the circle into both of which he conformably fits. Dee concludes that architecture is founded not in any action on, by, or through everyday things but in the science of number. Thus "the function of the architect is to produce the design of the building, and . . . this is not material but exists in the mind of the architect and is based on abstract considerations of mathematics and proportion." [14]

Analogy may proceed the other way round, from a point of departure in the discourse of reason to the worldly experience from which it is at least in part derived. Thus philosophical de-composing can be figured in relation to medical dis-section; when Descartes seeks to explain physiology by describing the heart and its functions, he suggests this help: "I should like anyone unversed in anatomy to take the trouble, before reading this, to have the heart of some large animal with lungs dissected before him (for such a heart is in all respects sufficiently like that of a man)" (*PW* 1:134). In the exposition that follows, the movement of the author's discourse is the very articulation of the movement of the blood and the operations of the apposite organs, all of which interconnectedness is assimilated into the inorganic, indeed into the mechanical: "This movement follows just as necessarily as the movement of a clock follows from the force, position, and shape of its counterweights and wheels" (*PW* 1:136). The clock appears to belong to a higher order than do some things in other analogies. It is not merely like other mechanical entities, it exemplifies mechanics, as Dee's architecture exemplifies the science of number. Such is the role of all worldly things in the *Discourse*, including even the animal spirits, which "like a very fine wind, or rather a very pure and lively flame . . . rise continuously in great abundance from the heart into the brain, passing from there through the nerves to the muscles and imparting movement to all the parts of the body" (*PW* 1:138–39).

If the arrangement of mechanical unity in the clock is governed by the rules of mechanics, and if the generation of animal spirits is also governed by these rules, what considerations govern the kind of being called human? The answer lies in the analogy with automata: Descartes suggests that should such machines be formed in the likeness of any animal wanting discourse of reason, one would not be able to tell whether or in what way they differed from the animal being mimicked. But an automaton made in the likeness of a man would be, by definition, of a different nature from the man, and for two reasons. Machines are not capable of discourse: "But it is not conceivable that such a machine should produce different arrangements of words so as to give an appropriately meaningful answer to whatever is said in its presence, as the dullest of men can do" (*PW* 1:140). Words are deemed discrete units or parts of the discursive whole, and they function according to the manner in which they were arranged. But, more than the mere arrangement of units, discourse requires the capacity of reason, which is universal and therefore available on all occasions, and the maker of the automaton could match this universality and availability only if he could design as many parts and as many arrangements as there are actions to be performed; "hence it is morally impossible for a machine to have enough different organs to make it act in all the contingencies of life in the way in which our reason makes us act" (*PW* 1:140). *Enough* organs; the criterion is purely quantitative.

The truth is either that Descartes simply does not believe that anyone but God can create human beings, or that this is what he wants to believe. He would distance himself as much as possible from those worldly things called animals because they are by definition subhuman, and subhuman differs from human as body differs from soul: "This shows not merely that the beasts have less reason than men, but that they have no reason at all" (*PW* 1:140). Descartes creates the situation from which he seeks to escape by assimilating from the everyday world a thing whose nature he has not thought through. Despite the generalizations about the automaton, he attends *from* it more than *to* it. What he says of automata derives directly from the correlate, which is that he attends *from* rather than *to* the nature of human being. The two criteria for distinguishing between human beings and machines that resemble them amount to making two statements about the way human beings are. They use language; they are capable of discoveries and of the discourse of reason; and brutes are beings that are not capable of language or reason.

Descartes would flee the contagion of likeness he himself has spread. By making the threatening likeness only a partial resemblance, man is saved from the brute in him. Yet the brute persists in the form of the animal spirits, a compound notion consisting half of "body," as it were, and half of "non-body"; its analogue in Hobbes is the angel, who, though spiritual, must possess some degree of materiality and is therefore conceived as being exceptionally thin.

After the first moral impossibility comes a second that might better be called spiritual, even theological. The discursive locus is a distinction between the ways in which the reasonable soul and the animal come into being. The reasonable soul must be expressly created, and since only God could put forth so superior a faculty, the divine trace is preserved. This leaves, in a state less clear and distinct, a lesser way of coming to be related. By this way nonhuman beings are "educed" from nature, meaning that, in creating it, God endowed nature with the capacity to continue creation, mediately, as it were. The distinction points the human in the direction of the divine, away from the contaminating zone of animality. Aside from the error of denying God there is no greater error "than that of imagining that the souls of the beasts are of the same nature as ours, and hence that after this present life we have nothing to fear or to hope for, any more than flies and ants" (*PW* 1:141).

Mortality is the threat, immortality the hope, and if Descartes attends to neither closely it is not for lack of attending from them. They form a well-spring from which the pathos of discourse flows. All of this sounds different from the preoccupation with the rules of mechanics, which proved to be the purport of the generation of animal spirits, of the heart, of the circulation of the blood, as of the objects of the eye and I. In fact, though only one is named, two sets of rules obtain, the rules of mechanics having their counterpart in the rules of reason (which a less rationalistic discourse might have called the rules of morality). Rules are universal, immutable, any set of them exhibiting the same quality of lawfulness as any other set, and each in its own way a whole consisting of parts. In what, if anything, lies the ground of this second, previously discussed belief, without which there could be no belief in rules? The broadest basis consists in the received idea of the *ens creatum* as a totality. Traditionally, that totality would have been deemed a harmonious hierarchy, a unity before units; and Descartes does not hesitate to repose high confidence in that state of being. It is just the sort of confidence that Nietzsche was to assail: " 'The well-being of the universal demands the devotion of the individual'—but behold, there is no such universal! At bottom, man has lost the faith in his own value when no infinitely valuable whole works through him; i.e., he conceived such a whole in order *to be able to believe in his own value*."[15] Descartes believes both that the whole is infinitely valuable, and that it works through him. If his epoch has not reached the stage of nihilism, of which Nietzsche is thinking, it already draws on presentment and on the value functions that it entails. The "whole of creation" that the Cartesian spectator sees is no longer the traditional plenitude of being; it is not, in a word, a unity, in the sense that Dee helped to overcome. "The creation" is an old name for the set of the largest example of the unit-arrangements the experimenter discovers and is governed by.

It counts neither as normative nor as supreme but as a complement of specular perceiving and doing. Bound as by contract to its other, *the creation is the value by which presentment compensates for the reduction of worldly things to specular objects*. The discourse of reason enables the mind, in presenting these objects to itself, to affirm its own ontological certainty. Only in its vision of things as objects *are* they—and what they are as objects is different from, and less, than what they were.

When very many kinds of qualitatively different things get reduced to entities with narrowly calculated characteristics, ontic plenitude reduces to something like ontic poverty. The universe becomes on the one hand an ensemble of objects that are seen to permit the passage of light and are entirely clear and transparent, or colored; and, on the other hand, that which is not such an object—the reasoning entity who understands himself as the spectator of such objects. Through presentment, objectifying calculation embraces the world as materiel and evidence: something for testing, numeration, proof. Even an endeavor in the strictly human sphere, such as Spinoza's attempt to determine norms of conduct, can take calculability (here in the form of extrapolations from geometry) as normative.

> There should be one and the same method of understanding the nature of things whatsoever, namely, through nature's universal laws and rules. . . . I shall, therefore, treat of the nature and strength of the emotions according to the same method as I employed heretofore in my investigations concerning God and the mind. I shall consider human actions and desires in exactly the same manner, as though I were concerned with lines, plains, and solids.[16]

Leveling once-concrete things into abstract objectivity, the light of presentment seems to shine equally everywhere. But there are notes of anxiety, and one is tempted by doubt. One can doubt, for example, that the things one experiences are, or one can dream that they are not and that other things are instead: at one point Descartes imagines a worldly arrangement in a manner entirely foreign to known creation. But dreams raise difficult issues in difficult ways. Even if we only dreamed that we were flesh, "it must surely be admitted that the visions which come in sleep are like paintings, which must have been fashioned in the likeness of things that are real, and hence that at least these general kinds of things—eyes, head, hands and the body as a whole—are things which are not imaginary but are real and exist" (*PW* 2:13). Even in the sphere of completely fanciful beings, such as sirens and satyrs, inspection uncovers only rearrangements of things already in being.

This discussion in the First *Meditation*, like those in the *Discourse*, attends from the anteriority of the world. Thinkers may well employ novel procedures; they may even combine with practitioners in other fields to study objects never before brought to view by presentment. But the indefeasible office of thinking is to recollect and remind. If Descartes can dream a centaur tonight it is because he could doubt a horse yesterday, and he can doubt a horse yesterday because yesterday there was a horse.

Even in refusing worldly things by refusing to desire them, one does not necessarily doubt their actuality. One attends always from the world as the course of things for every discourse. Nor does Descartes's discursive dreaming ever doubt the difference between it and that other, waking state that everyday experience takes as real. The illusion that life is a dream is sustained *as* an illusion. What pulls the thinker through time and again is memory, which reminds him that he thinks. Nonetheless the possibility that reason, and thus his being, may be illusory, just as a doubt or a dream is, cannot be easily dismissed; he must keep reminding himself that his reason is continuous with his being. Illusion must be denied, above all, when proffered by "a deceiver of supreme power and cunning who is deliberately and constantly deceiving me. In that case I too undoubtedly exist, if he is deceiving me; and let him deceive me as much as he can, he will never bring it about that I am nothing so long as I think that I am something" (*PW* 2:17).

The contiguity between putting forward and conceiving suggests a parallel between the discursive in the sense of utterance and discursive in the sense of forming an idea or apprehension. It also prepares the way for the more radical move, at once utterance and conception, by which the author of the *Discourse* can more nearly identify with his Author than with his human parents. As it denotes an idea, "the conception in my mind" connotes a procreation, *concevoir* carrying the same overtones in French as *conceive* in English. It is then an easy step to the suggestion that God is localized within the thinker to the extent that God generates himself there in the form of idea, in contrast to his parents, who merely established in him certain material dispositions:

> And indeed it is no surprise that God, in creating me, should have placed this idea in me to be, as it were, the mark of the craftsman stamped on his work—not that the mark need be anything distinct from the work itself. But the mere fact that God created me is a very strong basis for believing that I am somehow made in his image and likeness [*á son image et semblance*], and that I perceive this likeness [*ressemblance*], which includes the idea of God, by the same faculty which enables me to perceive myself. (*PW* 2:35; *OP* 453)

The trope of the craftman's mark derives from Plato, who saw in the workshop a site of action reconstructive in its very nature, as this is where worldly things are fabricated or repaired on the pattern of existing worldly things. The distinction Plato draws between knowing and making is of course inherently political, as the former, higher office is filled by those who lead and the latter by those who follow. At the same time, and more radically, Plato establishes a paradigm for borrowing from the everyday realm whatever the occasion warranted, a paradigm Descartes can be seen to follow, as I am suggesting, throughout the *Discourse*, not to mention the *Meditations*. Even a concept as "transcendental" as the *eidos* is redolent of such "humble" origins. In the words of Arendt,

> It is indeed true—and Plato, who had taken the key word of his philosophy, the term "idea," from experiences in the realm of fabrication, must have been

the first to notice it — that the division between knowing and doing, so alien to the realm of action, whose validity and meaningfulness are destroyed the moment thought and action part company, is an everyday experience in fabrication, whose processes obviously fall into two parts: first, perceiving the image or shape (*eidos*) of the product-to-be, and then organizing the means and starting the execution.[17]

This way of conceiving things serves two overlapping purposes. It practically separates knowing from doing, as must be accomplished if knowing is to gain the precedence that will allow the mentation of Descartes to seem natural. And it assimilates the process of making, the work of the craftsman, to the high plane of creation — or, more precisely, it makes of it a discursive resource, such that the very idea of deity implanted in the mind of the philosopher can be articulated through that process. What Descartes calls the craftsman's mark is the indwelling, discursive trace of God's presence in his creature. Such a mark cannot be identified with the Platonic *eidos*, which dwells at an infinite remove from "ordinary" worldly being. The mark that is ultimately responsible for the *Discourse* is simultaneously a proof and a prophecy. Proof: the mark not only records the implantation of the idea, it is the form in which that idea is, perpetually, possessed. Prophecy: the mark points to that time to come when the mortal life shall be exchanged for life without end. Whereas Plato explains any marking of things whatever, the Cartesian trope of marking has always one type, the Christian-divine, in view. The marking of the thinker that proves God is the very marking by which the thinker becomes that highest species of worldly being who is the human rational knower.

In the spectacle of self there is more to see than the implanted idea, however, for the idea is said to be contained in something else that is not an idea and not an entity; again: "But the mere fact that God created me is a very strong basis for believing that I am somehow made in his image and likeness, and that I perceive that likeness, which includes the idea of God, by the same faculty which enables me to perceive myself" (*M* 35). On a Derridean reading, the statement wants presence but betrays its absence, or better, its deferral, the deferring terms being, precisely, image, semblance, resemblance — figuring what does not appear otherwise than in those very words. But this implies a collateral move of deference, in the sense of "courteous regard such as is rendered to a superior, or to one to whom respect is due" (1660), or as the formation "in deference to" would have it, "in respectful knowledge of the authority of, out of practical respect or regard to" (1863). It is moreover a double deferring. On the one hand, Descartes acknowledges the superiority of God, whose authority is ultimately responsible for this entire course of articulation: the condition of possibility of a likeness *to* God is the existence *of* God, so that, however much *image et semblance* may be matters of appearance, matters of appearance are referable to an always actually existing God. On the other hand, Descartes is all the while deferring to the everyday world, of which much the same thing can be said: however much its existence may be represented by appearances—which is just to say, represented—all such appearances are referable to the reality of that existence. Even if painters "manage to think up something so new that nothing remotely similar has ever been seen before—something which is therefore completely fictitious and unreal—at least the colours used in the composition must be real [*véritables*]" (*PW* 2:13).

8. Discoursing of Made Things

The made things of which Plato discourses in *The Republic* include the products of the cabinetmaker, the cobbler, and the blacksmith, representative artisans in the earlier phases of the first great age of technology Lewis Mumford calls the eotechnic, which embraces all types of artifacts and procedures from "prehistory" to the industrial revolution of the eighteenth century. Descartes is equally of his age in taking his point of departure from light, which received new attention in an age of astronomical and microscopic investigation as well as experimentation in the arts, especially by painters alert to the possibilities of closely observed illumination. It was light that led Descartes to think of fire and then the products of the glassmaker, the paradigmatic artisan of the later eotechnic period: "But most important of all was the part played by glass in the eotechnic economy. Through glass new worlds were conceived and brought within reach and unveiled."[18] Descartes writes:

> Among other things, I took pains to make everything belonging to the nature of fire very clearly understandable, because I know nothing else in the world, apart from the heavenly bodies, that produces light. Thus I made clear how it can . . . produce different colours and various other qualities in different bodies; how it melts some bodies and hardens others; how it can consume almost all bodies, or turn them into ashes and smoke; and finally how it can, by the mere force of its action, form glass from these ashes—something I took particular pleasure in describing since it seems to me as wonderful a transmutation as any that takes place in nature. (*PW* 1:133)

This way of seeing things sacrifices producer in the interest of process. While Plato in Book X of *The Republic* evokes the workshop, the work of the craftsman, and the use of rein and bits by the horseman, Descartes discourses on an unmediated process, as if the formation of glass belonged somehow not to civilization but to nature; as if glass were more *phusis* than *téchnē*. Fire, moreover, resembles shining stars in that both generate light, the natural phenomenon that guides the course of reason. But it is perhaps the very intensity in fire, its ability to produce glass as if this were the reduction of fire to its own pure essence, that attracts a philosopher who is himself given to intensity and the search for essence.

If reason produces without the direct intervention of another entity or agency, which the stars and fire also do, it is otherwise with wax, which not only conforms its worldly way of being to the dictates of heat, but grotesquely inverts essentialization. A homely thing, wax can ooze, drip, contract, and harden; it can extend every which way, but when all is said and done the alterations culminate in no wondrous transformation. So impenetrable is the stuff of which wax is composed that it cannot even admit light, let alone transmit it, a property placing it among the lower terms in Cartesian discourse. Heat, belief, imagination, and so on—these lower terms—appear segregated from the higher terms—light, mind, intellect, and so on—belonging to the realm of glass. Which is to say, glass is affined to reason as wax is affined to body.

As the *Discourse* shows God present at the creation, so it shows the philosopher (as we have seen) present at the creation of glass, bearing witness to the fact that glass, its own phoenix, enters the world wondrously, quite as he does. Neither creation occurs *ex nihilo*. Glass finds its crucible in ashes, while the philosopher takes his departure from something proportionately humble, his parents, in whom he sees nothing but the source of "arrangements" on which God can work his creative craft.

Wax is never seen to enter the world at all, nor does the philosopher speculate on what might have transpired. Wax *already is*, now hardening, now expanding—pure extension, if not a parody of extension. In wax Descartes finds properties with which neither glass, nor Descartes himself, can be identified. To make a discursive abstraction of glass or wax, as he does, requires that one attend from things composed of it, the better to conform them to presentment. Attending to the things, making the implicit explicit, can help to explain why one thing or another—wax or what have you—forms with other components of the *Discourse* a significant nexus.

By his own account Descartes's rooms in Holland contained a stove, but glass things, windows, tableware, mirrors, and so on, must have graced the lodgings as well, Descartes being a man of means in a prosperous city. Now, standard window glass, in Descartes's day, was no more what it long had been. Medieval artisans had famously fashioned colored glass into pictures, transmuting light so as to figure, illuminate, reveal. Gradually, transmitting, not transmuting, becomes the dominant use, and the window stops interposing the images of a transnatural realm and in the process blocking access to what lies outside. It now lets in that world and its things, framing them, even as it illuminates and frames the worldly things inside. As the "highest" artifact of the late-eotechnic economy, glass affirms the sovereignty of the specular.

Although that nontransparent framing device known as the mirror had long reflected images, the images had grown much clearer and there were many more mirrors and thus more of such images, a development that reinforced a growing tendency to define the human in terms of the visual as well as the individual. By a kind of spontaneous portraiture the mirror enhances the self-fashioning that played so large a role in the Renaissance; which means not merely seeing oneself as another might, but so dwelling in the gaze of the other that the self-fashioning ego accustoms itself to being *that* subject's object while continuing to be a subject for itself.

As Mumford explains, the mirror conduces to the introspection that comes to be, for many modern sensibilities, the equivalent of meditation:

> The use of the mirror signalled the beginning of introspective biography in the modern style; that is, not as a means of edification but as a picture of the self, its depths, its mysteries, its inner dimensions. The self in the mirror corresponds to the physical world that was brought to light by natural science in the same epoch: it was the self *in abstracto*, only part of the real self, the part that one can divorce from the background of nature and the influential presence of other men.[19]

Descartes knew that other eotechnic artifact, the lens, through the new astronomy and its cosmography, in contrast with Spinoza, who knew it from daily practice as a polisher. In the lens the property of magnification joins the property of transparency, bringing worldly things into an unprecedented nearness. Contexts of familiar dimensions had long supplied the relations of near and far with an aura immediate and immutable. Through the mediation of the stained-glass picture window the Christian soul could experience directly her continuity with the continuity of some originary sacred belief or story. The lens offers different contexts, different dimensions. Its mediation is such that whatever it shows is shown immediately as other than it had appeared to be before the lens was trained on it. The lens instigates a revolution in appearance. Something now appears where nothing was seen before. The lens discloses some of what has been hidden in the world and promises that the hidden may forever be disclosed in the same way. Thus the hidden becomes closely associated with both a prospect of revelation and a promise of access.

Optical magnification demonstrates that in order to be right about things they must be viewed with detachment — literally detached from contexts familiar to anyone so as to be relocated in the domain of science or technology. Things previously situated in their own worldly context and aura are assimilated to the investigating subject's field as objects in that field — assimilated, in a word, to presentment. If the philosopher examines the lens no more closely than he examines the thing, it is also because glass in general, and the lens in particular, is already so close to the discourse of reason as to be practically invisible. The eye of reason looks through the lens, not at it, just as one looks through and not at one's eyeglasses. In this case proximity no longer refers to placement within a general environment. It refers to ontological nearness. Transmitter of natural light, the lens is a counterpart of the light of reason. It is light embodied and thus comes closest, among artifacts, to sharing the substance of reason itself.

9. Discourse, Fiction, and Fatefulness

Like the *Discourse on Method*, the *Meditations* is a history or tale of struggle. As before, the antagonists are doubt and certainty, but the fable also traces the thrusts and parries of a conflict between sleep, or delusion, and waking. Doubt is a shadow dreaming casts, a dark space of time from which the waking state forever seeks to distance itself. "For whether I am awake or asleep, two and three added together are five, and a square has no more than four sides. It seems impossible that such transparent truths should incur any suspicion of being false" (*M* 14).

The penultimate scene of the First *Meditation* witnesses a psychomachia, the traditional genre of the agon of the soul. Here the demon of doubt not only appears but invades, at least hypothetically, Descartes's own mind: "I shall think that the sky, the air, the earth, colours, shapes, sounds, and all external things are merely the delusions of dreams which he has devised to ensnare my judgement. I shall consider myself as not having hands or eyes, or flesh, or blood or senses, but as falsely believing I have all things" (*M* 4). If this all remains somewhat bloodless, it is because we are dealing with a discursive abstraction projected by the thinker to convince us of the rational rigor of his undertaking and the seriousness of the challenge. Such being the case, there may be a "formal" ground for the suspense the narrator creates by postponing the promised exertions and raising doubts about his own resolve — a strategy with overtones of the myth pattern in which the hero suddenly faces apparent defeat or fatal weakening of his powers: "But this is an arduous undertaking, and a kind of laziness brings me back to normal life. I am like a prisoner who is enjoying an imaginary freedom while asleep; as he begins to suspect that he is asleep, he dreads being woken up, and goes along with the pleasant illusion as long as he can" (*M* 15). Alone as he is, and at leisure, the philosopher seems half in love with easeful languor: he cannot be more than half in love because he knows that he should be up and doubting.

This doubting is, however, a dangerous discursive game. So is the donning of the deceiver's guise, advertised as deliberate role-playing. It is the sort of thing commonly ascribed to the Baroque, which, even in the act of conjuring grand illusions, grandly gives them away, inviting us to speak not only of illusion but of illusionism. Some of the ambivalence in the text stems from the discursive mode itself, which is confessional, both in the section concluding the first and the section concluding the final meditation. If the two confessions are thus finally symmetrical, they are not predictably so. The first, admitting to indolence and a desire for sleep, suggests a weakening of the resolve to reason. On this issue the second confession yields, admitting what was dubious in the doubting while stressing the virtues of wakefulness. A merit of the move is that it helps to overcome the preceding ambivalence, though recourse to the conditional suggests that doubt remains. Appealing to the testimony of his senses, his memory, and his intellect, Descartes concludes: "Accordingly, I should not have any further fears about the falsity of what my senses tell me every day; on the contrary, the exaggerated doubts of the last few days should be dismissed as laughable" (*M* 61). Descartes would have this apply to the main source of doubt, the difficulty of knowing whether you are asleep or awake; but what truly indemnifies reason is the relation between experience and the memory of things. What differentiates dreaming from being awake is the fact "that dreams are never linked by memory with all the other actions of life as waking experiences are" (*M* 61; *OP* 504).

He then deploys the fiction of an episode in waking life in which a man suddenly appears to him and as suddenly disappears, from which Descartes concludes "it would not be unreasonable for me to judge that he was a ghost or a vision created in my brain, rather than a real man. But when I distinctly see where things come from and where and when they come to me, and when I can connect my perceptions of them with the whole of the rest of my life without a break, then I am quite certain that when I encounter these things I am not asleep but awake" (*M* 62).

No less than any other must the discourse of reason draw upon memory and anticipate being remembered itself. Without such memory there is no posterity for the truth it would proffer. The power of recollection and reconstruction, implicitly exercised at every moment in Cartesian discourse, is never really in doubt and is sometimes directly in view: "and when I connect my perceptions [of things] with the whole of the rest of my life without a break"; here is a continuity as clear and distinct as any discursive enthymeme, however proudly skeptical the latter's credentials. For as Santayana says of Descartes, "his mind was not plastic nor mystical enough to be profoundly sceptical, even histrionically . . . Descartes could not lend himself to the disintegration of reason, and never doubted his principles of explanation."[20]

While Santayana describes himself as following Descartes, what he specifically accepts as worthy of faith, because confirmed in vital memory, is "discourse and (as an implication of discourse) my substantial existence."[21] Now, one's substantial existence can be an implication of discourse only if discourse has a claim as wide and encompassing as is made for it in the present study; and this is indeed Santayana's claim:

> Thinking is another name for discourse; and perhaps Descartes, in noting his own existence, was really less interested in the substance of himself, or in the fact that he was alive, than in the play of terms in discourse, which seemed to him obvious. Discourse truly involves spirit, with its intuition and intent, surveying those terms. . . . But discourse, no less than the existence of a self, needs to be posited, and the readiness with which a philosopher may do so yields only a candid confession of personal credulity, not the proof of anything. The assumption that spirit discoursing exists, and is more evident than any other existence, leads by a slightly different path to the same conclusion as the assumption of the self as the fundamental fact. In the one case discourse will soon swallow up all existence, and in the other this chosen existence, myself, will evaporate into discourse.[22]

Whatever alternative is chosen, or even if neither is, the story of the discourse of reason as told by Descartes is the story of a struggle to reduce the world to a more manageable objectness, and of the difficulty of bringing the process to what Dewey calls consummation.

With Vico our story takes a radical turn. The architect of the "new science" identifies "criticism," meaning the Cartesian analytic method, as the method of division by which a genus, for example, is broken down into species. In this he discerns a parallel with anatomy, which he sees as dividing the worldly things that God has put together. "We can observe in Latin idioms the traces of what we have been talking about. For the same verb *minuere* means both to lessen and to separate; as if what we separate may not fully be any longer what had been put together, but is diminished, changed, and corrupted."[23]

Vico is disturbed by Descartes's relative indifference to discourse that is not explicitly rational and to the concrete world of human experience. As Ernesto Grassi explains,

> Vico's rejection of the critical method, and of the Rationalism connected with it, is based on the recognition that the original premises are nondeducible and that the *rational process* hence cannot 'find' them: that, moreover, rational knowledge cannot be a determining factor for rhetorical or poetic speech because it cannot comprehend the particular, the individual, i.e., the concrete situation.[24]

Cartesian knowledge and judgment are for Vico a pre-knowledge and a pre-judgment, as the analytical philosopher decomposes things into their putative constituents before he can plausibly know even whether or how he knows them. To this, Vico opposes the awkwardly named "topical" method, which searches the world over for whatever things are there. Through a process of "finding" the *topoi* or "places" of the world the new science exercises its *ingenium*—not reason in the Cartesian sense but "mother wit, the creative power through which man is capable of recognizing likenesses and making them himself."[25] With the latter phrase we come to the postulate *Verum esse ipsum factum*, "The true is precisely what is made." The world being made by God, the first truth is divine, in contrast to the

> discursive thought [*cogitatio*], which is human. Just as divine truth is what God sets in order and creates in the act of knowing it, so human truth is what man puts together and makes in the act of knowing it. Thus science is knowledge of the genus or mode by which a thing is made; and by this very knowledge the mind makes the thing, because in knowing it puts together the elements of that thing.[26]

After Descartes takes things apart, we might then say, Vico puts them together. But the statement needs to be qualified. Vico does not dismiss analysis; he too considers the elements into which the things in question are broken down. The analytic procedure in Vico, however, is only one feature in a series, the overall thrust of which is indeed in the direction of putting-together on the basis of whatever is found. The result is an openendedness that would be anathema to Descartes, whose rationalism dives down with analytic speed to the minimal. Vico isn't necessarily sure what things he is looking for until he has found them. Relying on experience and experimentation, he envisages a greater or lesser degree of comprehensiveness, whereas the rationalist insists on a greater or lesser degree of exactitude.

The Viconian perspective is regarded as a breakthrough in Western thought because of its "new" way of being historical, which privileges interrogation, context, concreteness, and secular temporality. It is not the case that Vico knows with absolute certainty that this or that came about in this or that way and is therefore such and such. It is not the case with Vico that this or that merely *could* have come about in this or that way and *may* therefore be such and such. It *is* the case with Vico that by preponderance of evidence and rigor of examination it is more likely than not that this or that came about in this or that way and is therefore probably such and such.

Where the type of certainty sought by analytical philosophy tends to be abstract, the probability sought by Vico tends to be concrete, being guided implicitly by *sensus communis*. One could as accurately call the probability pragmatic, for Vico's truth is rooted in the rhetorical tradition, which depends for its efficacy on its concrete effect, outcome, or, again as Dewey would say, its consummation. "This sort of pragmatic approach to truth also brings Vico's *sensus communis* into the orbit of social praxis. Truth is what works, not in some crude utilitarian sense, but in the rhetorical sense, that is, truth is what *makes* sense out of a problem or situation."[27] Making sense of things entails extensive interrogation, and since we can only know what has been, interrogation must be recursive. Vico asks, "Thus, how can a clear and distinct idea of our mind be the criterion of truth unless it has seen through all [of the elements] that are in the things, or are germane to it? And how can anyone be certain that he has seen through all of them completely unless he has examined all the questions that can be asked about the matter at hand."[28] Since no program of research could examine every conceivable question, the point is to ask enough of the right kinds of questions, and the right kinds of questions are comparative and historical. This is why Vico, notwithstanding his reliance on an immemorial cyclical model of constancy alternating with change, has been credited with anticipating the interpretative practices that eventually branched into modern social and cultural history, on the one hand, and ethnology, on the other.

The concept of recurrence directly influenced Yeats's cyclical system, discussed in Part I. The same general concept informs as well the thinking of Nietzsche, who is close to Vico in his concern for historicity, interrogation, and the truth of experience. Nietzsche, however, has a particular concern with explicit secular morality, and, even more relevantly with the interweaving of discourse through what he calls *fatum*. Speaking of the conventional moralist, Nietzsche observes:

> He paints himself on the wall and comments, '*Ecce homo!*' But even when the moralist addresses himself only to the single human being and says to him, 'You ought to be such and such!' he does not cease to make himself ridiculous. The single human being is a piece of *fatum* from the front and from the rear, one law more, one necessity more for all that is yet to come and to be.[29]

As classical philologist the author of *Twilight of the Gods* knows that *fatum* first signifies "that which is said, an utterance." From a phenomenon specifically discursive, a statement as such without "content," *fatum* becomes an oracle or prophecy, or, more commonly, something ordained or fated, or, more darkly, an accident or calamity. To be a piece of *fatum* is to be, then, a piece of discourse on this or that fateful course. It is therefore no trivial matter that Nietzsche provides in quotation marks the utterance, statement, or declaration he would oppose: you can only get to the *fatum* through marked language. That is, you can be successfully discursive only if you are successfully metadiscursive. Thus, having quoted the moralist straw man, Nietzsche foregrounds another discursive formulation: "The most general formula on which every religion and morality is founded is: 'Do this and that, refrain from this and that — then you will be happy! Otherwise . . . ' " (*TI* 493). He can then deliberately transform the objectionable formula — literally change it into something else through his own production of speech: "In my mouth, this formula is changed into its opposite — first example of my 'revaluation of all values': a well-turned-out human being, a 'happy one,' *must* perform certain actions and shrinks instinctively from other actions; he carries the order, which he represents physiologically, into his relations with other human beings and things" (*TI* 493). The function of this metadiscourse is to represent on one level a "physiological" endowing that is already representational on another. The single human being who must perform certain actions articulates in the world its distinctive way of being a discourse and a destiny. To identify that being as a *fatum* in the type of inscription called discourse is to recognize an innate cofounding inscription or disposition from which or by means of which the performing human being becomes the realization of a destined performing type.

Such a type resembles what Christopher Caudwell calls the genotype: "When we speak of 'man' we mean the genotype or individual, the instinctive man as he is born, who if 'left to himself' might grow up into something like a dumb brute, but instead grows up in a certain kind of society as a certain kind of man — Athenian, Aztec or Londoner. . . . This genotype is never found 'in the raw.' Always it is found as a man of definite concrete civilisation with definite opinions, material surroundings, and education." [30] With this account Nietzsche would presumably agree. He would not agree with the view, developed by Caudwell, that the purpose of the genotype is to join in associated struggle with nature. Nietzsche acts the soliloquist, making up his script as he goes, thundering against the instinct of the "herd" in order to release humanity from causality and finality — from everything but his own discourse of fatality: "No one is responsible for man's being there at all. . . . The fatality of his essence is not to be disentangled from the fatality of all that has been and will be" (*TI* 500). His iconoclasm notwithstanding, Nietzsche is ready to accept not only the efficacy of fateful discourse, but the implications of the traditional part-whole dichotomy on which he directly draws. The purport is to subsume everything within a whole that is exclusively itself in the way that nature is itself, nature being a name for the ulterior necessity behind that "physiological" production of discourse in the form of utterance, which is, again, the *fatum* of the human being:

> One is necessary, one is a piece of fatefulness, one belongs to the whole, one is in the whole; there is nothing which could judge, measure, compare, or sentence our being, for that would mean judging, measuring, comparing, or sentencing the whole. But there is nothing besides the whole. That nobody is

held responsible any longer, that the mode of being may not be traced back to a *causa prima*, that the world does not form a unity either as a sensorium or as "spirit" — that alone is the great liberation; with this alone is the innocence of becoming restored. (*TI* 500–501)

In *The Birth of Tragedy* Nietzsche had suggested that when the lyric artist sings, the performing self is not the self in the usual sense but is somehow eternal yet existent, at one with the things of the world. This Eleatic account of the artist and the artist's inspiration anticipates the dynamic of the typical human being of the *Twilight*, who does what he is destined to do just by virtue of being who he is when and where and how he is. It is this fatefulness that, as suggested above, he himself signifies. In *The Birth of Tragedy* the artist Archilochus, however, signifies the spirit speaking itself *into* and *as* the artist, "a world-genius expressing his primordial pain symbolically in the symbol of the man Archilocus."[31] In the same passage Nietzsche negates every attempt to justify human existence except the esthetic:

> The entire comedy of art is neither performed for our betterment or education nor are we the true authors of this art world. On the contrary, we may assume that we are merely images and artistic projections for the true author, and that we have our highest dignity in our significance as works of art — for it is only as an *esthetic phenomenon* that existence and the world are eternally justified.[32]

If this sounds Emersonian, it is. To the author of "The Poet," railway and factory village are works of art; made things. The action of poetic discourse is verbal but so in a sense is any action: "Words and deeds are quite indifferent modes of the divine energy. Words are also actions, and actions are a kind of words."[33] Emerson would thus preserve the proximity of the discursive to the divine, at least when it is the poet who discourses. The poet, like Nietzsche's artist, is himself a symbol; for, again, all things are:

> We are symbols, and inhabit symbols; workman, work, and tools, words and things, birth and death, all are emblems; but we sympathize with the symbols, and, being infatuated with the economical uses of things, we do not know that they are thoughts. The poet, by an ulterior intellectual perception, gives them a power which makes their old use forgotten, and puts eyes and a tongue into every dumb and inanimate object.[34]

Dewey, having declared communication to be "the most wonderul thing," speaks in the same Emersonian vein when he postulates "a natural bridge that joints the gap between existence and essence; namely communication, language, discourse" (*LW* 1:132–33). It remained for Peirce to elaborate on the ubiquity of symbols and signification and, in particular, to establish the degree to which the realm of communicating, shared as it may be with other species, is indissociable from the realm of the human.

10. *Communicating*

For Heidegger communicating is as essential to being-in-the-world as the fact that we are always already with others in that world: "Communication is never anything like a conveying of experiences, such as opinions or wishes, from the interior of one subject into the interior of another. Dasein-with is already essentially manifest in a shared state of being [*Mitbefindlichkeit*] and a co-understanding. In discourse Being-with becomes 'explicitly' shared."[35]

Peirce approaches the general question of communicating through its relation to another, crucial feature of the human realm, namely, consciousness. Though sharing general presuppositions of his age regarding consciousness, he insists on its rational, even logical, character. Any state of consciousness is for him an inference, drawn from principles either essentially intellectual; or habitual; or based on sensation, emotion, or instinct. If every state of consciousness is an inference—a kind of enlightened "guess"—then "life is but a sequence of inferences or a train of thought. At any instant then man is a thought, and as thought is a species of symbol, the general answer to the question what is man? is that he is a symbol" (7.583). To answer the question more fully requires the comparison of one type of symbol with another, which means discovering what Peirce sometimes calls the correspondences between them.

Having ventured the proposition that a man has a consciousness while a word does not, Peirce proceeds to undermine it. For Peirce "consciousness" means only "the knowledge which we have of what is in our minds; the fact that our thought is an index of itself on the ground of a complete identity with itself. But so is any word or indeed any thing, so that this constitutes no difference between the word and the man." What then of feelings? Could they also belong to words? Peirce answers that words not only have but can themselves be feelings. "Every feeling is cognitive—is a sensation, and a sensation is a mental sign or word. Now the word has a world; it has itself; and so if man is an animal feeling, the word is just as much a written feeling" (7.586). What can feel can also perceive, and perception entails communicating—acquiring and disseminating not only feelings but ideas and judgment. In the great school of worldly things, words and persons and other things educate themselves as they educate each other. If the word "electricity" has come to mean more now than it meant in the age of Benjamin Franklin, this means that the word has proven to be capable of learning. For Peirce suggests, "since man can think only by means of words or other external symbols, words might turn round and say, You mean nothing which we have not taught you and then only so far as you address some word as the interpretant of your thought. In fact, therefore, men and words reciprocally educate each other" (7.587).

Writing in an age when philosophy could still treat perennial moral questions without feeling it must justify its doing so, Peirce deems himself responsible for the elucidation of conscience as well as for the elucidation of consciousness. Such elucidation turns on the conception that, just as a word can think, feel, and perceive, so too can it possess a conscience. For "good grammar is that excellence of a word by which it comes to have a good conscience, to be satisfactory not merely [with] reference being had to the actual state of things which it denotes, not merely to the consequences of the act, but to it in its own internal determination. Beauty and truth belong to the mind and word alike" (7.587). The allusion to beauty and truth is more than a token reminiscence of Keats. Peirce insists quite pointedly on the importance of both art and the artist, whom he sees as a coworker with the scientist: "nothing is truer than true poetry. And let me tell the scientific men that the artists are much finer and more accurate observers than they are, except of the special minutiae that the scientific man is looking for" (1.315).

In Peirce's thinking correspondence is not static but active, and its mode of action is communicative. Despite the quotation above, Peirce had the highest respect for science and scientists, and his optimism over the effectiveness of scientific inquiry presupposes that the inquirers, by virtue of communicating with one another, are ultimately working together. Moreover, as noted above, "men and words reciprocally educate each other," and the same applies to the relations between words themselves. Words learn from one another and they do so because they communicate. Indeed, Peirce goes so far as to suggest, by analogy, that they procreate: "If I write 'Let *Kax* denote a gas furnace,' this sentence is a symbol which is creating another symbol within itself. Here we have a certain analogy with paternity; just as much and no more as when an author speaks of his writings as his offspring,—an expression which should be regarded not as metaphorical but merely as general" (7.591).

If in Peirce's semiotic model everything is communicating with practically everything else, it does not follow that they "talk" to each other in identical ways. On the contrary, different things relate in different ways, and it will be the aim of the pages that immediately follow to inquire into these ways.

"A Sign, or Representamen, is a First which stands in such a genuine triadic relation to a Second, called its Object, as to be capable of determining a Third, called its Interpretant, to assume the same triadic relation to its Object in which it stands itself to the same object" (2.274). This dynamic develops from the enterprise of a speculative grammar, which would place Peirce's "semiotic" on a more solid methodological footing. It derives more generally from the problem of connecting such a grammar with the good grammar of the excellent word—the word's morality or good conscience, its ability to perceive and feel, and all other correspondences enabling communication of any type or mode.

The first class of signs, the icon, is exemplified by diagrams, algebraic formulas, or photographs, or by designs for a statue, a picture, a blueprint for a building, or a decoration, and relies upon some more or less immediate likeness. The second class of sign, the index, denotes a reference or relation, sometimes an actual connection. A weathercock lets us know the direction of the wind by pointing, being compelled to this by something other, namely, the wind itself. "A rap on the door is an index. Anything which focusses the attention is an index, insofar as it marks the junction between two portions of experience" (2.286).

The third and most complex type of sign is the symbol, which may have an icon or an index as a constituent, and which has the character of a law insofar as it depends not upon likeness or connection, but upon the habit of connecting an idea with it. "A symbol, once in being, spreads among the peoples. In use and in experience, its meaning grows. Such words as *force*, *law*, *wealth*, *marriage*, bear for us very different meanings from those they bore to our barbarous ancestors. The symbol may, with Emerson's sphinx, say to man, Of thine eye I am eyebeam" (2.302). The sphinx can so say just because, as we have seen, a word, having been produced in essentially the same manner as a human soul, can in a similar way learn and grow. Words and human beings are, again, symbols: the Emersonian mark on Peirce is indelible. But the constitution of the symbol, as a Third, requires its relation to a First and a Second, called respectively, in the preceding passage, "denoting" and "connoting." A First, in Peircean epistemology, is any quality or feeling, simple and positive, not in itself cognitive, but productive of cognition when you react to it (a Second) or interpret it (a Third), which is to say, when you comprehend both its thereness, or actuality, and its futurity, or lawfulness—where it is going and hence what it means. The one who denotes must be able to direct his or her attention to something that is, here called the object. The latter is simply and positively what the attention picks out, the target at which intentionality aims. Correlatively, the attention is just this simple and positive pointing, without reaction or the "brute force" of contact: as the *sine qua non* of such, it is what must be in order for anything further to be—for any act in the vein of interpreting or communicating.

This brings us to connotation, the richer process and the richer term, and one that accordingly requires a fuller exposition. For this, one turns to the reasonings by which Peirce, returning to the denotative-connotative tradition prevalent since the twelfth century, redefines the former term as what he calls application. To apply a term is to gather together all to which it refers; the application of a proposition "is the instances of its holding good." Connotation or signification, on the other hand, is "all the qualities which are indicated" by a term, the propositional version of which is the ensemble of its implications (2.431).

At least four ways of signifying may be distinguished. An *indispensable* signification embraces "all those elements of the meaning in the absence of any one of which the name would not be applied" (2.432); it is everything that counts toward whatever we agree to be the definition of the term (or proposition) in question. A *banal* signification is what everyone already knows, or what goes without saying, while an *informational* signification is what a particular occasion or situation calls for: "these, of course, vary with the different individuals to whom the proposition is given out — that oxygen is exhilarating is informational to the student of chemistry, and banal to the teacher of chemistry" (2.432). A *complete* signification "consists of all the valid predicates of the term in question. When I say, 'The one I saw yesterday was John Peter,' the indispensable signification of John Peter is simply an individual object of consciousness . . . whom it has been agreed to designate by that name, but the banal signification, to one who knows John Peter well, is very extensive" (2.432). Peirce does not explicitly mention that complete signification also entails the informational, answering as it does to the occasion of the utterance (for instance, the speaker has been asked who it was that he saw yesterday). This compounded sense of connoting stands behind the abbreviated account under discussion, helping to explain why it becomes as dense as it does, and indicating something of the range of signifying. It is dense, too, because "knows or feels" functions as a hendiadys (the rhetorical figure in which two words, usually similar, replace a noun and a modifier), not a distinction or opposition, and because this virtual doublet generates another "member," hence a kind of Third, in the drama of instantiation. What is instantiated is simply the type of signifying the hendiadys signifies — that of knowing or feeling — and who gets instantiated is simply the type of signifier who so signifies. To be in this way is to be essentially or ideally human.

The third chapter of Peirce's semiotic story tells of interpretation from the standpoint of the interpretant, who may be "the future memory of this cognition, his future self, or another person he addresses, or a sentence he writes, or a child he gets" (7.591). The interpretant, that is, plays the role of a Third in relation to a First and a Second. A First, again, is simple and positive, such as a quality of feeling or mere appearance: a shade of purple, or the sheer quality of stillness when aloft in a balloon, apart from and prior to, as it were, any direct experience of that state. Seconds embrace the phenomena of experience, of effort, resistance, or reaction, which exhibit "an aggressive unity" lacking in the pure quality of a First: "the explanation of it is that the quality involves no reference to anything else and so is one without any special emphasis . . . while reaction consists in the congress of two things, that might not come together, and every occurrence of them makes a distinct reaction" (7.532).

Besides qualities and reactions, every experience exhibits generality, regularity, continuity, significance; it has an intelligibility that is basically lawful, and can be thought of as a pattern of habit or necessity. It bears us through the mere reaction to a quality, the second's relation to a first, so as, in time, to yield sense: "generality and regularity are essentially the same as significance" (7.535). Such bearing is, to recall an earlier discussion, educational: "the mere experience of a sense-reaction is not learning. That is only something from which something can be learned, by interpreting it. The interpretation is the learning" (7.536). Interpretation as learning is the essence of discourse because the function of the sign is to bring inefficient relations to efficiency, so establishing a habit or general rule or law.

But, it may be objected, this is very general. Are we not losing specificity as to what gets communicated, and how? and to differences between different kinds of worldly things and communications? Is there no difference between writing a sentence and producing a child? The answer to such a question lies, again, in a peculiar character that words and human beings share: "When I communicate my thought and my sentiments to a friend with whom I am in full sympathy, so that my feelings pass into him and I am conscious of what he feels, do I not live in his brain as well as in my own—most literally? True, my animal life is not there but my soul, my feeling thought attention [sic] are. If this be not so, a man is not a word, it is true, but is something much poorer" (7.591). Soul, feeling, thought, attention are each and all discursive; they—it— communicate by a translation that is a trans-location. In this respect they are unlike these other worldly things such as trees, which are (following Heidegger's distinction) just there, present to us, or tools, which are there for us in readiness. The same ontological understanding that comprehends these distinctions appreciates the synonymity of the human and the discursive: being human is more like than unlike being a symbol. If such were not the case, there could be no trans-location, or communicating, and without communication there could be no society, dependent as it is on sympathy, or "fellow feeling," as Peirce, following Adam Smith, calls the sympathetic disposition of the species:

> A word may be in several places at once, Six Six, because its essence is spiritual; and I believe that a man is no whit inferior to the word in this respect. Each man has an identity which far transcends the mere animal;—an essence,

a *meaning* subtile as it may be. He cannot know his own essential significance; of his eye it is eyebeam. But that he truly has this outreaching identity — such as a word has — is the true and exact expression of the fact of sympathy, fellow feeling — together with all unselfish interests — and all that makes us feel that he has an absolute worth. (7.591)

The eyebeam trope from Emerson belongs with another Emersonian favorite that Peirce adopted, man's "glassy essence," by which Peirce suggests his commitment to a certain ideality. I say a certain one because ideality and the ideal, like connotation, can be taken in several senses. "Ideal" may signify that which partakes of idea. In common usage it indicates a being superlative or perfect in its kind or a state of such being.

Peirce's contemporary Husserl showed the importance of the ideal, *inter alia*, in the phenomenon of essence. The essence of anything is, in effect, what controls permissible predicates: what something is is all the things you can truly say of it. If a sound is to have a particular timbre, intensity, or pitch, it must have timbre, intensity, or pitch as such, and these must interact by the necessity of physical laws in such a way that the particular sonic phenomenon eventuates.[36] Such an essence is ideal in that it is other than the sonic quality in its concrete manifestation, while being the very condition of possibility for that manifestation. Ideal, too, though not in just this sense, is the essence of any symbol, which Peirce, accepting a type of distinction basic to philosophical tradition in the West, considers to be formal rather than material. The essence of the word "six," he argues, could not be material since, having once written it, he can erase it and write "six" again; the fact remains that six implies two times three or five plus one:

> This is eternal truth; a truth which always is and must be; which would be though there were not six things in the universe to number, since it would still remain true that *five and one* would have been *twice three*. Now this *truth* IS the word, six; if by six we mean not this chalk line, but that wherein six, sex, sechs, zes, seis, sei agree. Truth, it is said, is never without a witness; and, indeed, the fact itself — the state of things — is a symbol of the general fact through the principles of induction; so that the true symbol has an interpretant so long as it is true. And as it is identical with its interpretant, it always exists. (7.593)

If ideality is a rich dish on the Peircean menu it is because all of these ingredients go into it, though not always at the same time and not always in the same proportions. The drift is plain enough, nonetheless, hard as it may be to state with utter precision. Roughly, that which is ideal is the essential — a notion that informs all of the senses discussed, with the possible exception of the first. Nietzsche shows his understanding of this when he discusses the ecstasy or frenzy of the artist. While reveling in the physicality of the state of possession, he drives toward the consequence with a directness of the kind we associate with pragmatism:

> What is essential in such frenzy is the feeling of increased strength and full-ness. Out of this feeling one lends to things, one *forces* them to accept from us, one violates them — this process is called *idealizing*. Let us get rid of a prejudice here: idealizing does not consist, as is commonly held, in subtract-ing or discounting the petty and inconsequential. What is decisive is rather a tremendous drive to bring out the main features so that the others disappear in the process. (*TI* 518)

The consequence might be called a rendered essence or ideal — that which survives negation of whatever type. Nietzsche's type is discursive and prag-matic in its strong drive toward a kind of mainness of meaning. William James's colorful phrase "cash value," with its grotesque posterity in phrases such as "bottom line," can draw attention away from the fact that after purga-tion, after the thinker's alembic works its idealization, what remains is what counts most, what is essential — in a word, what means; and the field being discursive, the meaning may turn out to be, as here, the meaning of a word. Hence the concern here with "ideal" and its kind.

In discourse even the ideal is fateful, belonging as it does to the world, which, as suggested above, discourse is *of* and of which discourse *is*. What kind of worldliness is at issue when Nietzsche and Peirce, or for that matter Emerson, raise the question of the ideal? Nietzsche chooses for his context, we remember, the ecstasy of the artist; Emerson writes about the poet; and Peirce speaks of "the esthetic ideal." Peirce is considering what it means to accept for his own views the label of anthropomorphism:

> In the next place, anthropomorphism for me implies above all that the true Ideal is a living power. . . . That is, the esthetic ideal, that which we *all* love and adore, the altogether admirable, has, *as ideal*, necessarily a mode of being to be called living. Because our ideas of the infinite are necessarily extremely vague and become contradictory the moment we attempt to make them pre-cise. But still they are not utterly unmeaning, though they can only be inter-preted in our religious adoration and the consequent effects upon conduct. (8.263)

This goes against the notion, frequently associated with Plato, that ideas, being eternal, can't be bothered with worldly vocations, like a person of leisure who wouldn't dream of working for a living. What counts as ideal in the passage above does belong there, quite as Nietzsche's "idealization" does.

As it comes to pass in worldly time and place, it is the essence, the outcome, the main of meaning.

11. A Destined Center

To come to any such agreement requires the exercise of a faculty, not of reason, as Descartes would have it, but of imagination, as Vico would have it: "it remains true that there is, after all, nothing but imagination that can ever supply him an inkling of the truth. He can stare stupidly at phenomena; but in the absence of imagination they will not connect themselves together in any rational way" (1.46). Although the immediate concern here is the scientist, if this notion of imagination holds at all it holds for all.

Now, "nothing but imagination" can be a little misleading. It means that imagination is the faculty by which we genuinely know, not that no other faculty or factor comes into play. Time, for example, enters in, for only with duration can investigators communicating with one another develop methodologies that will answer the questions to which they are addressed. While investigators may get conflicting results at first,

> as each perfects his method and his processes, the results are found to move steadily together toward a destined centre. . . . The activity of thought by which we are carried, not where we wish, but to a fore-ordained goal, is like the operation of a destiny. No modification of the point of view taken, no selection of other facts for study, no natural bent of mind even, can enable a man to escape the predestinate opinion. This great hope is embodied in the conception of truth and reality. The opinion which is fated to be ultimately agreed to by all who investigate, is what we mean by the truth, and the object represented in this opinion is the real. That is the way I would explain reality. (5.405)

Imagination believes before reason knows and serves as animus to inference, "and the inferential process involves the formation of a habit. For it produces a belief, or opinion, and a genuine belief, or opinion, is something on which a man is prepared to act, and is therefore, in a general sense, a habit" (2.148). This signifies that the main meaning, whether the actor is a human being or some other being, is an enabling act.

Even in assimilating past experiences into present occasions, belief-habits are forward-looking: forming them enables us to act "when the time comes." The state in question may be the readiness that becomes Lear's ripeness when the future is poised on the edge of realization. It may exist for some time solely as the expectation of what one will do in certain imaginary circumstances. But if and when such circumstances come about, the belief-habit will effect the act. This does not mean that "predestination" dictates what will occur. The type of determination in question resembles a type examined by Roman Ingarden, whose theory of esthetic concretization prepared the way for what was to become "reader-response" criticism. To convey the sense of a city a narrative offers and holds ready certain "schematized aspects" that the reader then concretizes, "filling in" what has otherwise been left "empty." [37] In the communications of everyday life, a general idea—an idea that is not filled in with specifics—plays a role similar to the novel's schemata: "general conditions of potentialities *in futuro* . . . will under imaginary conditions determine *schemata* or imaginary skeleton diagrams with which percepts will accord when the real conditions accord with those imaginary conditions; or, stating the essence of the matter in a nutshell, you opine that percepts follow certain general laws" (2.148).

The difference here is the difference between two kinds of correspondence. The reader of a novel makes a concordant response by supplying what the schemata of the discourse make it felicitous to supply. In Peirce's example belief-habits provide schemata to which percepts correspond when expected circumstances arise because they were effectively agreed upon. The destiny each thus carries out is the specific lawfulness of this implicit but binding perceptual contract.

If the notion of a destined center has the advantage of a fateful suggestiveness, it has the disadvantage of implying a convergence, when in fact the coming to pass that Peirce calls "altogether admirable" is the vast movement on all fronts; an orchestration of growing vitalities; a rendering efficient of whatever relations the world may finally display. In this we see at once a mark of the place and of the time. Of the place: pursuit of perfectibility and commitment to realization are rooted in the collective disposition that to Santayana characterizes the character and culture of America. Of the time: the discourse speaks in familiar nineteenth-century tones of the positive joint prospects of science and evolution. What Peirce finally makes of the latter cannot be taken up here. But it is necessary to remember that the ultimate test of processes or powers is the pragmatic test, which is to say the test of conduct. As theist, Peirce's conduct borders on spiritual adoration. As scientist, his conduct is that of the professional scientific worker. And these modes of behavior complement more than they contradict one another. For theist and scientist both participate actively in the process of creation that has been, is now, and will continue:

> I look upon creation as going on and I believe that such vague idea as we have of the power of creation is best identified with the idea of theism. So then the ideal would be to be fulfilling our appropriate offices in the work of creation.

Or to come down to the practical, every man sees some task cut out for him. Let him do it, and feel that he is doing what God made him in order that he should do. (8.138.n.4)

Dewey shares with Peirce this fascination with the ways in which we do things and get somewhere, and a particular fascination with the ways in which this is accomplished in discourse (in this respect converging, as we shall see, with Santayana). The term "consummation," so privileged by Dewey, has had several valences. Since the late fourteenth century it has signified "the action of completing, accomplishing, fulfilling, finishing or ending" (1398). But when the focus shifts to a state, condition, or state of affairs, "consummation" signifies "a condition in which desires, aims, and tendencies are fulfilled; crowning or fitting end; goal" (1602).

The concept figures, for example, in the distinction Dewey famously draws between experience and *an* experience. By the former term we understand the range of processes that transpire as a living being interacts with the conditions of her milieu or, as he likes to say, environment. But *an* experience occurs when a course of action achieves a significant degree of consummation, which may be thought of as attaining the destined center. *An* experience occurs, says Dewey,

> when the material experienced runs its course to fulfillment. . . . A piece of work is finished in a way that is satisfactory; a problem receives its solution; a game is played through; a situation, whether that of eating a meal, playing a game of chess, carrying out a conversation, writing a book, or taking part in a political campaign, is so rounded out that its close is a consummation and not a cessation. (*LW* 10:42)

The kinds of conclusions reached in the experience of thinking, or "preliminary discourse" (*LW* 1:132), are not special cases but characteristic instances of any experiencing that is sufficiently integrated to be pragmatic — to amount to something and to get somewhere. Dewey specifically refutes the notion of two separate sets of abstract propositions, one consisting of premises, and another consisting of conclusions. In concrete thinking, he argues, premises develop in the very process of pursuing a conclusion:

> In fact, in an experience of thinking, premises emerge only as a conclusion becomes manifest. The experience, like that of watching a storm reach its height and gradually subside, is one of continuous movement of subject-matters. Like the ocean in the storm, there are a series of waves; suggestions reaching out and being broken in a clash, or being carried onwards by a co-operative wave. If a conclusion is reached, it is that of a movement of anticipation and cumulation, one that finally comes to completion. A "conclusion"

is no separate and independent thing, it is the consummation of a movement. (*LW* 10:44–45)

Dewey's philosophy of experience is equally a philosophy of discourse; because an experience exhibits sensuous qualities for apperception and appreciation, and a high degree of coherence, this philosophy is also an esthetic. As such it embraces activities in science, technology, or politics. In Dewey's view what is essential to an experience is in large part a conviction that the consummation attained is in no wise detachable (as a propositional conclusion might be). Whereas the latter "can be used in its independent entirety as factor and guide in other inquiries," this is not the case in the work of art, where "the end, the terminus, is significant not by itself but as the integration of the parts. . . . That which distinguishes an experience as esthetic is conversion of resistance and tensions, of excitations that in themselves are temptations to diversion, into a movement toward an inclusive and fulfilling close" (*LW* 10:62). As in philosophical discourse, the artist or writer acts toward goals that do not loom up like landmarks from which to take one's cues, but emerge gradually in the struggle with whatever materials are to hand; and by the same token there must be continual assimilation of whatever efforts have gone before into efforts currently undertaken. In such a continuum every stage has to a greater or lesser degree a consummative office to perform: "Fulfilling, consummating, are continuous functions, not mere ends, located at once place only. An engraver, painter, or writer is in process of completing at every stage of his work" (*LW* 10:62–63).

It would be a mistake to read too much finality into the processes at issue. Dewey is not privileging closure at the expense of anything preceding it, or for that matter at the expense of anything that might follow from it. To attain consummation presupposes ongoing processes, such as anticipating, assimilating, and reconstructing, as preparatory to consummation yet possessed of an aim and a thrust of their own:

> There can be no movement toward a consummating close unless there is a progressive massing of values, a cumulative effect. This result cannot exist without conservation of the import of what has gone before. Moreover, to secure the needed continuity, the accumulated experience must be such as to create suspense and anticipation of resolution. Accumulation is at the same time preparation, as with each phase of the growth of a living embryo. Only that is carried on which is led up to; otherwise there is arrest and a break. For this reason consummation is relative; instead of occurring once for all at a given point, it is recurrent. (*LW* 10:142)

Dewey believes that all such activity is an "affair" of what he variously calls discourse, communication, and language. For Dewey, as for other thinkers broadly anthropological in orientation, language is a tool par excellence, part of Kenneth Burke's equipment for living. To stress the originary and instrumental aspect of language, Dewey employs what is for him a rare trope, a maternal one: "As to be a tool, or to be used as means for consequences, is to behave and endow with meaning, language, being the tool of tools, is the cherishing mother of all significance" (*LW* 10:146).

Dewey approaches discourse and the worldly things of which it treats in a crucial chapter of *Experience and Nature* (1925):

> Of all affairs, communication is the most wonderful. That things should be able to pass from the plane of external pushing and pulling to that of revealing themselves to man, and thereby to themselves; and that the fruit of communication should be participating, sharing, is a wonder by the side of which transubstantiation pales. When communication occurs, all natural events are subject to reconsideration and revision; they are re-adapted to meet the requirements of conversation, whether it be public discourse or that preliminary discourse termed thinking. (*LW* 1:132)

Two years before *Being and Time* and close to two and a half thousand after Heraclitus, Dewey is here close to both. Reading Heraclitus, Heidegger identifies truth with "uncoveredness (unhiddenness)," which, when elemental words, such as the words of ancient thought, are forgotten, "sinks back into hiddenness. Thus to the *logos* belongs unhiddenness—*a-letheia*" (*BT* 220). Through discourse, things let themselves be seen, so to say: they reveal themselves to human beings even as they reveal themselves to themselves. To suggest that things are revealed to themselves by communication, Dewey moves again in the direction of Heraclitus and Heidegger, and indeed of Parmenides: "We know from Heraclitus and Parmenides that the unconcealment of being is not simply given. Unconcealment occurs only when it is achieved by work: the work of the word in poetry, the work of stone in temple and statue, the work of the word in thought, the work of the *polis* as the historical place in which all this is grounded and preserved."[38]

Dewey attends to a similarly wide range of worldly events, but in his concern for public and preliminary discourse he conceives of a more directly educational mission. By speaking or writing "learning and teaching come into being, and there is no event which may not yield information. A directly enjoyed thing adds to itself meaning, and enjoyment is thereby idealized" (*LW* 1:133). Dewey is interested, moreover, in the "naturalization" achieved by words, in their capacity for sustaining "a natural bridge" (*LW* 1:132–33), or even for being that bridge. If Dewey speaks of nature, the natural, and naturalization he also speaks of ideality and idealization, and, in the present text, of the type of idealization arising from discursive representation.

Far from being contradictory, the relation between these seeming polarities is an ontological necessity. Every being who communicates meaning is, at a minimum, "the live creature" who is the first theme of *Art as Experience*, a vital action belonging as much to the realms termed corporeal, physical, material (or incorporate, in the terminology of Part IV, below) as to the realm of discourse. That experience which figures in Part V below is a natural bridge not only between essence and existence but also between sensation and office: "Even the dumb pang of an ache achieves a significant existence when it can be designated and descanted upon; it ceases to be merely oppressive and becomes important; it gains importance, because it becomes representative; it has the dignity of an office" (*LW* 1:133). Dewey's discourse of things in nature roughly covers, in other words, what is described in Part II as endowing, and the relations among what he terms "nature, communication and meaning" (*LW* 1:132ff.) are cofounding relations.

Notwithstanding differences in temperament and terminology, Dewey and Heidegger are not only capable of "dialogue," but, as here, their paths run parallel and even intersect.[39] Heidegger believes with Dewey in the naming power of words—in their capacity for world-making, and even in their capacity for nature-making, as it were—inasmuch as access of meaning enables "crude or raw events" (*LW* 1:132), through interactive communicating and experimenting, to cohere into patterns. "Where communication exists, things in acquiring meaning, thereby acquire representatives, surrogates, signs and implicates, which are infinitely more amenable to management, more permanent and more accommodating, than events in their first estate" (*LW* 1:132). Dewey further believes, with Heidegger, that in the worldliness of discourse "natural events become messages" (*LW* 1:138) only and always in the process of social interaction: "Everything that exists in as far as it is known and knowable in interaction with other things" (*LW* 1:138). Like Heidegger, Dewey repudiates the individualist psychology in which introspection contemplates "a wholly private realm of events disparate in kind from other events, made out of mental stuff." He who takes that tack "is only turning his attention to his own soliloquy. And soliloquy is the product and reflex of converse with others. . . . If we had not talked with others and they with us, we should never talk to and with ourselves" (*LW* 1:135).

And Heidegger writes, more broadly still: "As an existential state in which Dasein is disclosed, discourse is constitutive of Dasein's existence" (*BT* 204). It is in this context that Heidegger, turning from everyday oral discourse to discourse with specifically esthetic aims, instances that capacity for revealing things to themselves of which Dewey speaks above. Heidegger goes on: "In 'poetical' discourse, the communication of the existential possibilities of our mood, of how we 'find' ourselves (*Befindlichkeit*), can become an aim in itself, and this amounts to a disclosing of existence." (*BT* 204–5; cf. 172 n. 2)

Dewey and Heidegger may differ in their apprehension of the tendency or disposition of things overall. The quest compelling Heidegger is for the *nature of being* as such. By contrast, Dewey's verges on being a quest for *the being of nature*: "Nature may not be worshiped as divine even in the sense of the intellectual love of Spinoza. But nature, including humanity, with all its defects and imperfections, may evoke heartfelt piety as the source of ideals, of possibilities, of aspiration in their behalf, and as the eventual abode of all attained goods and excellencies" (*LW* 4:244). If at the same time both authors discourse on need—Dewey, for example, in *Art as Experience*, Heidegger in "Recollection in Metaphysics"—they discourse differently.

For Heidegger need emanates from *being*, not from *human* beings, whose role is rather to reflect back to being its own worth: "Only from human being, that is, from the manner in which man grants the word of response to the claim of Being, can a reflection of its dignity shine forth to Being. . . . Being needs the reflection of a radiance of its essence in truth."[40] Dewey's notion of need is grounded in something closer to natural instincts, or to Nietzschean physiology, and the language he employs is a reminder of the prevalence, at the time of writing, of organic models of elucidation: "Impulsions are the beginnings of complete experience because they proceed from need; from a hunger and demand that belongs to the organism as a whole and that can be supplied only by instituting definite relations (active relations, interactions) with the environment" (*LW* 10:64).

Having delimited the human role with respect to the higher dignity of being, Heidegger meanwhile effectively erases even the need first attributed to being: "At times Being needs human being, and yet it is never dependent upon existing humanity."[41] Thus, insofar as worldly things reflect back to being the latter's dignity, and insofar as this is a natural thing for them to do, nature is a scene for the authentic appearance of being. For Dewey, human being is inescapably oriented toward the being of nature. In that realm of experience the function of communicating or discourse is, we recall, to color, temper, and compose the course of the mainstream of naturally valenced events, having each and all their respective consummations. Ultimately, the process is less transcendence of nature than nature transcending, through dynamic relation with the human community; the being of nature is such as to elicit the piety of this community toward nature-*cum*-humanity, where the nature of being in Heidegger is such as to elicit piety toward, simply, being.

Dewey declares: "Communication is consummatory as well as instrumental. It is a means of establishing cooperation, domination and order. Shared experience is the greatest of human goods. In communication, such conjunction and contact as is characteristic of animals become endearments capable of infinite idealization; they become symbols of the very culmination of nature" (*LW* 1:157). In sum, the nature that is deserving of piety is a nature defined specifically as including humanity, the corollary of which definition is the inclusion of nature in the human. When we speak of a natural event such as fire "we speak proleptically; we do not name an immediate event; that is impossible. We employ a term of discourse; we invoke a meaning, namely, the potential consequences of the existence" (*LW* 1:150). The meaning of this term of discourse, as of all other such terms, is what is consummated in, by, and through natural event and human event interacting: "the ultimate meaning, or essence, denominated fire, is the consequence of certain natural events within the scheme of human activities, in the experience of social intercourse, the hearth and domestic altar, shared comfort, working of metals, rapid transit, and other such affairs" (*LW* 1:150).

Mutual entailment of the natural and the human informs Dewey's discourse of fateful interaction and its consequences: "Some consequences of the interaction of things concern us; the consequences are not *merely* physical; they enter finally into human action and destiny" (*LW* 1:149). "Things" embraces whatever in the world interacts: fire, for example, and the working of metals that fire helps make possible, together with the words that enable the conduct and comprehension of that process. Worldly things are anything of which anyone may have an experience. In one of the longest surviving senses the word denotes entities of any kind, in comparison with Old English, which exhibits the sense of a gathering of persons at which deliberative or judicial discourse held sway. This latter meaning is thus as much a matter of processes or activities as of entities, for it is understood that the gathered are there to *do* as much as to *be* things. In medieval usage "thing" could be a possession or property, or more particularly a discourse, say, or a piece of music. Thus "worldly things" means happenings, acts, events, or states and conditions as well as entities as such. "How are things today?" asks after an existing condition or state of experience. "Things" may be equally the "things themselves" to which Edmund Husserl aspired to return, or the "things as they are" as Wallace Stevens plays them on his blue guitar.

Mutual entailment of interacting things is another way of expressing the interrelations (described above in Part II) in constitutive terms. Certain events in the course of nature, such as fire, endow the human realm with enabling possibilities through which human beings achieve what their nature (what they are in essence and the cosmic sphere in which they are) entitles them to do and be. It is in aspects and activities such as these that "things" appear in the context of what is called the universe or the cosmos; they manifest their destiny. Oxymoronically, it is "the moving unbalanced balance of things," our relative slightness against that force, but our courage too, and our belief; for "we know that though the universe slay us still we may trust, for our lot is one with whatever is good in existence" (*LW* 1:314).

Whether preliminary or public, discourse becomes active in "the field of criticism" (*LW* 1:315), in an expanded sense of the term, when it educates itself in the ways of nature transcending. Through critical discourse "the office of intelligence" (*LW* 1:315) comes to be understood as a mode of realization of the course of nature broadly conceived: "The striving of man for objects of imagination is a continuation of natural process; it is something man has learned from the world in which he occurs." (*LW* 1:315).

Such learning is not passive and specular but active:

> to act upon what has been learned, thereby to plunge into new and unconsidered predicaments, to test and revise what has been learned, to engage in new goods and evils is human, the course which manifests the course of nature. They are the manifest destiny of contingency, fulfillment, qualitative individualization and generic uniformities in nature. To note, register and define the constituent structure is not then an affair neutral to the office of criticism. (*LW* 1:315)

Ultimately, Dewey embraces as the expression of that office precisely the type of discourse from which Descartes keeps trying to distance himself. The descriptions and stories of the poets enter his discourse explicitly to work mischief. They suffer guilt by association with chaos: even if God were to make the natural world "a chaos as confused and muddled as any the poets could describe, the laws of nature are sufficient to cause the parts of this chaos to disentangle themselves and arrange themselves in such good order that they will have the form of a quite perfect world" (*PW* 1:91). By contrast, Dewey, while accepting the utility of calculation in the scientific realms that Descartes espouses, finds superior merit in a discourse of description and storytelling:

> To explain is to employ one thing to elucidate, clear, shed light upon, put in better order, because in a wider context, another thing. It is thus subordinate to more adequate discourse, which, applied to space-time affairs, assumes the style of narration and description. Speaking in terms of captions familiar in rhetoric, exposition and argument are always subordinate to a descriptive narration, and exist for the sake of making the latter clearer, more coherent, and more significant. (*LW* 1:216)

A discourse that is more adequate in this sense stands in contrast not only with the rationalist preferences of Descartes but with the preferences of the founder of discursive reason—if that is not too limiting a label for Plato. Plato makes every effort to distinguish exemplary from dangerous discourse, and it is to this important distinction that we may now turn.

12. Dangerous Discourse

Exemplary discourse is found, for example, in the *Symposium*, where we are told that the youthful learner, if properly instructed by his preceptor, "will fall in love with the beauty of one individual body, so that his passion may give life to noble discourse" (*Symp.* 210a).[42] Dangerous discourse is perhaps most famously addressed in Book X of *The Republic*, where Socrates, having banished from the state all poetry save hymns to the gods and paeans to virtuous men, avers that "the honeyed muse" may yet show cause why she should after all be admitted. His own awareness of her sorcery evidently inoculates him against it. Precisely because "we ourselves are very conscious of her spell" he "would gladly admit her." Those who listen to the muse's dangerous discourse are further shielded by the requirement that she speak without the advantage of meter. But if this is enforced, wherein lies the danger? It lies, Socrates suggests, in "the love of this kind of poetry inbred in us by our education in these fine polities of ours" (*Rep.* X.607e). While Socrates approaches this love as a motive for letting the muse defend herself, in fact it is part of the background of fear, especially the fear of civil disorder, that informs the text. Granting admission to the muse, warns Socrates, will make pleasure and pain, rather than law, the rulers of the city; he who listens to the discourse of the muse risks the personal counterpart of that usurpation, the overthrow of order in the soul. Thus the need for a counter-discourse with a charm of its own:

> But so long as she is unable to make good her defense we shall chant over to ourselves as we listen the reasons that we have given as a countercharm to her spell, to preserve us from slipping back into the childish loves of the multitude, for we have come to see that we must not take such poetry seriously as a serious thing that lays hold on truth, but that he who lends an ear to it must be on his guard fearing for the polity in his soul and must believe what we have said about poetry. (*Rep.* X.608ab)

An agon consists in the exertions of opponents whom we customarily assume to be unlike. The *polemos* of combat myths supports such an assumption, as does the *polemos* of dramatic works. In the present dialogue, too, unlikeness figures prominently. For, if admissible discourse did not differ importantly from dangerous discourse, why would Socrates hold forth as he does? The problem is that unlikeness is wound round with likeness. While in principle the conduct that Socrates envisages should be the same for all, it is far from being so, since, besides those receptive to the Socratic position, such as Glaucon, there are those who remain supporters of Homer, believing that his discourse alone can properly educate. Socrates would overcome this opposition; he holds that the discourse of hymn and paean, like as they are, may together educate. Whereupon another unlikeness dissolves: no longer will the affective nexus of pain or pleasure contend with law for civic authority; law alone will reign. The Socratic argument, then, establishes the primacy of two like discursive modes, the hymn and the paean, the better to distinguish both from the dangerous discourse that is poetry as such.

If dangerous discourse would put the polity of the city and the polity of the soul at risk, it is because it aims at the usurpation of both by identical means. The plural polities are already contaminated; for the education that here remains in force derives directly from Homeric discourse, and is therefore unlike the education, and unlike the discourse, that Plato would establish.

The problem of curing ourselves of the unlike discourse is made the more difficult by the fact that it not only breeds the habit of assuming that it is best; in addition, as we have seen, it overturns the polity of the auditor's very soul; hence the counterdiscourse or countercharm. Once more unlike gets wound round with like. Socrates has called for two like kinds of poetry, the hymn to the gods and the paean to virtuous men: no other type shall appear in the well-ordered state. But Socrates' own discourse is, conspicuously, neither. It is agonistic, dialectical, dramatic. It is even, to a degree, magical, depending upon an incantation to ward off an incantation; which is to say that the charm and the countercharm, the magical discourse of the muse and the counterdiscourse of the Socratic party, seem more like one another than either is like the discourse of paean and hymns.

Plato is poet enough to know how good a defense against the poetic the poetic can be. His position is something like this: drawing upon sensibilities fostered by the very education one resists, one fights the illness homeopathically; the process grounds a new education. Or more precisely, it lays the ground for such through the discourse itself. Does this mean that the discourse is noble, rather than dangerous, that its words are rational rather than selective?

Yes and no. Yes: it is edifying to counsel another in a manner conducive to civic order; then, too, this makes for a beauty having no need to be merely beautiful, for what is unbeautifully beautiful becomes so by being ordered, lofty in character and high in excellence: *kalos*. On the other hand, no. However edifying the aim, the discourse is ambiguous, possibly ambivalent. It is, again, agonistic, but in a peculiar way. For, even while being presented as an uncertain process, the outcome is preordained; which is to say that the discourse works in a way that a Sophocles, for example, would recognize. But a venerable mythic structure is wanting, so that the struggle is not merely a struggle of Socrates, Glaucon, and the other countercharmers against the muse. The struggle also pits Socrates against Socrates, Plato against Plato, and is agonistic about being agonistic. The truth of the myth that Socrates thus improvises, in lieu of a venerable one such as the myth of Oedipus, discursively delivers a fiction susceptible of belief. To put it another way, Plato's phenomenological and ontological aspirations interpenetrate. The ontological aspiration would declare what must be the case—what is structural and necessary; here is the order of likeness, for all things "of due measure" are governed, according to the *Laws*, by the rule that like belongs with like. Deity establishes the rule, being itself the measure of all things (against the view, doubtfully attributed to Protagoras, that man is the measure):

> So he who would be loved by such a being must himself become such to the utmost of his might, and so, by this argument, he that is temperate among us is loved by God, for he is like God, whereas he that is not temperate is unlike God and at variance with him; so also it is with the unjust, and the same rule holds in all else. (*Laws* IV.716cd)

But in the everyday world all things are not of due measure, since their measure depends on the way they actually act, and acting is the concrete "line of conduct" one pursues—the sphere not of *is* but of *does*.

This question of measure is not only a recurring theme in Western discourse but figures centrally in a highly important if largely forgotten political tradition, already touched upon in this study. Conceptualized by Jefferson, then developed and memorialized by Arendt after a brief attempt at revival by Dewey,[43] this is the tradition of the small-scale unit of political representation, the ward. Although we are nearly in a position to do this, we need to continue for a time in Platonic contexts as they bear on this and related issues. After inquiring into Plato's discourse of the city, his paradigmatic venue for the exercise of authority and representation, we will be able more readily to inquire into the later venue and manner of discourse—into, in short, wards and words.

13. *Wards and Words*

Plato tends to imagine human destiny—insofar as the discursive context is earthly—within an essentially urban construct. It is, moreover, a very particular kind of construct, keyed to a citadel (*Laws* V.745bc), and so ordered and equipped as to guarantee its military superiority over rival cities.

> In the citadel, the new mark of the city is obvious: a change of scale, deliberately meant to awe and overpower the beholder. Though the mass of inhabitants might be poorly fed and overworked, no expense was spared to create temples and places whose sheer bulk and upward thrust would dominate the rest of the city. . . . What we now call "monumental architecture" is first of all the expression of power, and that power exhibits itself in the assemblage of

costly building materials and of all the resources of art, as well as a command of all manner of sacred adjuncts.[44]

Although Mumford develops his composite from many specific historical instances, his description brings clearly into view the authoritarian nature of the monumental. Mumford recognizes, at the same time, Plato's insistence on small scale: thus the ideal city must be small enough to permit all inhabitants to hear the sound of one voice. Two matters here require consideration. The first is that the criterion reflects the importance of words; the fate of the *polis* depends upon spoken discourse, which can assume as many modes (exhortation, announcement, prayer, command, and the like) as necessary. The second matter is that the other criterion — small scale — is subordinated to a more powerful operator, which is proportion in general and numeration in particular. How this works can be seen in Book V of the *Laws*:

> Our immediate concern, now that we have resolved on the division into twelve parts, must be precisely to see in what conspicuous fashion these twelve parts, admitting, as they do, such a multitude of further divisions, with the subsequent groups which arise from them down to the five thousand and forty individuals — this will give us our brotherhoods, wards, and parishes, as well as our divisions of battle and columns of route, not to mention our currency and measures of capacity, dry and liquid and weight — to see, I say, how all these details must be legally determined so as to fit in and harmonize with each other. (*Laws* V.de)

Subdividing produces relatively small civil groups, somewhat like the wards and parishes in which a modern citizen detects a "neighborhood" feel. It is true that a ward, for example, could allow more and better interaction than would be feasible in any of the twelve larger regions into which the city is divided. But the statement on fitting in and harmonizing shows where the discourse is actually moving. Conformity to a predetermined ideal pattern is the end in view, and the units that go together into the ultimate harmony are mainly means to that end.

A city design of strict proportions such as those that Plato spelled out was, according to Herodotus, what distinguished Babylon from the older Greek cities. Perhaps influenced by such models, the Milesian architect who has been taken to epitomize reliance on mathematical proportion created a style that Aristotle could appreciate: "Aristotle calls it 'the modern or Hippodamic style of architecture' and regards it — we in the United States might agree — as an expression of the democratic spirit in contrast to the 'oligarchical' city plans of older periods."[45] The Platonic design is hardly democratic, of course. The subdivisions into which Plato would sort populations are little like the political units that the term denotes in the United States. For one thing, Plato's merely illustrate a method powered by a pure ideal. For another, they want concreteness. We are never told what advantages might accrue to an organization small enough to enable people to discourse in close proximity to one another. We already know, of course, that if the *polis* is to be discursively preserved, scale and voice must be so proportioned as to assure the audibility of the latter; just there, apparently, lies the rub—for a latter-day democrat, at any rate. For the one voice that must be heard hardly aims to converse or to debate, but pronounces words of solemn power, the political discourse that the Guardians alone deliver.

State monumentality of the type embodied in the citadel seems not to enter into reciprocal relations with small-scale organization, embodied in the ward. With the design of a republic in North America, by contrast, an opportunity arose to consider just such a reciprocity. For Jefferson the monumental did not repose in the citadel—in a Carcassonne or a Castel Sant'Angelo. He found it instead in the Hotel de Salm, which he repeatedly came to the Tuileries to contemplate, and on the Maison Carrée in Nîmes, a monument to the beauty, nobility, and purity of Roman classicism. Leading the way toward the Classical Revival in the United States, Jefferson's designs for the Richmond state capitol adapted the venerable building in Nîmes to the political functions—executive, legislative, judicial—necessary in a modern democracy. Featuring "a monumental hall, in which George Washington's statue was to stand," the capitol presented "an impressive symbol of the majesty of a republican state. . . . Thus did he introduce the temple form into his country, and from this beginning monumental classic forms came to dominate the public architecture of the United States."[46]

Jefferson's concern for the ward came later and, far from achieving public dominance, all but slipped from the realm of political discourse. In retirement from public life, Jefferson reconsidered and finally rejected his earlier views about permanent revolution, substituting the concept of "little republics" in which the voice of the people could distinctly and consistently be heard (J 1308). As he explained in an important letter to John Adams in 1813, his original proposal, which the new national legislature might have acted upon in 1776 but did not, was educational in origin:

> It was a Bill for the more general diffusion of learning. This proposed to divide every county into wards of 5. or 6. miles square, like your townships; to establish in each ward a free school for reading, writing and common arithmetic; to provide for the annual selection of the best subjects from these schools who might recieve [sic] at the public expence a higher degree of education at a district school; and from these district schools to select a certain number of the most promising subjects to be compleated at an University, where all the useful sciences should be taught. (J 1308)

Without the division of counties into wards, the new nation, Jefferson feared, might not survive. But he never saw the institution of these novel worldly things. The ward remained a word, by means of which the author of the Declaration of Independence could hand on to posterity something of his long reflection on political representation and organization.

A discursive trope served to figure Jefferson's vision of this new order, in which natural law could be already incorporate and at the same time be authored into being through words, or through analogy with words. "Our Revolution . . . presented us an album on which we are free to write what we pleased. We had no occasion to search into musty records, or to investigate the laws and institutions of a semi-barbarous ancestry. We appealed to those of nature, and found them engraved on our hearts" (J 1491). Such innate inscription could be diffused through education, as he suggests in the same letter of 1824. The university he was then helping to establish would exhibit not only a professor of government and a professor of agriculture, but a professor of a privileged primal discourse, Anglo-Saxon: "As the histories and laws left us in that type and dialect, must be the text books of the reading of the learners, they will imbibe with the language their free principles of government" (J 1495–96).

Organizing counties into wards would be only the beginning, but a very important beginning, as only by this means of representation could the democratic republic remain genuinely democratic. The lost treasure of the revolutionary tradition, as Arendt calls it, is precisely the small-scale organization that appeared spontaneously in the *sociétés révolutionnaires* of the French Revolution, the sections of the Paris Commune, the local assemblies of the American Revolution, the political societies of the early republic, the *soviets* of the Russian Revolution, and, I would add, in the factory councils Antonio Gramsci helped to found in 1919.[47] Suffice it to note that each of these improvisatory organizations is at the least a nexus of discursive formations. They were talked and written into being, formed in the felt commonality of a historical generation before playing themselves out for complex reasons that remain a subject of controversy and speculation. A brief look at the last organization, the soviet, will help nonetheless to throw into relief at least one important consideration.

The soviet is only the most conspicuous political construction of the relatively small-scale, grassroots council system that emerged in the French Revolution, sprouting up more or less spontaneously as local revolutionary societies, but failing to become permanent. For, as Arendt points out, the professional revolutionists were schooled to such an extent in the revolutionary past, and were so tied to the precedents they knew, that they could not deal with something this unknown and untried: "So great is the fear of men, even of the most radical and least conventional among them, of things never seen, of thoughts never thought, of institutions never tried before."[48] If professional revolutionaries are so bound by the past, does this make revolutionary politics Platonic? Do binding historical precedents play the same role for revolutionary politics that Lachesis plays for souls preparing for a rebirth? No such claims are being attempted here; both questions presuppose too close a similarity between the modern and ancient cases. But without being anachronistic one may discern a recursive tendency in the modern case toward a brand of Platonism. Challenged with something radically new, even the most radical political practitioners may, while producing a discourse of the revolutionary future, face backward to venerable ideals.

When it comes to words, professional revolutionaries are heavy users—as much so, in their own way, as the artists and writers who are their contemporaries. The political and artistic users of words resemble one another as well, at least since the nineteenth century, in opposing to the bourgeoisie that quasi utopia called Bohemia: "The artists and writers joined the revolutionists because 'the very word bourgeois came to have a hated significance no less esthetic than political'; together they established Bohemia, that island of blessed leisure in the midst of the busy and overbusy century of the Industrial Revolution."[49] The enabling freedom from ordinary worldly work that the activist planners of revolution enjoyed was a freedom to theorize not easily distinguishable, paradoxically, from the ease and leisure enjoyed by the anti-bohemian, anti-theoretical, anti-revolutionary bourgeois, though differently lived out. For, if the bourgeoisie delights in the consumption of commodities, the professional revolutionary revels in the production of a discourse antagonistic to that delight. When Arendt notes how much time the revolutionaries spend sequestered in libraries, coffeehouses, and jails, she does not point out that this time is typically filled with the reading, writing, hearing, or speaking of words.

The small-scale, council type of organization that to Jefferson epitomized representative democracy thus anticipated the fate of the soviet. To be sure, the latter figured in the name "Soviet Union," but that was more an onomastic memorial than an accurate designation. Despite the important differences between the apposite modern context and the context of the Platonic discourse discussed above, here too memory, through naming, preserves that which remains unrealized. In Jefferson's vision the delegation of power that begins with the ward provides a counterpart to the structure of checks and balances that run across the government from legislative to executive to judicial divisions. In this counterpart, power flows from the ward through the county to the state to the federal level, ensuring that the words uttered in the wards will be heard in the Federal City. Jefferson remained vague about details, though he stipulated that each ward should cover an area of approximately six square miles. This may reflect the circumstance that, like Marx and Lenin, he just never got around to thinking the matter through. It may also be that Jefferson did not consider wards to belong to the sphere of means. Had he done so, he might have had to expend many more words on the wards, specifying the manner in which their voices would be orchestrated with the voices of the other organizations without turning the process into something too rigidly vertical. Jefferson saw the wards, evidently, not as a means but as an end of revolutionary and constitutional founding. This would make it hard to lay up stores of specific words on the subject just as it would make it desirable to do what he did: to utter few but strong words, and to reiterate these with singular passion.

The failure to recognize the institutional potential of the ward epitomizes the loss of the revolutionary tradition. It can be recovered only, Arendt argues, by recollecting and remembering. On this view, the communitarian spirit that appeared in the first half of the American nineteenth century looks more nostalgic than utopian, if utopianism is not already a species of nostalgia. The idealism and the straining to embody abstractions persists into subsequent efforts to revive the sense of the lost tradition, frequently called the sense of lost community. The Knights of Labor, for example, may be seen huddling around a communal core, the District Assembly, positioned organizationally in roughly the same relation to higher units of governance as the ward was to be, but with a Grand Master Workman at the top. "Ineffectual as a means of responding to the economic needs of the workers," this organization "served an entirely different purpose. It was the geometric replica of a philosophical principle, and contemporary reformers, who also conceived of organization as an embodiment of the ideal, appreciated it precisely for that archetypal quality."[50]

Arendt assigns primary responsibility for memory and recollection to poetic rather than political discourse. The poets alone furnish "an approximate articulation of the actual content of our lost treasure."[51] Frankly compensatory, this articulation consists in the affirmation of action over mere existence and of the public over the private. The Resistance poet René Char found, ironically, that he could perform emancipatory deeds and utter freeing words under the German occupation more readily than in the prewar years, and feared that "liberation," welcome as it was, meant a return to the sterility and routine of private life. "These reflections are significant enough as they testify to the involuntary self-discourse, to the joys of appearing in word and deed without equivocation and without self-reflection that are inherent in action."[52]

The spirit of that curiously suggestive phrase, "involuntary self-discourse," blows steadily through Emerson's words, which are those of a man who, though not active in Char's way, was a shaper of public opinion. His theory of poetry is thought to be driven by a kind of discursive necessity rooted in nature: "Poetry finds its origin in that *need of expression* [Emerson's emphasis] which is a primary impulse of nature. Every thought in man requires to be uttered, and his whole life is an endeavor to embody in facts the states of the mind." [53] While "endeavor" may suggest a cool business, in speaking through the persona of a representative man his passion ignites: "I must say what is burning here: I must do what I shall perish if I cannot do, I must appear again in my house, in my fortune, in my marriage, in my speech, or else I must disappear" (E 3:349). Expression is involuntary and what flows forth is precisely self-discourse. Emerson would have savored Hopkins's coining of the verb "selve"; Emerson everywhere assumes that selving is what the poet's words do, and the words of any other human being do it too. This by no means deprives the public dimension of its prominent place as in discourse it moves from self to other. That his self-discourse features *my* this and *my* that reflects Emerson's loyalty to the individual as a medium through which nature, and through nature God, become themselves expressive. Having insisted on the public side of expression, he can then look to particular institutions in order to disclose the genius of poetry that was waiting to articulate itself in the American scene.

Such genius may be found both in Senates and in bethels, though more often in the latter than in the former. Like Jefferson, Emerson never transferred his affections from the countryside to the city. To Jefferson even the organs of national political power smacked of the foreign, and if Emerson does not go that far, he nonetheless feels the Senate to be an alien place in contrast with the American wilds. Still speaking of the genius of poetry, he reports:

> You may find it, though rarely, in Senates, when the forest has cast out some wild, black-browed bantling, some great boy. . . . In the folds of his brow, in the majesty of his mien, nature shall vindicate her son; and even in that strange and perhaps unworthy place and company, remind you of the lessons taught him in earlier days by the torrent, in the gloom of the pine woods, when he was the companion of crows and jays and foxes, and a hunter of the bear. (E 3:362)

A more precise equivalent of the Jeffersonian ward is, as suggested above, the "bethel," a word referring originally to a place of religious worship, and first recorded by Richard Henry Dana in 1840, the year before "The Poet" was delivered, in reference to a chapel or meeting-house. Being modern, American, and democratic, Emerson prefers this humble setting to that of the lofty legislature: "Perhaps you may find it in some lowly Bethel by the seaside where a hard-featured, scarred, and wrinkled methodist whose face is a network of cordage becomes the poet of the sailor and the fisherman, whilst he pours out the abundant streams of his thought through a language all glittering and fiery with imagination" (E 3:362).

But for Emerson words are symbols, as all things are, and symbols turn dangerous precisely when employed by genius; at the same time, expressive as they are, they are rarely expressive enough from an intellectual point of view. Emerson addresses the first consideration by describing a virtuous per-formance in another small-scale setting:

> Every gardener can change his flowers and leaves into fruit, and so perhaps is this man who astonishes the senate or the parlor by the splendor of his conversation, who seems to stride over all limits,—this genius who today can upheave and balance and toss every object in nature for his metaphor, capable in his next appearance in human nature of playing such a game with his hands instead of his brain. (E 3:354)

Fascinated by eloquence, as was his age, and eloquent himself, Emerson holds the discourse of the orator to partake of the highest expressive power, and contends that genius itself, like poetry, is, first and last, expression: "I know no more striking instance of the representative character of genius than we have in the rare fact of genuine eloquence" (E 3:82). To achieve eloquence is to exert power: "The orator masters us by being our tongue. By simply saying what he would but cannot say, he tyrannises over our wills and affec-tions" (E 3:82). Emerson seems to hint at possible demagoguery and its con-sequences: at a typical meeting in Boston's Fanueil Hall, "when fate hangs on the vote of the morrow" (E 3:83), a gathering of "dark, irregular thickening groups" becomes a multitude, then a mob, fidgety and vaguely threatening. The reader may suppose that the sinister note is preparing the way for an equally sinister event, such as the crowd disorder to which Augustine bore witness in Book VI of his *Confessions*. But Emerson has hatched a democratic plot. The lackluster speaker loses the crowd, which accounts for its restless-ness, and retreats to silence, whereupon true eloquence speaks forth:

> At last the chosen man rises, the soul of the people, in whose bosom beats audibly the common heart. With his first words he strikes a note which all know; his word goes to the right place; as he catches the light spirit of the occasion his voice alters, vibrates, pierces the private ear of every one; the mob quiets itself somehow,—every one being magnetized,—and the house hangs suspended on the lips of one man. Each man whilst he hears thinks he too can speak; and in the pauses of the orator bursts forth the splendid voice of one or five thousand men in full cry, the grandest sound in nature. (E 3:83)

In the hall we find an organization small enough to allow everyone to communicate, large enough to allow for big effects. The description confirms that eloquent discourse, like all things, depends upon proportion, whether or not one can stipulate exactly what it should be. Masses could never be eloquent because they are too widely distributed to hear a single voice, and for the same reason they are unable to speak in a voice of their own; which is to say that a norm is built into the situation by the dependence of politics on oratory. Only in a later age whose technology can carry the voice to mass hearing may the immediately accessible political arena be "national," but then only a few voices, those of the leaders, tend to dominate; the more powerful constituencies function on a scale much larger than that of the assembly hall, and the ward-chosen man disappears, there being no ward to choose him.

The second consideration, concerning intellectual expressiveness in oratory, comes to the fore when Emerson lauds the speakers in current senates or assemblies: "It is easy to see that every man represents a new and perfect style of oratory, and each, if he speak long enough, and the matter is important enough to show his genius, will actually come to the verge of good deliverance;—comes so near that the professional poet or orator begins to feel himself quite superfluous" (E 3:354–55). The question signals the turning point foreshadowed here by "come to the verge" and "comes so near," and in the earlier lecture on genius by the "spell" to which everyone who hears the chosen man succumbs: "Each man whilst he hears thinks he too can speak . . ." (E 3:83). What is more, each hearer may so identify with the speaker as to find in him a democratic self-as-other: "An obscure old instinct revives in the beholder, that this man who does what the beholder had panted in vain to do, or said what he was bursting to speak, is himself, himself with some advantages,—and he begins to love him as himself. We love, we worship the expressors of that which we have at heart" (E 3:355). Previously appearing as need, impulse, function, and criterion, expression now becomes a person, another and higher chosen one who is "the head of the party" (E 3:355) and may even become the chief executive. The expressor who heads a party is not, however, a commander but "an interpreter" who reports his constituents' conversation because he can find the words and they cannot.

Although Jefferson fulfilled that office in his own way, and one may imagine him tolerating the term "expressor," it is not only the Jeffersons with whom Emerson is concerned at this juncture. It is also from here on mainly the poets, as with Arendt. For these, no one since Shelley makes higher claims than Emerson (and no one higher, after Emerson, than Heidegger). If Shelley's poet is the unacknowledged legislator of the world, Emerson's is, as it were, the essence of that world:

Man knowing and man speaking is he. This is he whose speech is music; who gives name to whatever he beholds, and the name clings thenceforward; who announces news — the only teller of news, of news that never get old [sic] or not in a thousand years. . . . This is the man who makes all other men seem less, the very naming of whose name is ornamental and like good news, and the sounds of his words for ages makes the heart beat quicker, and the eye glistens, and fills the air with golden dreams. (E 3:356)

This discursive rhapsody seems to give the poet more power than the other chosen man, who devotes himself to a more specifically political discourse. But in Emerson all power is ultimately the same, differences lying in the how, when, and where of its appearance. In this text, he politicizes the poetic: after building up the one or two who achieve true eloquence, and after explaining why we worship the head of the party, he passes the scepter to someone who stands for intellect rather than will; to someone who may not even vote; to someone who possesses indeed only one weapon, discursive endowment. As if to offer a corrective, Emerson elsewhere poeticizes the political: all worldly things, he says, "ought to be located poetically, — religion, war, law, politics, money, housekeeping. It would be easy to show that they must all be handled poetically in action in order to have any success. A judge and a banker must drive their craft poetically as well as a dancer or a scribe" (E 3:239). The state itself must be treated poetically, which means, negatively, to remove from it what is secondary, though regarded as primary; positively, it means to discern wherein its disposition truly lies. What is secondary, though regarded as primary, is law, by which Emerson means positive law in the sense of statutes and other types of legislation. "Law is therefore always only a memorandum. We are too superstitious. We think the statute somewhat. So much life as it has in the character of living men is all its force. The statute is a memorandum only. It stands there to say, 'Yesterday we agreed so and so, — but how feel ye this article today?' " (E 3:241).

For Emerson the discourse of positive law belongs implicitly, together with politics, to the sphere of will; the poet belongs to the sphere of intellect; while the sphere to which the state belongs is the one that ultimately governs these others — what he calls fate. A mnemonic procedure, law tends to look back, while fate tends to look forward, driving the state before it. The wise know "that the state must follow the character and progress of man and does not lead it, that the state goes not by will but by fate" (E 3:241). While both concepts, character and progress, are central, character, in both the collective and the individual sense, is perhaps the more insistent. Character denotes what is essential in human being; but it also carries the sense of the symbol, feature, or trait (1502), and, given Emerson's belief that all things signify, the sense of character as symbol or expression probably contributes too. But even as character is mediated by the type of discourse called the statute, it somehow governs *through* the statute, a necessary distinction in light of character's implicit priority over any positive law. What gives it that priority is, again implicitly, what character expresses, which is the always given, binding orderliness that in the West traditionally goes by the name of natural law, but might better be called, in the Emersonian context, the natural divine. It is this that the poet-sage himself mediates in *Nature* (1836), where, as transparent eyeball, he senses universal being coursing through him.

Nature symbolizes spirit, which is to say that spirit appears in history as that which history expresses, as it were, "in nature," a recurring phrase that situates the scene of any event or entity always in the same ideal place. "We say next that the great antidote and corrective in nature to this abuse of Formal Government is the Influence of Private Character, the growth of the Individual, the appearance of the principal to supersede the proxy, the appearance of the Wise Man" (E 3:242). Implicitly, Emerson distinguishes between two types of individual, one whose words express the political or legal and one whose words express the fateful or natural. Again he gets at the distinction, partly, through will. Schematically stated, in politics or law will is a property of the individual, in nature the individual is a property of fate. The great man is he who, mediating fate through his public discourse, can express a collective character consonant with his personal character. Such discourse consists in those "forms in nature" (E 3:354) that are the poetry of politics:

> See in the political processions Lowell in a loom, and Lynn in a show, and Salem in a ship. They fancy they hate poetry and they are all poets and mystics. Witness the striped pig, the cider barrel, the old Hickory, the log-cabin, and all the cognizances of party. . . . What does all this love for signs denote, if not that the relation of man to these forms in nature is more intimate than the understanding yet suspects . . . ? (E 3:353–54)

Euler's statement on the law of arches (that it is true even though it denies experience), which Emerson quotes in *Nature*, translates another great sphere of public life, architecture, into another expression of nature. Emerson deems it "sublime" because it transfers that nature, in turn, into mind, or spirit—yet these only name what is already consubstantial with natural law. Not only is natural law above and beyond parties, it is above and beyond any political organization. Even the public discourse of the ward or senate or bethel can be dispensed with. The true member remains such at all times and everywhere because membership, like conscience, is wholly internalized. The most perfect union comes with the isolation of "all the uniters"; the "secret soul" of every member ensures that "he will go up and down doing the works of a true member, and, to the astonishment of all, the work will be done with concert, though no man spoke."[54]

This consummation of communal existence means much more, it would seem, than a sum of parts or the parts in this or that combination. It means that the individual is so integrated with the community as to understand, as if by instinct, that destiny which is the ultimate disposition of all particular existences within a historical epoch. Though the limits of an epoch are sometimes difficult to define, there are many instances of agreement as to what constitutes an "age," and clearer still is the shape of a generation, the concept of historical periodicity developed by Wilhelm Dilthey and elaborated upon by Ortega y Gasset and Julián Marías.

Emerson had already pondered the issue:

> There is a great destiny which comes in with this as with every age, colossal in its traits, terrible in its strength, which cannot be tamed, or criticised or subdued. It is shared by every man and every woman of the time, for they are as leaves on this tree which bears them. In solid phalanx the generation comes on; the pattern of their features is new in the world: all wear the same expression, but it is that which they do not detect in each other. The Genius of the time is one spirit but of many operations. (E 3:364)

The analogy of the leaves may draw attention away from what is peculiarly human as distinct from natural. Emerson is too near to Spinoza to overrate that distinctness. The analogy of the leaves proposes that what is human cannot be discerned apart from the context of the so-called natural world; that destiny resembles a force in nature, even nature itself; that destiny therefore exemplifies the involuntary and the self-discursive. Emerson, for his part, seems to downplay the particular existence when he speaks of "this resistless onward Fate, which makes the Individual nothing" (E 3:364), which is another way of stipulating the primacy of all existences, which in fact he does by shifting from the "Individual" to "us": "But the grandeur of our life exists in spite of us—all over and under and within us,—in what of us is inevitable and above our control. Men are facts as well as persons, and the involuntary part of their life is so much, as to fill all their wonder, and leave them no countenance to say anything of what is so trivial as their private thinking and doing" (E 3:365). Like Spinoza before and Peirce after him, Emerson is alive to human participation in the great work of creation. Inevitably because involuntarily, every one is a character—a personage and a symbol—in the fateful discourse of existence.

Emerson's analogy of the leaves contrasts informatively with Plato's analogy between a citizen of the *polis* and a puppet. In the first place, the former is an organic analogy, the latter just the opposite; more specifically, the puppet is an artifact whose human origin befits Plato's eventual emphasis, the domination of the city and its laws. And yet Socrates appears to assume that some degree of will or cooperation is necessary if the puppet is to move as the law requires. In the following, Plato's point of departure is what he calls "interior states," such as pain and pleasure or confidence and fear: "These interior states are, so to say, the cords, or string, by which we are worked. . . . In fact . . . a man must always yield to one of these tensions without resistance . . . must yield, that is, to that golden and hallowed drawing of judgment which goes by the name of the public law of the city" (*Laws* I.645a). The suasive animus becomes even clearer when Socrates goes on to speak of the necessity of "self-conquest and self-defeat," "the individual's duty," and the obligation to "live in obedience" to the "true doctrine" of which he discourses (*Laws* I.645b).

If Socrates argues for a doctrine, Emerson reports an observation, or so he would have us believe. As the organic character of his analogy prepares us to expect, the purport of his words is the inherence of human fatefulness in the fatefulness of the natural world. It is not that he devalues the organizing that human beings undertake in order to do as they must. This organizing is recognized in the military trope of "the solid phalanx," which renders in a flash the solidarity and discipline of the human race. But it is a "generation" that moves, a born-together collectivity whose natality the author subtly underlines by letting the trope come just after the analogy of the leaves, which have all come forth from "this tree." What is missing here in Emerson is *voluntas*, which appears as etymon only in the negative "involuntary." Onward fate is resistless, it has no such "otherness"; in Emerson's unitary vision there is only "withness."

When the puppet citizen in effect chooses which string to be pulled by, the city accepts the performance in conformity with that entitling discourse which is its set of laws. Necessity, at least where the *polis* and its environs are concerned, is precisely this mutuality of assent, this weaving of quasi-voluntary strands into pervasive context. Or so runs the inference one may draw from the story of the puppet. One also infers a key opposition in Plato's thinking between the "inside states" of human experience and the public space of the city, a relation that translates in a more general way into an opposition between immanence and transcendence: the reader is never allowed to forget the difference between what goes on inside the citizen and what goes on outside, nor the fact that the discourse of the civic law reigns supreme.

In the Emersonian analogy of seed or leaves, by contrast, the opposition disappears; it is only an expository necessity that justifies introducing it in the first place. For the seed of the plant is *phusis*, the coming into being that occurs without human mediation. In recognizing this one recognizes also that the analogy with the natural thing is itself no thing of nature but a hypostasis of discourse enabling *poiesis*, the coming into being that requires human mediation and thus belongs to another realm of being. To call the analogy "enabling," then, is to say that it is formative, even performative, of the world. This discourse, this Nature of nature, is through and through a way of being worldly, for a natural thing is a worldly thing just *as* it is realized discursively. To suppose otherwise, to hypostatize a word for nature in which no trace of nature can be found, is to suppose that there could be relation without relation.

14. A Design in a Web

Emerson assumes that, as the maker of the world ultimately determines the nature of its things, whether puppets or seeds, an author of a discourse determines the nature of the discourse. But daily discourse has no author in this sense. Its characters cannot trace themselves back to some all-determining other because they are at least partly self-authorizing—they draw motive power from circumstance and chance and whatever else the world has to offer, just as they find themselves at times balked or baffled by these. Their stories are extraordinarily profuse and complex, and it is with the aim of managing the complex profusion that philosophies of history take recourse to an actor behind the scenes, a puppet-maker, an author. Nietzsche's author is a kind of enemy; Emerson's is nature or spirit or fate; Adam Smith's, the invisible hand to whose action every worldly thing may ultimately be traced.

Ascribing all to authorship does not reveal the destinies of daily discourse but, if anything, provides a destiny *for* it. The entitlement of authorship enables the hand to write its version of things across daily discourse as the uppermost script of a palimpsest. To the extent that it conceals the underscript, it passes for that script, leaving the characters of the other story, that of daily discourse, in obscurity. It thus appears, in other words, that the fateful discourse of worldly things is whatever the author-hand declares it to be because only this can authorize. It declares that the characters are determined by the declarer, whereas in fact the characters look to no authors, being protagonist-producers of a story that is theirs. Which does not mean that they recognize its turning points or foresee its outcome—its destiny. It only means that its destiny is finally of their own making.

A human life story may show significance rarely, or often, or never. In any case, the realization of such significance as it has, Arendt suggests, can emerge only when it ends, after death. If this is the case, those whose medium and milieu are daily discourse cannot know for a surety the destinations to which they are going.

"Storytelling," as though to combat that limitation, endeavors to reveal and to memorialize, as Arendt writes: "acting and speaking men need the help of *homo faber* in his highest capacity, that is, the help of the artist, of poets and historiographers, of monument-builders or writers, because without them the only product of their activity, the story they enact and tell, would not survive at all."[55] Works of art are memorials as well as inaugurals: they keep alive the meaning and tenor of a time, hence the linking of the poet's work to the work of the historian and to the monument. Art thus preserves, but in times called modern it does something else. Pater tries as hard as anyone to say what the something is, and concludes, anticipating Sartre, that it has to do with freedom. Having-to-do indicates that art's bond with freedom is somehow problematic, which is only the case, for Sartre, in some art. Pater asks: "And what does the spirit need in the face of modern life? The sense of freedom" (R 173). The status of freedom depends upon the status of the term "sense," which is ambiguous in the way that "perception" is. Perception can mean, and is used only to mean, actual cognition. It can equally mean, and in current conversation has come primarily to mean, a cognition that you suppose you have—your opinion, merely, or your view. Sense may therefore be the proof of freedom in your experience, or the illusion of freedom, or both. Not being sure, perhaps, that he has a soul to save, Pater eschews a Pascalian wager, which might at least in part have sheltered his freedom. He tries instead to preserve of life, of his own and of any who will listen, just, so to say, the savor. His renaissance is a reawakening to something as classical as anything in the Renaissance: the fact that a literary discourse can importantly shape the conduct of life.

One recognizes at the same time "the intricacy, the universality of natural law," the old phrase for the patterning that modern systems and sciences transcribe into a discourse peculiarly their own. Another name is "necessity"; the sense of this, however, has changed:

> For us, necessity is not, as of old, a sort of mythological personage without us, with whom we can do warfare. It is rather a magic web woven through and through us, like that magnetic system of which modern science speaks, penetrating us with a network, subtler than our subtlest nerves, yet bearing in it the central forces of the world. Can art represent men and women in these bewildering toils so as to give the spirit at least an equivalent for the sense of freedom? (R 185)

This seems to concede that the older, more positive sense of freedom cannot hold. Pater then settles for the substitution of made-up "value" for a lost intrinsic worth. He does so because the omnipresence and omnipotence of those forces whose filaments weave the web leave no room for choice. The "fatal combinations" of natural life have more than a will of their own, they have all the will there is. To the human being falls no opportunity to volunteer; caught up wholly in and with and *as* the central forces, everyone is always already doing and being done to. Self-discourse in such a state is quite as involuntary as its counterpart in Plato or in Emerson. A voluntary dimension nonetheless remains, for, while death insures that all human stories end, it does not determine how they end, which depends in part on what we choose to contribute to them. To end is to consummate, and every story consummates in its own way; the attitudes adopted unfold more nobly, or less, in each, and in each discloses, as they unfold, the labor of its love: "In those romances of Goethe and Victor Hugo, in some excellent work done *after* them, this entanglement, this network of law, becomes the tragic situation, in which certain groups of noble men and women work out for themselves a supreme *dénouement*" (R 185).

"Dénouement" is far more than a euphemism. Signifying as it does the process of untying or loosening, it is, in the context, the *mot juste*. The interplay of active and passive and of attitude and work is the richer as a result, and we are ready to recall the elaboration on the web in the "Conclusion." Referring to "our physical life," Pater writes:

> Fix upon it in one of its more exquisite intervals, the moment, for instance, of delicious recoil from the flood of water in summer. What is the whole physical life in that moment but a combination of natural elements to which science gives their names? But those elements, phosphorous and lime and delicate fibres, are present not in the human body alone: we detect them in places most remote from it. . . . Like the elements of which we are composed, the action of these forces extends beyond us: it rusts iron and ripens corn. Far out on every side of us those elements are broadcast, driven in many currents; and birth and gesture and death and the springing of violets from the grave are but a few out of ten thousand resultant combinations. (R 186)

Looked at more or less abstractly, the combinations had seemed fatal; viewed concretely, they look more like simple effects; then too entanglements of a tragic situation seem less troubling when the elementary forces are seen to constitute our very being, or at least, as Pater calls it, its physical aspect. While these combinations cannot be rejected they can be organized in imagination, and continually are. Here the analogy of the web becomes explicit again: "That clear, perpetual outline of face and limb is but an image of ours, under which we group them — a design in a web, the actual threads of which pass out beyond it" (R 187). Such a vision would steer a course between the reefs of freedom and necessity, the course not being an altogether clear one, however, since neither freedom nor necessity is transcended. Pater seems to locate what freedom we do possess within a larger necessity; this is, roughly, the meaning of the design, which is "in" the web, discursively woven into it, along with countless others not attended-to. Since such freedom as may exist is fugitive and fragile, it is not surprising that the image of the flame connotes mutability more than light or heat: "This at least of flame-like our life has, that it is but the concurrence, renewed from moment to moment, of forces parting sooner or later on their ways" (R 187).

15. *Destiny Is Discursive*

Pater's discourse of renaissance is, however, as we have seen, recollective and reconstructive, figuring a world in which the author felt himself somehow, like Rousseau, already deceased. When Rousseau discourses of rebirth, he tells in effect the tale of one who survives his own death, garnering for the interval of life between resurrection and final dissolution richer possibilities than he had heretofore known. "I can well say that I did not begin to live until I looked on myself as a dead man. Estimating the things that I was about to leave behind me at their true value, I began to concern myself with nobler preoccupations, as if in anticipation of the duties I should soon have to fulfill and which I had seriously neglected till then." [56] Pater comments:

> One of the most beautiful passages of Rousseau is that in the sixth book of the *Confessions*, where he describes the awakening in him of the literary sense. An undefinable taint of death had clung always about him, and now in early manhood he believed himself smitten by mortal disease. He asked himself how he might make as much as possible of the interval that remained; and he was not biassed by anything in his previous life when he decided that it must be by intellectual excitement. (R 189–90)

In fact the preoccupations and the duties to which Rousseau refers are those traditionally associated with retirement and contemplation, especially as these incline to some ultimate discursive production. Thus Rousseau blends the tending of animals, and similar chores, in the little realm of nature owned by Mamma, with the study of great discourses, from Virgil's *Eclogues* to the more philosophical writings not only of Voltaire (whom Pater also mentions) but "the logic of Port-Royal, Locke's Essay, Malebranche, Leibniz, or Descartes" (C 226).

As introspective in his *Confessions* as Descartes is in his *Meditations*, Rousseau arrives at a state of certainty as redolent of clearness and distinctness, and as self-evident, as the certainty of Descartes, though differently grounded. Descartes predicates his sureties on the fact that in order to be thinking he must exist: he cannot after all doubt that he thinks. Rousseau for his part cannot doubt that he feels, and is pledged to the authenticity of his affective experience as Descartes is pledged to the rationality of his. Rousseau declares:

> I have only one faithful guide on which I can count; the succession of feelings which have marked the development of my being, and thereby recall the events that have acted upon it as cause or effect. I easily forget my misfortunes, but I cannot forget my faults, and still less my genuine feelings. The memory of them is too dear ever to be effaced from my heart. . . . The true object of my confessions is to reveal my inner thoughts exactly in all the situations of my life. It is the history of my soul that I have promised to recount, and to write it faithfully I have need of no other memories; it is enough if I enter again into my inner self, as I have done till now. (*C* 262)

A story of this type may be distinguished from the involuntary self-discourse of action. The times and spaces are no longer those in which the recollected events occurred, but the times and spaces as they appear in the process of recollection, as Rousseau endeavors to justify a destiny that is partly his own creation, partly the consequence of circumstances beyond his control. The way to effect the desired consummation — to obtain for oneself as great a measure as possible of that worldly thing called justice — is precisely to increase the degree of control, such that the destiny can mean being reconciled to one's nature, to the dispositions native to one's self. Rousseau's confessions could be described as spiraling between two poles, the one representing being at ease with one's destiny, the other just the opposite, with an intensification, toward the end of his discourse, of his sense of being the more unreconciled to his destiny as he has not received the justice he deserves. Persecuted, ostracized, and libeled, he yet believes in the spirit of justice as an ideal, and indeed in the fact that he is its representative if not its incarnation: "I dare affirm that never did my burning desire for impartiality, never did uprightness or the generosity of my soul, never did my confidence in that spirit of justice innate in every heart, show themselves more plainly, more palpably than in that wise and affecting memoir in which I unhesitatingly chose my most implacable enemies as arbitrators between my libeller and myself" (*C* 285).

For Rousseau, to suffer injustice is to be reminded at every turn that others in the world are too much other — too distant from one's desires and feelings. It is to learn that one who cannot be at ease with his destiny is essentially alone. And so the natural course, the course to which Rousseau feels innately attracted in a specifically social context, is to lament the lack of fraternity, and to see in this lack the very figure of his undeserved fate:

> How could it be that, with a naturally expansive nature for which to live was to love, I had not hitherto found a friend entirely my own, a true friend — I

who felt so truly formed to be a friend. . . . Devoured by a need to love that I had never been able to satisfy, I saw myself coming to the gates of old age, and dying without having lived. These melancholy but moving reflections drove me back upon myself with a regret that was not without its own pleasure. It seemed to me that fate owed me something she had never given me. To what purpose had she sent me into the world with delicate faculties, if they were to remain to the end unused? (*C* 396–97)

As a spokesman of modern individualism as well as social reconstruction, Rousseau associates friendship with the proprietary and the affective: the ideal friend, though a member of society, would be entirely his own and no one else's, and together each would feel his or her oneness with the other. Given the currency of this concept of friendship, it has become difficult, as Arendt explains, to conceive of friendship in the expressly political terms, which is at the same time to say discursive terms, employed by early Greek authors:

> But for the Greeks the essence of friendship consisted in discourse. They held that only the constant interchange of talk united citizens in a *polis*. In discourse the political importance of friendship, and the humanness peculiar to it, were made manifest. . . . For the world is not humane just because it is made by human beings, and it does not become humane just because the human voice sounds in it, but only when it has become the object of discourse. However much we are affected by the things of the world, however deeply they may stir and stimulate us, they become human for us only when we can discuss them with our fellows.[57]

The things discoursed of may be said to be all things, any one of which may equally be said to be any thing. Here at least is one way of sidling up to the fact that "thing" is, again, one of the most encompassing words in the language. Michael Oakeshott takes a broad view of the matter, possibly the broadest, when he states: "A thing, then, is whatever behaves (and can sustain such behaviour) as a single whole or unity. Whatever shows some kind or degree of independence and competence to exist in its own right, we call a thing." In the same discussion he makes a connection between thing and environment: "It is, in fact, impossible to say, in detail, where the environment ends and the thing begins."[58] This has the virtue of warding off premature definitions or the application of exactness where exactness does not belong. I would only emphasize that Oakeshott does not say we can't make a distinction but that we can't make it in detail, to which I would add, in a Deweyan vein, that things and their environments can seem to blur together because of the thoroughness of their interaction: they are saturated with each other.

On a less general level, worldly things include entities called human but do not obviously exclude entities said to be natural. For, while any part of nature is nameless in itself—*phusis* exists as bush and boulder as well as "bush" and "boulder"—very many parts of nature are named in human discourse, and it is largely in that nexus that they are revealed and experienced: they are the things that are "said to be natural." For their part human beings as entities are also things. In a number of languages *thing* signifies a public assembly of persons, as in a council or parliament, as well as the matters or affairs with which such a body deals. Old English likewise provides, as noted above, the equivalent of the first of these meanings; in three centuries we acquire "that which is done or to be done" and in another three "that which is said . . . a story, tale . . . a part or section of an argument or discourse." With these articulations the essential role of language in each and every one of these phenomena becomes the more explicit.

All of which is to suggest some ways in which destiny may be said to be discursive.

PART IV

Incorporating

1. Introductory Overview

Part I inquired into reconstructing. The world, seen from the perspective
of the constitutive modes of endowing, enabling, and entitling, served as the
theme of Part II. Part III turned to discourse in relation to the "fate" family
and the discourse of reason, as problematized by Vico and Heidegger among
others. Part IV now inquires into the constitution of incorporate being, or
flesh, as distinguished from body. In Western tradition the latter term signifies a discrete material entity; but flesh, I argue, is not such an entity; it is a
relation. If body serves as an object of presentment and research (see Part III
above), flesh embraces all interactive doing and being.

In reducing flesh to body, Galileo serves as exemplar. With Galileo primary qualities are demoted to secondary status, and vice versa: what is primary in an orange is not its scent when sniffed but its rate of descent when
dropped. Yet Galileo, no less than Descartes, works from a shared understanding of everyday worldly being, his own discourse representing the Italian humanist tradition that peaks with Vico.

My point of departure for going "beyond" body is Merleau-Ponty's statement, "The flesh is not matter, is not mind, is not substance. To designate it we should need the old term 'element' . . . that is, in the sense of a *general thing* . . . a sort of incarnate principle." Flesh appears when a "body" couples with the world, "forming tirelessly with its hand the strange statue which in turn gives everything it receives." "Element" may also be thought of as environment or milieu, atmosphere, or even air. For a thinker like Pascal it is the human milieu between animality and divinity, for it is in that in-between that the thinker, as species being, is capable of attaining salvation through grace.

Pascal invites comparison with Hopkins, who shares his preoccupation with piety, grace, and salvation, and who, through "selving," articulates the unique nature of each worldly thing within the sacred economy of the supernatural. Investigating the being of one of his own fingers, for example, Hopkins discovers that "grace or merit, fortune or fate" inhere in that portion of his flesh while being at the same time an aspect of universal mind. Quite as remarkable is the capacity of another worldly being, a bird, to flame out as the transcendental being who is Christ. Hopkins's perspective is further examined by comparing and contrasting his ideas of individuality, proprietorship, and God with those of Hobbes. Discussion subsequently turns to Valéry, then Sartre, who are seen to pursue their own, complementary inquiries into the being of the hand as a way of exploring worldly being.

Flesh, as I am defining it, is a key theme of *Rameau's Nephew*, where the title figure rhapsodizes over compelling needs and appetites, rising to that analogue of the musical crescendo which is sexual climax. Nonetheless, I suggest that for Diderot incorporate being is a social, educational enabling in which the child is endowed paternally with the capacities to which society believes him or her to be entitled.

Equally fascinated by flesh, Baudelaire explores correspondences among the senses as well as the transcendental dimensions that imagination, working in flesh, aspires to attain. Here the *locus classicus* is Pater's concept of the "*Anders-streben* of all art" and his worry that the very materiality of sculpture limits its ability to become Merleau-Ponty's more general kind of thing. Understandably, it is in the very incompleteness of works by Michelangelo, where form is suggested more than realized, that Pater finds the element of infinity he desires.

I continue the discussion by examining other major writers who also approach the theme of incorporating through sculpture. From his experience as assistant to Rodin, Rilke discovered the seemingly paradoxical ability of surfaces to open outward and around them, into an elemental horizon, and the way in which air influences, alters, and unites surfaces into something solid yet in a sense aerial. The closely related paradoxical effect of ecphrasis, of

motion / no motion, is found not only in Rilke but in Luis Cernuda's treatment of Michelangelo's *David*. Cernuda posits that the *David*, having fallen
into time, now exists in a state of slumber and unawakened sexuality from
which the reader is not to rouse him: "Hush. Let him not wake." Such letting-
be leaves the work as it is, and as it will forever remain. Lessing's *Laocöon*,
figuring the penultimate moment of life-or-death struggle, remains, I believe,
even more completely in the world than Rilke's angel or Cernuda's *David*. Indeed, Lessing asserts that art has a major role to play in the constitution and
maintenance of civil order.

Rilke's Rodin, in an effort to go beyond state and society, creates a kind
of marble margin between immediate and infinite. For his part Rilke would
define the archaic torso of Apollo by a series of Spinozist negatives, in a way
similar to how the sculptor chips away at stone to release its expressive potential. Linguistically enabled, the sculpture beholds the beholder and utters the
admonition, "You must change your life," which is not a command but an expression of wisdom to be followed.

Yeats attests to the importance of such wisdom in "The Tragic Theatre."
Yeats, however, tends to make the wisdom otherworldly whereas it is properly regarded, I believe, as an aspect of incorporate being-in-the-world. The
Plotinian element in Yeats helps sustain his belief in an earlier unitary state
of being, as well as a belief in the possibility of releasing immanent beauty by
emulating the practice of the sculptor, which is to say, by eliminating what is
superfluous. We gather nonetheless, from a poem like "News for the Delphic
Oracle," where Plotinus revels in distinctively sensual pleasures, that flesh
stays stubbornly on.

By contrast Hopkins sees nature not only as something inherently appealing but as a medium of divine regeneration. In "Felix Randal" the farrier's fate
is the tragedy of all finite, incorporate "manshape," which inevitably passes
from the world like "burnt matchwood." But in supernatural terms it becomes at the same time, thus carbonized, "immortal diamond," in a miraculous transformation parallel to the transformation of the bird into Christ in
"The Windhover."

It falls to Vallejo, through a highly original exploration of incorporating,
to attempt an integrative poetic-political vision. Like Marx, the Peruvian poet
envisages a world in which theory and practice, working and thinking, are
not only not divorced but are integrated in a social figuring of flesh analogous
to Gramsci's "muscular-nervous effort towards a new equilibrium." Although
Vallejo uses the Venus de Milo to problematize Romantic spiritualization of
the work of art, and indeed the very being of sculptural high art, he leaves
considerable room for reconstructive possibilities, as his vision spreads from
the immediacies of his own flesh to the politics of the entire human con-

dition. When he speaks of "the distant state of the forehead and the recent nation of the stomach," he envisages the phenomenon of a geopolitics that is equally a geopoetics.

My discussion concludes with a Vallejo poem of the Spanish Civil War, in which a fallen soldier's book endures after him as, on the verge of dissolution, hence of regeneration, his sleeve becomes "gaseous, infinite." Such passing from immediate existence into another phase of the cosmic economy reconfirms the poet's sense of the continuity of incorporate being and the need for an integrative vision to keep that sense poetically alive.

2. *From Body to Flesh*

A discursive formation such as incorporate being may be approached in relation to certain familiar assumptions about corporeality. The most familiar, perhaps, is that body exists in opposition to soul, spirit, and the like. Another assumption is that body is an unavoidable wherewithal, a kind of necessary evil. A third assumption is that the body can be examined in isolation from other worldly things, as a thing-in-itself. In contrast to all of these conceptions, flesh is concrete and environmental. It is real in the most immediately worldly way and it interacts with everything around it that is real in the most immediate worldly way. And even as flesh is more inclusive than body, environment is more inclusive than any mere setting or background:

> The words "environment," "medium" denote something more than specific *continuity* of the surroundings with his own active tendencies. . . . The things with which a man *varies* are his genuine environment. Thus the activities of the astronomer vary with the stars at which he gazes or about which he calculates. Of his immediate surroundings the telescope is most intimately his environment. (*MW* 9:15)

Such tendencies and actions are of the flesh, and not merely of the body; which is to say that they are at all times interactive with everything that environs them. Flesh is not, like body, an entity; it is a *relation*, and, moreover, a relation *in perpetual process*. Since the unfamiliarity of that relation is a function, again, of the assumptions stated above, it may be helpful from a heuristic point of view to approach the former by way of the latter, or at least by way of some issues entailed in these assumptions. To take this tack is to border on definition by negation, since the concreteness of flesh must be seen in contrast to a corporeality abstracted from the world of everyday things and its discourse.

Such abstraction is a feature, needless to say, of the presentment described above, in which the course of worldly things is radically altered through their "objective" representation by a subject, an alteration in which *concrete things* are administered as if they were *abstract objects*. By reducing primary qualities to secondary status, by measuring the time it takes a rock to fall while discounting the color, heft, and texture of the rock, mind can affirm itself as matter's master; only by thus constructing a framework of experimentation that they can be ordered into can the things of the world be predicted and controlled. Although this new conceptual system organized research on a scale and with an efficiency hitherto unknown, it did so on a problematic foundation. Scientific abstraction of the world created the illusion, according to Whitehead, that the objects abstracted were in fact concrete things:

> Thereby, modern philosophy has been ruined. It has oscillated in a complex manner between three extremes. There are the dualists, who accept matter and mind as on an equal basis, and the two varieties of monists, those who put mind inside matter, and those who put matter inside mind. But this juggling with abstractions can never overcome the inherent confusion introduced by the ascription of *misplaced concreteness* to the scientific scheme of the seventeenth century.[1]

It is no easy matter to reverse this process or even to trace its course. The discussion that follows, by discriminating among relevant phenomena in a wide range of discourse, tries at least to clarify the nature of the problem. For this purpose Descartes's and Hobbes's contemporary Galileo, as paradigmatic scientist-philosopher of the modern age, provides a useful point of departure. He sets a framework for the comprehension of "matter," "body," and related concepts, which are relevant not only to Hobbes and Descartes, but to a number of other important thinkers and poets to be considered here.

3. From Statue to Man

In *The Assayer* of 1623 Galileo makes an attempt to locate sensation:

> I move my hand first over a marble statue and then over a living man. As to the effect flowing from my hand, this is the same with regard to both objects and my hand; it consists of the primary phenomena of motion and touch, for which we have no further names. But the live body which receives these operations feels different sensation according to the various places touched. When touched upon the soles of the feet, for example, or under the knee or armpit, it feels in addition to the common sensation of touch a sensation on which we have imposed a special name, "tickling." The sensation belongs to us and not to the hand.[2]

This radically revises the way we think of worldly things. The crisis comes in the final sentence: "The sensation belongs to us and not to the hand." In a flash, Galileo changes the nature of the hand, which is no longer the familiar enabling organ engaging in work or play. The hand is now an object for observation and experimentation, not essentially different from any other research object. If such an object is dropped, it falls due to gravity, and the quantity of mass and velocity is the only matter that really matters. A research object exists to instantiate the calculable; and if we call to memory its origin as a worldly thing, the memory may be small consolation for the quality of being that has been lost. Galileo continues: "A piece of paper or a feather drawn lightly over any part of our bodies performs intrinsically the same operations of moving and touching, but by touching the eye, the nose, or the upper lip it excites in us an almost intolerable titillation. . . . This titillation belongs entirely to us and not to the feather; if the live and sensitive body were removed it would remain no more than mere words" (G 275). The passage abstracts a lived world of differences into a system of sameness. The "us" appearing as non-feather is the same "us" that appeared as non-hand. The scientist who abstracts continues to exist in the same life-world, the world of things colored or textured, things cold or warm to the touch; it is simply that the scientist's discourse would remake the work in his or her own image, or rather the image of presentment. Galileo goes on to report that "whenever I conceive any material or corporeal substance, I immediately feel the need to think of it as bounded, and as having this or that shape, as being large or small in relation to other things, and in some specific place at any given time; as being in motion or at rest; as touching or not touching some other body, and as being one in number, or few, or many" (G 274).

Separate from daily discourse, this new way of reckoning inhabits a realm of being all its own. In structure such a dualism is essential to Galileo's recension of Platonism: "One domain is assumed to be subordinated to the other and to lead a merely borrowed existence; it has to be explained in terms of the domain of higher order. Galileo's work may be said to mark a turning-point in the historical development of 'Platonism' in this sense of the term."[3]

Yet somehow this "I" who discourses on the new order, this "I" who can speak, feel, and think, still belongs to *us*. What is more, this "Now I say" is the statement of a living man powered by strong beliefs strongly espoused, in a practiced worldly rhetoric not so different from that of Italian humanism. He relies too on something more easily overlooked, the "as" relation — as bounded, as having this or that shape, and so on: "That which is disclosed in understanding . . . is already accessible in such a way that its 'as which' can be made to stand out explicitly. The 'as' makes up the structure of the explicitness of something that is understood. It constitutes the interpretation."[4]

Even as something framed for observation, experimentation, calculation, the research object cannot escape from its grounding in the everyday incorporate world. In Pisa or Padua this I goes about its daily business along with all the other I's, relying on their endowment of worldly understanding, exercising their capacity for doing and being. It is because we can function in this basic sense that we can interpret. Based on the implicit understanding with which we live, we can project another kind of understanding that enables us to relate to other worldly things both like and unlike ourselves. The very accessibility of Galileo's discourse presupposes shared worldly experience and knowledge. Galileo can be credible because the observations that he makes and the experiences he draws on are the observations his readers could in principle make or draw on in similar circumstances.

More complex, and more paradoxical, is Galileo's relation to another great worldly phenomenon, music. His father, Vincenzio Galilei, taught music to his son, engaged in debates about musical theory and practice, and influenced his son's scientific development. Galileo conducted research that won him a chair in mathematics while his father conducted research to disprove ancient hypotheses about musical sound. According to the Pythagorean theory that was widely accepted at the time, music is not to be explained by corporeal audition but by sonorous numbers expressed by fixed intervals determined in turn by equally fixed arithmetic ratios. But no such ratios could offer consistent guidelines to audible changes of pitch in the human voice, to the fretting of stringed instruments, or to the sounds that real musicians had learned to produce. As such a musician, Galileo's father pointed out that the primacy of number over sense had not been accepted by all the ancients. "Any sound was as natural as any other," he argued. The ear, "not the number system, determined musical pleasure," he argued, "for mathematics had no power over the senses, which in turn were the final criterion of excellence in colors, tastes, smells, and sounds."[5]

Anyone familiar with the schism between primary and secondary qualities will recognize in the father's criterion the worldliness from which the distinction departs. Precisely how it departs through the medium of Galileo's now discredited musical theory need not detain us here. But a passage from a dialogue, followed by a comment from one of the scientist's leading interpreters, shows how Galileo's hands-on experimentation, when screened through his bi-world theory, leads inevitably to the same hypostasis of separation. A speaker objects to the blandness of the octave, which, in Galileo's experimental model, offers pulsations in the lower and upper string, between which

> there is interposed a solitary pulse, occurring at equal intervals and in such a manner as to produce no disturbance. The result is that such a harmony is rather too bland and lacks fire. The fifth, however, is characterized by its displaced beats; that is, by the interposition of two solitary beats of the upper string and one solitary beat of the lower string between pairs of simultaneous

pulses. . . . Thus the effect of the fifth is to produce a tickling of the eardrum so that its gentleness is modified by sprightliness, giving the impression
simultaneously of a gentle kiss and of a bite.[6]

The discussion finally foregrounds the same primary phenomena of motion
and touch that were foregrounded in the touching of the statue and the man.
The tickling named now is identical to the tickling named before, and is not
"in" the eardrum any more than the kiss or the bite are: "For the first time . . .
the quality of pitch is removed from the sounding string and placed in the
sensitive being; to the string, the air, and the eardrum are left only mechanical motions, devoid of tonal properties."[7]

To put the issues I have been pursuing in another way, Galileo's words
here suggest an interplay of two voices: on the one hand the voice we hear in
daily discourse when it abides with things, on the other hand a kind of ventriloquist voice uttering words as though one wished they were numbers. In
the present text "things" is one example and "imagination" another. The word
"things" does not indicate worldly things but research objects. If our hearing does not readily pick up the difference between the voices, it is because
the objectifying ventriloquist is speaking through the daily voice; yet, filtered
by the former, the latter still sounds. To do otherwise, to be transvocal, as it
were, is no easier than to be transdiscursive—to discourse of worldly things
without words like "things," to discourse of nature without "nature." In the
case of "imagination" we are evidently meant to hear both the usual accep-
tation and a new one, which equates imagination with the rational, reason
being equated in turn with the mathematical, as exemplified by geometry.
The imagination that can't stretch enough to conceive of secondary qualities
is not the faculty that inspires us when the statue-maker chisels stone. It is
the faculty that, investigating the physics of this enterprise, finds in the chisel
and in the sculptor the same phenomena that it finds in the stone.

4. From Matter to Flesh

Galileo's discourse speaks, as we have seen, both in the voice of flesh and
in the voice of the new science, for which flesh is matter and matter the object of *mathesis*, itself a projection of the immaterial mind. In this section the
direction will be reversed: the matter that sought to supersede flesh will give
way to flesh. Flesh will be envisaged, however, as something other than corporeality in the usual sense, or rather as something more. What this more
amounts to has been hinted at by Merleau-Ponty:

In general, [the flesh] is not a fact or a sum of facts "material" or "spiritual."
Nor is it a representation for a mind: a mind could not be captured by its own

representations; it would rebel against this insertion into the visible which is essential to the seer. The flesh is not matter, is not mind, is not substance. To designate it, we should need the old term "element," in the sense it was used to speak of water, air, earth, and fire, that is, in the sense of a *general thing*, midway between the spatio-temporal individual and the idea, a sort of incarnate principle that brings a style of being wherever there is a fragment of being. The flesh is in this sense an "element" of Being. Not a fact or a sum of facts, and yet adherent to *location* and to the *now*. Much more: the inauguration of *where* and the *when*, the possibility and exigency for the fact; in a word: facticity, what makes the fact be a fact.[8]

As element, flesh interacts of necessity with other elements, such as air, to which I will turn below, and other processes.[9] It is such a ubiquitous where, when, and how of our being that, as Octavio Paz writes, "to think is to breathe because thought and life are not separate universes but communicating vessels: this is that. The ultimate identity between man and the world, consciousness and being, being and existence, is man's most ancient belief and the root of science and religion, magic and poetry."[10]

The present discussion privileges the aerial medium in part because that medium is famously allied with the "light metaphysics" of the Western tradition, which posits a correspondence between illumination and truth, reason, revelation, and the like. Now, it is very difficult, and possibly needless, to distinguish light from air, or air from space, taking these terms in a broad sense. Generally, the medium or element of air gives light a where and when and how, filling the same office in behalf of darkness and the shades of illumination in between. But in the history of thought there are different kinds of "air." Plato, for example, knows of a higher sphere, more ethereal, which would feel as different to breathers of terrestrial air as an environment of water. In the middle ages "ether" signifies pervasive exterrestrial substance, becoming in the seventeenth century a substance permeating the entire cosmic environment. Henry Adams locates the ethereal, now conceived as a form of thought, between electricity and space, from which arise "Hyper-space" or "Hyper-thought."[11] Images of such an ethereal or aerial element, Bachelard suggests, tend to dematerialize, a concept about which two clarifying points need to be made. The first is that dematerialization—transformation into a mode "ethereal" or insubstantial, yet actual—serves the interest of Galilean revision. Such a discourse does not destroy matter but rather redefines it, so that even if the same name is applied to its new mode, it is not the same mode. The statue Galileo touched and the man he tickled, the felt but toneless pulsation of the air and its register as tickle, kiss, and bite, are composed of this same stuff; *de*materialization is *re*materialization. The second consideration is that dematerialization as rematerialization would—like its corollary, the

Galilean presentment of worldly musical sound—eliminate the helter-skelter of impressions and interests of the flesh. Its efficacy would be uniform and predictable, not aleatory.

In objectified space, in space as a slate for calculation, the vectors, angles, planes, what have you, must conform to whatever imperative the research agenda imposes. But traditional worldly air appeals to the freer power we call imagination, which may be vertical in orientation or, as it were, nondirectional. It aspires, for example, to rising or soaring, to flight. On the other hand, air as in-spiration, as breathing in and with the environment, is more a matter of relation than of direction. That such an aspiration takes shape against a horizon reaching beyond and before modern science is a consideration of which another seventeenth-century figure reminds us. For Pascal the human being is a *milieu* or middle between extremes, a middle between flesh and matter, spirit and thing. To succeed in mathematics, as in any science, is, for Pascal, to transcend, as it were, the immanent world, the life-world touched upon above. When Pascal weighs air as a scientist, he does not quit the element embracing himself with other worldly things:

> In Pascal, at the summit of the Puy de Dôme in his native Auvergne, experimenting on the weight of the invisible air, proving it to be ever all around by its effects, we are presented with one of the more pleasing aspects of his earlier, more wholesome, open-air life. In the great work of which the "Thoughts" are the first head, Pascal conceived himself to be doing something of the same kind in the spiritual order by a demonstration of this other invisible world all around us, with its really ponderable forces, its movement, its attractions and repulsions, the world of grace, unseen, but, as he thinks, the one only hypothesis that can explain the experienced, admitted facts.[12]

Milieu also signifies environment, the sense that enters English as a loan word: he is himself a kind of place poised between other, higher or lower places. But he also inhabits, as by synecdoche, a larger place as well. "We sail on a vast in-between [*milieu*], ever uncertain and floating, driven from one end to the other."[13] This *agon* expresses horizontally the vertical situation to which the human world is fated, with animality growling below and divinity shining above. In such a milieu discourse struggles. The higher world, where grace is sought and may be obtained, cannot be captured by scientific procedures. Its weight is entirely spiritual. One turns then to what one knows immediately of the world, invoking names, which in their own way have weights just as do things that we lift. On such knowledge are science and life alike grounded. "For knowledge of first principles, like space, time, movement, numbers, is just as solid as any that reason gives us. And it is on such knowledge of the heart and of instinct that reason must lean, and there that it must ground all its discourse."[14] If there is a fallacy in the opening assumption, it is a fallacy of *misplaced abstractness*.

Concrete cases make Whitehead's straw-man philosopher founder because the cases are really abstractions in disguise. In Pascal the situation is reversed. *Espace, temps, mouvement, nombres* may sound abstract; they are in fact, in their figuring of everyday experience, concrete. When Pascal weighs air he weighs it somewhere at some time, he moves in doing so, and when he numbers the pages of the discourse he is composing, he does so somewhere at some time. Essentially these instances are neither scientific nor, though the first one involves an experiment, proto-scientific. They are just plain experiences, no different in principle from the experiences of anyone else. Pascal writes of himself as single person and as species-being, never doubting that he will be understood, because what we all know is what our heart and instincts endow, enable, and entitle in us, and only because this is so can they come to serve as rational foundation, when occasion warrants a search for such foundation. The fallacy consists not in anything Pascal does but in something a reader might not do. The reader might not recognize that space, time, movement, numbers are, like flesh, general things rather than general ideas.

To this relation of heart and instincts reason brings the power of discrimination and demonstration, narrowing things within its field of operation in such a way as formally to destine their disposition. Logic and mathematics, and scientific disciplines generally, tend to be fateful in this way. As projections of mind, with exact and exacting protocols, they bring the object of thought into conformity with thought, even making it thoughtlike. This is what Peirce is getting at when he observes "that the only object to which inquiry seeks to make our opinion conform is itself something of the nature of thought; namely, it is the predestined ultimate idea, which is independent of what you, I, or any number of men may persist, for however long, in thinking, yet which remains thought, after all" (8.105).

5. Guilt or Merit, Fortune and Fate

Their mutual engagement in spiritual meditation is only the most apparent ground on which Pascal invites comparison with Gerard Manley Hopkins. Hopkins subscribes to Pascal's vertical differential, with human existence as a milieu between lower and higher powers. At the same time he shares Pascal's sense of himself as an incorporate species-being endowed as other members of the species are, and thus able, in speaking of himself, to speak for others.

Working his way toward the heights of spiritual elevation through the twists and turns of selving, Hopkins becomes in a manner of speaking his own milieu insofar as any human way of being elemental is subsumed synecdochically in a greater being (which Hopkins calls the universal mind). This makes each human milieu the inscape of an inscape, the latter being on a higher plane and, as origin and destination, both prior and subsequent.

Hopkins strives to capture his individual thisness as he strives to capture the essence of any worldly thing:

> I caught this mörning morning's mïnion, king-
>> dom of daylight's dauphin, dapple-dáwn-drawn Falcon, in his
>>> riding
>> Of the rólling level únderneáth him steady aír, and stríding
>> Hígh there, how he rung upon the rein of a wimpling wing
>> In his ëcstasy! then off, off forth on swing,
>>> As a skate's heel sweeps smooth on a bow-bend: the hurl and
>>>> gliding
>>> Rebuffed the bíg wínd.[15]

Equally big is that stretch in which the speaker-reader must sustain sufficient breath to reach the first break, which comes with the exclamation point, or, for the shortwinded, with the caesura after "there." And of course in silent reading one still feels the the poem's basic aerial dynamic. In the air of the environment in which we live there also blows that vaster breath which is a big wind. The aural-aerial experience consists then in the acted interdependence of the speaker-reader's performance and the riding striding of air by the bird, the balancer, whose being attains thereby its incorporate thereness. The effect of intimate proximation is not unlike the one Keats achieves when, in "Ode to a Nightingale," the first person is suddenly "already with thee." It is also not unlike the "self-presence" of which Wordsworth speaks in the *Prelude* of 1799 (Second Part, l. 28). If neither comparison quite serves it is because Hopkins's appeal is more direct, from being to being, as though he thinks it possible to reach and touch, almost to be, that equally enfleshed other. This is part of what he means by "instress," which unfortunately smacks of pure immanence — of being right *into* something — whereas it is more a matter of being altogether as close as one can possibly be. And it is part of what he means by "pitch," a tuning term to connote an intensity of self-sameness, the endowed enabled state of being to which every being is entitled by grace of being. When that something is not of the same species as we are, we may have to work to connect, and the direct appeal is one way of doing so.

Much as the poet apprehends the bird, he apprehends himself: "I find himself both as man and as myself something most determined and distinctive, at pitch, more distinctive and higher pitched than anything else I see."[16] If this self-discourse is so far less concrete than the description of the bird, the motivational principle that animates the poem is in force here as well. By "motivational principle" I mean the idea that the being of divinity belongs to a higher sphere than that of unregenerated nature, which is why the "brute beauty and valour and act" of the bird must flame out as Christ, chevalier. The essential relations here, as developed in Hopkins's commentary on the *Spiritual Exercises* of Loyola,[17] are 1) between species-man and myself, 2) between that pair and all that is other than that pair ("anything else I see"), and 3) between that pair and the highest being of all. As man, the author incorporates the species *Homo sapiens*, whereas his self signifies the more concrete existence of his incorporate being as he lives it day by day.

What makes being a self higher than being an entity as such is just that the former so clearly and distinctly selves. That clarity and distinctness carry Cartesian overtones is not to suggest that Hopkins owes the main of his thought to this source. But the dualism of the latter is consonant with the Christian worldview, which the Cartesian theodicy was, like that of Pascal, so largely concerned to justify. Ratiocination in Hopkins serves, as is so often the case in Pascal, to tease out what is already certainly known—or better, what is certainly because incorporately experienced. This is the quality of being essentially individuated:

> Each mortal thing does one thing and the same:
> Deals out that being indoors each one dwells;
> Selves—goes its self; myself it speaks and spells,
> Crying *What I do is me: for that I came.*
>
> (H 141)

If each thing becomes itself by doing what it must do when and where and how it must do it, then all things are uniquely individuated; it is just that beings who are human are more highly selved or pitched, more endowed with what Hopkins calls "selftaste." Such, then, is the second relation.

Given the human disposition to transcend, selving itself must be explained by the existence of some other force, "not by the working of common powers but only by one of finer or higher pitch and determination than itself . . . for this power had to force forward the starting or stubborn elements to the one pitch required."[18] Without such a one there could be no *other* other, such as Hopkins himself. The poet requires at this point what the possessive individualism discussed in Part I already supplies: a theory of origin and derivation that is also a justification of self-determination—a kind of theodicy of self. Hobbes, as we have seen, envisages a natural milieu in which all parties, endowed, enabled, and entitled equally, possess themselves and are free to dispose themselves by contract: "The individual, it was thought, is free inasmuch as he is proprietor of his own person and capacities. The human essence is freedom from dependence on the wills of others, and freedom is a function of possession."[19] If Hopkins does not discern self-possession in the same sociopolitical way, he does understand selving as something at least analogous to proprietorship, to the condition of an ownmost property that is a propriety in the seventeenth-century sense of own or proper character, disposition, individuality. Hobbes says bodies when Hopkins says minds, and thinks of contracts when Hopkins thinks of covenants, but Hopkins's freedom consists largely, as in Hobbes, in his capacity to dispose himself.

A danger has arisen meanwhile. It consists in the application of a single universal criterion—selfsameness, thisness, individuality of being—to all existence, an application that stresses likeness at a conceivable risk of sameness. That God founds both man and nature, to use a traditional terminology, only increases the danger. The solution will be to establish that man and nature are the same in respect of being both founded by divinity, but different in respect of the pitch of their being. Hobbes for his part handles a similar danger in a similar way. Since all human beings as species-beings are roughly the same in their capacities and concerns, only a differentiation of pitch will keep them apart and so control primal conflict, which is their condition in the state of nature. There must be a one-and-only who is higher than any other type of being, a one-and-only possessed of perspicuous difference, such that those who among themselves are the same understand this one, the sovereign, as the possessor in trust of their otherwise separate powers and rights.

Both men are saved by hierarchy, each in his own way. In Hobbes the hierarchy of society, with a sovereign as supreme authority, makes possible the shift from a dynamics of the same—his description of the "facts" of human life in a warring state of nature—to the stable vertical structure of differential powers. Once the model is complete, citizen and sovereign are seen to have become, through the establishment of a covenant with obligations both from above and from below, cofounded. In Hopkins, by contrast, hierarchy makes possible a dynamics of difference without which all things could confront—as in Hobbes, but without Hobbes's mechanics of motion—the danger of being exactly the same. Structurally equivalent in the hierarchy to the civil sovereign, Hopkins's God is ontologically mightier in that He shares credit for creation with no one. Each arrangement is deemed, by virtue of being perfect in its own right, universal yet unique—that is, a concrete universal:

> Nothing finite then can either begin to exist or eternally have existed of itself, because nothing can in the order of time or even of nature act before it exists or exercise function and determination before it has a nature to "function" and determine, to selve and instress, with; how much less then when the very determination is what the determiner itself is to be and the selving what its self shall be like! And this is above all true of that inmost self of mine which has been said to be and to be felt to be, to taste, more distinctive than the

taste of clove or alum, the smell of walnutleaf or harts'horn, more distinctive, more selved, than all things else and needing in proportion a more exquisite determining, selfmaking, power.[20]

Although Hopkins exploits a sense of flesh remarkable for its immediacy, a degree of reluctance can be felt in the statement that the self "has been said to be and to be felt to be, to taste," and this is so, possibly, because of a danger complementary to the danger of being only natural. This is the danger of becoming or desiring to become God. Like the previous danger, it arises from the priority of selving, which manifests itself not only as idea but as power. To yield lovingly to that power seems a temptation Hopkins can scarce resist, and indeed most of the major poems express that surrender vivaciously. But if the self that is myself is somehow part of the higher self that is divine; if, as I have suggested, the former is a kind of inscape in the inscape of the latter; if all this is the case, then one may be tempted to feel oneself to be possessed of a higher being than one is properly endowed with or entitled to. It is a form of the sin of pride, and Hopkins perhaps comes close to committing it when he speaks of "that selftaste which nothing in the world can match. The universal cannot taste this taste of self as I taste it." [21] The statement complements "I Wake and Feel the Fell of Dark":

> I am gall, I am heartburn. God's most deep decree
> Bitter would have me taste: my taste was me;
> Bones built in me, flesh filled, blood brimmed the curse.
>
> (H 181)

Pride chastened, the mortal self feels fate in the flesh. This last makes for a dangerous norm, however, insofar as the speaker is like them, the lost. But at the same time—and here is the solution to the dilemma of becoming lost himself—he is also unlike them: grievous as his miseries are, theirs are worse. Their miseries seem rooted, largely, in fleshly being; and in the commentary, too, incorporating has a maieutic effect. But in the very act of using it this way, Hopkins escapes the danger of being *too* like the universal. That is, by putting "myself" in its lower place *vis-à-vis* the universal, he demonstrates that the latter really is different and higher, and yet, at the same time, he retains the right to claim inherence in that being:

> Put it thus: suppose my little finger could have a being of its own, a personal being, without ceasing to be my finger and my using it and feeling in it; if now I hold it in the candleflame the pain of the burning, though the selfsame feeling of pain, experienced by me in my finger and by my finger in itself, will be nevertheless unlike in us two, for to my finger it is the scorching of its whole self, but to me the scorching only of one finger. . . . Though then I most intimately share my finger's feeling of pain, for indeed it is to me and to

it one and the same, I do not share its feeling of self at all and share little, if I share any, of its guilt or merit, fortune and fate. So then the universal mind is outside of my inmost self and not within it; nor does it share my state, my moral standing, or my fate. And for all that this universal being may be at work in mine it leaves me finite: *I* am selfexistent none the more for any part the selfexistent plays in me.[22]

If the guilt or merit, the fortune and fate of the finger are not shared by the self, it follows that in the analogous relation of self and universal being, the former's guilt or merit, fortune and fate are not shared by the latter. But with this affirmation of difference comes an affirmation of the same insofar as the flesh in question inheres in that higher, purely selfexistent state. If finger is to self as self is to universal being, than this impromptu theodicy is sufficiently complete. Creation provides the human realm with a medium through which to unfold its element of flesh or incorporate being.

From the element of thinking flesh could be separated only if one could act in the world without the breathing of air or the circulation of blood, not to mention water and food—without, in a word, participating in incorporate being. When Paul Valéry, as though following Hopkins, turns his attention to his hand, a "philosophical stupor" arises from the fact that he is in his hand and at the same time not in his hand: "And in effect this presence necessitates a contradiction, inspires, imposes contradiction; and it is this property which would be fundamental in a theory of the living being. . . . And the same is true of a thought, of this thought, of all thought. They are *me* and *not-me*."[23] Contradiction names a nexus of properties that seems, in the thinking of prose (which Valéry likens to walking), not to cohere. But in poetic thinking, which he likens to dance, and above all in music, they do cohere, revealing their cofoundation. Poetry deals with the same worldly things as "abstract thought," but more harmonically than dissonantly. In the poetic state all manner of things or ideas representing things "somehow change in value. They attract one another, they are connected in ways quite different from the ordinary; they become . . . *musicalized*, resonant, and, as it were, harmonically related."[24] The universal being in which the Hopkins *self* is stressed has its counterpart in the universe that the music of poetic discourse constitutes. "Whereas a *noise* merely rouses in us some isolated event—a dog, a door, a motor car—*a sound evokes, of itself, the musical universe*."[25] The evocation can occur because the musical universe is, so to speak, preorganized, such that on the proper cue of sound it emerges fullblown. The cue in Valéry's example is the note of a tuning fork, from whose sounding an ambient mood instantly emanates that is the tacit, felt-in-the-flesh experience of worldly organization taking shape.

If incorporate being offers thinking a helpful instance in such hearing, it offers another in walking, which the French poet describes as peculiarly conducive to composition, and which comes to pass through him as through an involuntary medium. This kinetic point of departure looks different from the one that Sartre employs when, in a moment Valéry anticipates in the passage above, Roquentin confronts, as for the first time, his own hands. He has been writing about the historical figure Rollebon, he concludes, because without the living Roquentin the deceased Rollebon would not exist, and without the occultating presence of the latter the hero of *Nausea* could not hide the fact of his own incorporate existence, which at times becomes unbearable. Roquentin fluctuates between stasis, immobility, petrification, on the one hand, and liquefaction, dampness, flowing, on the other—a fluctuation that Bouville, or Mudville, the town in which he is working, brings to uneasy stability. "Slime is the agony of water," says Sartre.[26] But mud is not so much a state of any one thing as it is a liminal milieu between the extremes of petrifaction and liquefaction, signifying, respectively, the type of being that is in-itself, *en soi*, and the type that is for-itself, *pour-soi*. On the meaning of mud for another modern, Ezra Pound, I will have more to say below.

When Roquentin observes his own hands, the milieu becomes Roquentin himself, as the two poles, liquefaction and petrifaction, pull through him in different directions. First, he feels the frothy saliva in his mouth and throat, glazing his tongue; his hand, conversely, looks like something that has crawled from water into stasis: "The fingers are claws. I entertain myself by making them move, very fast, like the claws of a crab that has fallen on its back. The crab is dead. . . . I feel my hand. It is I, these two animals."[27]

The duality in Sartre's novel is, as has often been said, between "exists" and "is." Rollebon *en-soi* is; Roquentin *pour-soi* exists. Readers agree too that the discovery of existence is the source of the mood of nausea. But another mood, a conflation of shame and repugnance, arises in the crucial conclusion. To understand the role of shame, recall that Roquentin abandons conventional historical study in order to attempt *histoire* in the sense of story, in particular an adventure of a type that could never have actually occurred: "It would have to be beautiful and strong as steel and make people ashamed of their existence."[28] The motif of petrifaction recurs, purified, its beauty the beauty of steel, which will never slip into the viscosity, which is to say the impurity, of mud. The petrifaction is pure because it displaces the shame associated with impurity onto those still mired in mud; these, of whom Roquentin was one, it shames for existing.

The other, compounding mood is repugnance, or, more precisely, repugnance overcome. Once the new endeavor is complete it remains so. It will ever possess the beauty of an *en-soi* through the medium of which the history of one's existence, of one's being-*for*-oneself, is illuminated: "I think that a little of its clarity would fall on my past. Then perhaps I would be able, through it, to recall my life without repugnance."[29] This hard-steel beauty is a God-term, signifying a type of almost supernal incorporate being that never suffers or grows or dies because it never really lives. Although this is another way of saying that it is for-itself, the statement does not cover the present case entirely. For the artifact in question comes to be through an existence. As author, Roquentin makes the discourse in question for himself; and though he can never own it or identify with it, nothing prevents him from using it. As product, the *aventure* can tell the producer something about the producer. In this, it has something of the practico-inert in it, this being Sartre's later term for materiality in which a praxis is embodied. Through this medium of the made the producing self escapes the fate of those shamed by their failure to escape, which is to say, by their existence. Feeling no repugnance, safe in the repose of purity, such a self feels no shame. What makes Sartre's version of the purgatory of discourse distinctive is the fact that the discourse that purges *me* contaminates *them*.

The unwritten adventure will belong to *la poésie pure*. "Beautiful and strong as steel" congeals a fate as solidly, and as luminously, as Mallarmé's "Le vierge, le vivace et le bel aujourd'hui." It is not merely that they both typify the musicalized universe; any true poetry does. But the "purest" poetry, such as Mallarmé's, like the "purest" prose, such as Pater's, intensifies the music's pressure on meaning, as it were, as though to give mood the final turn of the screw. Sartre helps build the effect through the popular American refrain: "Some of these days, / You'll miss me honey." Harder than any steel, purer than any worldly thing, is the sound of this music: "at the bottom of all these efforts which seemed without constraints, I found again the same desire: to drive existence out of me . . . to purify me, so as finally to render the clear and precise sound of a saxophone note."[30] This is more than making oneself into a medium of music, which anyone does when singing, for example. It is to make oneself into a peculiar incorporating medium of which the music being pro- duced—the saxophone note—signifies the producer's very mode of being.

This would be a trope of impossible reconciliation, of ineffability ex- pressed; for observe—man *is* an *existence*: he is the it, the it is he, hence an entity uniting the for-itself and in-itself. Such a strong coupling is hardly wanting in precedent. On Sartre's account of Baudelaire, it is the very defi- nition of beauty, a visionary reality in which existence and being merge. For that matter, if the pineal gland of Descartes could vocalize, it would sound a lot like the note of the Sartrean saxophone, for what is this incorporate site but the medium through which "body" and "mind" demonstrate their in- separability?

In mud, the theme to which we may return in concluding this discussion, polarities fuse. Mud is elemental, like flesh understood as incorporate being. Pound begins Canto 51 with a transition from light to mud and a radical revision of the latter:

> Shines
> in the mind of heaven God
> who made it
> more than the sun
> to our eye.
> Fifth element; mud; said Napoleon[31]

The semicolon after "element" in lieu of the expected colon, if not an oversight, links "fifth element" and "mud" metonymically even as it echoes a key line from Canto 34: "The fifth element: mud, said Napoleon." In the latter passage Napoleon's witty expansion evidently reflects his experience when the merger of two of the traditional elements, earth and water, created an obstacle for military maneuver. Overarching, the idea of elemental mud reposes in the later Canto unchanged but in a changed context. From an Italian medieval poem Pound assimilates a supernal light to worldly circumstance: it is to *our* eye that the light is more than the sun; and, while nothing could be more ordinary than mud, it is something truly elemental that here vies with earth, water, air, and fire as an indispensable wherewithal in the very constitution of incorporate being-in-the-world.

The appeal of mud is primordial: mud is sublimity and spontaneity, like the light to which Pound juxtaposes it or the music to which he devotes so much poetic energy. In the grain of the voice, to borrow Barthes's phrase, we hear incorporately the audible breath and feelable flesh of a timeless world that is yet experienced in time. Here is the appeal of Sartre's singer and saxophone note in Santayana's reconstruction of that idea. "The lion's roar, the bellowing of bulls, even the sea's cadence has a great sublimity. Though hardly in itself poetry, an animal cry, when still audible in human language, renders it also the unanswerable, the ultimate voice of nature. Nothing can so pierce the soul as the uttermost sight of the body."[32]

To be bathed in light, in music, in mud, is to become a familiar of chaos, of a coursing that comes before discoursing, perhaps, or overlaps it or informs it, or helps in its way to produce it: "In this muddy torrent words also may be carried down; and if these words are by chance strung together into a cadence, and are afterwards written down, they may remain for a memento of that turbid moment."[33] From such primordial poetry, Santayana believes, all discourse derives, for discourse must possess indefeasible interest; as its signs are something by knowing which we know more, they must be signs in which we are interested. The poetry here in question has a kind of molding power that compels, the power of a passion formed in an incorporate mode of being whose nature will be explored more fully in the section that follows. This is what Santayana is getting at, I think, when he speaks of body and volume: "Poetry has body; it represents the volume of experience as well as its form, and to express volume a primitive poet will rely rather on rhythm, sound, and condensed suggestion than on discursive fulness or scope."[34]

Such a body is inseparable from corporeality, the peculiar volume of which, in its dispositions through the world, shapes the strange statues that Merleau-Ponty calls flesh.

6. Strange Statues

His point of departure is the context of the visible and the invisible. The former, he suggests, offers a depth without end through a surface, and "this is what makes it able to be open to visions other than our own." When this occurs,

> for the first time, through the other body, I see that, in its coupling with the flesh of the world, the body contributes more than it receives, adding to the world that I see the treasure necessary for what the other body sees. For the first time, the body no longer couples itself up with the world, it clasps another body, applying itself to it carefully with its whole extension, forming tirelessly with its hands the strange statue which in its turn gives everything it receives; the body is lost outside of the world and its goals, fascinated by the unique occupation of floating in Being with another life, of making itself the outside of its inside and the inside of its outside.[35]

In speaking, we are both "outside" and "inside": what the other sees as external we experience, more nearly, as an extension of our inmost. In the correspondence of seen with being seen, of touch with being touched, of speaking with being heard, cofounding reigns. If Merleau-Ponty privileges the auditory, as he does elsewhere in this passage, this is linked to the peculiar sense we have when speaking or hearing, or when thinking about speaking or hearing, of having entered another dimension without leaving the dimension we are in when touching or being touched, when seeing or being seen, or when thinking about these correspondences. But Merleau-Ponty almost takes, at this point, too distant a view, as though voice and voicing were wholly of the surface; the movements of the throat appear strange, when another speaks, even though they communicate sounds that I can understand, because I do not feel the vibrations as I feel the vibrations in my own throat when I do the speaking. Insofar as the other and I are beings of the same species, there is, of course, an important sense in which the two experiences are essentially the same, and it is to such a recognition that Merleau-Ponty wants, I think, to move. Hence he breaks down distance, moving so near the other as nearly to touch:

If I am close enough to the other who speaks to hear his breath and feel his effervescence and fatigue, I almost witness, in him as in myself, the awesome birth of vociferation. As there is reflexivity of the touch, of sight, and of the touch-vision system, there is a reflexivity of the movements of phonation and of hearing; they have their sonorous inscription, the vociferations have in me their motor echo.[36]

How near is near enough? Here, proximity to another's phonation suffices. For a Helen Keller, a nearer near would be in order: now the hand touches the speaking throat's very covering, riding the signifying rhythms there. In either case, the surface does not deflect access but is itself a medium of access, enabling something otherwise invisible to become manifest.

In the incorporate mode called flesh, proximity may be determined in various ways. One may for example form strange statues in intimate conversation, speaking and being heard, gesturing with hand or head while the partner stands nearby, in which case nearness may be measured in terms of sympathy or understanding: the other's phonation, the "body language," the texture of words, brings the partner near or holds the partner away according to each participant's knowing and imagining and feeling, weaving all the while a contexture of interdependence.

Diderot makes this a leading theme of *Rameau's Nephew*, where the eccentric musician takes his cues for behavior from the needs of the flesh and of what he calls his position in the world: "I am in *this* world and here I stay. But if it is natural to be hungry—I always come back to hunger, for it is with me an ever-present sensation—I find that it is no part of good order to be sometimes without food."[37] He also keeps coming back to sex, whose animal power he detects behind disguises of propriety:

> The woman who mortifies her flesh, who visits prisons, who attends all meetings organized for charity . . . who is continually on guard against the temptations of the senses—does any of this keep her heart from burning, her breast from sighing, her flaming desires from obsessing her?[38]

The Nun uncovers a similar discrepancy between private sexual behavior and public decorum. Thus the Mother Superior fondles the flesh of Suzanne while carrying on a devout discourse.

In the face of the nephew's sensualism, the *philosophe* finds himself exposing his own, confessing that he has a palate and likes to possess pretty women. The eroticizing of discourse begins in fact with the opening description of the attitude the *philosophe* assumes when walking in the Palais-Royal area: "I give my mind up to all its wantonness [*libertinage*]. . . . My thoughts—they are my whores."[39] Thus Diderot is the first to raise the topic of sex, the first to use racy language, the first to speak of libertinage. But if this brings him into a certain complicity with Rameau, it also helps, by contrast, to make the life of the *libertin* musician more vivid. It is a question, again, of where one sees or fails to see a difference. To Diderot thinking and sexual licence may resemble one another in some respect — here, in vagrancy and opportunism — but they are not fundamentally the same. The sign of difference is simile. Rameau, on the other hand, erases the difference. His "physiology," expressed in the strange statues of his gesticulations, does his thinking for him; and if Diderot thinks about thinking as prostitution, Rameau's nephew actually prostitutes himself.

In the state of nature, according to Rameau's nephew, the relation that is flesh is such that youthful (male) passion knows no restraint:

> MYSELF. If the little savage were left to himself, he would retain all his imbe-
> cility and would unite the bit of reason that a child in the cradle has with the
> violence of a thirty-year-old man's passions, he would strangle his father and
> go to bed with his mother.
>   HE. That proves the necessity of a good education . . . (*RN* 76)

If we are to believe *Philosophy in the Bedroom*, it only takes a day for the liber-tine Dolmance to train the virginal Eugénie in the arts of incest, sodomy, and matricide. How Diderot's conception of education would counter the nephew or Sade is left unclarified and is part of Diderot's attitude of reticence. He seems not to see the rendering of his own incorporate thereness as an issue. The nephew gestures for us, Diderot does not. It is only in the movements of Rameau's nephew, and in the words that sometimes accompany them, that flesh comes into its own, frequently in a way that suggests a parallel between Diderot's antics and sexual intercourse. Notable in this regard is the long mime on music in which the performer's enthusiasm comes so close to madness that Diderot cannot be sure that the other will return to normality. All ends in a climax in which the nephew loses himself completely, only to return to his senses, sweaty, spent. The pattern repeats itself in works as various as *The Nun* and the *Encyclopedia*: "Diderot has managed to introduce a suggestion of the sexual act itself: the perturbation of the senses, consummation, and relaxation. . . . no reader can fail to sense immediately the physiological rhythm of an erotic moment, isolated from the historical flow."[40]

The nephew sees his incorporate figurations as genetically determined. Like Roderick Usher he carries the curse of his race in his blood, and his son may be expected to experience the same fate. By way of antidote education is unlikely to help:

> HE. I'll try it, but (I think) in vain. If he is fated to become a good man,
> trying won't do any harm. But if the molecule decides that he shall be a
> ne'er-do-well like his father, the pains I might take to make him an honest
> man would be very dangerous. Education would work continuously at cross-

purposes with the natural bent of the molecule, and he would be pulled by two contrary forces that would make him go askew down the path of life.[41]

This comes a little before the philosopher's speculation on oedipal prospects, preparing the way for the reversal wherein the musician proposes the antidote. The reversal puts the nephew in an ironic position. According to the scenario by which the paternal molecule dominates, education dooms the child to conflict and errancy. The proposal of the philosopher would therefore warrant rejection. But in his speculation on the oedipal instinct, he discloses a worse scenario: the child strangles his father and sleeps with his mother, a prospect putting Rameau in the position of accepting the philosopher's educational proposal after all. The switch tilts the balance of the argument, evidently, in the latter's favor. But a caveat is in order. In response to the imagined parricide and incest the musician replies, "Which only proves the need of a good education. There's no argument. But what is a good education if it is not one that leads to all the enjoyments without trouble or danger?" [42] As Rameau's nephew lives it, incorporating is essentially a solitary, abortive process, discontinuous. As Diderot would live it, it is social, productive, continuous. For Diderot heredity—the paternal molecule—is a precondition and not, as for Rameau's nephew, a predestination. Education can enable what the natural molecule endows in order to entitle the social.

What Diderot opposes in *Rameau's Nephew* takes such a different shape in *D'Alembert's Dream* that it does not appear immediately recognizable, but it is entirely consistent with the disposition of that other work. In brief, he seeks to discover what is unique about flesh by a kind of detour through another proximal human being, an imaginary statue by Falconnet. After being pounded in an imaginary mortar, with an imaginary pestle, this strangest of statues would seem to have disappeared altogether; would seem, in its decomposed state, to be as wholly other to the hands that ground it down as to the hands that first gave it shape. But Diderot mixes the powder with humus or soil, adds water, and waits—up to a hundred years—until it rots, whereupon it proceeds toward incorporate being once more.

> D'ALEMBERT. Your notion may or may not be true, but I like the idea of this transition [*passage*] from marble to humus, from humus to vegetables, and from vegetables to animals—in the end to flesh.
> DIDEROT. Well, that's how I make flesh, or, as my daughter says, a soul—that is, matter that possesses active consciousness.[43]

The experiment epitomizes continuity as the statue, proceeding through decomposition to recomposition, emerges reborn in an incorporate human state; had he gone on with the story another Falconnet would have reappeared along with another statue and another philosopher, another mortar and pestle along with powder and humus and water and soil, and so another recomposed man and another proof of ontological continuity. Framed in negative terms, the process says no to irreversibility as Diderot had said no to the predestining molecule. Again, the no is neither explicit nor unequivocal but playful and speculative. In contrast to the sculptor, who fears irreversibility, Diderot disdains it, for, whatever happens to the shape of matter, matter must persist as permanent endowment, and generative into the bargain. What can be undone can be redone; *there* is the winning hand. As continuous, irreducible, generative endowment, matter, epitomized in incorporate human being, is here seen to be educable. *Educare*, to draw forth, hence to bring up: this gardening of Diderot's *is* education; when the being who is produced later goes to school, that is education too. Form never precludes re-form. "Nature" and "nurture" are not antagonists and do not operate in separate spheres but interpenetrate.

The poetic concept of nature suggested by Baudelaire brings additional helpful perspectives to the nexus of issues under consideration and focuses on the "correspondences" between and among various modes of figuring flesh.

7. Nearing the Statue

"Who is the man who, in the street, in the theater, or in the woods, who has not enjoyed in the most disinterested manner a knowledgeably composed toilette, and who has not carried away an image inseparable from the beauty of the woman to which it belongs, making thereby of the two, of the woman and her dress, an indivisible totality?"[44] Even more pertinently, the poet wonders, in his "Praise of Makeup," whether *maquillage* does not aim "to create an abstract unity in the texture and the color of the sky, which unity, like that produced by the tights [*maillot*], draws human being immediately near the statue, that is, to a being divine and superior?" (B 562).

If the male spectator is "disinterested," and if the unity of a nearly sculptured woman is abstract, it is because both are viewed from afar. Here the dominant tendency is ascent, corresponding to what Baudelaire sometimes calls desire (*désir*), in contrast to joy or delight (*joie*), which corresponds to descent. It is the latter that dominates when Baudelaire proceeds from "higher" to "lower" orders of society. Now, the further one penetrates into the latter, one might suppose, the more difficult it becomes to transform human female flesh into the divinely sculptural, or to present it thus transformed. So we are shown women with minimal adornment, dispossessed even, in that some do not own the adornments they wear. But if this is poverty, it is a poverty rich in prospects, like Jerzy Grotowski's poor theater, which makes an asset of its liquidations. Denuding the figure lets flesh stand out in attitudes expressing a general orientation toward the world: "Sometimes they discover, without looking for them, poses of an audacity and a nobility which would delight the sculptor if the modern sculptor had the courage and wit to gather up nobility everywhere, even in the mire." (B 564). Gone are the gorgeous possessions, the dresses and jewels, the elaborate makeup; yet no less theatrically than those who can afford the theater, these dispose and display: "attitudes of ennui" are not the less attitudes for being "desperate" (B 564). A pose is ultimately something of which incorporate being cannot be dispossessed, a strange statue ordering itself into that which, by this ordering, comes to envision it (an arrangement that Baudelaire expresses in pictorial form by referring to portrait and frame).

The surrounding environment takes on, as the descent continues, an artificially elemental quality: "We have descended to the last stage of the spiral, to the femina simplex of Latin Satire. Soon, on the background [*fond*] of an atmosphere where alcohol and tobacco have mixed their vapors, the inflamed emaciation of consumption or the rondures of obesity, that hideous health of the indolent, stands out" (B 463). On reading passages like these, Rodin finds something different from the sort of thing expected of literature; for, in Rilke's words, "there are places which stick out from the writing, which seem not to be written but to be moulded [*geformt*], words and groups of words, fused in the hot hands of the poet, lines which feel like a relief, and sonnets which carry, like columns with intricate capitals, the burden of an anxious thought."[45] He envisages things that so function in another environmental medium as to approximate the medium—in this case sculpture—that is his own. The analogy of the arts, drawing comparisons between this or that "sister," has long filled this office: teasing out the likeness between one art and another can throw into relief what is unique in each as well as what they have in common. It is as if one glanced away from a thing of interest to another thing so as to return and, in the returning, know the original thing for what it is.

There is a further dimension. We have seen it already in Baudelaire and it figures prominently in Rodin, as Rilke remembers him. It is the transcendental dimension wherein flesh in imagination strives to become higher in becoming other. A modern *locus classicus* is Pater's remark that "All art constantly aspires towards the condition of music," often cited out of context, as if it were not woven into a dense discursive artifact. A key filament of the web is Pater's fascination with the mortality of flesh, of which the tempering correlative is one or another esthetic compensation. There lurks in the background too, like a religious afterthought in a secular age, a suspicion that some state of still incorporate being might follow death after all. Meanwhile one makes everything around one as beautiful as possible, experiencing in worldly things whatever of beauty they may possess. "These Tuscan sculptors of the fifteenth century worked for the most part in low relief, giving even to their monumental effigies something of its depression or surface, getting into them by this means a pathetic suggestion of the wasting and etherealisation of death" (*R* 50). In low relief less of the worked material rises to prominence, as though the figures presented are not committed to the state of being they occupy in the same way that a three-dimensional figure would be. When the low-relief figure is an effigy, the spectator may read it in two interrelated ways. Pater calls these "the wasting and etherealization of death." What etherealization means is plain enough: dissolution renders the person figured less incorporate, less earthly, more nearly assimilated to such thoughts of them as the living may have. This would seem to make wasting the more somber side, if one takes wasting to indicate the sheer decay of what was once vital. But the wasting can also mean the wasting away that death undergoes through the esthetic process. As death lessens life by wasting it, life lessens death by etherealizing it.

All this is transcendental too in the sense that the flesh the artist works with, the "material" of sculpture, must be in some sort overcome. When material is worked into sculpture, it risks approximating too closely other three-dimensional things. So at least Pater assumes, attending as he does from the nonabstract mainstream of the Renaissance and its antecedent tradition represented by Phidias and others. All such sculpture is so fully modeled environmentally, is so present in the medium of air and so extremely individuated, that it risks never coming to life as a more general kind of thing. To lack general power is to be weighed down and deadly. The special limitation of sculpture

> results from the material, and other necessary conditions, of all sculptured work, and consists in the tendency of such work to a hard realism, a one-sided presentment of mere form, that solid material frame which only motion can relieve, a thing of heavy shadows, and an individuality of expression pushed to caricature. Against this tendency to the hard presentment of mere form trying vainly to compete with the reality of nature itself, all noble sculpture constantly struggles, each great system of sculpture resisting in its own way, etherealising, spiritualising, relieving its stiffness, its heaviness, and death. (*R* 51)

In his overdetermined use of the term "presentment" several senses appear to be conflated. One is Milton's "the appearance, aspect, form, or mode in which anything is presented" (1634). Another is "the action of presenting to notice or mental perception" (1611). A later entailed sense comes closer to what I have been calling presentment: "All the modification to consciousness directly involved in the knowing or being aware of an object in a single moment of thought" (1842). All this may be compared with the Brunelleschi scenario discussed above, in which the artist self-consciously isolates and fixes an appearance for perception. With Pater standing by, this may be the place to note that Brunelleschi's mode of presentment gives everyone who peeks through the hole a simulacrum of the painter's own originating moment. This may be one of the earliest instances of the modernist fascination with the moment (that we find, for example, in Pater and Woolf) and with the challenge somehow to make the given moment last. What Pater in particular adds to our theme, and what brings him toward the position I am arguing in the present study, is an element of reductiveness. For he discerns that presentment per se tends to be one-sided, hard, and a matter of mere form—characteristics readily associated with the properties of the research-object, in the same contradistinction from the worldly thing suggested by my constrast between extreme individuation and the more "general" kind of thing in life.

Pater appears to believe, in any case, that sculpture offers relief doubly: as verb and as noun. While the latter indicates the elevation of one figured surface above another, the former indicates those sorties from stasis by which sculptural flesh can overcome too much inertness or heaviness. Such qualities must be fined, worn away, even as sculpted things of great age are worn away by time and the elements. This reduces the purity, which Pater savors because it is extreme, but which he tempers—because it is extreme. Purity, essence, idea, and companion concepts are, like music, a condition to which one or another art aspires. If any ever attained the condition, the condition would no longer be ideal, as there would cease to be any extreme or limit to move toward. If the sculptors of Greek antiquity are admirable, it is because they are "like some subtle extract or essence, or *almost* like pure thoughts or ideas" (*R* 51; italics mine). The "likes" alone ensure that they only approximate purity; the "almost" subtly emphasizes the remaining distance. Similarly, only when the aura of a work is not rigidly particular can extreme purity be tempered: "That was the Greek way of relieving the hardness and unspirituality of pure form" (*R* 52).

Michelangelo's commitment to ancient Greek sculpture is tempered, Pater suggests, by a spiritualism rooted in the middle ages, whose soulfulness helps to acount for the "individuality and intensity of expression" found in the best of Michelangelo's strange statues. Expression may be fed by inward sources, as Pater implies, but in the process of communication it becomes deindividuated, as all art must: otherwise it is publicized privacy. Time and the elements have performed a relieving office on the Venus of Melos "by fraying its surface and softening its lines," the effect achieved when Michelangelo leaves most of his pieces "in a puzzling sort of incompleteness, which suggests rather than realises actual form" (*R* 55). The life this brings out, in Pater's conception, is almost a stage of dying, a polarization between duration and dissolution. That

Michelangelo's strange statues are incomplete compensates for a finitude by suggesting infinity. "Something of the wasting of that snow-image which he moulded at the command of Piero de' Medici, when the snow lay one night in the court of the *Pitti* palace, almost always lurks about it, as if he had determined to make the quality of a task, exacted from him half in derision, the pride of all his work" (*R* 53). After the wasting away of the snow figures, the sculptor creates fleshlike figures whose duration answers dissolution: in such fashion is finitude to a degree overcome.

What guarantees life in sculptures of stone is precisely their relieving incompleteness, which "is Michelangel's equivalent for colour in sculpture; it is his way of etherealising pure form, of relieving its stiff realism, and communicating to it breath, pulsation, the effect of life" (*R* 53). The state in which he leaves these works raises three further issues. First, incompleteness is suggestive. Hence the power, in Lessing's interpretation, of the Laocöon group: because the artist shows a moment before the last moment, the viewer's imagination is prompted to project. Similarly, because the entire story has not been told, the sculpture retains a semblance of life. That is to say, as incompleteness is an equivalent for color, so is it an equivalent for story, which becomes what it is only when it is over. This consideration suggests another sense in which a statue can have life and be possessed of flesh.

Second, incompleteness entails the issue of the discursive fragment, which the Romanticism preceding Pater had elevated to an unprecedented status. Fragments often get that way by accident; Michelangelo's are deliberate. If they incite to completion, it is because the concept of totality has such a hold on us. It is said that if someone failed to resolve a keyboard sequence, Haydn awoke and had to strike the missing chord before he could sleep again. The incomplete work must move toward its destined wholeness, analogue for Pater of the condition of music: wholeness is where the story is supposed to end. With no one to impose a limit to which imagination may extend, aspiration is practically infinite. Valéry will be seen, in a later discussion, to engage this illimitability as a major theme.

Third, incompleteness in the sculpture eternalizes its own emergence. The completed work is separated from its original element, the incomplete one is not. It shows what it grew from, and it does so permanently. The primordial matter is not origin but a state prior to origin, and its necessary precondition. If one kind of wholeness looms as a possibility for the completing imagination, another kind is found already in the stone unworked.

8. Surface

It is important in three-dimensional works such as these that what is immediately visible, "surface," works reciprocally with its surroundings to intertwine the visible and the invisible, the near and the far. At the margin of the marble, where air embraces contour, another strange statue subtly forms, sculptured by and sculpturing this intertwining; a worldly thing that is itself not flesh but partakes of it and would not *be* were it not for flesh, to whose world it belongs: a thing operating in the world so as to throw into relief something in the realm of incorporate being which is specifically human.

In his recollections of Rodin, Rilke makes much of the master's devotion to surfaces, which he encounters when palpating stone. And when he has done his making, it is surfaces that show. But what precisely is a surface? In *The Kiss*, is the surface that slant of light, this curve, these undulations? Is the surface entirely on the "outside," or is it some near aspect of what is hidden in the mass? The sculptor, Rilke remarks, makes his surfaces the way they are made primordially, meaning that in its proximation to flesh what does not become entirely visible is implied in the treatment of that which does, always in the context of the medium, or elemental horizon, in and through which the work comes to be. The medium in which the sculptor lets it be is in the first place the proximate air of its environs: "One must fit the sculpture into the air that surrounds it as into a niche" (*AR* 359). Elsewhere the sculpture resembles a monad: it does not see out because, being self-sufficient, it need not, and yet, like the monad, it reflects what surrounds it. "With such methods he could make things visible from afar, things which were not only of the nearby surrounding air, but things of the entire sky. With a living surface he could, as with a mirror, seize and move distances, and when a gesture seemed great to him he could shape it and force space to take part in it" (*AR* 404). Here the zone of the proximate expands through the power of gesture, or more precisely, through the power it embodies when the artist enables it.

Surfaces such as these conceal no depth — if any surface truly does. Rather, by bringing their surroundings into an intimacy of relation, they open to breadth. From the surface outward, all around, is where the elemental horizon, the medium or environment, lies. The poet calls it again, traditionally, the air. The sculptured figures grouped as *The Burgers of Calais* engage in "a kind of touching . . . attenuated through the medium of air which lay there between, and by which they were influenced and altered. . . . For Rodin the participation of air was always of great significance" (*AR* 405). If the air participates, then the medium in question is more than a backdrop; it belongs with the sculpture no less than the air we breathe and in which we gesture belongs to flesh. Incorporate being is no more body than sculpture is stone. It is, if you will, the *worlding* of body, as sculpture is the worlding of stone. Air as medium is not a thing in itself, not an "other," but a participant in an interactive relation.

Another major modernist, Luis Cernuda, while closer to the more chthonic orientation of many visionaries, is equally concerned with incorporating the liminal and the latent. The poem is "Escultura inacabada," or "Unfinished Statue," and the sculpture is Michelangelo's *David*:

> Sorprendido, ah sorprendido
> Desnudo, en una pausa,
> Por la selva remota,
> Traspuesto el tiempo.
>
> Adherido a la tierra
> Todavía, al tronco
> Y a la roca, en la frontera
> De infancia a mocedades.[46]
>
> Surprised, ah surprised
> Naked, beyond time,
> While paused
> In remote wilderness.
>
> Still rooted to the earth
> To tree-trunk
> And rock, on the frontier
> Between childhood and youth.

The pausing and the frontier motif express a liminal quality, as tree, rock, and earth connect the figure with the original element from which it has not yet emerged.

> Reposo y movimiento
> Coinciden, ya en los brazos,
> El sexo, flor no abierta,
> O los muslos, arco de lira.
>
> Repose and movement
> Coincide, now in arms,
> In sex — unopened flower —
> O thighs, the bow of a lyre.

Here is the moment of ecphrastic equilibrium, when the stillness moves, as it is also — to turn from liminality to latency — the pause before the creature has come into the full flesh of his endowment, here consisting mainly of the capacity, in embracing, to generate. The inwardness Pater sees in the sculptor this poet glimpses in the sculpture:

> Por el dintel suspenso
> De su propria existencia,
> Se mira ensimismando
> Y a si se desconoce.
>
> Dentro, en el pensamiento,
> Escucha a su destino,
> Caída la cabeza,
> Entornados los ojos.

> At the lintel of his own existence
> He hesitates, wholly self-involved
> He stares at himself
> And fails to recognize.
>
> Head fallen,
> Eyes half-closed,
> Lost in thought he listens
> Inwardly to his own fate.

"Se mira ensimismando" might be rendered, somewhat more literally, as "he stares at himself being in himself," or "he contemplates himself being within himself," and so on, the first verb being less striking than the second, from *ensimismarse*, which is the state of withdrawing from the world into a kind of inwardness. José Ortega y Gasset objects to calling this state by such customary names as meditation or contemplation because "these expressions hide the most surprising thing in the phenomenon: man's power of virtually and provisionally withdrawing himself from the world and taking his stand inside himself—or, to use a magnificent word which exists only in Spanish, that man can *ensimismarse* [be inside himself]."[47] Ortega contrasts this capacity with the condition of the animal, which is fated to the polar condition, *alteración*, a state of being beside oneself within an environment in which the animal must be ever on the alert in order to survive. The familiar concept of animal innocence, viewed as something positive, becomes in this case a concept of menace and impairment, an insufficiency of endowment: the animal has not that capacity for being consciously within oneself which is the portion of human endowment. By contrast, this is precisely what Cernuda's statue is possessed of, and yet the possession is incomplete, for in contemplating himself he does not see himself for what he is. Therein lies his innocence, which is not so much an insufficiency in endowment as in enablement; only by entering incorporate temporality will he be capable of continuity and cognition, the ability to know that the being one is looking at is both the same one who was looked at before and the one who is doing the looking.

The *David*'s fate emerges as the mood of the poem turns imperative, shifting, in the process, to the relation of the artwork to its audience. It is the fate of the figure to fall into time, losing eternity as it does:

> Calla. Que no despierte,
> Cuando cae en el tiempo,
> Ya sus eternidades
> Perdidas hoy.
>
> Mas tú mira, contempla
> Largo esa hermosura,
> Que la pasión ignora;
> Contempla, voz y llanto.

Hush. Let him not wake
When he falls into time.
Already his eternities
Are lost this very day.

But you must contemplate
At length that beauty
That knows no passion;
Contemplate: voice and lament.

Anyone, by waking the figure, can terminate his innocence. To do so would make it more nearly approximate the fate of flesh. Yet, though anyone has the power, no one—here is the moral drift of the poem—is entitled to do so. Rather, let this being, transcendent in his fashion, stay that way: transcendent, not because he escapes from the temporality of the world, but because he does not know that he does not. As the figure pauses, so then should the reader, the better to obey the discursive imperative of contemplation.

A return to contemplation is arguably in order because, at least in the West, contemplation, as a privileged mode of incorporate being, began in the seventeenth century a decline from which, Arendt notes, it has never recovered:

> The reversal of the modern age consisted then not in raising doing to the rank of contemplating as the highest state of which human beings are capable. . . . The reversal concerned only thinking, which from then on was the handmaiden of doing as it had been the *ancilla theologiae*, the handmaiden of contemplating divine truth in medieval philosophy and the handmaiden of contemplating the truth of Being in ancient philosophy. Contemplation itself became altogether meaningless.[48]

If one now contemplates, one serves in effect to revivify the traditional concept of contemplation as the experience of the eternal, but in a highly modified way. As suggested above, by its incompleteness the sculpture eternalizes its own emergence from the elemental background of its material. The figure preserves forever its own incorporate coming into being, and it is this that the reader of the poem is called upon to contemplate.

It may be objected, on the one hand, that the figure, being fated to fall into time, is not itself eternal, and, on the other, that the reader isn't either. In the first place, the contemplative attitude is what makes the eternal possible in relation to the statue, not its fall into time. What the poem eternalizes is in effect the attitude of contemplation. So long as we let the statue sleep, which is to say so long as we let it be, just so long do we perpetuate its innocence, hence its infinity. The poet commands his reader, then, not to passivity, but to a kind of protective restraint. The *David* has the possibility of being eternal, and, by preserving that infinite innocence, it preserves that possibility. Indeed, such preservation *is*, in this context, the eternal. In the second place, where the contemplative attitude is concerned, the fleshly mortality of the reader changes nothing. Loyola did not fail to contemplate because Augustine, being dead, no longer could. Anyone may contemplate who will choose to do so.

> Fué amor quien la trajera,
> Amor, la sola fuerza humana,
> Desde el no ser, al sueño
> Donde latenta asoma.

> Love, the only human power,
> Has brought it here:
> From nothingness to this slumber
> Where, latent still, yet it emerges.

Sex is here regarded both in its present explicit and its future implicit state. Presently, the figure's sexuality is to be fulfilled. But the entry of *David* into a different, enabling temporality, that of worldly experience, is a "when," not an "if," and the only uncertainty attending it pertains to the admonition not to wake him. Here is a key distinction, for the *David* differs in a crucial respect from other creatures who "fall" into flesh. On doing so they awaken; he continues to sleep. Here the great *sueño* theme of the Hispanic literary tradition joins the themes of ecphrasis and emergence that appear in the poem even as they do in Michelangelo's sculptural art. In the very process of becoming differentiated, the statue remains a part of the earth, of the tree trunk and the rock, which I have called the elemental background. It dwells on a threshold, so to speak, between earth and world, in a liminal stage for which "dormancy" is as apt a name as "latency." The unopened flower of sex, as an aspect of incorporate being, is precisely analogous to the unawakened condition of the figure on the brink of falling into worldly time.

As endowment, sex relates intimately both to beauty and to love. To be sexed is to be predisposed to the experience of the beautiful. Santayana writes:

> If any one were desirous to produce a being with a great susceptibility to beauty, he could not invent an instrument better designed for that object than sex. . . . sex endows the individual with a dumb and powerful instinct, which carries his body and soul continually towards another; makes it one of the dearest employments of his life to select and pursue a companion, and joins to possession the keenest pleasure, to rivalry the fiercest rage, and to solitude an eternal melancholy.[49]

More is needed, however, than sheer endowing. The passion carrying "body and soul" incorporately together requires love's enabling; the very idea of passion entails something like the amorous crystallization of which Stendhal writes in his book *On Love*. This celebrated trope derives from the practice of dropping a leafless bough into an abandoned salt mine in order to fetch it back, after two or three months, as a little tree of sparkles. The governing notion is that the crystallization that is love is likewise a complex development, enabling sex to infuse a wider area of experience—a higher one too, possibly, and a more enduring one, certainly. What permeates this wider area is no longer endowing but endowing enabled toward a distinctive fleshly purpose: sex transfigured into love.

Love and beauty converge no less than love and sex, as many canonical texts attest. Many attest also to the existence of a beauty somehow other than, or "higher" than, the beauty known to passion. Of this Cernuda speaks. Precisely such a beauty suits the attitude of contemplation. But the transcendence of passion means a certain loss for experience, as does the exchange of eternities for the temporality of the world. Hence the poet links the giving of voice and lamentation. The imperative nonetheless remains, since contemplation alone could bring the apposite beauty in question from nonbeing to sleep. "Could bring": the subtlety of the imperfect subjunctive *trajera*, which makes the process a matter of interpretation rather than reportage, accords with the conative dimension so evident in the poem. The moment that dominates the first five stanzas is one of suspense as the figure pauses, a blending of movement and repose, still adhering to the elemental. To regard himself, to listen to his fate, are his only acts. The following stanzas then pivot toward the reader, as we will see a Rilke poem do, declaring what ought to be done, which is to let the work be what it is entitled to be through the poem's enabling.

The poem summons the reader to enable this entitlement. Silence, letting be, prevents the interruption that the act of waking the *David* would be. Hence it is all that need be done. The "ought" of the poet's argument stakes in this way its indefinite future claim: that this certain kind of beauty that already is will always be. The futural emphasis suggests a phenomenon crucial to an understanding of human love: "And the first condition," says Emerson, "is that we must leave a too close and lingering adherence to facts, and study the sentiment as it appeared in hope and not in history."[50] Hope here figures those elements within incorporate existence which aspire to transcend; it figures the ideal that could be rather than the actual that is. The wonder is that hope can enable its own realization, achieving in the future what was in the past mere possibility. To those who would perceive it love shows its madeness; such a one is Stendhal, who argues, in effect, that we can explain its construction, but never suggests that we can or ought to comprehend just what the madeness is made of. The mistress abides on the horizon of desire, just beyond the reach of knowing, though not of recollection:

The statue is then beautiful, when it begins to be incomprehensible, when it is passing out of criticism and can no longer be defined by compass and measuring wand, but demands an active imagination to go with it, and to say what it is in the act of doing. The god or hero of the sculptor is always represented in a transition *from* that which is representable to the senses, *to* that which is not. Then first it ceases to be stone.[51]

What cannot be attained cannot be represented; what enables poetry to express the infinitude of desire and the desire of infinitude is precisely the radical otherness of the unattainable unnameable. "And of poetry the success is not attained when it lulls and satisfies, but when it astonishes and fires us with new endeavors after the unattainable. Concerning it, Landor inquires 'whether it is not to be referred to some purer state of sensation and existence.' "[52]

An alternative approach hinges on the critical juncture singled out in the *Laocöon*. In Lessing's interpretation, this juncture is the penultimate moment in a sequence of actions. The need to focus on only one moment, as any of the plastic arts must necessarily do, appears at first to be a limitation. On reflection it proves, however, to be an opportunity, enabling the imagination to pursue further a seemingly incorporate configuration of the sculpture. Like Cernuda, Lessing realizes that this requires a duration beyond the moment, and a contemplative attitude as well. "Now that only is fruitful which allows free play to the imagination. The more we see the more we imagine, the more we must think we see. But no moment in the whole course of an action is so disadvantageous in this respect as that of its culmination."[53] The sculptor must abstain from depicting consummation, else the beholder remains passive, there being nothing for imagination to do. By the same token the artist must refrain from too closely approximating the distorting that an incorporate being undergoes, for example, in extreme pain. Lessing's term for what the artist does in the realm of flesh dimensionally rendered is *softening*. Only a softened passion, grimace, or other expression is conducive to beauty, which Lessing traditionally associates with a greater or lesser degree of idealization.

Like Plato, Lessing views the plastic arts, and statues in particular, in connection with the state and its order of laws and institutions: "The plastic arts especially, besides the inevitable influence which they exercise on the character of a nation, have power to work one effect which demands the careful attention of the law. Beautiful statues fashioned from beautiful men reacted upon their creators, and the state was indebted for its beautiful men to beautiful statues."[54] The veracity of the assumption about the influence of art is to some degree confirmed in our own time by the vagaries of Soviet realism, and yet more grotesquely by the official art of the Nazis. Lessing in any case reverses the direction in which Plato holds that art must move. Here it is no longer incorporating that provides a model for art but art that provides a model for incorporating; whereupon only a small step is required to conclude that society in general, and the state in particular, pattern themselves to a considerable degree on the work of artists who are meanwhile patterning themselves correlatively on aspects of society and state.

By contrast with Lessing, Rilke's *Rodin* follows the direction of sculpture not only beyond the state and society but beyond the endowment from which it is made: "When Rodin aspired to draw the air as close as possible to the surfaces of things, it was as if he immediately dissolved the stone in it: the marble seems only the firm, fertile core and the vibrant light its ultimate, finest contour" (*AR* 408). Light makes manifest the interplay of near and far, the margin of marble, near and definite, connecting with the far of light, immediate and infinite: this much can be said, Rilke implies, of any statue by Rodin. What may be said of that sculpting in words which the poet undertakes in his poem on the sculpted torso of Apollo?

> Wir kannten nicht sein unerhörtes Haupt,
> darin die Augenäpfel reiften. Aber
> sein Torso glüht noch wie ein Kandelaber,
> in dem sein Schauen, nur zurückgeschraubt,
>
> sich hält und glänzt. Sonst könnte nicht der Bug
> der Brust dich blenden, und im leisen Drehen
> der Lenden könnte nicht ein Lächeln gehen
> zu jener Mitte, die die Zeugung trug.
>
> Sonst stünde dieser Stein entstellt und kurz
> unter der Schultern durchsichtigem Sturz
> und flimmerte nicht so wie Raubtierfelle
>
> und bräche nicht aus allen seinen Rändern
> aus wie ein Stern: denn da ist keine Stelle,
> die dich nicht sieht. Du musst dein Leben ändern.[55]

> We did not know his legendary head,
> in which the eyeballs ripened. But
> his torso still glows like a candelabrum
> in which his gaze, only turned low,
>
> holds and gleams. Else could not the curve
> of the breast blind you, and in the slight turn
> of the loins could a smile be running
> to that middle, which carried procreation.
>
> Else would this stone be standing maimed and
> under the shoulders' translucent plunge
> nor flimmering like the fell of beasts of prey
>
> nor breaking out of all its contours
> like a star: for there is no place
> that does not see you. You must change your life.

In this version of the sculptural-divine one feels the influence of Hegel's account of the god's entry into the temple through the mediation of just such a work as this. The tendency to transcend through dissolution, notable in the poet's aerial undoing of marble, also resembles the Hegelian progression through less and less matter to more and more spirit. But if anything, Rilke holds poetry in higher esteem even than the philosopher, who insists that, vast as may be the domain of that highest art, his own genre of discourse, the philosophical, could but supersede them. Given all this, a poetic approach to such a piece would be peculiarly suited to a kind of discursive divinization wherein the god, ironically, is humanized in entering the realm of flesh.

The present poem differs from the text on Rodin, *inter alia*, in that the dissolving impetus here turns from aerial medium to grammar. The way of the poem is almost exclusively a *via negativa*, with every statement but the second and last employing negation. And even in the second the "but" ushers in a contradiction of the previous sentence, which had introduced the state of not being known. Inasmuch as the torso still glows, it declares for the *not* not-known. The light of the figure's gaze, furthermore, is qualified by the quasi-negative *nur*.

It is by way of the negative, as Spinoza is always there to remind us, that definitions are made, a process not entirely unlike the process the sculptor employs in negating this or that area of a block of marble, eventually eliminating all of the areas not needed for the ultimate "definition" of the form of flesh envisaged. The piece of sculpture of which Rilke discourses in the Apollo poem has undergone a subsequent stage, not envisaged by its creator, when by unforeseen events and means the work as originally defined has been designedly negated. If the result is a diminution of the being with which the sculptor endowed his creation, it is only a partial diminution, for the work remains essentially what it was; indeed, Rilke's poetic tour de force so transfigures the torso that the reader has no sense of lack or absence. It is as if the torso, in becoming a fragment of the original, had become its quintessence — not so much its residue as its concentration. Again, such a process could only be undertaken within the tradition of the fragment, which so places existing part in relation to absent whole that the whole is somehow experienced in and through the part: that something is missing from the synecdoche in no way jeopardizes the operation of the implicit synecdochic *relation*. In fact, the absence to which the fragment is connected creates both an air of mystery and an aura of ideality, as if to say that the things unseen, so long as they are figured in what *is* seen, are felt influences in the experience the fragment enables.

Redolent of origins, the fragment, persisting as the still valid pledge of what was once complete, epitomizes Aristotle's preference for the probable impossibility over the improbable possibility. Did Zeuxis paint human beings as they never were and never could be? Well and good. He showed how the impossible might actually look, the impossible being higher in Aristotelean terms than the merely probable, which is by definition always possible. The impossible that this poem makes probable, and to which it attends, is that a statue lacking head and limbs can yet be a complete work of art. The impossible from which the poem attends is that an incorporate being similarly deprived could yet be a complete being. Only in art could such a fragment be, which means that any treatment of the fragment is tacitly a celebration of art per se. It is also, finally, a sly way of keeping immortality alive, at least as a notion.

The poem makes up for the absence of head, hence of eyes, by distributing the "impossible" gaze throughout the figure, thereby increasing its confrontative and hortatory claim. "You must change your life" is not a command, which assumes some competent authority, but is rather, like an oracle or a summons, directive, in the manner described above. If it is also a little gnomic, it is because, speaking solely to entitlement, it says what ought to be done but furnishes no clue as to any relevant endowing or enabling. Its office is essentially the office of wisdom, which is as decisive on policy as it is elusive on program. The power of wisdom to inform is spelled out by Yeats in various places, the most pertinent of which is the essay on "The Tragic Theatre" (1910). There Yeats distinguishes between the experience of J. M. Synge's *Deirdre of the Sorrows* as reported by professional reviewers and the experiences of those who, like Yeats and his circle, feel in their very flesh every phase of the drama's maternal moon. To such as these wisdom is far more than a residual presence of something greater and spiritually prior:

> And at last when Deirdre, in the paroxysm before she took her life, touched with compassionate fingers him that had killed her lover, we knew that the player had become, if but for a moment, the creature of that noble mind which had gathered its art in waste islands, and we too were carried beyond time and persons to where passion, living through its thousand purgatorial years, as in the wink of an eye, becomes wisdom; and it was as though we too had touched and felt and seen a disembodied thing.[56]

News tells its audiences what they need to know now, while wisdom tells them what they should always know; drama, for its part, conveys both the long and short of it, the wisdom that still abides and the news that just arrived. In his poetic practice Yeats so underlines the long of it that wisdom verges on the transworldly, the imagined state in which incorporate passion passes into a kind of noncorporeality. The course of worldly things continues to subtend this process nonetheless because a binding relation persists, as in the sculptural fragment, between what is here to be seen and felt in the flesh and what is absent yet experienced: though "disembodied," passion-as-wisdom can still be felt and seen.

To verge on the transworldly is to exist in the peculiar state of liminality that the anthropologist Victor Turner has brought into our vocabularies. Liminality characterizes a process of transition, a threshold between some stage of inception and some stage of closure. Such closure is necessarily wanting, by contrast, when the place you want to go to is a supernal realm beyond incorporating, such as Yeats's Byzantium, in which case desire, being denied the consummation it wishes, turns on itself, producing, in a text like "Among School Children," a polarization between unattainable Ledaean possibilities and the present actuality of the poet as scarecrow.

9. *Working at the Statue*

The mode of transcendence considered here aspires from some prior state of metaphysical unity that in itself can never be expressed. The Plotinian element in Yeats sustains his sense of such an anterior state of ontological unity of which the *First Ennead* is a paradigmatic text. The point of departure is the connection between a prenatal state and the world of living flesh:

> What accordance can there be between the bodily and the prior to the bodily? That is like asking on what grounds an architect, who has built a house in keeping with his own idea of a house, says that it is beautiful. Is it not that the house, aside from the stones, is inner idea stamped upon outer material, unity manifest in diversity? When one discerns in the bodily the Idea that binds and masters matter of itself formless and indeed recalcitrant to formation, and when one also detects an uncommon form stamped upon those that are common, then at a stroke one grasps the scattered multiplicity, gathers it together, and draws it within oneself to present it there to one's interior and indivisible oneness as concordant, congenial, a friend.[57]

Paradigms of the prior, such as this, may be approached in various ways. What is prior could be deemed superior in principle, such that anything subsequent comes about by derivation: the prior as antecedent. Or the prior could be deemed, in evolutionary fashion, the animus for what comes later: once upon a time there was a superior state of being, the prior, and so on. Or one could take the path of Plotinus in his attempt to release beauty, a path that seems a closer approximation of the first approach than of the second and third:

> If you do not yet see beauty within you, do as does the sculptor of a statue that is to be beautified: he cuts away here, he smooths it there, he makes this line lighter, this other one purer, until he disengages beautiful lineaments in

the marble. Do you this, too. Cut away all that is excessive, straighten all that is crooked, bring light to all that is overcast, labor to make all one radiance of beauty. Never cease "working at the statue" until there shines out upon you from it the divine sheen of virtue.[58]

As in the illustration of the house, attention is directed away from the material substrate, as it were, to what is truly at issue, the inherent quality that makes for apprehended beauty, under the name of idea or form. Now, this idea Plotinus locates first in the maker, in whom it dwells during the fashioning of the statue-soul, then in what he calls the artist's participation in the work. Derivative and diminished, the beauty of the statue is a kind of shadow cast by ideality onto a lesser realm. This is not the dualist relation that Neoplatonism fosters in the Christian Gnostic tradition, but a hierarchy of ontological gradations, the aim of life being to mount back up through these into the paradigmatic "prior" of origin. Long before the strange statue of mundane incorporating, much the same dynamic is working in Plotinus in the reverse direction, as it were. There flesh, rather than reaching into the world as its co-creator, reaches *before* the world.

If Santayana's path is not that of Plotinus's mysticism, because of the latter's fondness for worldly things, especially beautiful ones, spirit in Santayana has something nonetheless of the Plotinian aura: "Spirituality likes to say, Behold the lilies of the field! For its secret has the same simplicity as their vegetative art; only spirituality has succeeded in adding consciousness without confusing instinct. This success, unfortunately so rare in man's life as to seem paradoxical, is its whole achievement."[59] "Instinct" is a strong clue. No more than Pater does Santayana propose a Neoplatonist withdrawal from incorporate existence. On the contrary, what a casual reader could take to be a rejection of "primitive" or "earthly" features of worldly living is precisely the opposite: "But it hardly follows that animal feelings are not spiritual in their nature and, on their narrow basis, perfectly ideal. The most ideal human passion is love, which is also the most absolute and animal and one of the most ephemeral."[60]

10. One Way of Incorporating and Another

From Santayana's perspective there is no need to reconcile polarities such as absolute and natural, spirit and flesh; these, being already subtended by the givenness of the world, are already reconciled. The question is how to distinguish between the claims of one kind of flesh, which is also to say one kind of discursive representation, and another. This question is the focus of this concluding discussion, in which attention will turn, as promised, to Yeats, Hopkins, and Vallejo. To Yeats, who would recuperate individual and species through a self-discourse that is at the same time visionary cosmogony-*cum*-history. To Hopkins, who would recuperate individual and species through a self-discourse in pursuit of grace. To Vallejo, whose self-discourse redefines the fate of individual and species by redefining flesh in terms of an integration at once social, political, and cosmic. To put the issues another way, using Santayana's sense of the natural as a point of departure, we will see, first, the de-naturing of nature which is for Yeats an important discursive objective; then the imaginative operation of Hopkins by means of which nature is recuperated as a kind of trans-nature—divinity breaking out in the world, incorporate. Finally, on the way to a materialism that is fully dialectical, if not politically orthodox, Vallejo will subvert claims to identity and the absolute, including those made for art, as the price of integrating a phenomenal nature within a concrete geopoetics and geopolitics.

In "Leda and the Swan," as we have seen, we have a bird without whose mediation there would be no rape, hence no history, yet from the outset the text deprives this creature of its being; it can only be bird-*like*, having been possessed by another flesh, hence denatured. Does the bird return to itself, or is it consumed in the transformation? Yeats seems not to have answers to such questions. Hopkins does.

> My heart in hiding
> Stírred for a bird,—the achieve of, the mästery of the thing!
>
> Brute beauty and valour and act, oh, air, pride, plüme, here
> Buckle! AND the fire that breaks from thee then, a billion
> Tímes told lovelier, more dangerous, O my chevalier!

Here the bird is not denatured but naturally is anew. Nature being God-informed, creatures may break forth at any time through poetic imagination, in epiphany. If the breaking forth is part transformation, it is also part annunciation: it declares the moment and declares it momentous. That it transpires through a bird (the poet may here be sounding a Franciscan note) testifies to a love connecting each incorporate being to every other. Although the action follows a trajectory of descent, from sky to ploughed field, the "fall" is most fortunate, its consequence being nothing less than a kind of instant transubstantiation.

It is as if the beloved being of the bird decided suddenly to speak, "Crying *What I do is me: for that I came.*" As original as Hopkins's words are, the redemptive transformation of the bird follows a model that is not only traditional within the Christian framework but orthodox within the Catholic. Not so Yeats's treatment in "Leda and the Swan," where from one destination to another, destiny, beyond or outside of grace or mercy, runs out its line: the broken wall, the burning roof and tower, and the death of Agamemnon seen as inevitable as the sexual convulsion that, once initiated, not even the god himself can prevent from reaching its climax.

The Platonic Yeats reduces almost to parody the vision of natality inform-ing the conversation of Diotima and Socrates in *The Symposium*. In human propagation Diotima finds a divinity, "an immortal something in the midst of man's mortality which is incompatible with any kind of discord." Going further, she amends the common notion that love is a longing for the beauti-ful; it is rather "a longing not for the beautiful itself, but the conception and generation that the beautiful effects." She continues, "And why all this long-ing for propagation? Because this is the one deathless and eternal element in our mortality" (*Symp.* 206cde). All of this occurs in the realm of what she calls (in the Michael Joyce translation) "the flesh." [61] In the realm of ide-ality a similar story unfolds, as the poet fulfills his office by begetting wisdom and her sister virtues, the most important of which are the justice and mod-eration that alone can govern society. Friends who undertake one another's education, with a view to propagating friendship, will enjoy a more complete consummation through such progeny than that which comes from begetting and raising children. Homer and Hesiod in poetry or Lycurgus and Solon in law exemplify this type of generation.

In "The Mother of God," an early poem on propagation, Yeats's speaker, having described the flamelike announcement and the terror in the mother's womb, implies through a rhetorical question that she was not properly con-tent with the world and with her role:

> What is this flesh I purchased with my pains,
> This fallen star my milk sustains,
> This love that makes my heart's blood stop
> Or strikes a sudden chill into my bones
> And bids my hair stand up?
>
> (*CWY* 249)

A cyclical theory of history such as Yeats developed risks removing the pur-pose and freedom that make a livable world possible. And fittingly, the gyre as figure of time, in a poem like "The Second Coming," is a torsion away from precisely that point of reference which the poet so values: "Things fall apart; the center cannot hold . . ." (*CWY* 187). Spiraling off from the center, worldly things drift into one or another extreme, we are told; "lack of all conviction" marks the best people, "passionate intensity the worst" (*CWY* 187), and all certainty of knowledge dissolves. Of such a center one might say with Shelley that as a deep truth it is imageless. Yet something of its quality can be con-veyed:

> ... but now I know
> That twenty centuries of stony sleep
> Were vexed to nightmare by a rocking cradle,
> And what rough beast, its hour come round at last,
> Slouches toward Bethlehem to be born?
>
> (*CWY* 187)

On a first reading there is no reason to suppose that the climactic "what" clause is anything but an element of the persona's knowledge: he knows that the centuries of sleep were vexed and he knows that the rough beast will be born. Only with the shift toward the sublime interrogative does the gap, retroactively, loom. All the poet now knows, we see, is that the sleep was vexed; what beast will be born is what he does not know. For, though he has put on some knowledge, it does not satisfy. The characterization of the beast as rough, and the fact that it is a beast rather than the Christ child, make it plain that the creature is terrifically bad, and that we can expect a future whose dismal reaches will compare with those arising from the violence of Zeus in "Leda and the Swan."

The worst construction one can make of Yeats's fateful discourse of knowledge and power is that no one in the world truly has any knowledge or power to speak of. Such knowledge and power as we possess are only the sort that "Sailing to Byzantium" would flee in fear of "sensual music" and in quest of "monuments of unageing intellect" (*CWY* 193). The poet's report of Leda's rape estheticizes the sexual politics of the act more than one might have wished, and this is dehumanizing, in the first place, to Leda, and by implication, to anyone else in her position. It is not that the center of the vision cannot hold, but that there is no center, there is only incorporate agony crying, but without a voice of its own. All of which gives way to an attempt at a more human-centered perspective in a work like "Sailing to Byzantium," which depicts old men with whom the poet may more readily identify, but only to revolve toward a transcendence wherein, as the realm of flesh dissolves, another flesh begins to glimmer, if not fully to form. Such a work is "Byzantium." As we have seen, there remains in turn, in a play like *The Resurrection*, a prospect of reincarnation whereby, as the human being dies the death and lives the life of the god, the god does the same, manifest now, through epiphany, as incorporate.

In "Anima Hominis" action characterizes the public hero or the saint, and the handling of "paper or parchment" the poet, but what they share is living "flesh and blood" (*M* 333). Dante or Shakespeare "sought no impossible perfection but when they handled paper or parchment." So too will saint or hero, because each works in his own flesh and blood and not in paper or parchment, and thus has more deliberate understanding of that other flesh and blood.

Two modes of flesh are entered upon here. In one the incorporate state is the very medium of action: the hero active on the battlefield or in the senate, the saint on the stake or in the town square. The other mode makes paper and parchment the medium; the flesh and blood of the poets must be sheltered rather than risked, held back perhaps in a sort of ascesis. The advantage here falls, at any rate, to the men of action, who embody what Yeats in his autobiography calls the moral element, an idea that sheds light on the ambiguity of "deliberate understanding." For this can mean either that the saint or the hero possesses an understanding of that flesh and blood which the other may lack or that the understanding the former possessed is more deliberate than the understanding possessed, if at all, by the other flesh and blood. "Deliberate" inclines in the second direction, indicating that when saint or hero act in flesh and blood, deliberation precedes and determines choice; that choice, being the commitment one makes to this rather than that course of action, is the expression of what is moral in the moral element, and that such is the path on which saints or heroes advance to their destinies.

The dying generation, the aged man, and the other hints of dissolution that attend the entreaty of "Sailing to Byzantium" — "gather me into the artifice of eternity" — suggest an end to this world that the beginning of the concluding stanza affirms:

> Once out of nature I shall never take
> My bodily form from any natural thing,
> But such a form as Grecian goldsmiths make
> Of hammered gold and gold enamelling
> To keep a drowsy Emperor awake:
> Or set upon a golden bough to sing
> To lords and ladies of Byzantium
> Of what is past, or passing, or to come.
> (*CWY* 194)

Readings that emphasize the first two lines underline renunciation, dying from life, and so on. But the lines that follow, specifying what takes the place of "nature," serve as a counterbalance. Even in the process of dying from nature the persona preserves the identity of the worldly self in its incorporate state. In retrospect nature looks like mere endowment, whereas the artifice of post-nature enables a supreme entitlement, release from mortal time. Hence flesh is not surrendered but forged into something different from what it was. It was a natural form. Now, like the golden bird the Grecian goldsmith makes, it will be a beautiful worldly form patterned on a beautiful worldly thing: "Beauty is indeed but bodily life in some ideal condition" (*M* 349).

The poem makes two large moves, the first of which corresponds to stanzas one and two, and the second to stanzas three and four. The first stanza

offers a retrospect on "Whatever is begotten, born, and dies," the second a re-
prise of this in the form of the aged man as tattered coat, in the process raising
the prospect of something redemptive. For the aged man is a poor thing

> unless
> Soul clap its hands and sing, and louder sing
> For every tatter in its mortal dress
> (*CWY* 193)

which means that his destitution is not insuperable. Glimpsing some prospect
of a better state, the second stanza concludes with a transition as the speaker
sets sail for holy Byzantium. If the first two stanzas deal, then, with the circumstances of a departure, the second two will deal with the circumstances
of an advent.

In stanza three the sages are apostrophized: "Come from the holy fire,
perne in a gyre, / And be the singing-masters of my soul" (*CWY* 193), after
which the supplicant makes what may be either a promise or a pledge. As
promise the statement is straightforward enough: he makes a commitment to
what he deems it right to do. As pledge the statement assumes that a story
line develops between stanzas three and four as it did between stanzas two
and three: that is, the speaker's commitment may meet a condition for being
gathered into the artifice of eternity through the mediation of the sages. Insofar as one views this discursive act as a means of assimilating the individual
to one or another social order, one is inclined to take the commitment as a
pledge. For the speaker posited in early drafts of the poem—a medieval Irish
seeker after salvation—would have good reason to make a pledge the moment
Byzantium is seen to be the society he has envisaged. Since that persona has
been assimilated into a more general one, we may infer that while a residue
of the pledge may remain in the final stanza, what it articulates is essentially
a promise.

The assimilation of the specific to the general, in the case of the persona,
parallels the transposition of the action from "that" country of the flesh to a
hypostatized ideal condition. Again, it is misleading to regard the idealizing
as nothing more than a world-denying gesture. It strives rather to create the
world all over again. In the promise the poem spells out another kind of incorporating, one that is reborn, though patterned on a familiar worldly thing.

Flesh stays on elsewhere as well. In "News for the Delphic Oracle" the
immortals, such as Oisin and Pythagoras, may be golden, but they are codgers just the same, lying about as they do, and Plotinus with them, stretching,
yawning, and sighing like anyone else. The poem concludes:

> Slim adolescence that a nymph has stripped,
> Peleus on Thetis stares,

Her limbs are delicate as an eyelid,
Love has blinded him with tears;
But Thetis' belly listens.
Down the mountain walls
From where Pan's cavern is
Intolerable music falls.
Foul goat-head, brutal arm appear,
Belly, shoulder, bum
Flash fishlike; nymphs and satyrs
Copulate in the foam.

(*CWY* 338)

As for Byzantium, the poet's vision may be dreamlike, it may even be a dream, but it conduces importantly to wakefulness, rousing the sated ruler that he may savor flesh as the golden codgers do. The Yeatsian office of singing is a complement to that of the "sylvan historian" whose depictions Keats ecphrastically represents. Though Yeats's singing creature is avian and auditory, it is not less a historian. Though it sings to creatures of another flesh, to emperors and lords and ladies, these are at the same time figures of a once-actual world of which the poet has reconstructed at least a measure of the beauty and the atmosphere.

Writing in the country that Yeats would be "out of" even as he would be out of nature, Hopkins can discourse dithyrambically of another mode of incorporate being with as much otherworldly potential as that envisioned by Yeats, but more attuned with nature both in its own right and in its role in human destiny. The title "That Nature is a Heraclitean Fire and of the Comfort of the Resurrection" identifies as its point of departure Heraclitus's vision of a cosmos constituted of fire at the same time that it identifies as its destination the Christian mystery of regeneration through divine grace, with the caveat that the latter operates through the agency of flesh in the most mundane sense of the term. Indeed, the specifically human factors in the scene are of the humblest.

Million-fuelèd, | nature's bonfire burns on.
But quench her bonniest, dearest | to her, her clearest-selvèd spark
Mán, how fást his fíredint, | his mark on mind, is gone!
Bóth are in an ünfáthomable, áll is in an enórmous dárk
Drowned. O pity and indig | nation! Manshape, that shone
Sheer off, disseveral, a star, | death blots black out; nor mark
Is ány of him at áll so stárk
But vastness blurs and time | beats level.

Hopkins's choice of a Heraclitean point of departure is as physical as it is metaphysical. "Nature's bonfire," pointing to the constitution of the cosmos by a single element, is a venerable instance of the material imagination studied by Bachelard. But Hopkins is ecumenical, for despite the title, all four traditional elements figure: not only fire but air (the "air-built thoroughfare"), water ("yestertempest's creases; in pool and rutpeel parches / Squandering ooze"), and earth ("squeezed dough, crust, dust . . . / . . . treadmire toil"). Not too far in the background, indeed, is the doleful Christian discourse of "earth to earth and dust to dust," together with the redemptive potential with which the words are invested just because the discourse is Christian. The obligation of work and earthly production entails, in the general sense, environmental praxis, and in the particular sense, as here, the collaboration of earth and earthly materials with one or another forms of fire. Both destructive and creative, fire can use things — fuel, oxygen, and so on — in order to make things — pottery, sculpture, and so on. It is that element in which *Homo faber* is most immediately at home, the power that in Hopkins's day drove a range of industrial technologies, from textile factories to the maritime vessels for which the poet's father underwrote insurance: the foundering ship in "The Wreck of the Deutschland" is such a vessel. But too exclusive a focus on what was then more or less state-of-the-art technology can be misleading. "The Loss of the Eurydice" concerns the sinking of a royal training ship equipped with a larger fitting of sail than any other craft of her tonnage and therefore epitomizing the "state of the art" in maritime technology. When Hopkins speaks in line 18 of the present text either or both could figure as types of disaster and dissolution.

In "Felix Randal" we see the poet turn to a still earlier technology, memorializing the work of the farrier who depends upon the iron forge — a transformer of earthly materials through fire — and such of its products as hammer, horseshoe, and nails:

> How far from then forethought of, all thy more boisterous
> years,
> When thou at the random grím fórge, pówerful amídst péers,
> Didst fettle for the great grey drayhorse his bright and battering
> sandal!

> (H 165)

The farrier's portion is to work up strange statues with his vocational environment — the things, as Dewey says, with which he varies — including the domestic animal itself. The poet's fascination with such environments is matched only by his fascination with the fact that everything and everyone belonging to them belongs equally to the larger cosmic scene. Like Vallejo's, his eye is on the continuum of being, and like the Peruvian poet he weaves the artifacts of the vocational environment and their cosmic counterparts into an integrated fabric. The author who would write of nature as Heraclitean fire is the same man who collected dialect and technical terms from the crafts or trades of spinning and weaving, thatching, plowing, and, more to the point of the present text, blacksmithing.[62] It is entirely fitting then that Felix Randal should perform his work in metonymic nearness to the natural phenomena kinetically rendered in the preceding lines:

> Delightfully the bright wind boisterous | ropes, wrestles, beats earth
> bare
> Of yestertempest's creases; in pool and rutpeel parches
> Squandering ooze to squeezed | dough, crúst, dust; stánches, stárches
> Squadroned masks and manmarks | treadmire toil there
> Fóotfretted in it.
>
> (H 198)

Thus does nature in its own way erase its own marks, even as the marks of manshape will be erased in the lines that follow. As earth is beaten bare of the creases from the storm, so is it stripped of human marks, those of published public discourse being arguably an exception: "vastness blurs and time beats level."

Heraclitus saw cosmic strife through the entire universe. But in Hopkins's hands energies are spontaneously affirmative — more harmonious processes than conflicting ones — and they run in a continuum as "Nature" does its work and human beings do their work: "and manmarks treadmire toil there / Footfretted in it." It is crucial to the organization of the poem, in any case, that nature's dearest spark and manshape is blacked out, its mark erased, for this is the condition of possibility for the mystery that redefines, that revolutionizes, if you will, the fate of flesh:

> Enough! the Resurrection,
> A héart's clarion! Awáy grief's gásping, | joyless days, dejection.
> Across my foundering deck shone
> A beacon, an eternal beam. | Flesh fade, and mortal trash
> Fáll to the resíduary worm; | world's wildfire, leave but ash:
> In a flash, at a trumpet crash,
> I am all at once what Christ is, | since he was what I am, and
> This Jack, jóke, poor pótsherd, | patch, matchwood, immortal
> diamond
> Is immortal diamond.
>
> (H 198)

Here, for a time, Hopkins reverts to the Christian figure of carnal abjection: "Flesh fade, and mortal trash / Fall to the residuary worm," where the hendiadys "flesh/trash," reminding us that flesh has long been a term for meat, is the more shocking as it immediately contrasts with the prospect that this same incorporate being will after all be saved.

Yet even the ascetic Hopkins is not of a mind to dwell on carnal abjection: only a semicolon and a line mark separate the clause from "world's wildfire, leave but ash," where the entire world is consumed by divinely ordained fire, beyond all mortal control. With the fate of flesh suspended between the prospect of Resurrection and its realization in the text, the rhyming carry-through of "ash" into "flash" and "trumpet crash" prepares for the sudden identification of the speaker with Christ, an identification based on the incorporation of the species in the individual: "he was what I am." The denigration immediately following recapitulates the perspective of carnal abjection as a kind of trial and viaticum for the transformation of earthly incorporate being into another kind of flesh altogether:

> This Jack, jóke, poor pótsherd, patch, matchwood, immortal diamond,
>   Is immortal diamond.

The poem thus brings to pass, in its climax, the same kind of miraculous transformation witnessed in "The Windhover." Mackenzie derives Hopkins's concatenation from the list of materials from which the Christian symbolic repertoire was built up over the centuries: "gold, silver, precious stones, wood, hay, stubble . . . the fire shall try every man's work, of what sort it is." Hopkins's reconstruction tenders a more immediate human presence in Jack, the representative marker, who is also a joke, perhaps because, as in First Corinthians, Christianity seemed folly to the Greeks (or perhaps for the echo of Pope's "Glory, jest, and riddle of the world").[63] In the second triad of materials, each thing is the inverse of the kind of thing a diamond is. A potsherd is easily broken, a diamond hardly. "Patch" is a name for a misfit and for a mere part of a whole, and a makeshift part at that; a diamond is a whole thing and the epitome of natural perfection. Matchwood is something consumed by heat, diamond a pure crystallization of the element of carbon itself. If the introduction of "immortal" then seems gratuitous it is, as grace is gratuitous; not having been taken for mortal, there is no "need" to represent it as such, but neither is there "need" to resurrect faded flesh and mortal trash. All of which is at the same time a way of saying that flesh thus transubstantiated is finally what the maker of marks already is, once the Resurrection is.

Even more than Hopkins, Vallejo in his references to deity or communion or Christ strains the bonds of creedal authority, yet he feels the need to experience different kinds of being and to express that experience in a way that reintegrates alienated, de-natured human beings into a common, essentially secular world. What is "of the spirit" in Vallejo is precisely what is "of the flesh." It can only be explored by the kind of continual quest that his life as a writer represents, zigzagging across some of the same terrain traversed by Yeats in his quest for a theory of history, a credo of corporeality, and a vision of anti-nature—in his quest, in short, for a politics of the human condition.

In a text concerning the Venus de Milo, Vallejo explores the ways in which the sculpture is informed by and informs its environment, and the fateful fact that its being is continually impaired by natural forces. In the damaged Venus, whose revered status in high culture is problematic from the moment she is named in the text, nature more than subtends the work's mode of being; it ventures to reassimilate the entirety of what the sculptor and the tradition have made. In the spirit of Vallejo's neologistic art, we could say that in *Trilce* 36 art can be "de-arted" more readily than nature can be "de-natured" or flesh "de-fleshed."

11. Figuring Flesh

That the Venus de Milo was once "all one radiance" may be supposed, but it is not a certainty of our esthetic experience, the sculpture's original figuration having been impaired. But neither is it certain, Vallejo suggests, that we can recover its unimpaired condition or reconstitute its original aura. Vallejo rejects the possibilities of an ecphrastic experience such as Keats depicts in "Ode on a Grecian Urn" or Eduard Mörike in "Auf eine Lampe." Problematizing restoration, Vallejo radicalizes the element of interrogation already evident in Rubén Darío's Venus de Milo poems, "Venus" and "Yo persigo una forma" ("I Pursue a Form"). His iconoclasm is in any case remarkable in its ramifications, as evidenced in Poem 26 of *Trilce*.

> ¿Por ahí estás, Venus de Milo?
> Tu manqueas apenas pululando
> entrañada en los brazos plenarios
> de la existencia,
> de esta existencia que todaviiza
> perenne imperfección.

> Are you there, Venus de Milo?
> You are maimed,
> scarcely sprouting buried deep in the plenary arms
> of existence,
> of this existence that "yets"
> perennial imperfection.[64]

In countering shallow spiritualization, Vallejo comes close to questioning the very being of the statue: Does Venus de Milo even exist? Even if—as the rest of the poem seems to accept—that entity really *is* there, it is severely impaired. Rather than compensate for the statue's impairment, the text underlines the absence of arms both by 1) refusing to refer to them, even as something missing, and by 2) assigning the diagonally opposite trope, "plenary arms," to existence itself. The sculpture no longer figures the one Plotinian radiance, the harmony and symmetry, valorized by traditional esthetics; it figures rather "perennial imperfection," which is said to be "yet-ed"—continued, furthered—by existence. If this is the case, then the imperfection is not unique to the Venus as work of art but is a condition of incorporate existence as such—whether instantiated in the strange statue formed by the sculptor's shaping gestures, by the strange statues formed by the movement of onlookers around the displayed figure, or by that strange statue which, as here, surrounds the figure in the modalities of discourse.

Vallejo goes further:

> Rehusad, y vosotros, a posar las plantas
> en la seguridad dupla de la Armonía.
> Rehusad la simetría a buen seguro.
>
> (V 163)

> Refuse, and all of you, to place your soles
> in the double security of Harmony.
> Refuse symmetry at all costs.

The admonition aims to remove from the discourse of flesh, in which all worldly things are connected, the term and concept representing the targeted tradition. Upper-case "Harmony" suggests the degree to which the concept has been enshrined, even deified in the discourse of those who search in art for something of the fulfillment once supplied by religion. By not capitalizing "symmetry," the text further suggests that even outside of that tradition there lurks the same temptation to hypostatize, to borrow Wallace Stevens's phrase, "the idea of order." So that when the poet's lines denounce symmetry, in nature or anywhere else, they are, at a minimum, denouncing "symmetry." For it is the office of the poem to inform and environ the represented figure in discourse, and to interrogate its relation to incorporate being.

Nearing the end, the text turns rather more inward:

> Tal siento ahora al meñique
> demás en la siniestra. Lo veo y creo
> no debe serme, o por lo menos que está
> en sitio donde no debe.
>
> Y me inspira rabia y me azarea
> y no hay como salir de el, sino haciendo
> la cuenta de que hoy es jueves.
>
> ¡Ceded al nuevo impar
> potente de orfandad!
>
> (V 164)

So now I feel a little finger
superfluous on the left. I see it and believe
that it should not be me, or at least that it is where
it should not be.

It inspires me with rage and I'm rattled
and don't know what to do, except to consider
that today is Thursday.

Cede to the new uneven number
potent with orphanhood!

In this move toward self-discourse, transferring attention from the Venus de Milo to the speaker's anatomy implies a parallel between the two figures, more specifically an analogous impairment. And here indeed is the demon imperfection doing its work again, but with this twist, that for the first time the deontological rhetoric ("must not," "should not") aims at a being whose very endowment (represented by the little finger) is disenabling. If his finger were missing, making him resemble more closely the maimed Venus, this would only throw into relief the essential problem of his own imperfection and everydayness, signified by the fact that today is rather meaninglessly Thursday.

In "Piedra negra sobre una piedra blanca" ("Black Stone Over a White Stone") the day on which the poet predicts he will die is Thursday, a temporal placement more meaningful than may first appear, for nothing is more "ordinary" than mortality, which may come at any day or hour; it is a time to focus not on the author's anatomy as such, but on the fate of flesh in the very act of writing.

Jueves será, porque hoy, jueves, que proso
estos versos, los húmeros me he puesto a la
mala y, jamás como hoy, me he vuelto, con todo
mi camino, a verme solo.

(V 310)

Thursday it will be, because today, Thursday, as I compose
these verses, my forearms make me
ache and never as today, with all
my travel, have I felt myself so lonely.

It belongs to incorporating to be named—to be born of beings with names and in turn to bear one name or more—and thus the poet, in declaring his own, at a stroke individualizes himself (every *one* is called something) and generalizes in behalf of the species (*every* one is called something):

César Vallejo ha muerto, le pegaban
todos sin que él les haga nada;
le daban duro con un palo y duro

también con una soga; son testigos
los días jueves y los huesos húmeros,
la soledad, la lluvia, los caminos . . .

(V 310)

César Vallejo is dead, they all beat him
without his having done anything;
they hit him hard with a stick and hard

as well with a rope; his witnesses
the Thursday days and the forearm bones,
the solitude, the rain, the roads . . .

A word of singular resonance in Spanish-language poetry, *camino* indicates a
road or way, here broadly suggesting the entire course of incorporate being;
the plural then opens the text beyond the closure that the finality it addresses
might have led a reader to expect. It now seems that there were other trails
or roads in the past or that there will perhaps be other roads or witnesses to
come; or it may be that the weight bearing down, the discursive accumula-
tion of tradition, say, obliges already punished flesh not to annihilation but
(as implied by the ellipse) to sheer indeterminacy.

How different from the fate of flesh in the Hopkins passage, in which the
suffering of the finger demonstrates the difference between the individual's
"inmost self" and his anatomy, and by analogy the difference between the
universal mind and his own! "And for all that this universal being may be at
work in mine it leaves me finite: *I* am selfexistent none the more for any part
the selfexistent plays in me." For Vallejo, again, the notion of immaterial mentation is illusory; there is *only* flesh, and mortal destiny, hence any attempt to
envisage "incarnation" in any traditional Christian sense is without warrant:
in "Lomo de las sagradas escrituras" ("Spine of the Holy Scriptures"), the
incarnation of the word of which the poet speaks not only carries no otherworldly overtones but is entirely a phenomenon of flesh. Attending again to
his own anatomy, now in the context of the engendering and nurturing provided by his mother, he writes:

Mi metro esta midiendo ya dos metros,
mis huesos concuerdan en género y en número
y el verbo encarnado habita entre nosotros
y el verbo encarnado habita al hundirse en el baño
un alto grado de perfección.

(V 251)

My meter is now measuring two meters,
my bones agree in gender and number
and the word made flesh dwells among us
and the word dwells, as I sink into the bath,
a high degree of perfection.

If perfection exists, it does so ironically and mundanely: the degree of perfection in the immediate lived environment, composed of earthly gravity that conditions his sinking, of his own sensuous being obeying that law, and of that rejuvenating worldly vessel, the implied bathtub—of all the things, in short (again in Dewey's formulation), with which a man varies.

The poet's ironies imply the possibility of reconstruction: "Implicit in this deconstruction is a ceaseless dialectical reconstruction that the structure of allegory affords: the infinite recontextualization of meaning emanating from the power of signification places metaphoricity a hair's distance from a linguistic truth always about to emerge."[65]

> Venus de Milo, cuyo cercenado, increado
> brazo revuélvese y trata de encodarse
> a través de verdeantes guijarros gagos,
> ortivos nautilos, aunes que gatean
> recién, vísperas inmortales.
> Laceadora de imminencias, laceadora
> del paréntesis.
>
> Venus de Milo, whose clipped, uncreated
> arm turns round and tries to elbow itself
> by way of greenish, stammering pebbles,
> ortivius nautilus, evens that crawl
> recently, immortal nights before.
> Lassoer of imminences, lassoer
> of the parenthesis.

As "uncreated" raises the question of the sculpture's actuality, the passage, as it jerks disjunctively along, endows the figured flesh with compensatory capacities. Unable to embody the transcendental harmony dear to the Symbolist and Parnassian esthetic, the work of art becomes a modality of self-discourse, "the author of her own allegorical meaning; her lack, her spatial inadequacy, propagates signifiers of pure imminence."[66] Enclosed like a parenthesis, inclining to narcissism psychologically and to tautology linguistically, the artwork, though thus empowered, is at the same time limited and isolated, like the individual in the Hobbesian-Lockean social model. Vallejo indeed identified this model, in his explicitly political writing, with the capitalist system, and in his later work spoke openly against it:

> The word of the individual with regard to collective experience has been truncated and suppressed in the mouth of the individual. We are dumb in the midst of our incomprehensible babble. It is the confusion of tongues arising from exaggerated individualism on which bourgeois economy and politics are based. Rampant self-interest has filled everything with its selfish intent, even words. The word is stifled by individualism. The most human form of social relationship—the word—has thus lost its collective essence and attributes.[67]

Comparable qualification is in order when it comes to the more positive, retrospective dimension alluded to above. Consider how, in the interaction of the two forward-looking nouns *vísperas* and *imminencias*, the latter counters and darkens the former. For, while the notion of an eve or night-before is relatively neutral as a proleptic, the *imminence* family comes from the Latin "to overhang," to impend, hence to be threatening. There is, to be sure, in the dialectically disposed Vallejo, plenty of upward, transcendent movement to go along with the downward tendency evident here; in his poem on miners, to be discussed below, both directions come into play. In the present text, nonetheless, the sense of something about to come down emphasizes the weightiness or gravity of earthly life and its burdens. Thus in "Heces" ("Dregs"):

> Esta tarde en Lima llueve. Y yo recuerdo
> las cavernas crueles de mi ingratitud;
> mi bloque de hielo sobre su amapola,
> más fuerte que su "¡No seas así!"
>
> (V 55)

> This afternoon in Lima it rains. And I recall
> the cruel caverns of my ingratitude;
> my block of ice over your poppy,
> heavier than your "Don't be that way!"

Seeing the lassoer of imminences as also the lassoer of the parenthesis underlines the particularity of the processes in question. The lassoer delimits a discursive locus that could be filled with practically anything: the perfect place indeed for the imperfection of self-discourse, the more autonomous as the filler it provides for is the more arbitrary; the perfect place to punctuate and puncture the inflation, in the age of presentment, of the individual and individualism.

Discourse embraces the poet in the incarnate particularity that he is. Which is to say that the poet, at least in modern times, has a degree of self-discourse, reflexive and metalinguistic, to work through — to use up and surpass. For if the poet's words are sometimes about the poet's words, this is in order to get at what the poet's words endow, enable, and entitle: that other of discourse which is no longer easily termed the referent, the signified. We arrive at the situation of Octavio Paz, who follows the "languagey" Vallejo into the relation of the word to what Paz calls physiology:

The language turns in upon itself. Not the language of books, that of the street; not the language of the street, that of the hotel room with no one inside. Fusion of the word and physiology. . . . Hunger not as a dissertation topic but speaking directly, with a faint and delirious voice. A voice more powerful than that of the dream. And that hunger becomes an infinite desire to give and be given: *his corpse was full of world.*[68]

To link word and physiology is to emphasize their connection in flesh, or, better, their convergence there, where cosmos is as well, and species in all their plenitude. The vision is as inclusive as it is integrative, and even suggests some of the terms on which a satisfactory politics of the human condition could be articulated. It is a vision Vallejo comes to have, but only after confronting the actualities of disintegration. "Los desgraciados" ("The Wretched Ones") is addressed to everyone and anyone in that dis-integrated and all-too-familiar condition; the title calls them "the unfortunate ones," or those without grace who seem scarcely to exist, so that it has become necessary for the poet to tell them what to do, and what he tells them to do is to embrace, in the cosmos that is, flesh as it is. The text begins:

> Ya va a venir el día; da
> cuerda a tu brazo, búscate debajo
> del colchón, vuelve a pararte
> en tu cabeza, para andar derecho.
> Ya va a venir el día, ponte el saco.
>
> Ya va a venir el día; ten
> fuerte en la mano a tu intestino grande . . .
> (V 337)

> Already the day is coming; wind
> up your arm, search under
> the mattress, return to upright in your head
> to go straight.
> Already the day is coming, put on your jacket.
>
> Already the day is coming; hold
> firmly in your hand to your big intestine . . . [69]

The refrain, occurring eleven times, intensifies the eschatological mood, which is not, however, otherworldly. The poet speaks of last things by way of worldly things at hand: of what is now, and what the wretched ones should do about it. "Should," because the text is as much deontology as ontology. It says what to do in order to gear up for the world that will come if you make it come. Wind your arm as you wind your watch, embracing "physiology" and technology. Ready yourself in the upright cerebrating posture to which, by Darwinian evolutionary processes, this poet deems you entitled; then clothe yourself for appearance in society. But with loss of grace there is still the sense of a coming day that may be the last day, and the access of horror when the overhanging at last comes down, so get a good hold on the flesh that you are.

> ¿Tiemblas? Es el estado remoto de la frente
> y la nación reciente del estómago.
> (V 337)

> Are you trembling? it is the distant state of the forehead
> and the recent nation of the stomach.

Incorporating as politics: the poet brings new life to the traditional trope of the body politic by merging the head, roughly the intellect, and the stomach, roughly endowment, the sheer need to survive, into the discourse of polity. And as part of the merger there is attention both to geopolitical generality and geopolitical specificity, the forehead punningly indicating the former and the stomach indicating the material needs of nations recently emergent, in political or socioeconomic terms, such as the poet's native Peru. The same phrase, more concretely still, indicates a contrast between the cerebral assured existence of Spanish Peninsular culture and more "physiological" polities, in which lower strata of the populations are struggling even to feed themselves. That the body politic is equally a soul politic is clearly stipulated: "Already the day is coming, put on your soul," then "Already the day is coming, put on your body." The intervening imperative, "put on your dream," employs one of the most resonant nouns in Hispanic literature in order to imply that in some way this "natural" power of imagination, as mediated by the "artifice" of discourse, can handle reality well enough.

The poem takes a nightmarish turn as the poet, embracing at once the cosmic and the social, portrays a dramatic disjunction between the phenomenon of the solitary individual and the phenomena of the environment.

> Ya va a venir el día;
> la mañana, la mar, el meteoro, van
> en pos de tu cansancio, con banderas,
> y, por tu orgullo clásico, las hienas
> cuentan sus pasos al compás del asno,
> la panadera piensa en ti,
> el carnicero piensa en ti, palpando
> el hacha en que están presos
> el acero y el hierro y el metal; jamás olvides
> que durante la misa no hay amigos.
> Ya va a venir el día, ponte el sol.
>
> (V 338)

> Already the day is coming;
> the morning, the sea, the meteor, are
> pursuing your fatigue, with banners,
> and, for your classic pride, the hyenas
> count their steps in time with the ass,
> the baker's wife is thinking of you,
> the butcher is thinking of you, palpating
> the cleaver in which are captured
> the steel and the iron and the metal; never forget

that during mass there are no friends.
And already the day is coming, put on the sun.

The environment envisaged is as wide as possible; it is the morning brought by the rising sun and the sea that the sun renders visible, the meteor flaming in the sky, and the cosmos itself—the day becoming, with access of clarity, a fateful convergence of time and place. But rather than exploit the Longinian potential, the poet, as though looking through the wrong end of the telescope, narrows the last scene to the fatigue of the individual alone in himself, a Cartesian I in a burnt-out secular age. To evoke the morning, the sea, and the meteor and then to set them in pursuit of the individual's exhaustion is to move the sublime toward the ridiculous—the kind of merging so characteristic of effects traditionally called grotesque, and representative of a good deal of Vallejo's writing. The hyenas pursuing the beast of burden in expectation of inevitable carrion are clearly in the same vein.

Suddenly the poet's alienation-effects turn social and vocational. First, the baker's wife, a cipher suggesting alienation of person from person, and possibly of class from class. A cipher: we do not know if her interest is erotic, therefore adulterous since she is married, or if she merely seeks distraction. Her identity being no more than an appendage of her husband's vocation, she may be entirely marginal, but she could also be a transitional figure for the next vocational cipher, the butcher, whose interest in the graceless individual is anything but individual; he cares nothing for commonality in flesh, or for the integrity of the other, but is the social actor at his most menacing. Even the technology is alienated. Steel and iron are to metal as species is to genus, which is at once the more inclusive category and the epitome of these materials—the very stuff of which all worldly things, and the very cosmos, are composed. Chemically, iron is a metallic element derived from naturally occurring ores, and from a certain "ecological" perspective lays claim to be left natural. Such is the preference of Ruskin, who subordinates metal tools to "the main service" of "making the ground we feed from. . . . For these are nothing but metals and oxygen—metals with breath put into them."[70] No less earth-oriented than his Victorian predecessor, Vallejo is more concerned with the estrangement in technology, wherein materials of the inhabited cosmos undergo an alienation as grotesque in its own way as the notion that the morning, the sea, and the meteor are in pursuit of an individual exhaustion. The sobering touch in the present instance is the relation of the butcher's metonymic tool to the object of his thought, who is precisely an object—not the kind of fellow human being you find in the solidarity poems of the Spanish Civil War, but a target for violence; *palpando*, like the English cognate "palpating," surpasses the more general term "feeling" as suggestive of tactile sensation and implied intent, the point apparently being that the butcher, eyeing the other, is examining the readiness of his blade for fearful use against flesh.

When in the end day comes,

> tu . . . has soñado esta noche que vivías
> de nada y morías de todo . . .
>
> you . . . have dreamed tonight that you were living
> on nothing and dying of everything . . .

The dream has become the worst of nightmares.

12. An Integrative Vision

The dark mood of these lines finds its counterpart in a poem like "Telú- rica y magnética" ("Telluric and Magnetic") or "Los mineros salieron de la mina" ("The Miners Came Out of the Mine"), which are virtual companion texts. Each is as rhapsodic in its own way as Hopkins's Christian-Heraclitean celebration of a flesh transformed from bird to savior. Vallejo's vision is sto- ically secular, however, and his focus is the incorporate interacting of human beings with a concrete environment that is both a given (the things we call natural are already there) and a place in which human beings give (of the things that are already there we make other things—the mining of ores, for example, leads to the production of the metal that makes its way into the butcher's cleaver). It is a wide range that the poet sees, the widest, extend- ing from the strange statues of the miners acting here and now, from the cultivators in "Telluric and Magnetic" acting since time immemorial to the remotest reaches of the cosmos. Such reaches are not so remote after all, for the distant sun illuminates the immediate daily world; and the constituents of the cosmos, as Pater, Yeats, Hopkins, and Ruskin also attest, are themselves constituents of the actors and their acts: the iron in the earth is one of the materials of which we are made—the ground we feed from, as Ruskin says— and is one of the worldly things from which we make new worldly things.

The difference between "Telluric and Magnetic" and "The Wretched Ones" is that the poet now steps back for a broader view, enabling the per- ception of very large patterns: cultivated fields, for instance, rather than dis- crete cultivators. Cultivation is then revealed in an assimilated state, as some- thing developed by work into what it is now seen to be, even as the natural features of the scene are revealed as developing themselves by virtue of the enabling wherewithal of intelligence, desire, need, and practical competence they shared with their human counterparts. Any piece of discourse applicable to the latter is applicable to the former, and vice versa. The result looks like, but is not, an instance of the pathetic fallacy.

¡Mecánica sincera y peruanisima
la del cerro colorado!
¡Suelo teórico y práctico!
¡Surcos inteligentes; ejemplo: el monolito y su cortejo!
¡Papales, cebadales, alfalfares, cosa buena!
¡Cultivos que integra una asombrosa jerarquía de útiles
y que integran con viento los mugidos,
las aguas con su sorda antigüedad!

(V 272)

Sincere and most Peruvian mechanics,
that of the colored hill!
Ground theoretical and practical!
Intelligent furrows; example: the monolith and its cortege!
Potato fields, barley fields, alfalfa fields, good thing!
Cultivated lands that an astonishing hierarchy of tools integrates,
and that are integrated by lowings in the wind
and waters of mute antiquity!

This is not pathetic fallacy because the poet is not projecting human qualities onto things not human. His interest is not so much psychology as it is history and ontology. The poet discourses of qualities in a continuum of being at once heterogeneous and homogenous: heterogeneous because incorporated one way here, another there; homogenous in that everything that is, is, and partakes in what are ultimately the same or similar capacities of being. Vallejo's cosmos is of the earth, earthly, as it is of the flesh, fleshly.

It is on earth and as flesh that everything enters into everything else, polymorphously but not perversely; or if you prefer, Vallejo bears witness to polymorphous *normality* in which a "purely natural" thing such as a hill can epitomize both the mechanical and sincerity. If this is at the same time the quintessence of what is Peruvian, it is because the language of geology and geopolitics is being integrated into a geopoetics. *Integrar* means to integrate, to bring together, form, or compose. The "magnetic" in the title points to the attractive power of the lodestone as a site to which iron filings, say, are brought together, and "telluric" signifies not only the earthly but the larger scene in which cosmic things and processes interact and integrate. This is not to deny difference or struggle, whether between things or processes, ranks and powers. The text indeed indicates a hierarchy of tools; the integration that results in cultivated fields presupposes effort and contestation — the hard work of agriculture; and in stanza two there is a curious, seemingly incidental agon between earth and sky. All of this transpires through the explicit mediation of the speaker, who understands the integration of his own incorporate being into the life processes he illuminates, but understands equally well, as a later stanza will show, how infinitesimally small he is in comparison with the succession of maize crops grown since the emergence of that species of grain in the Quaternary epoch.

> ¡los oigo por los pies como se alejan,
> los huelo retornar cuando la tierra
> tropieza con la técnica del cielo!
> ¡Molécula ex abrupta! ¡Atomo terso!
>
> (V 272)

> I hear them with my feet as they go away,
> I smell them return when the earth
> stumbles into the technics of the sky!
> Sudden molecule! Shining atom!

The speaker can hear through his feet because so endowed: the senses of the flesh are interactive, not passive or inert; unitary, not isolated or discrete; and everything that is sensed—potato fields, barley fields, alfalfa fields, and maize crops—is made possible by the interacting of earth and sky, envisioned (as Lewis Mumford would also say) as a technics. In the context of the scientific terms "molecule" and "atom," which immediately follow, the same primordial laws and forces that are seen at work in technology or science are at work in the sky. If everything is at some level molecule and atom, if grain species develop because of their atomic-molecular structure and evolutionary potentiality, and if the lightning in the sky and the falling rain are liable to the same physical laws of electricity and gravity—in short, if everything enters in or into everything else, then it is as fair to speak of the natural in technical or scientific terms as it is to speak of the technical or scientific in terms of the natural.

By the same geopoetic and geopolitical logic, all things being liable to the same kinds of laws and being constituted from the same ensemble of cosmic qualities, the things they make of what is already there, and they themselves, may be spoken of in like terms.

> ¡Oh campos humanos!
> ¡Solar y nutricia ausencia de la mar,
> y sentimiento oceánico de todo!
>
> . . .
>
> ¡Oh campo intelectual de cordillera
> con religión, con campo, con patitos!
> ¡Paquidermos en prosa cuando pasan
> y en verso cuando páranse!
>
> (V 272)

> Oh human fields!
> Solar and nutritious absence of the sea,
> and oceanic feeling of everything!

. . .
Oh intellectual field of the mountain range,
with religion, with fields, with ducklings!
Pachyderms in prose when they pass
and in verse when they stop!

Just as he has included species of grain, so the poet, in embracing flesh, includes animal species other than the human:

¡Roedores que miran con sentimiento judicial en torno!
¡Oh patrioticos asnos de mi vida!
¡Vicuña, descendiente nacional y graciosa de mi mono!
(V 272–73)

Rodents who look around with judicial sentiment!
Oh patriotic asses of my life!
Vicuna, national and gracious descendant of my monkey!

The notion of judicially disposed rodents is itself descended from various discursive strategies for playing human beings off against beings of other species, in order to play them off against one another. La Fontaine's "The Wolf and the Lamb" concludes with the Wolf, roughly representing strength, carrying off the Lamb, roughly representing weakness, because that is the Wolf's desire, which acts without proper judicial procedure. The Wolf as jurist knows the only "legal" system that matters is the fact that he is endowed with the capacity to consummate his own desires, and the reader knows that this scene of "nature" signifies the social, political, and cultural order resonating in the subtext. But the term "procedure" or *procès* "has at least two meanings: the judicial meaning (trial), and the etymological meaning (process). A process includes a predecession and a succession: it is an order."[71] The order that the Wolf employs against the Lamb turns out to be after all the order of sheer power, of which the satirical purpose is whatever moral a reader decides to draw. The order Vallejo depicts is more primordial, if you will, but is equally a matter of hierarchy and power, whether the context is the behavior of species or of particular social actors. Rodents feel judicial because in their own way they do indeed judge; it is only that what they judge, in the astonishing order of animal hierarchies and jurisdictions, is a practical-theoretical nexus involving: the situation in which it finds itself; the identity of another species entering into the scene or game; the strategy to be employed in order to carry away and consume the other entity; the execution of the strategy; and so on, all thanks to molecules and atoms, to the cosmos in which they inhere and interact, to the oceanic feeling of all and everything, to the fact that everything enters into everything else. So that what matters most is not the classification of species or individual into abstract, preemptive categories but the recognition that where rodents are concerned, "Judicial is as judicial does," while for asses, "Patriotic is as patriotic does."

> ¡Sierra de mi Perú, Perú del mundo,
> y Perú al pie del orbe; yo me adhiero!
>   . . .
> ¡Rotación de tardes modernas
> y finas madrugadas arqueológicas!
> ¡Indio después del hombre y antes de él!
>   (V 273-74)
>
> Sierra of my Peru, Peru of the world,
> and Peru at the foot of the world; I am embracing!
>   . . .
> Rotation of modern afternoons
> and fine early archeological mornings!
> Indian after man and before him!

In the poet's geopolitical geopoetics Peru is at once a nexus of geological and archaeological features and of politically determined cartographic and social representations. Without what is already there before such determination and representation — what is already Peruvian or Andean before there are "Peru" and "the Andes" — there is no *suelo*, no ground, for those determinations and representations. "Nature" being easy to silence as the inarticulate other (by the convention of feminization, for example), Vallejo gives it a voice by listening to and communicating to the reader what it already is and says. This means recognizing that the ground, the hill, the fields, the sierra must no longer be hypostatized as merely prior to theory and practice, any more than the Indian is merely prior to the human; they must be experienced as *already* practical *and* theoretical. Geopoetically everything in Peru cultivates or is under cultivation, everything is theoretical and practical, everything is national and patriotic, modern and archaeological; but the common assumption running otherwise, the poet throws his perception into relief, exemplifying capacities where it is usual to assume they cannot exist, while slyly rendering them recognizable: the monolith with its (or his) following, as of retainers; the intellectual field; the sequential rather than hierarchical ordering of religion, field, and ducklings. In the succeeding sequence the happily overdetermined term "rotation" figures the relation of afternoons to mornings on both cosmic and cultivating patterns: the rotation of earth and other orbs in the cosmos, the rotation of crops (*rotación de cosechas*) in the tilled or fallow fields. "Indian after man and before him" is a highly condensed perspective on the history of the Americas, a perspective privileging native peoples. The Indian existed there, in the area that became "Peru" and other geopolitical entities, before "man" came, the poet ironizing the generic male flesh by placing him in the position of a latecomer and a middle term, whose historical existence, no longer that of the conqueror, is assimilated into the term "indio," that already was and is to be.

The poet's orientation toward collective action is even more emphatic in "The Miners Came Out of the Mines," which, like "Telluric and Magnetic," was composed after Vallejo began what were to become three journeys to Russia (1928–31). In the aftermath of the Bolshevik Revolution, Vallejo, like other visiting intellectuals, could believe that the new Soviet state was laying the groundwork for a humane and secular, and conceivably worldwide, polity. Although Vallejo's paean to the rising miners is more thematically revolutionary than "Telluric and Magnetic," both texts subvert the reified distinctions by which modern capital-based economies ensure the coercion and exploitation of underclasses and indigenous populations. These practices being discursive as well as political and economic, Vallejo published a counter-discourse in the form of a novel, *Tungsten* (1931), exposing the manipulations of Peruvian *peones* by U.S.-financed mining operations in the same Peruvian highlands in which he was reared. As a former mining-company employee, and the grandson of a Chimú Indian woman, Vallejo experienced firsthand the brutalization of native peoples. In the novel the process has been so effective that the only hope lies in the fledgling existence of a cell organized for political protest. But the miners in the poem are shown already emerging from bondage to take charge of their collective destiny:

> Los mineros salieron de la mina
> remontando sus ruinas venideras,
> fajaron su salud con estampidos
> y, elaborando su función mental,
> cerraron con sus voces
> el socavón, en forma de síntoma profundo.
>
> (V 268)

> The miners came out of the mine,
> conquering their future ruins,
> enwrapped their health with explosions,
> and, elaborating their mental function,
> with their voices closed
> the excavation, in the form of a profound symptom.

The subtext is a strike in which the miners face ruin, but through solidarity find safety in the very violence (*estampidos*) of their vocation. They do so in large measure by developing the necessary mental functions; but *elaborar* also means to work metal (or some other material), to produce or manufacture, or to prepare or work out (as in the case of a plan), and the senses interweave. Indicating the mental function, far from denying incorporate existence, re-

veals an aspect of it too easily excluded from the realm of labor. The miners
were able to think to begin with and are now elaborating the thinking function by means of oral discourse, for it is their voices, their specific ability to
communicate with one another, that closed the mine. To underline the interconnectedness in flesh of aspects and functions conventionally segregated
and reified, Vallejo writes:

> Craneados de labor,
> y calzados de cuero de vizcacha
> calzados de senderos infinitos,
> y los ojos de físico llorar,
> creadores de la profundidad,
> saben, a cielo intermitente de escalera,
> bajar mirando para arriba,
> saben subir mirando para abajo.
>
> ¡Loor al antiguo juego de su naturaleza,
> a sus insomnes organos, a su saliva rustica!
> ¡Temple, filo y punta, a sus pestañas!
> ¡Crezcan la yerba, el líquen y la rana en sus adverbios!
>
> (V 268)

> Craniumed by labor,
> and shod in vizcacha skin,
> shod in infinite paths,
> and eyes physically weeping,
> creators of profundity,
> they know, by the sky glimpsed from the ladder,
> the stairway, to descend looking up,
> to ascend looking down.
>
> Praise for the ancient play of their nature,
> for their sleepless organs, for their rustic saliva!
> Temper, edge and point, for their eyelashes!
> May the grass, the lichen and the frog grow in their adverbs!

"Craniumed by labor" reworks "elaborating their mental function." In both
phrases labor is seen as enabling, and what it enables is inter alia thinking capacity, that aspect of endowed incorporate being which is the human
counterpart of the intellectuality in the cultivated fields. Showing what labor
does for the cranium shows as it were the anatomical nature of the process,
lest the reader construe the earlier phrasing in a narrowly mentalist way. In
an alienated economic system, as described by Marx, working and thinking
are divorced. Vallejo does not dispute that view, but in his own way endeavors to show, as did Marx, not only that alienation can be overcome, but how
a new order based on the integration of working and thinking might look if it
actually came into being. That such an integration was a credible possibility

is a view Vallejo shares with his contemporary and fellow socialist Antonio Gramsci:

> The problem of creating a new stratum of intellectuals consists therefore in the critical elaboration of the intellectual activity that exists in everyone at a certain degree of development, modifying its relationship with the muscular-nervous effort towards a new equilibrium, and ensuring that the muscular-nervous effort itself, in so far as it is an element of a general practical activity, which is perpetually innovating the physical and social world, becomes the foundation of a new and integral conception of the world.[72]

Basing such conceptualization in muscular-nervous effort is a figuring of flesh, and indeed is very much the same kind of figuring that Vallejo offered above in "craniumed by labor" and "elaborating their mental function." As it happens, "elaborate" is a key term in Gramsci's vocabulary as well.

That new order which is based on integration is glimpsed in "The Miners Came Out of the Mine," when the poem brings together something as immediate and finite as the *vizcacha* skin the miners wear on their feet with the utopian implications of infinite paths. It is only because they are thus equipped that they carry forward their endless quest and only because they have this quest that they are thus equipped. As the skin of an indigenous rodent belongs together with infinite movement, so does an orientation toward, respectively, the "lower" realm of worldly things and the "higher" realm of ideals. The miners know that when they are moving toward the latter they need to bear in mind the former, and vice versa; for if the poet speaks in terms of knowledge, it is a knowledge dialectically conceived—and above all dialectically carried out.

As he had looked back to integrate ancient waters with the hierarchy of tools and the lowing of cows, so the poet reveals the temporal "profundity" of the flesh, which is (organs and saliva being added to craniums) as anatomical as ever, and as natural. That the saliva is rustic moves in the direction of pastoral conventions, which Vallejo is partly assimilating and partly subverting. Pastoral plays with nature, plays with its own nature and with anti-nature, and is always invested with political significance. It is a mode well suited to meta-discourse, as here, where the growth of the vegetable and the animal world is mediated, as Vallejo himself points out, by the workers' *adverbs*, "The part of speech which indicates the mode in which an action is accomplished, for it is in their activity that man and nature are reconciled."[73] It is to further that reconciliation, which I am calling integration, that this call follows immediately, without transition and without the necessity of explanation, a technological troping not at odds with some pastoral texts (one thinks of the armaments in Sidney's *Arcadia*) but relatively rare: the workers' eyelashes, among the most delicate of anatomical features, are to be treated metallically—tempered, provided with edges and sharpened to a point, in the manner of a tool or, in a revolutionary context, a weapon. Just fate for an anatomical feature intimately connected to the eye, previously shown only in tears.

> ¡Son algo portentoso, los mineros
> remontando sus ruinas venideras,
> elaborando su función mental
> y abriendo con sus voces
> el socavón, en forma de síntoma profundo!
>
> (V 269)

> They are something portentous, the miners
> overcoming their future ruins,
> elaborating their mental function,
> and with their voices opening
> the excavation, in the form of profound symptoms!

Here is a worldly thing with a unique resonance that is far more than the sum of its parts. In the collective being that the miners constitute there is something of the phenomenon of the thing, meaning an assembly or judicial gathering, a thing of persons, if you will (to this day *mafiosi* refer to their collective identity as "our thing," *cosa nostra*). In this sociopolitical formation of flesh the portent lies in the very nature of the depicted action, which is collective, momentous, and also dangerous—the action, at the very least, of protesters, and, at the most, of revolutionaries. The poet does not stipulate the class of persons at whom the action aims, assuming that their identity is sufficiently obvious. The combination of the imminent and the indefinite is evocative, in esthetic terms, of the sublime; it is like some vaster version of overhanging threat in "Black Stone Over a White Stone," underlining the fact that a portent signifies not only omen or prodigy but something that could be—for those who, in the present case, would stand in the miners' way—downright calamitous.

The implications of "something portentous" emerge when lines from the opening stanza turn into a refrain—with a crucial variation in tense and vocabulary: "They are something portentous, the miners overcoming their future ruins, elaborating their mental function, and with their voices opening the excavation. . . ." Tense: in the opening stanza, "overcoming" and "elaborating" are participial, giving a sense of ongoing activity, but within the context of the past: "came out," "enwrapped," and "closed" are in the preterite indicative. In the second version, the present takes over, everything is concrete and in process here and now, including the miners' action in shafting the mine; if anything, the present participle heightens the felt actuality of what they are doing.

The anguish of flesh in war inevitably infuses Vallejo's dealing with the Spanish Civil War, which broke out in the summer of 1936; that he died in 1938 on the edge of spring on a Thursday is the more ironic as the final text to be considered here, "Pequeño responso a un héroe de la República" ("Little Prayer-for-the-Dead, for a Hero of the Republic"), is a testimonial to hope and memory in the spirit of spring, and begins indeed with the sign of new life:

> Un libro quedó al borde de su cintura muerta,
> un libro retoñaba de su cadáver muerto.
> Se llevaron al héroe
> y corpórea y aciaga entró su boca en nuestro aliento
>
>   (V 407)

> A book remained at the edge of his dead waist,
> a book was sprouting from his dead cadaver.
> They carried off the hero
> and corporeally and fatefully his mouth entered in our breath

Thus is mortal flesh confirmed in its historicity, for, anonymous as the dead man may be, he has all the identity that is needed: he is a man fallen in the cause of the Spanish Republic, and a hero. He is sanctified as the recipient of a *responso*, a prayer for the dead, here freed from ecclesiastical context but replete with the kind of religious associations on which the poet nonetheless frequently draws. He is sanctified by the existence of a book, the first of the explicitly discursive terms that weave through the text. The preterite tense is another way of historicizing: the hero passed and a book remained, suggestively situated "at the edge," rather than beside or alongside, as though something further were on the verge of taking place. And something indeed does, or was; first the "what" (a book remained), then the "how"—a book was, in the more general sense of *retoñar*, reappearing, or more concretely, and more tellingly, was sprouting. More tellingly because "sprouting" sounds more organic, and fits better with the cadaver, the last recognizable state of flesh-as-organism before decomposition; the book coming into its own comes from this state, which Hermann Broch, with a similar sense of integration, liminality, and regeneration, calls "the very humus of existence growing instinctually in this incessant change, in this constant self-renewing, sprouting and pushing . . . and he, who even while in its midst might watch it, could watch it, must watch it, moved on by the animally-invaded plant-life, became like a plant himself . . . though still remaining human."[74] The difference between two similar senses of integration is also telling, for Broch is discursively mediating the process of Virgil's dying as Virgil experienced it, while Vallejo is depicting death at the edge—in an inchoate state of liminality—as the condition of discursive regeneration. Vallejo, like Broch, works through all the senses. Here he renders flesh both kinetically and tactilely: they carry the hero away and in the process his organ of speech is integrated into the very breath of the survivors, fellow supporters of the Republic, and other readers. A fateful moment of profound continuity is formed as the poet focuses now on one strange statue, now on another, from the deceased individual to those who by breathing him are incorporate with him and with their shared environment: "Todos sudamos . . . / también sudaba de tristeza el muerto" ("we all sweated . . . the dead man was sweating of sadness too").

The association of the book with a specific military engagement in a specific war gives it a concrete historicity:

> Y un libro, en la batalla de Toledo,
> un libro, atrás un libro, arriba un libro,
> retoñaba del cadáver.
>
> (V 407)

> And a book, in the battle of Toledo,
> a book, a book behind, a book above,
> was sprouting from the cadaver.

The book is not "of" or "about" the Battle of Toledo but is said to be "in" it; the book existed before and through and after the named historical event, and in its doing so consists its own historicity. The book survived the battle as it will survive the war because the power of the word is generative and regenerative: discourse grows like something in nature, being in its own way incorporate and vital.

> Poesía del pómulo morado, entre el decirlo
> y el callarlo,
> poesía en la carta moral que acompañara
> a su corazón.
> Quedóse el libro y nada mas, que no hay
> insectos en la tumba,
> y quedó al borde de su manga, el aire remojandose
> y haciéndose gaseoso, infinito.
>
> (V 407)

> Poetry of the purple cheek, between speaking
> and silence,
> poetry in the moral letter that should accompany
> your heart.
> The book remained and nothing else, for there are no
> insects in the tomb,
> and at the edge of his sleeve the air remained, soaking itself
> and becoming gaseous, infinite.

The cheek is deathly purple, and if it is poetic as well, it is because this is one of the important ways, since time immemorial, in which loss engenders and flesh becomes strangely regenerative: "Death," as Wallace Stevens famously says, "is the mother of beauty."[75] Except that here everything is fatefully discursive because on the edge, from the book in relation to the dead hero to the liminality of a poetry suspended between life and death, on the verge of expression or of extinction. That poetry is in a moral letter assumes its consanguinity with the sprouting process and for the first time explicitly situates the martyrdom in the ethical realm; here, however, there are no guarantees — avoiding the preterite employed in the first line of the text and in the line to follow, the poet avers only that the letter *should* accompany his heart.

What is certain is the survival of discourse: besides the book nothing else remained, not even the cadaver; there is moreover the charnel detail, which deviates from the *memento mori* tradition in abstaining from any appeal to exemplarity. The air also remained, providing a crucial transition toward the surprisingly hopeful resolution of the poem. Adumbrated by "our breath," the air, soaking itself in the hero's blood, becomes the most rarefied form of water. A worldly thing suggesting a state of being not the less actual for being liminal, gas is something given off, as we say, like a vapor, passing from one phase in the cosmic economy to another and, in that sense, is a phenomenon seemingly "beyond" all chthonic constraints. The metonymic sequence is all threshold and border crossing, with each moment at the edge of another: the dead man, then at the edge of his flesh the sleeve, then the air at the edge of the sleeve, soaking itself and becoming gas, after which: infinity. It is all in confirmation of the poet's sense of the essential continuity of incorporate being and of the need for integrative vision and solidarity. Only such a vision can credibly unite feet that are shod in *vizcacha* skins walking in infinite paths, and a dead man's flesh, and air becoming infinite too.

PART V

Experiencing

1. Introductory Overview

Part I explored reconstructing, Part II the constitution of the world. Part III explored the nature and processes of discourse and Part IV the realm of incorporate being. Part V now explores "experiencing" in a variety of modes and perspectives.

I begin by pointing out that, in contrast with the "-stance" family of Part II, members of the "ex-" family variously signify "out of," "by way of," or "from." They are active, emergent, instrumental, as illustrated by the word "experience" from the Latin *experientia*, for trial or testing, or as illustrated by "experiment" from the Latin *experimentum*.

With these terminological patterns established, discussion turns to vicissitudes of experience of both historical and methodological interest. Among Renaissance humanists, discourse and experience gradually become separated, a process that makes it difficult later to comprehend that the humanist no less than the merchant is immersed in things of the world. At the same time, the rise of an overly conscious or mentalist view of experience separates theory from practice and reduces action to specular passivity in a manner consistent with presentment's reduction of things to objects for observation and calculation.

Experience has been further distorted by preoccupation with the individual and individualism. The quality of being owned by one individual is not originary, Dewey reminds us, but "additive; it marks the assumption of a new relationship, in consequence of which the house, the common, ordinary house, acquires new properties. . . . Substitute 'experience' for 'house,' and no other word need be changed." Experience is not a static entity but a process, much as occupants of the "house" are processes, interacting variously with things in the environment. A related architectural analogy is offered by John Adams, who advocates that misbehaving youths be confined to a mirrored *boudoir*, there to see for themselves the "deformity" of their "persons." Adams's purpose is to give the person sequestered an experience of, hence an education in, their own individual imperfections, and by implication the imperfections of the collective past.

The most far-reaching efforts at educational development are found, arguably, in Plato, whose dialogic tactics help to prepare the investigation of dialectic and experience in Hegel and Brecht. Plato's dialectic is seen to be radically interruptive. When a speaker performs formulaically, in a way long venerated, and the dialectician forces him to stop and examine abstractly what is being said, continuity of experience is broken. For this and related reasons, Plato pragmatically cautions that dialectic should not be studied too early.

Another vicissitude: Experience is sometimes concealed behind abstraction. Such is the case with Hegel, whose ideas seem to emerge from pure ratiocination. What underlies his *Logic*, however, is the Western cultural experience in all its concreteness. The experiential character of Hegel's thinking is nowhere more apparent, I argue, than in his examination of the way in which, by passing through "nodal points," quantitative increments can turn a thing or a state of affairs into something qualitatively different. Here the story is that when you increase the temperature of water a degree at a time it eventually disappears into steam, whereas by the reverse process water is miraculously transformed into something you can skate on. Hegel then extrapolates from these consequences to the political scene, where small additions to a state of territory or population at first have small effects, but in time alter the very nature of the state. Most if not all of the other abstract propositions in the *Logic* also derive, in my view, from worldly experience and example.

When he remarks that the indigenous populations of the New World are dying out due to "brandy and guns," experience and agency split apart: we are not told who the suppliers were, or why they went to the New World.

We know only that when brandy and guns appear natives become extinct. The European, Hegel adds, "wants . . . to make this Other confronting him his own." Abstractly, this means to "bring to view the genus, law, universal thought, the inner rationality in the particular form of the world." But concretely, it means domination of the "Other" by European colonialism.

In his thinking on experimental theater Brecht makes significant use of Hegel's nodal points: "We made a short film of the performance, concentrating on the principal nodal points of the action and cutting it so as to bring out the gests in a very abbreviated way." This and other experiments with everyday experience lead to the famous alienation effect. To achieve the effect one has only to regard an ordinary incident as illustrative of a general principle, and what is particular and unique in the incident suddenly stands out.

Sharing Dewey's interest in experience in relation to education, Brecht creates a genre, the *Lehrstück*, or "didactic cantata," as a vehicle for experimenting with both. Dispensing with the audience, Brecht's performers act and experience—they do things and at the same time they undergo—for themselves. The problem that arises is the way in which the *Lehrstück* deals with subsumption, Hegel's term for that in dialectic which is negated and at the same time preserved. For, in Brecht's new genre, subsumption entails an almost abject subordination of the individual to authority. In *The Measures Taken*, the erring Young Comrade, brought to account, arrives at knowing consent, *Einverständnis*, over his own elimination. Here I point the sobering fact that Brecht created the *Lehrstück* at a time when Stalinism set guidelines for leftwing political action, and in this respect one may speak of Brecht's theater as a theater of danger.

Elimination as an acceptable price for social "progress" is nowhere more memorably rendered than in the myth of the Roman Lucretia, whose sexual violation and sacrifice enable the founding of the paradigmatic republican state. In the myth and its variants, Lucretia's experience as victim is typically subsumed within a nexus of male interests. Thus the Florentine statesman Salutati stresses the consequences of Lucretia's rape from a political point of view, which is to say from the point of view of the state's male leaders. His only gesture toward Lucretia and her feelings is to have her speculate on the pleasure she may have experienced in being violated. In general Lucretia assumes the role of a *pharmakos*, who removes the taint of corruption by taking her own life, a sacrifice that serves as an enabling moment in the endowing of political liberty, to which the Romans believe themselves to be entitled.

By contrast, that other Florentine statesman, Machiavelli, makes no attempt to experience Lucretia's experience, as it were. Women have "occasioned many divisions" in cities, he complains, pointing out that those who did "the outrage to Lucrece took their position from the Tarquins." But on balance Machiavelli marginalizes the sacrificial female: it was not the rape of Lucretia that drove the tyrant out but his own tyranny.

Chaucer for his part depicts in Lucretia the paradox of innocence-in-experience. Whereas in Shakespeare Lucretia is given full opportunity to express herself, Chaucer's heroine is largely unable to do so. That Chaucer Christianizes Lucretia helps to explain why he makes no mention of the motive of vengeance so central to the pagan narrative. Here he shows his debt to St. Augustine, who argues for the superiority of Christian female martyrs to any of their ostensible pagan counterparts.

In Shakespeare's version of the myth, I note, a certain discrepancy emerges between the expression of the heroine's experience and expression for its own sake. The shedding of Lucrece's emblematic blood serves to suggest that the poet's display of expressive virtuosity has as much to say about chivalric rivalry with Sidney as it does about the heroine's own felt experience.

Lucretia subsequently figures in an experiential mode representing both an age and a genre, respectively—the eighteenth century and the epistolary novel—which offered an arena for exploring intensities, both in themselves and as aspects of contemporary social experience. The authenticity of each correspondent's experience is insisted upon by novelists like Goethe and Richardson and attested to by, for example, the intervention of social authority in the figure of the "editor," whose reliability is an article of faith. In *The Sorrows of Young Werther* the editor takes on the additional task of reflecting upon Werther's socially unacceptable behavior; lest the reader should regard that behavior as exemplary, the author gives a balanced picture of social normality by introducing the complementary authority figures of the father and the judge. In English literature the counterparts of Goethe's hero are Pamela and then Clarissa Harlowe. Looking for prior experiences and attitudes that she can imitate, Pamela finds a notable one in, precisely, Lucretia. Richardson's ultimate Lucretia, however, is Clarissa, who recognizes but has trouble expressing her likeness to that figure. In a crucial scene Clarissa imitates Lucretia by pointing a penknife to her bosom and declaring to Lovelace and his minions that the Law will finally make her safe from every violence. The distance between the experiences and reflections of the two protagonists is here unforgettably enforced.

Clarissa is a great character, one concludes, because she is a great "social individual" (Mead). Richardson has transformed the Lucretia figure from a specular object to someone who expresses her experiences for others to re-experience and reflect upon. Her tragedy is that, although she is prophetic of an imagined new social order, the old order to which she is effectively sacrificed continues to exist very much as it was before she entered the scene.

2. Deriving "Experience"

"Destiny," "constitution," "hypostatize," "substance," "state," and a range of related terms in the "-stance" family express a sense of place or placement, evoking in turn a sense of sufficient standing or staying to inhere in an identity. Members of the "ex-" family, by contrast, take as their point of departure the sense of being out of, by way of, or from. *Ex-* in Latin derives from the Greek syncategorem and prefix *ec-*, as in *ecstasis*, from which we get English "ecstasy" and German *Extase*, as the state or condition of standing outside of oneself, from which Heidegger extrapolates temporality as such: "We therefore call the phenomena of the future, the character of having been, and the Present, the '*ecstases*' of temporality."[1] In spatial terms the Latin prefix indicates what comes out of or issues from, in temporal terms the idea of since or after, and in more general terms a relation or responsibility to origins, as in the Latin *ex officio*, or such rich English terms as "experience," "experiment," and "expression," which together constitute, as the present discussion will endeavor to show, a crucial worldly nexus.

"Experience" derives from the Latin *experientia*, for trial, or learning from experience; trial is equally expressed in *experimentum*, from the same root, the close connection between experience and experiment enjoying thereafter a long life in English usage. If Francis Bacon is remembered for the prestige he gave to that linkage, experience as testing is already the sense employed by Wycliff in 1388. Experience as procedure, operation, or experiment is Chaucer's sense in 1384.

Tracing "expression," we are led back to *exprimo*, for pressing or forcing out (1400), shaping or portraying something in the likeness of something else (1382). Meanwhile Chaucer furnishes representation specifically in words, as in the utterance of feeling or intention (1386), which in Shakespeare becomes a kind of linguistic self-fashioning: "It charges me in manners, the rather to expresse myself" (1602).

A further caveat touches on lexicographical authority, which, as I suggested in Part I, should not go unquestioned, even where the *Oxford English Dictionary* is concerned. Its way of defining "experience," for example, tilts too far toward the specular and the passive: "The actual observation of facts or events, considered as a source of knowledge." But this is too detached to express the felt life in Goldsmith's "Just experience tells . . . That those that think must govern those that toil" (1764); for the overtones of social hierarchy, division of labor, and governance make it clear that more is involved than mere mentation. And surely when we hear a practiced barrister state that "daily experience informs us of the consequences" (1862), we have a similar feeling of lived process.

An analogous overrating of mentation and passivity appears in "the fact of being consciously the subject of a state or condition, or of being consciously affected by an event" (1382), which admittedly sorts well enough with the self-reflexiveness we encounter in Laurence Sterne's Yorick; but to assume with *OED* that this experience is what people were getting at in the fourteenth century is anachronistic at best. It is surely not what Chaucer is getting at when the Wyf of Bath asserts that experience "were ynough for me / To speke of wo that is in mariage."

By this overrating of the mental, the specular, and the passive, ideas are torn from their concrete "contexture," which is at once the action of weaving together (1649), and more specifically "the weaving together of words, sentences, etc. in connected composition" (1603).

A similar sundering occurs when Cosimo de' Medici partitions off from the overall corpus of humanist and mercantile discourse certain writings of use to the state. What he thereby interrupts is a flow of "composite culture" constituted by humanist writing devoted to the recension and transmission of texts honored for their general cultural worth, and by mercantile writing keyed to the experience of the marketplace and to the preservation of family history. As Stephanie Jed notes, these discursive practices are composite by virtue of overlapping ideals and acts, as illustrated by the parallel between humanist strategies for idealizing received narratives, such as the sacrifice of Lucretia for republican liberty, and merchant strategies for idealizing commerce as directly expressive of such liberty:

> This severing of the ties between humanistic literature and the writing of merchants contributes to our own conceptual distinction between "thinkers" and "producers." Once "writing" comes to refer only to the kind of text represented in the humanistic library, we not only stop regarding the merchants as writers, but we stop looking, as well, for links between the reproduction of narratives such as the rape of Lucretia and mercantile thought. This thought, characterized by its goal of producing, by means of "*ragione* accompanied by force," present "realities" of property, liberty, and honor, easily disappears from the meaning of the humanistic text.[2]

The thought in question needs to be seen not as abstract mentation but for the role it plays in the concrete activity by means of which the merchant writer, alongside his humanist counterpart, comes to enjoy security and esteem.

But, as is often the case when we try our hand at reconstructing experience, we risk replacing one lopsidedness with another. In the present instance, this could occur if, having recovered something of the contextures in which merchant and humanist writing coexisted and complemented one another, we were to stop at the rehabilitation of the former as a respectable analogue of the latter. For that would leave out of account the fact that the humanist is in his way just as immersed in worldly things as the merchant. The term *umanista* applies to the workaday practices of scholarship and not to the sphere of sometimes rarefied reflection with which that discourse has come to be associated. We are witnessing an irony wherein the balance beam of reinterpretation "lifts" the mercantile writer toward the idealist plane of humanism while at the same time "lowering" the humanist to the more "mundane" level of the everyday world of work and want. In the process experience as activity in the world fades into the specular passivity of mere consciousness. To approach this issue in another way: If consciousness really is the secret to understanding experience, it is hard to explain why "experience" flourished for so many generations before anyone found it necessary or desirable to invent the "consciousness family" of terms, which is almost entirely a construction of the seventeenth century, and which would have seemed a strange business indeed (as suggested above) to the Wyf of Bath.

The mentalizing of experience reduces particular real actions and states of being to occasions for observation or contemplation, illustrating the process of presentment described above in Part III. The notion of separate spheres of meaning separately expressed exposes a worldview in which earlier, more practically oriented states "progress" through linear time into "higher states" in the manner of Darwinian species. Such a template reproduces as linguistic history the supposed separation of lower from higher, of active from passive, of mental from physical, of ideal from actual. To put all this into narrative terms one has only to see the second member of each pair as transcending the first. With a change in emphasis, one could say that earlier linguistic forms have a way of becoming obsolete, a proof of which is that terms so classified have ceased to occur in certain established locutions — for instance, "to make experience of." This does not alter the fact that subsequent usage may keep on doing the work supposedly superseded. A John Dewey can then try reconstructing what vanished into the void separating, for example, the worldly activity of "the action of putting to the test" from the subjectivity and passivity of "the fact of being conscious of a state or condition, or of being consciously affected by an event."

But it doesn't take a Dewey to see that even within the latter category the sense of experience as a kind of experimentation remains active. Thus Hawthorne speaks of "a man of science who . . . had made experience of a spiritual affinity more attractive than any chemical one" (1846). Here for anyone to see is the active process of trying — not a mere *state of being affected* but the *act of affecting*. That the actor is a scientist underscores the experimental character of what he does, indicating the degree to which, given the science analogy, what he does is equally *effective*, a consideration underscored, for its part, by the predicate "make." But construed as sense four, which emphasizes consciousness, the experiment is polarized into the event and its effect — which effect is nothing more than the passive pole in which the event is registered. To construe in this way is to repeat the error that occurs when "the popular mind" separates the lightning from its flash, as though the lightning were a discrete doer "behind" the doing: "But there is no such substratum," says Nietzsche, "there is no 'being' behind doing, effecting, becoming; 'the doer' is merely a fiction added to the deed — the deed is everything."[3]

The dualist imperative is not satisfied, in other words, with positing a separative sequence, a before and an after matching up, respectively, with cause and effect; it must posit all relations of two as vertical values, and it must do so in line with paradigms of dualist dominance of the type that the pragmatist tradition has contested and endeavored to replace. Dewey, concerned to uphold the integrity of human experience, disputes the received conception of human activity as something separable into oppositions such as theory versus experience or practice, or body versus mind:

> In changed form, we still retain the notion of a division of activity into two kinds having very different worths. . . . Instead of being extended to cover all forms of action by means of which all the values of life are extended and rendered more secure, including the diffusion of the fine arts and the cultivation of taste, the process of education and all activities which are concerned with rendering human relationships more significant and worthy, the meaning of "practical" is limited to matters of ease, comfort, riches, bodily security and police order, possibly health, etc. (*LW* 4:224–25)

Such dis-integration could never have become second nature were it not for the *cordon sanitaire* between theory and experience.

> The problem of the relation of theory and practice is not a problem of theory alone; it is that, but it is also the most practical problem of life. For it is the question of how intelligence may inform action, and how action may bear the fruit of increased insight into meaning: a clear view of the values that are worth while and of the means by which they are to be made secure in experienced objects. (*LW* 4:224–25)

If the integrity of experience is endangered by dualistic separation and polarization, as it is by the correlative overrating of consciousness as the "higher" of a "lower," it is not less threatened by the individualist imperative, which, in keeping with the overrating of consciousness, overrates the possessiveness enjoyed by the so-called private self. In this manner the theme of possessive individualism comes again into the foreground. This theme is closely connected to Dewey's exploration of nature, mind, and subject in *Ex-*

perience and Nature, where his use of the trope that constitutes the section heading that follows provides a link to the present discussion.

3. The Architecture of Experience

Dewey takes as his point of departure the practical circumstance in which mention of experience prompts the question of whose experience is at issue. Such a question misleadingly presupposes that personal possession is the decisive consideration: "Its implication is that experience by its very nature is owned by some one; and that the ownership is such in kind that everything about experience is affected by a private and exclusive quality" (*LW* 4:178–79). As in the conceptual world of possessive individualism, ownership is the constitutive center around which other factors and interests must gravitate, whereas by almost any other reading such ownership is but one consideration among many.

So far in this discussion a misleading interpretation of experience has been traced to unwarranted separation. But not every separation is unwarranted; without some separating it is impossible to make distinctions or discriminations. Thus we can see that the notion of experience as something possessed fails from insufficient discrimination. It fails in particular to recognize that, if the act or state of possession could not be distinguished from what is possessed, there would be no point in the idea of possession. The condition of being owned by one individual "is not an all-absorbing maw in which independent properties and relations disappear to be digested into egohood. It is additive; it marks the assumption of a new relationship, in consequence of which the house, the common, ordinary, house, acquires new properties" (*LW* 1:179).

The crucial move that Dewey is making here recalls the architectural tropes through which Henry James inquires into the types of experience made possible by literary art, the most familiar of his tropes being the "house of fiction." An extended conceit in the manner of the English Metaphysical poets, the house of fiction has many windows, "mere holes in a dead wall, disconnected," at each one of which "stands a figure with a pair of eyes, or at least with a field glass."[4] Since there is in principle no limit to the number of these figures, the trope expresses a plurality of perspectives. Like the residence at Bly in *The Turn of the Screw,* this house plays the same basic role as the phenomenon James elsewhere calls element, medium, or atmosphere. Such is a more concentrated trope bearing explicitly on the question of experience: "Experience is never limited, and it is never complete; it is an immense sensibility, a kind of huge spider web of the finest silken threads suspended in the chamber of consciousness, and catching every airborne particle in its tissue.

It is the very atmosphere of the mind; and when the mind is imaginative . . . it takes to itself the faintest hint of life, it converts the very pulses of the air into revelations."[5] If this seems a more fitting tropological architecture, it is because it does more justice to sensibility, which is connected through percipience to any and every potential experience within its ken.

Meanwhile Dewey's house, "the common, ordinary, house," emerges specifically as the house of experience. To repeat an important proposition:

> Substitute "experience" for "house," and no other word need be changed. Experience when it happens has the same dependence upon objective natural events, physical and social, as has the occurrence of a house. It has its own objective and definitive traits; these can be described without reference to a self, precisely as a house is of brick, has eight rooms, etc., irrespective of whom it belongs to. (*LW* 1:179)

Like Whitehead, Dewey takes for granted that the conception of a house, or of any other entity, is as much a matter of process as experience itself. A house as an environment is, as I suggested above, a scene of interrelating things, an occurrence even as its occupants are occurrences. Although such a relation could be called symbiotic, it might better be called interconnecting, which is the same quality of process Dewey is getting at in the proposition to which we have been returning, that "the things with which a man *varies* are his genuine environment" (*MW* 9:15).

The self for its part is largely left to take care of itself, a circumstance to which readers brought up on individualist assumptions will understandably object. Others, myself included, will see in Dewey's downplaying of such assumptions a tolerable overcompensation for the consequences of separating the individual as self, mind, or soul from that enabling endowment of environment which is their entitlement. Dewey, possibly underrating differences between epochs but making nevertheless a crucial point, traces the isolation of the individual to a dilemma arising from the preeminence of natural over positive law in medieval recensions of classical thought. Historically, as interest moved gradually away from divine and toward human concerns, thinkers began to question what might be called their institutional environment. The dilemma was that this environment was so grounded in the received theological, political, and cultural order, as epitomized in the Church and theological discourse, that "it was not possible to put institutions as such in contrast to nature, but by accepted theory existing institutions were in the main expressions of the law of nature." The solution to this dilemma

> was to place the mind of the individual as such in contrast to both nature and institutions. This historic fact, reinforced with the conspicuous assertion of medievalism that the individual soul is the ultimate end and ultimate sub-

ject of salvation or damnation, affords, it seems to me, the background and source of the isolation of the ego, the thinking self, in all philosophy influenced by either the new science or Protestantism. (*LW* 1:173)

All the same, Dewey acknowledges that the individual as private owner of property has a counterpart in the experiencing self. Far from being a static center or immutable substrate, the self is an active, organizing orientation toward a complex of environing occurrences—taking the latter term in the broad sense already discussed. "Among and within these occurrences, not outside of them nor underlying them, are those events which are denominated selves." And as events, selves are susceptible of description "just as are sticks, stones, and stars" (*LW* 1:179) or any other worldly things.

Recognizing the self as one node of experience in a world constituted of many other nodes widens our sense of human needs and desires, motives and acts. It becomes less important to claim the individual self as originary, for example, than to appreciate the experiential "productivity" flowing from the interanimation of self and environment. For, if a statement of desire is a projection from self, it is also an articulation of a possibility inhering in the environment, an occurrence seeking a correlative occurrence.

But this is still to favor what Dewey calls "authorship," or the notion that the origin of an expressed thought is uniquely in its thinker. Such a notion confers on self an originary capacity somehow prior to worldly being as environment, whereas the self and the environment are more accurately regarded, in my view, as mutually responsible because mutually operative. Dewey goes further, and possibly too far, in arguing that the expression of a thought, belief, or desire "signifies that the self as a centered organization of energies identifies itself (in the sense of accepting their consequences) with a belief or sentiment of independent and external origination" (*LW* 1:180). Here the problem is a rare lapse into an exclusionary mode of interpretation tending to legitimate one explanation to the disadvantage of another: origins are either in the self or, as here, in some "independent and external" realm. I have been arguing, on the contrary, for a both/and rather than an either/or explanation, such that "I desire" (for example) is a convergence of expression with the existence of this or that thing in the environment.

In any event, Dewey's case against authorship is perhaps less significant than his case for the alternative, which is "liability." In contrast with authorship, which looks to what was, liability looks to what can or will be. Where authorship finds a self operating *ab ovo*, liability finds a future participant in a covenant. In such a conception the "I" that experiences something looks less like a Hobbesian or Lockean ego than a Shaftesburyean seat of sociability or a Humean locus of "public affection": "To say '*I* think, hope and love' is to say in effect that genesis is not the last word; instead of throwing the blame or the credit for the belief, affection and expectation upon nature, one's family, church, or state, one declares one's self to be henceforth a partner. An adoptive act is proclaimed in virtue of which one claims the benefit of future goods and admits liability for future ills flowing from the affair in question" (*LW* 1:180).

When an "I" expresses in this way it functions, as George Herbert Mead would say, as a *social* individual. The separated, solitary "I" is either a deviation, bespeaking some impairment or pathology, as in the temperamental makeup once called melancholic; or such an "I" is a philosophical construct, a device for psychology, a legal fiction. The person who experiences anything, and who in any way expresses what was experienced, is always concretely situated, as Sartre taught us to recognize, and a situation is a social nexus, which is to say a political, economic, and cultural nexus as well. So much is this the case that "social individual" ought to be a pleonasm.

What is expressed as the experiences named thinking, believing, or desiring is a relation to that same nexus, for which the term "environment" is being used synonymously in this discussion. For, as Dewey observes,

> the whole history of science, art and morals proves that the mind that appears *in* individuals is not as such individual mind. The former is in itself a system of belief, recognitions, and ignorances, or acceptances and rejections, of expectancies and appraisals of meanings which have been instituted under the influence of custom and tradition. (*LW* 1:170)

The notion of a private language has been dismantled by Wittgenstein, who offers in its stead a language game requiring interaction in a context of socially agreed-on rules. This does not of course dismantle the notion of private experience; but such experience is "unworldly" insofar as it does not issue in expression or in some other mode of action. Both thinking and desiring, says Dewey, "are 'overt' behavior of a communicated and public form in process of construction" (*LW* 1:171). The quality of being private and incommunicable might better be termed *temporarily* private and *not yet* communicated. Private experience is a preparatory stage that takes on worldly significance only when it reaches a stage of expression or some other mode of action. Dewey protests that "it is absurd to call a recognition or a conception subjective or mental because it takes place through a physically or socially numerically distinct existence; by this logic, a house disappears from the spatial and material world when it becomes *my* house; even a physical movement would then be subjective when referred to particles" (*LW* 1:171).

The point seems to be something like this. In the sharable world the house that I experience as mine would still be a house even if it should come about that somehow it was not mine. Conceiving or recognizing the house connects the numerically distinct individual, the putative thinking subject or "I," with the thing thought. Because it really *is* the worldly thing called a house, the house does not disappear in the relation; it is an inhabitant of an environment of which the individual who conceives or owns it is but another inhabitant. The "individual mind," sequestered from its own experience, is a chimera because it is a recognizing or conceiving process without anything recognized or conceived, hence without concrete relation to the very environment it inhabits.

An earlier architectural analogy, drawn by John Adams in 1787, turns to ancient Greek history to edify the realm of contemporary experience:

> The history of Greece should be to our countrymen what is called in many families on the continent a *boudoir*, an octagonal apartment in a house, with a full-length mirror on every side, and another in the ceiling. The use of it is, when any of the young ladies, or young gentlemen if you will, are a little out of humor, they may retire to a place where, in whatever direction they turn their eyes, they see their own faces and figures multiplied without end. By thus beholding their own beautiful persons, and seeing, at the same time, the deformity brought upon them by their anger, they may recover their tempers and their charms together.[6]

One of Adams's main points is that his countrymen should "study the history of ancient Greece in order to amend their political behavior."[7] But his architectural trope spreads out in so many directions relevant to the present discussion that it calls for a more thorough reading.

In requiring young ladies or gentlemen to withdraw from company, Adams contributes to the large literature of confinement, separation, and sequestration explored by Michel Foucault.[8] The particular retirement envisioned by Adams does not, however, entail punishment so much as a benign confinement for the reform of social behavior. Hoping for the type of improvement we think of as educational, it takes its place among "fabrications in narrative of the power of confinement to reshape personality."[9] In the narrative of Clarissa's confinement, to which I will turn below, it is almost everyone *but* the person confined who needs improvement. (To the family, *boudoir* would reveal its root in the French *bouder*, to pout, so that this type of apartment would be a "pouting place.")

Exploring passional experience, Hume employs much the same nexus when he posits that beauty and deformity are both closely related to one's ideas about one's self, the former being "an object of pride," the latter of "humility."[10] By the fact that a pillar must be narrower at the top than at the base a sense of security is engendered, hence a sense of pleasure, "whereas the contrary form gives us the apprehension of danger, which is uneasy. From innumerable instances of this kind . . . we may conclude, that beauty is nothing but a form, which produces pleasure, as deformity is a structure of parts, which conveys pain." Although the latter statement may seem to imply an antinomy between "form" and "structure of parts," Hume's wording elsewhere in the passage suggests that this is not the case. For beauty is said to be "such an order and construction of parts, as either by the *primary constitution* of our nature, by *custom*, or by *caprice*, is fitted to give a pleasure and satisfaction to the soul." Parts, then, are a given; what is decisive is their ordering and construction.

The same reasoning operates in Adams, as we can see from the concluding statement of the passage quoted above. The assumption behind the appeal to historical experience is the equivalence between past deficiencies and the present deformity in the otherwise beautiful young ladies and gentlemen:

> A few short sketches of the ancient republics will serve to show, not only that the orders we defend were common to all of them; but that the prosperity and duration of each was in proportion to the care taken to balance them; and that they all were indebted, for their frequent seditions, the rise and progress of corruption, and their decline and fall, to the imperfection of their orders, and their defects in the balance.[11]

Orders as modes of political organization require a proper balance among the powers they represent, as Adams, following the Polybian argument for mixed government, continues to insist. When the proper balance is not provided, experience teaches that the orders become little better than parts of an unsteady whole, like the factions and parties he speaks against in other passages; a polity so sundered disintegrates into such further illustrations of imbalance as sedition and corruption.

The architectural example adopted by Adams has a distinctly specular orientation, even an element of theatricality, as the persons to be reformed watch the impressions they make on that audience which is themselves: experience as a controlled experiment with expression. In the preceding paragraph, Adams indeed refers to Greece as Socrates' "principal theatre,"[12] indicating that the latter is a general scene of public action, and remembering that Socrates expresses his views in dialogues with dramatic overtones. Hume, of course, speaks of the mind itself as a theater of sorts, but one in which perceptions appear briefly before gliding out of sight, leaving the knower with no distinct idea of the place where the scenes transpired or the stuff of which they were constituted.

Adams, less concerned with epistemology, takes a more sanguine view. His tropological staging is supposed sufficient to induce in those who are in seclusion a measured self-awareness captured by the sense of "conscious" found in Locke, Defoe, and Edmund Burke: "having the witness of one's own judgment of feeling" (1620). The distortions in the *boudoir* are not in the mirrors but in the mirrored persons, who, through the reflections they see, recognize their deformities in the same way that the student of Greek historical experience understands the deformities in the orders or balances in the polities of ancient Greece.

Underlying Adams's re-collective model are certain assumptions regarding experience and education. One assumption is that experience is the best teacher, and another is that the focus of education is the youth as future republican citizen. That Adams first associates the *boudoir* with young ladies suggests that his stance is implicitly patriarchal: owners of houses boasting of *boudoirs* were very likely at the time to be both men and fathers, and it is the authority of these that typically sets the terms of educative confinement. But the inclusion of young gentlemen is more than an afterthought: writing in his diary a year before the *Defence* was published, Adams describes "what he calls his boudoir — a little room between his library and drawing-room," while Cowper, one year before that, applies the same term to the "nook" in which he composes. It thus appears that location and use may have been more important issues than the gender of the persons being enlightened. It is also assumed that the experiential development enabled by this architectural arrangement is fairly class-specific. As a matter of statistical proportion in an entire population, "many families" would more accurately read "few families." The original statement is not, for all that, inaccurate, given the framework of a hierarchical society in which the study of ancient history is a privileged wherewithal on which individuals of a certain station are uniquely entitled to draw.

In antiquity itself we encounter some of the most far-reaching explorations of education as experiential development. Of particular interest is the dialectical model of experience envisioned by Plato.

4. Experience, Story, Dialogue, and Dialectic

Prior to Plato, use of dialectic might mean nothing more than getting a speaker to repeat himself so as to elucidate his meaning. Eric A. Havelock explains the decisive implications of the process when the discourse in question involves matters of cultural import conveyed through traditional oral expression. The challenge comes as a shock to the speaker; it does not solicit rhythmic recollection of traditional matter but requires some new, nontraditional formulation, analytical and summative, on the order of the prose paraphrase. "As the question was asked, and the alternative prosaic formula was attempted, the imaginations of speaker and teacher were offended, and the dream so to speak was disrupted, and some unpleasant effect of calculative reflection was substituted. In short, the dialectic . . . was a weapon for arousing the consciousness from its dream language and stimulating it to think abstractly." [13]

"The best way to obtain a confession of the truth," Socrates will wryly propose, "may be to put the statement itself to a mild degree of torture" (*Soph.* 237b). Whether the overtone of cruelty could be heard in earlier dialectic is an open question. But the agonistic tendency is easily discerned: interrogation of the initial utterance, breaking the rhythm of customary discourse, forces the speaker not to repeat the utterance but to reformulate it. The shift is profound. To accept the imperative of reformulation, to submit to the mild torture that will replace the initial utterance with a discursive "other" called "truth" rather than "tradition," is to infer that the initial saying was somehow deficient; that the animating collective experience may have been somehow deficient as well.

In a single stroke two things happen. First, the utterance, no longer a matter of discursive "second nature," calls into question the role and the competence of the speaker. Second, in the same process, the moment the speaker acquiesces to the challenge put to him, the discursive tradition itself comes into question together with the experiential legacy the tradition embodies. Notwithstanding the dialogical nature of Socratic dialectic, Plato has recourse to narrative when an occasion offers—as when Protagoras asks whether he should express himself in that mode, and on being told that he can do as he pleases, decides that it will indeed be pleasant to tell a story. Story draws power from experience. Everyone wants to hear what others have done or felt or been, and to be counseled and informed by the storyteller, who relates past experience to the present and may even suggest or imply what future experience might be. Memory, news that stays news, is prior to, more powerful than, a cognition that is merely retrospective. We believe "once upon a time," and even "it was a dark and stormy night," because our experience of such discourse endows a memory that belongs to us and to which we belong. Only later, and less powerfully, does "knowing" believe otherwise. The primordial power of narrative is in its being taken at a "face value" to which one commits oneself, not in subjection but voluntarily. Narrative creates from the same shared stock of worldly experience new worldly experience. Such novelty is the essence of creativity as a singular moment wherein, in Whitehead's words, "the various special ways in which various sorts of entities are 'together' in one actual occasion." [14] Creativity as story as a unique instance of experiential integration is described by Whitehead:

> There is togetherness of the component elements in individual experience. This "togetherness" has that special peculiar meaning of "togetherness in experience." It is a togetherness of its own kind, explicable by reference to nothing else. For the purpose of this discussion it is indifferent whether we

speak of a "stream" of experience, or of an "occasion" of experience. With the former alternative there is togetherness in the stream, and with the latter alternative there is togetherness in the occasion. In either case, there is the unique "experiential togetherness." [15]

In our text from Plato, to the discussion of which we may now return, the author posits an essence or principle to be unfolded—in this case, the principle that civic virtue is equally distributed; from this synchronic state of affairs he derives a conclusion to be arrived at diachronically through narrated incidents or stages. If the process seems tautological, it is, for the conclusion is the premise: the story of Hermes' equal distribution of the civic virtues is narrated into the principle of such equalization because that is what the stability of the state requires.

If it is the unique experiential power of the story that carries the auditors through this transition, a good part of that power flows from the element of repetition seen as "archaic," as a kind of predialectical togetherness incorporating the speaker and the listeners. For, when Protagoras comes to the first moment of narrative crisis, he does not merely describe what happened, he describes it twice. The following may suffice to indicate the effect:

> Prometheus . . . stole from Hephaestus and Athena the gift of skill in the arts, together with fire. . . . In this way man acquired sufficient resources to keep himself alive, but had no political wisdom. This was in the keeping of Zeus, and Prometheus no longer had the right of entry to the citadel where Zeus dwelt. . . . But into the dwelling shared by Athena and Hephaestus . . . he penetrated by stealth, and carrying off Hephaestus' art of working with fire, and the art of Athena as well, he gave them to man. Through this gift man had the means of life. (*Prot.* 321de)

While it is true that Protagoras makes his living by giving instruction through reading and writing as well as through speaking, it is also true that speaking remains a crucial mode of performance, that speaking is intimately associated with storytelling, and that storytelling derives much of its mnemonic power through the experiences of rhetorical and rhythmic reinforcement. Hence the repetition of Promethean thefts, the second description varying just enough to provide incremental interest. As a charismatic speaker and educator, the storyteller mediates cultural memory for the audience—a dangerous game, in Plato's eyes, in that "any poetised statement must be designed and recited in such a way as to make it a kind of drama within the soul both of the reciter and hence also of the audience. This kind of drama, this way of reliving experience in memory instead of analysing it, is for him 'the enemy.'" [16]

In a lively exchange Socrates problematizes the relativism of Protagoras, who, in saying that wisdom can be taught just as well as anything else, re-

duces that unique faculty to a sameness with other phenomena. Socrates'
provocation is in line with experiential dialectic as conceived in the *Republic*: "The experiences that do not provoke thought are those that do not at
the same time issue in a contradictory perception. Those that do have that
effect I set down as provocatives, when the perception no more manifests one
thing than its contrary, alike whether its impact comes from nearby or afar"
(*Rep.* VII.523bc). Notwithstanding that Hegel credits Aristotle with pointing
the way toward the phenomenology of the spirit, the piling up of negatives in
the first sentence is already suggestive of the Hegelian method, and even more
so is the valorization of the aporia, and the fall into confusion from which
the soul must fight its way up to transcendence. Before the discussion closes,
Plato shows his pragmatic bent by connecting dialectical education with the
level of experience of the learners themselves. Those who tackle dialectic too
early, taking it for a mere game, fall into disputing for the sake of disputing,
the worst consequence of which is that they come to doubt what they formerly held to be valid and true. In so reasoning, Plato opens the way for what
will become experiential methods of education like those of Vico, Friedrich
Froebel, and Dewey, who ask not only what shall be taught, but specifically
how and when. At the same time he provides, with other exemplars of early
dialectic, points of departure for Hegel's intriguing inquiries into experience.

5. Dialectical Experience

In Hegel the worldly things we experience seem nearer to Aristotelian *con-
creta* than to the constructions of an apperceiving mind that we find in Kant.[17]
Early dialectic helped Hegel find the route to follow in order to describe the
self-realization of Absolute Spirit. Moreover, his roots can be traced in part
to Eliatic argumentation and to the Socratic dialogues, which exploited the
phenomenon of contradiction wherever they could. Hegel noted in particular
the fact that Socrates' interlocutors subjected themselves to such "immanent"
development, which their compliant attitudes assisted on its way. This theme
of subjection will be taken up again in connection with dialectical experience
in Bertolt Brecht.

To say that these ancient texts dealt more effectively with contradictions
than did Kant is not to imply that Kant ignored them: he saw them clearly
in the operations of human understanding. Hegel criticizes him rather for
recoiling from the recognition that contradiction is active in worldly things
themselves, and not merely in our passive cognition of that world. Kant believes in worldly experience, but as it were from a distance, while Hegel believes that worldly experience is contradictory because it is experience of a
contradictory world.

Dialectic in Hegel is so much the story of experience that, even when he abstracts his discourse into categorical segments, they frequently have explicit stories to tell about concrete persons and what they have done or undergone. This centrality of experience might have been more evident if Hegel had left the title of the original 1807 edition as he first had it: *Science of the Experience of Consciousness*. Replacing this with *Phenomenology of Spirit* assimilates the central role of experience into a phrase that may have appealed to him as sounding more scientific and transcendental. Hegel was nothing if not a rhetorician; and as a Swabian, he was enough of a discursive practical joker to take an occasional lead from the thief of Poe's purloined letter, who concealed it by placing it in view but sufficiently disguised to keep it from the notice of any but initiated investigators.

In the original introduction Hegel tells a relatively straightforward story, in which, at a critical juncture, natural consciousness emerges "as the path of the soul which is making its way through the sequence of its own transformation as through way stations prescribed to it by its very nature, that it may, by purifying itself, lift itself to the level of Spirit and again attain cognizance of what it is in itself through the completed experience of its own self." [18]

In what follows I will briefly discuss passages from other of Hegel's crucial "story" texts, the *Logic* and the *Philosophy of Mind*, with a view to elucidating the experiential basis of Hegelian dialectic. [19]

In the *Logic* Hegel suggests that essence is a kind of otherness throwing light on being that is reciprocal to it: "firstly, Essence, as simple self-relation, is Being, and secondly as regards its one-sided characteristic of immediacy, Being is deposed to a mere negative, to a seeming or reflected light. . . . That reflection, or light thrown into itself, constitutes the distinction between Essence and immediate Being." (*HL* 162). More plainly, whenever we think or reflect, we perform something like a mirroring in which experience is an immediate fact while being also "transmitted . . . or mediated" (*HL* 162). This latter process Hegel implies is in some sort epiphenomenal; it follows from and after what is immediately given. We have the mirror surface as such, which is the immediate fact, then the reflection that derives from it when illuminated. What we have in a discursive, temporal, fully experiential sense, then, is a very short, very fast story. Further on, Hegel brings out the necessary pastness in his concept of essence, noting that in German the verb to be, *sein*, expresses in its past tense

the term for Essence (*Wesen*): we designate past being as *gewesen*. This anomaly of language implies to some extent a correct perception of the relation between Being and Essence. Essence we may certainly regard as past Being, remembering however meanwhile that the past is not utterly denied, but only laid aside and thus at the same time preserved. Thus, to say, Caesar *was* in Gaul, only denies the immediacy of the event, but not his sojourn in Gaul altogether. That sojourn is just what forms the import of the proposition, in which however it is represented as over and gone. (*HL* 163)

Again and again, as here, it is the recourse to everyday life that brings the main exposition down to earth, even authoring a kind of condensed *Bildungsroman* wherein a youth undergoes the process of social enabling we call education:

> The reason, which at first exists in the child only as inner possibility, is actualized through education: and conversely, the child by these means becomes conscious that the goodness, religion, and science which he had at first looked upon as outward authority, are his own and inward nature. As with the child so it is in this matter with the adult, when, in opposition to his true destiny, his intellect and will remain in the bondage of the natural man. Thus, the criminal sees the punishment to which he has to submit as an act of violence from without: whereas in fact the penalty is only the manifestation of his own criminal will. (*HL* 198–99)

In a sense Hegel is writing of his own experience in reflecting, during his early years as a student of theology, on the interdependence of crime and punishment; to that extent the story of *Bildung* that he tells here is a matter of concrete remembered experience. He turns more explicitly to history when he goes on to distinguish between what he calls substantial and formal interests. The former include "patriotism, justice, religious truth, and the like," the latter "vanity, ambition, avarice, and the like." Hegel faults the practice of those historiographers who belittle public heroes by charging that their outward and inward motives differ, their "outer" patriotism masking "inner" vanity, and so on. Hegel insists that on the contrary inward and outer motivation possess "the same content": if the hero behaves patriotically he does so from patriotic motives.

The story of judgment, a mode of what he calls "the notion," is equally the story of the term itself and the story of its instantiation in nature. Judgment is "an infinite form of boundless activity, as it were the *punctum saliens* of all vitality, and thereby self-differentiating" (*HL* 232). This is apparently the same phenomenon touched on elsewhere as the kind of bursting-forth we experience in *phusis*, the type of being that comes into its own without the mediation of another type of being. What Hegel proceeds to offer near the end of the discussion appears to confirm this conjecture:

> the germ of a plant contains its particulars, such as root, branches, leaves, etc.: but these details are at first present only potentially, and are not realized till the germ uncloses. This unclosing is, as it were, the judgment of the plant. The illustration may also serve to show how neither the notion nor the judg-

ment are merely found in our head, or merely framed by it. The notion is the very heart of things, and makes them what they are. (*HL* 232)

In "Draft for a Critique of Historical Reason," Dilthey takes his departure from the physiology of the concrete experience which is *Erlebnis*. Operating in a context not connected explicitly with Hegel, but discussing the same subject, judgment, Dilthey observes:

> Experience is followed by judgments about what has been experienced in which this becomes objectified. It is hardly necessary to describe how our knowledge of every mental fact derives entirely from experience. We cannot recognize in another person a feeling we have not experienced. But for the development of the human studies it is decisive that we attribute general predicates, derived from experience and proving the point of departure for the categories of the human studies, to the subject who contains the possibilities of experience in the confines of his body.[20]

Returning to the *Logic*, we find Hegel undertaking nothing less than a condensed narrative of Western culture. Here as before the narrative in the appendix unfolds from the preceding general postulates. But now we see what one otherwise only surmises: that in so doing Hegel is narrating experiences that precede the same exposition. The story concerns the conception of the universal, "a thought which, as we know, cost thousands of years to make it enter into the consciousness of men" (*HL* 227). The Greeks, who appear early in the story, drew a distinction of species between themselves and others, who could only be barbarians. They failed, in other words, to recognize the concept of human universality that had to wait until the chapter written by the Christians. It is from the latter that we learn how a narrative-within-a-narrative of Western culture — the story of slavery — came to a happy ending: "the real ground why there are no more slaves in Christian Europe is only to be found in the very principle of Christianity itself, the religion of absolute freedom. Only in Christendom is man respected as man, in his infinitude and universality" (*HL* 227). How this relates to the experience of European colonization will be considered below.

One of the more dramatic junctures in Hegel's narrative dialectic is a sequence of stories he tells about, *inter alia*, water, wheat, and the nation-state. In the first narrative, raising the temperature of water produces a radical transformation typical of those that occur in the narratives that follow: the water wonderfully turns to steam. By contrast, as the temperature is reduced by quantitative increments, the same water turns to ice, whereupon that which one could swim in is, as it were, revolutionized into something to skate on. Hegel also wonders at the dramatic change that comes about when a single grain of wheat gets enough company to become a very different kind of thing: "a point is finally reached where a single additional grain makes a heap of wheat," in the same way that pulling one hair at a time from a horse's tail eventually results in a bald tail. When a nation-state with a given number of citizens and a given territory starts adding citizens and territory, the changes are at first of little moment. But keep on adding and "we finally get to a point where, apart from all other circumstances, this quantitative alteration alone necessarily draws with it an alteration in the quality of the constitution." When he goes on to say that "the constitution of the Roman republics was unsuitable when transferred to the small imperial towns of Germany" (*HL* 159), he gives a glimpse of the sorts of concrete historical experiences that can be seen to inform even his most abstract pronouncements.

The originary role of such experience may also be discerned in the conclusions he draws about the merits of monarchy. The subjectivity embodied in the unifying will of the state, he argues, "is not a so-called 'moral person,' or a decree issuing from a majority . . . but an actual individual — the will of a decreeing individual, — *monarchy*" (*PM* 270). The experiential ground is finally revealed as the very type of hereditary monarchy incorporated in Hegel's Prussia in Friedrich Wilhelm I, the "*one* person" who is seen as concretely uniting all the single wills that are otherwise atomistic, and for whom "the dignity of the princely power is fixed by inheritance" (*PM* 271).

An earlier portion of the same sentence suggests another, implicit point of experiential reference: "That subjectivity . . . partly leads on to the proviso that the name of the monarch appear as the bond and sanction under which everything is done in the government" (*PM* 271). The point of reference here is the practice of legal fiction as such, and doubtless, in a collateral way, the specific European corpus of all such creations in law. At the risk of belaboring the point, such fictions are discursive formations in which are condensed countless equally concrete experiences by means of which particular social organizations, classes, and interest groups direct, perpetuate, and regulate their political, social, economic, and spiritual existence.

In these discursive instances of time, what-happened is conceived to be what-is. That is to say, under particular historical circumstances, particular persons employed linguistic performatives to call into being discursive formations that took on a life of their own by that very act. As phenomena of a "second nature," these become lenses whose foci permit phenomena to be seen in certain ways. To interpret such foci is not to dissolve the formation but to bring into view its job of work. The same applies when Hegel creates such powerful discursive formations as the Individual, Specific, and Universal Moments, whose work it is to demonstrate the nature of governmental functions and the distribution of those functions in a hereditary, constitutional monarchy. As J. N. Findlay points out, Hegel's account matches up with the British version of that royal institution in the concrete form it had attained in Hegel's day: "Though the monarch may have the Individual Moment of making last decisions, he also has the Specific Moment represented by his advisers, and the Universal Moment represented by the Constitution and Laws, which it is not in his power to alter."[21]

The transformation of temporal experience into the abstractly essential characterizes the biological sphere as well, reflecting the fact that this ostensibly "first" nature is just as much a second nature as the legal fictions already discussed. In the philosopher's fateful discourse the worldly things ascribed to nature are brought into focus through fictions constituted in ways precisely analogous to their legal counterparts. There is indeed reason to regard Hegel's biological facts as biological fictions. They are fictions, moreover, with specifically narrative roles to play.

As Hegel moves to considerations of race, the ratio of the main text to explanatory appendices continues in favor of the latter, as is generally the case in the first part of the *Phenomenology*; for here, in contrast with, say, the third part, the Idea is in an early stage of self-realization, hence the plethora of "mundane" data and stories. Some of the commentary approaches the nature of reportage, as in his account of the aborigines of the New World. Discourse of this type derives from a particular diachronic process that has been unfolding and is unfolding still. This process is fundamentally a narrative of experience: "The indigenous races of this continent are dying out; the Old World is refashioning itself in the new" (*PM* 41).

Returning to this theme at the end of his discussion, Hegel notes that "the original inhabitants of America . . . are a vanishing, feeble race"; then again he makes concessions, this time in deference to a known historical reality: "It is true that in some parts of America at the time of its discovery, a pretty considerable civilization was to be found," but this was not compatible with European civilization and so it disappeared. In the next two sentences the focus is now essentialist, now reportorial, as the story of extinction nears its end: "In addition, the dullest savages dwell there, e.g. the Pecherais and Eskimos. The Caribs of earlier times are almost completely extinct," after which the history of colonial expansion is condensed to "When brought into contact with brandy and guns, these savages became extinct" (*PM* 45). To postulate historical events in this way is to divorce human experience from human agency. The reader is not provided with the identity of the brandy and gun suppliers, their motives, or their sources of supply, nor is the reader provided with the identity, motives, and responses of the original inhabitants. The complex phenomena the discourse thus occludes could find expression only in an account that is commensurately complex. Hegel offers instead what amounts to parataxis: brandy and guns appear, savages become extinct. The automatism derives from a characterological assumption, grounded in a notion of inalterable racial endowment, that only emerges in the sentence that follows: "In South America, it is the Creoles who have made themselves independent of Spain; the native Indians were incapable of doing so. In Paraguay, they were just like small children and were even treated as such by the Jesuits" (*PM* 45). In view of this inherent debility, which the main exposition would explain as merely one way in which "the nature-governed mind specializes itself" (*PM* 40), and in view of the experiences thus related, a liminal juncture arrives at which the philosopher can first pronounce unequivocally upon the natives' fate, and then, turning futural, write the story of what will inevitably happen: "The natives of America are, therefore, clearly not in a position to maintain themselves in face of the Europeans. The latter will begin a new culture over there on the soil they have conquered from the natives" (*PM* 45).

Falling somewhere between tunnel vision and downright blindness, Hegel's fateful discourse on race is about as economical an illustration of European ethnocentrism and racism as you are likely to find in a philosopher of such stature. The theorist of contradiction is unable to see the contradiction between his judgment of the New World races and the more general commentary that precedes it. Here the philosopher lays aside the problem of human descent, interpretations of which led to many spurious conclusions about race; descent, Hegel states, "affords no ground for granting or denying freedom and dominion to human beings" (*PM* 41). The further conclusion that Hegel himself draws is that the human species is universal in the sphere of entitling: "Man is implicitly rational; herein lies the possibility of equal justice for all men and the futility of a rigid distinction between races which have rights and those which have none" (*PM* 41). The difficulty arises from Hegel's inability or unwillingness to link entitling with endowing and enabling, and stems in large part from the fact that what differentiates the spheres is itself a matter of inequality, specifically the inequality of power, or if you prefer, of freedom.

The appeal to justice and rights on racial matters is weak because race, epitomizing subjection to necessity, is nature-bound, unfree. Somewhat grimly, Hegel observes that the division of the earth into geographical zones reveals "an element of necessity" (*PM* 41), which is immediately passed over as appropriate only to the field of geography. The tacit experiential point of departure here is the organization of knowledge, with its divisions into autonomous fields of investigation based largely on past professional experience. The assumption on which this in turn depends is the organization of values around knowledge as a privileged norm: "In Europe . . . there prevails this infinite thirst for knowledge which is alien to other races. The European is interested in the world, he wants to know it, to make this Other confronting him his own" (*PM* 45).

In Hegel's ideal agenda, making the other one's own means to "bring to view the genus, law, universal thought, the inner rationality, in the particular forms of the world" (*PM* 45). But in its concrete use of worldly power this drive means the domination, then the extinction of the other through the same kind of demonic instrumentality that Mephistopheles puts at Faust's disposal. Goethe, who believed that improving transportation technology could effect the unification of Germany, hoped that he would live to see a canal system for the Danube and Rhine rivers as well as canals in the Suez and Panama.[22] A similar commitment motivates Faust, with the important distinction that Faust is endowed with enough worldly power to impose his technological imperialism wherever he wishes. It is a part of his tragedy, and of the logic he in part embodies, that actual human costs experienced by actual people are deemed less significant than realizing imperial imperatives. Thus the willingness of Faust to displace Philemon and Baucis, the idyllic old couple of legend whose hospitality caused a grateful Zeus to spare them from inundation. The process by which the two are eliminated problematizes the relation between Faust's felt experience and the "objective" domain in which will is exercised through the mediation of Mephistopheles.

That the dialectic of experience is in both authors a dangerous balancing act does not prevent Lukács from viewing it in a positive light:

> The seeds of good can be hidden in evil, but at the same time, there can be something satanic in the most lofty feeling, or the satanic can even grow out of it. This balancing on the razor's edge is what constitutes the inner drama of Faust. But as in all dramatic, tragic, wisdom, this constant and dangerous oscillation does not engender nihilism. Goethe incorporates moral and social relativism poetically as an element in the total dialectic in the same way that Hegel does philosophically.[23]

Dialectical process has always its uncertainties. In antiquity, as we have seen, the interruptive innovations in dialectic endanger just because they increase uncertainty; there is a world of difference between, on the one hand, the experience of listening to a storyteller use rhythm and formulae within an immemorial poetic tradition, and, on the other, forcing her to repeat herself in order to produce a more prosaic intelligibility. As suggested above, experiential continuity is broken, the dream is disrupted, and discontinuity is lived as a fact before it is known as a danger.

Plato measures the danger in dialectic in relation to stages of life. Thus the young are at risk when exposed to the thrills of confutation because, in their limited experience, they cannot distinguish between the ultimate seriousness of dialectic and the playing of mere games. As their experience of dialectic increases, so does their endangerment: "And when they have themselves confuted many and been confuted by many, they quickly fall into a violent distrust of all that they formerly held true, and the outcome is that they themselves and the whole business of philosophy are discredited with other men" (*Rep.* VII.771c). If the danger, then, consists in being experienced in dialectic before being experienced in life, the solution is to guarantee the latter as the prior condition of the former.

The dialectical balancing act we have seen in Hegel seems, by contrast, to be more precarious. He would nonetheless insist on the feasibility of avoiding missteps; though sacrifices must be made and risks taken, final victory awaits in the inevitable self-realization of absolute spirit.

The discussion that follows will consider how Bertolt Brecht, in his attempt, partly inspired by Hegel, to "dialecticize" experience, deals with a danger that is partly of his own making, but that inheres in the very nature of the project with which he challenges the theater in challenging himself.

6. Experiencing, Experimenting, and Theater

In his epic theater Brecht forged a crucible in which to explore experience and dialectic through experimentation. In doing so, he rivaled Hugo von Hofmannsthal in drawing on European tradition and Antonin Artaud in dramaturgical innovation. The dynamic interplay of narrative, song, instrumental music, visual documentation, and theory-in-practice that Brecht provided had never been experienced before, at least in the West. Late in life, the playwright focused anew on the challenges he had earlier taken up, creating in the *Lehrstück* a concrete dialectics of experience for the stage; this being an enterprise for which neither the name of epic theatre nor of *Lehrstück* seemed apt, he at one point substituted the working title "dialectical theater." From first to last, Brecht kept his attention trained on everyday experience. As my heading here indicates, the present discussion concentrates on experience in relation to dialectic, with particular concern for a problem that leads the playwright *beyond* Artaud's Theater of Cruelty and toward, if you will, a theater of danger, in which his approach risks dissolution at the very height of its success. To these considerations Hegel can provide a transition.

In a 1926 interview Brecht already underscores the connection between dialectical process and everyday experience: "I may confine my plays to raw material, but I show only what is typical. . . . Even when a character behaves by contradictions that's only because nobody can be identically the same at two unidentical moments." [24] To be effective in the theater contradictions must be demonstrated, hence the famous alienation-effect; hence too his distillation of demonstration into "the general gest of showing, which always underlies that which is being shown, when the audience is musically addressed by means of songs" (*B* 203).

Seeing himself as in some sort scientific, Brecht was willing to operate experimentally on any and every aspect of experience, "experimental" meaning in this case analytical, the not surprising consequence of which is that narrative breaks down into the episodic, the serial, and the gestic. In dramaturgical terms, the trick, he discovered, is to throw into relief the ways in which the story gets from one episode to another—to point out unmistakably where its knots are tied. Indeed, Brecht has recourse to the famous nodal points discussed above: "We made a short film of the performance, concentrating on the principal nodal points of the action and cutting it so as to bring out the gests in a very abbreviated way" (*B* 55).

In ideal dialectical terms, such a juncture enables the negation, part or whole, of what has preceded, such that, being itself no less liable to negation, a subsequent state can realize in its own sublated terms whatever is for its purposes worthy of being preserved from the stages preceding. A little less technically: in a liminal juncture too much seems to happen, and everything that happens seems to happen at once, yet something is all the while undergoing a conflation of continuity with transformation. In epic theater and the *Lehrstück* something hitherto unnoticed suddenly looms up at the audience, simultaneously demonstrating to its members that they are having an experience and that the experience is of something they have not experienced previously in this way. Such experience imposes the imperative of having somehow to deal with it. This process will be considered more fully when the discussion turns to the relation of sublation to subsumption and the significance of both for the theater of danger. Here we need only note the means by which experience becomes "alienated" for theatrical purposes:

> A simple way of alienating something is that normally applied to customs and moral principles. A visit, the treatment of an enemy, a lovers' meeting, agreements about politics or business, can be portrayed as if they were simply illustrations of general principles valid for the place in question. Shown thus, the particular and unrepeatable incident acquires a disconcerting look, because it appears as something general, something that has become a principle. As soon as we ask whether in fact it should have become such, or what about it should have done so, we are alienating the incident. (*B* 201)

It should be noted, first, that alienation here involves what are basically narrative *gests*. Portraying a visit or a lovers' meeting requires the telling or retelling of that visit or meeting. At the same time, the purport of that experience is what it boils down to, its ultimate pragmatic consequence. To alienate the incident is at the same time to make it stand out from the rest of the story in a liminal juncture that by its very nature cannot last. A crisis is created and the audience subjected to shock by being denied the experience it thought it was having and is in a sense cruelly being forced to create another experience in its place. Such incessant destruction and re-creation—such negation and negation of negation, in the language of dialectic—is crucial to creating the seemingly chaotic effects for which Brecht has been both praised and criticized. But if this is chaos, it is a chaos uncomfortably like the murk and jumble of the everyday life on which it draws.

An earlier text by Brecht serves as a reminder of Dewey's suggestion that an experience can generate any number of theories. The experience in question involves the enactment of a common street scene in which an eyewitness to a traffic accident demonstrates to bystanders how it came about. In this simulated situation the imaginary eyewitness performs actions but is not an actor according to the theatrical norm, which holds that action derives from character: the actor acts as he does because he identifies with an antecedent, author-created character whose nature is such that he cannot do otherwise. By contrast, the street eyewitness or demonstrator has no such antecedent to identify with. How can he know, for example, the kind of person the driver of the vehicle may be? The demonstrator knows only what he can demonstrate, and that is the action that he experienced as eyewitness. The issue here is not alienation in the previous sense but the manner in which the audience's experience is shaped by the ordinary experience (the accident) mediated by the demonstrator. For such a role no Stanislavsky graduates need apply, the demonstrator having too little experience of the persons involved in the accident to identify with them as Stanislavskyan actors are expected to do. The demonstrator communicates no more and no less than what he directly experienced, and what he experienced were precisely another's actions. To approach the matter from a different angle, the demonstrator must differentiate between his performance as communicator of actions and the subject giving rise to that performance.

> One essential element of the street scene lies in the natural attitude adopted by the demonstrator, which is two-fold; he is always taking two situations into account. He behaves naturally as a demonstrator, and he lets the subject of the demonstration behave naturally too. He never forgets, nor does he allow it to be forgotten, that he is not the subject but the demonstrator. That is to say, what the audience sees is not a fusion between demonstrator and subject, not some third, independent, uncontradictory entity with isolated features of (a) demonstrator and (b) subject, such as the orthodox theatre puts before us in its productions. The feelings and opinions of demonstrator and demonstrated are not merged in one. (*B* 125)

This is to say that in the epic theater the basic rendering of experience, of which the street scene is an epitome, is allegorical. The Stanislavskyan program, however, is inherently symbolic, calling for the actor, through attempted identification, to signify and ideally to merge with the adopted character. Epic theater demands that the *dramatis personae* and their impersonators retain their separate identities. Charles Laughton as Galileo never ceases to be Charles Laughton; rather than bring Galileo to life, the actor brings life, his own and that of his society, to Galileo. Equipped with "his own opinions and sensations" (*B* 194), rooted as these are in shared social experience, the actor is a lens through which that experience can shine on, in, through the character in question. In the process the character, the actor, and the audience's own "meta-experience" of the two-way experience thus allegorized come under interrogation. At all times the otherness and artificiality of the relation between actor and character, like the relation between demonstrator and subject in the street scene, remains in view in much the same way as Brecht's visual documentations (signs announcing songs, screen projections, and the like) remain in view.

The experience of the audience is just as interpretive as the experience of the actor: through the actor's interpretive experience the audience experiences interpretively. If the alienation effects and the *gests* and instrumental music and costumes and songs and visual documentations are successful—if, that is, the members of the audience are forced to see themselves as Laughtons too, not to mention Galileos, and ultimately as themselves—then their interpretive experience is an enabling one on the basis of which they can not only better comprehend the world but begin to change it.

That world is not "outside" the theater; you do not check your experience at the door before entering the auditorium to receive sedation in the dark—though that is precisely the state of the audience, according to Brecht, when "advanced music" is performed (*B* 89). A theatrical phase of experience is, notwithstanding the discontinuities it may embrace, ultimately continuous with other phases of experience: I use the term "phase" because theater is a duration within the world, so that, whereas one cannot say either that the world is outside the theater or that the theater is outside the world, one can say of such and such an experience that it transpired, for example, "after" the theater. This means, not that the particular theatergoer's life began immediately thereafter, but that the duration went on, reaching back out into the street and its scenes.

The street scene, then, is where the spectator returns because the street experiences occur before, during, and after the theater experience. This is partly a statement about lived time. When you go to the theater you bring with you, in you, of you, what you have experienced before going; during the time in which the scenes of the play take place, scenes of the street take place too. But when you make your way again to the street, the experiences you undergo are "after-theater" only in the sense described above: you do not necessarily cease experiencing the theater merely because you leave the auditorium, any more than you necessarily cease experiencing what you have been reading when you lay down your book. When you go home the theatrical duration endures, ringing in your memory, and tingling in your nerves. The statement also points to the street scene as a source of patterns or models. The power of such a scene is forcefully put: "The street scene determines what kind of experience is to be prepared for the spectator" (*B* 122).

Back on that street we find our demonstrator coming under interrogation: "One of the spectators might say: 'But if the victim stepped off the kerb with his right foot, as you showed him doing . . .' The demonstrator might interrupt saying: 'I showed him stepping off with his left foot' " (*B* 126). The experimental attitude toward experience so typical of Brecht is here made the clearer by the use of the conditional tense. In the experimental attitude the playwright shows that the dialectical rhythm of epic-theater narrative operates in the street much as it operates in the theater, the difference being that in the present instance we hear the playwright thinking aloud, as it were. He shows as well that the agonistic tempo runs faster and is more reciprocally polarized than in early dialectic; for no sooner has the demonstrator been interrogated, which is to say interrupted, than he interrupts in turn. In a moment the contradiction finds itself contradicted. The experimental focus becomes an alteration in the demonstrated experience, such that an alienation-effect is achieved. To accomplish this, however, a turn of the screw is required, an intensification of attention to detail together with a radical deceleration of tempo:

> By arguing which foot he really stepped off with in his demonstration, and, even more, how the victim himself acted, the demonstration can be so transformed that the A-effect occurs. The demonstrator achieves it by paying exact attention this time to his movements, executing them carefully, probably in slow motion; in this way he alienates the little sub-incident, emphasizes its importance, makes it worthy of notice. (*B* 26)

Comprehending the scenic unit requires the breaking down of its wholeness into the units of which it is constituted. The process, disclosing tensions and contradictions not otherwise perceived, proceeds if necessary down to the micro-level of the individual *gest*. In preparing with Laughton for the Los Angeles production of *Galileo*, "our first concern throughout was for the smallest fragments, for sentences, even for exclamations—each treated separately, each needing to be given the simplest, freshly fitted form, giving so much away, hiding so much or leaving it open" (*B* 165). That the process aims finally at synthesis, at re-composing what such "scientific" analysis has decomposed, is indicated in the title of the essay in question: "Building Up a Part: Laughton's Galileo."

In the street scene the largest constituent unit of experience, the scene itself, is divided into the critical incident and the sub-incident. But however scientific Brecht wants his experiments to sound, the scientific approach is itself seen to be instrumental, a mediator between the scientific community and the larger community whose experience remains the ultimate point of reference of theatrical art. In elucidating the role of the latter, as the discussion of the street scene does, Brecht first indicates the debt of the street corner to the theater, then contradicts that thesis, then turns it into its reciprocal polar position: "And so the epic theatre's alienation effect proves to have its uses for the demonstrator too; in other words it is also to be found in this small everyday scene of natural street-corner theatre, which has little to do with art. The direct changeover from representation to commentary that is so characteristic of the epic theatre is still more easily recognized as one element of any street demonstration" (*B* 126). What is here called commentary is called discussion in a *Lehrstück* such as *The Measures Taken* (*Die Massnahme*). Each is like a knot in the series of episodes forming a narrative, a nodal point whose energies require redirection into further episodes, new nodal points. In principle, the energies can lead practically anywhere; I will consider below the dangers inherent in an experiential process so open-ended.

This discussion has itself reached a juncture sufficiently liminal to suggest the value of the following preliminary summing-up: Brecht's theatrical practice, whether in the epic theater or what I am calling the theater of danger, is dialectical because of the way in which it is narrative, narrative because of the way in which it is dialectical, experiential because of the way in which it is narrative and dialectical, and experimental because of the way in which it is narrative, dialectical, and experiential. It should be recognized that the *because* is in fact a free syncategorem that could be repositioned anywhere in the clausal series, the ultimate effect of which would still be to indicate that dialectic, narrative, and experience are precisely cofoundational. The reader is thereby made "safe" for the essentializing in Brecht's observation that "Everything hangs on the 'story.'. . . . The 'story' is the theatre's great operation, the complete fitting together of all the gestic incidents, embracing the communications and impulses that must now go to make up the audience's entertainment" (*B* 200). Theatrical experience nonetheless remains the element, as Henry James would say, in which the story comes to the fore: epic theater is epic *theater*, incorporate, and enacted in concrete experience here and now.

Precisely how this enactment proceeds is one of the least understood of experiential, and more particularly esthetic, phenomena. Nor has anyone made entirely clear what concretely happens in the alienation-effect. We do know, of course, that in Brecht, as in Hegel and Marx, alienation conduces to consciousness, the *sine qua non* of subsequent action with respect to whatever is envisaged as the object of such consciousness. On this whole question, and on the relation of consciousness to drama, Dewey proves surprisingly helpful. "Every case of consciousness is dramatic," he states aphoristically; "drama is an enhancement of the conditions of consciousness" (*LW* 1:232). Language in drama, Dewey suggests, illuminates in a way unknown to immediate consciousness: we have the experience of sweet or red without the explicit mediation of words, because of which absence the having is neither communicated nor known:

> But words, as means of directing action, may evoke a situation in which the thing in question is had in some particularly illuminating way. It seems to me that anyone who installs himself in the midst of the unfolding of drama *has* the experience of consciousness in just this sort of way; in a way which enables him to give significance to descriptive and analytic terms otherwise meaningless. There must be a story, some whole, an integrated series of episodes. This connected whole is mind, as it extends beyond a particular process of consciousness and conditions it. (*LW* 1:232)

"There must be a story" epigrammatically announces a guiding narrative, the precise nature of which is not, unfortunately, a point on which the philosopher is especially lucid. What he suggests, however, is again a sense of element, of a condition of possibility and of that possibility realized as medium, ambiance; in which case what Dewey calls "mind," associated by him implicitly with meaning, perception, significance, knowledge, and communication, is that concrete continuum in which *any* experience is experienced. Such is the case despite the fact that no thematization can make the elemental, functioning as a "background," directly accessible as a whole any more than the "elemental presence of the earth" can be made accessible as a whole: "The earth as a theoretical object is a globe, a planet. But the earth is also constantly present in the background of our sensorial experience, as the original reservoir of solidity and repose, upon which landscapes are at rest. Lacking profiles, its contours being impossible to encompass with our gaze, unexplored, it is not susceptible of becoming an object of perception."[25] Such elemental presence functions as a tacitly acknowledged continuum much in the manner of Dewey's "mind," which, precisely because of its continuous nature, persists in being despite the fact that it is never immediately present in its entirety. Dewey thus speaks of "the operative presence of a continuum of meanings," emotional and intellectual, that are constitutive of a dramatic experience; a continuum which, like worldliness itself, or more especially like the light of day, affords such "suffusive presence in what is now said and done" that "the purport of past affairs is present in the momentary cross-sectional idea in a way which is more intimate, direct and pervasive than the way of recall" (*LW* 1:232). The story that must be is a continuous real experience—not some abstract totality gliding in the ether, to be materialized on command, but already concrete connectedness.

Plays consist in an integrated series of episodes, and may be distinguished according to the degree of tension, and thus of potential contradiction in a dialectical sense, between the integration and the seriality. For illustrations one may look to the classical drama in seventeenth-century France; and if these practices don't always match up with received ideas (on the unities, for example), the theory often does. For illustrations of such theory one can look to the modern dramatic tradition, which, at least since Georg Büchner, has used to advantage fragments, abrupt transitions, change of pace, and shocking contrast. Unless or until the audience gets used to such practices, the effect is one of disturbance and disruption; yet even disturbance and disruption are educational insofar as they redirect attention to the madeness and contradictoriness (for lack of better terms) of what transpires on the stage; they point out to the spectators that the thoughts and feelings they are having are those of *consciously* theatrical experience. For playwright and philosopher alike, redirection is of the essence, consciousness being "that phase of a system of meanings which at a given time is undergoing re-direction, transitive transformation" (*LW* 1:233).

To speak of phases of meaning that undergo redirection and transformation is to speak of an educational process. But if the terms are Deweyan, the thinking is no less Brechtian, the creator of the *Lehrstück* being as concerned over *Bildung* within and outside the theater as Dewey is concerned about it within and outside the classroom. The medium or element in which education takes place, insofar as the dramatist is concerned, is to a large degree the theatrical experience itself.

From at least as early as the Renaissance, theater has proffered on its site a simulacrum of the relation between the piece being performed and the audience experiencing that performance. And while this meta-relation we call a play-within-a-play is more the exception than the rule, the exceptions compose a memorable repertoire extending from Hamlet as playwright, director, and stage manager to the dispersed Pirandellan ensemble that wants to find out in what if any play its members are playing. As radical as these moments are in their own way, they still derive from an experiential paradigm that tends to be inactive and specular. The members of the audience are not invited into the stage world but, as it were, to the edge of it. They may see and hear people like themselves on stage and before the lights, but they are still seeing and hearing as members of an essentially passive collectivity. The old practice of seating privileged spectators on the stage, still popular late into the eighteenth century, is only a qualified exception to the rule. On the one hand, the spectators occupy positions in view of the audience; on the other hand, they do not figure among the *dramatis personae*. True, whatever they do while on stage belongs in some sort to the audience's experience as a whole, but only as experience of a *spectacle*. The orbit of gazes is complex and inclusive as the audience in the hall watches the audience on stage as well as the acting company, the members of the audience on stage watch the members of the acting company, and probably the audience in the hall as well, to that extent giving that audience a taste of that being-looked-at which is central both to the stage audience and to the acting company. Peter Shaffer's revival in *Equus* of on-stage spectators underscores the obsolescence of the former practice. For his part, Brecht threw it into relief—alienated it from its "second nature"—by shifting the musicians from the pit onto the stage, where they could watch their watchers while watching themselves being watched.

The situation is very different in the *Lehrstück*, or "didactic cantata" (*B* 90), where experience is designed to be more participatory, direct, and concrete. Resisting specularity by dispensing with an audience, dispensing therefore with an assumed transcendental point of reference, the *Lehrstück* is acted by performers for one another; or the professional acting company can be replaced by a worker's council, a student group, or some other type of "grassroots" cultural organization.

This is a crucial point: how well a political agenda will be carried out depends in no small measure on the unit of organization in which people are brought together and on the level of experience characterizing that unit. In practice, a rough correlation obtains between unit and level, the former tending to be smaller as the level is lower, and vice versa. The minimal unit of collectivization must be modest enough in size and low enough in level to permit broad participation with an effective procedure for decision-making. Otherwise the organization faces the danger of dissolving into a Sartrean seriality, dispersed along an axis at once arbitrary and random, as in the queueing of prospective passengers at a bus stop: arbitrary because they have to line up in a certain way and random because who happens to be lining up for a certain bus at a certain place and a certain time is a matter of chance.

Such dissolution threatens from the moment when theory, with its cool abstractions, enters the stage of practice, where temperatures run high. *Pace* Brecht, Lukács acknowledges the problem by noting that "on the level of pure theory . . . antagonisms are only expressed in the form of discussions which can be contained within the framework of one and the same organization without disrupting it." In a sort of dramatic nodal point, hidden contradictions then spring forth: "But no sooner are these same questions given organizational form than they turn out to be sharply opposed and even incompatible." Whereupon the principle to be drawn from this condensed story line finds expression in connotation: "Every 'theoretical' tendency or clash of views must immediately develop an organizational arm if it is to rise above the level of pure theory or abstract opinion, that is to say, if it really intends to point the way to its own fulfillment in practice." [26]

Which is just what any politically oriented group aspires to do. When the group in question is revolutionary, the question of unit and level can be decisive. Jefferson suggested, we recall, that governance on a local level should be carried out by "small republics" with broad responsibilities and rights, including the right to elect representatives. Organizations of just this type became a recurring feature of subsequent (that is, post-1776) revolutionary periods, from the Paris Commune of 1870 to the councils or soviets set up in Russia in 1905 and again in 1917. In the next two years German workers, soldiers, and peasants organized councils of their own; as it happens, Brecht was in Munich in the winter of 1919 when these councils staged a demonstration at the Deutsches Theater. Characterized by relative spontaneity of formation and by active participation, the councils could look utopian to observers who knew only too well that their relative want of partisanship represented an imminent danger. Other organizations, which were united precisely by party interests as well as common experience, could plan and implement programming for which the improvisatory councils had no immediate counterpart.[27]

It is within the context of these participatory, small-scale groups that *Lehrstück* performers dialectically negate the conventional audience as origin of educative experience. This is sublated in that the audience function is preserved and elevated in the ensemble, whose members are not the less members of an audience for being at the same time performers. Educational convention is negated to the extent that responsibility for learning is assimilated by the empowering group, whose members are at once those being educated and the educators. This amounts to a fuller negation, it seems to me, than is accomplished by Antonin Artaud, who endeavors to move the audience closer toward unmediated participation without negating the existence of the audience in order to sublate it in the Brechtian way. Artaud moves in a similar direction, nonetheless; and if he is sufficiently dialectical, and Hegelian, to speak of Tibet and Mexico as the "nodal points of world culture," he also sees himself, with Brecht, in a revolutionary capacity, as illustrated by his design for the grand anti-imperial spectacle called *The Conquest of Mexico*.[28]

In any case, my description of the *Lehrstück* clearly has a "pure" model in view, not the mixed and volatile piece of fateful discourse that the Brechtian didactic cantata often proves to be. It is pure because it takes dialectical sublation at face value, whereas the latter, whether as abstract concept or concrete process, is as problematic as it is provocative. Merely to list the authorities who have come to such a conclusion would take far more space than the boundaries of this discussion allow. Here it must suffice to suggest the extent to which dialectical sublation, in the concrete case of the *Lehrstück*, is problematized by the possibility of an inherent contradiction between sublative and subsumptive process.

7. Sublation and Subsumption

In English, "to sublate" is to deny, whereas Hegel uses the concept to posit both a denying and a preserving. In J. H. Stirling's wording, "A thing is sublated, resolved, only so far as it has gone into unity with its opposite" (1868). A much more venerable term, "subsume" means to bring something, such as a statement, under something else that is more inclusive or stronger (1535), a definition modified by Hegel's contemporary Coleridge to cover the process by which an idea, principle, or term is brought under a rule or is included in something larger or higher. In its nominal form emphasis falls less on the notion of including than on the notion of being brought under, except in the case of Scottish law, where a subsumption is a narrative of an alleged crime (1639), that is, something brought under an action (such as libel) in support of that action. In the preceding century supportive use of "story" to state pertinent facts is already in use.

For present purposes, then, "subsumption" signifies *a hierarchical relation of supportive subordination inclusive of factual representation in a narrative mode.*

To lend more concreteness to the discussion, *The Measures Taken* (*Die Massnahme*) will serve as exemplary text. In this instructional play everyone enters into the experience of everyone else: the cadre of agitators, switching roles, become the Young Comrade, the Coolies, the Trader, and so on, in order to justify themselves in the eyes of the Control Chorus for having exterminated the Young Comrade. In their narratives the latter is shown committing a series of errors, as a consequence of which the revolutionary mission is aborted and the lives of the cadre jeopardized. In one of several "discussions," which interrupt the narrated action for a give-and-take between the cadre and the chorus, the Young Comrade arrives at the state of *Einverständnis*, or knowing consent, which enables him to submit to execution in the knowledge that in the long run the Communist Party has been correctly served.

A knowing consent is in this context essential to sublation, for if it is one thing to be negated in the ultimate way (that is, killed), it is another, "higher" thing to negate that negation in turn, so as to continue enabling the revolutionary cause. Acceptance, a conscious act, is a doing and an undergoing, such that revolutionary spirit can rise to a higher state, not despite the sacrifice of the individual but because of it. Hegel himself speaks of the phenomenology of *Geist* as the Golgotha of the Spirit—its "dialectical-speculative crucifixion," in Heidegger's phrase.[29]

Every feature of this process that can be embraced as sublation conduces as well to subsumption. The process is hierarchical through and through, the organization of power conforming to the conventional structured model of the pyramid, with the performing group, whether of workers, peasants, students, or soldiers, constituting the broad experiential base. The next level is occupied, to borrow from a 1943 presentation by Mao, by the party's "own excellent cadres endowed with rich personal experience," the latter being in fact the organizations the Chairman was then addressing.[30] At the apex of the pyramid we find, of course, the Party. But what *is* the Party, the Young Comrade wants to know, to which the three other Agitators reply:

> We are the Party,
> You and I and you all—all of us.
> The Party is in that suit you are wearing, Comrade,
> And is thinking in that head of yours.[31]

Contradiction: if it really is incorporated in the Young Comrade, the Party, being self-identical, cannot negate itself as it would if the Young Comrade should split with it. The very fact that the latter has a choice to make enables the attempt at negation initiated by the other Agitators: if they convince him of their thesis, and if he accordingly subordinates his private feelings to Party interests, the state of contradiction will be resolved. Thus their appeal: "We may be wrong and you may be right. / Therefore do not cut yourself off from us!" (*M* 279).

To make a choice correct for the Party, the Young Comrade need only follow The Teachings of the Classics, which is the title of Scene 1: "We bring you nothing. But over the frontier to Mukden we bring the Chinese workers the teachings of the classics and the propagandists, the ABC of Communism: to the ignorant, instruction about their condition; to the oppressed, class consciousness; and to the class conscious, the experience of revolution" (*M* 259). The narratives and songs that follow make these abstractions more concrete. In Scene 3, for example, the Agitators instruct the Young Comrade to tell the coolies of wooden-soled shoes to keep them from slipping as they tow barges. He is to operate, in other words, at level one, which consists of putting the coolies in touch with their own experience, a point on which the Agitators are quite explicit (*M* 263). But the Young Comrade attempts in effect to operate on the third level; being already class conscious, he is ready for the experience of revolution — but the revolution is not ready for him. When he gives in to pity and challenges the overseer openly, he gets himself and the other cadre members debarred for a week from the central city, where they need to work.

Again, when we hear the Four Agitators say, "Daily we fought those old associates: Oppression and Despair" (*M* 270), we are getting a narrative distillation of a virtual infinitude of social, political, and economic experiences. Brecht is equally at pains to draw upon specifics of historical circumstances: "Then we heard there was conflict between the merchants and the British, who ruled the city, on account of tariffs. In order to exploit this rulers' quarrel for the benefit of the ruled, we sent the young comrade with a letter to the richest of the merchants. It said: 'Arm the coolies!' " (*M* 270).

Not a few commentators have labored under the illusion that this and other references to Chinese situations are exotic touches or coded allusions to contemporaneous German or Russian developments. While this may in part be the case, Brecht was clearly drawing on experiences recorded in China in the five years preceding his composition of the play.[32] The conflict cited by the Agitators was a documented datum in a China exploited in the 1920s by British and other foreign capitalist interests. During this period the Chinese Communist Party, dependent on a Comintern controlled from 1924 by Stalin, saw no alternative to forging a front with, or even subordinating itself to, the Kuomintang, the party of the "rulers," in the language of the Agitators, since that party also sought the removal of foreign presences together with the existing Peking government.

When the other comrades tell their youngest member to do all he can to facilitate the arming of the coolies, they are doing just the sort of thing that their historical counterparts actually did in order to achieve identical goals. Their action, that is to say, is at once typical and concrete. Brecht makes the rice trader with whom the Young Comrade has to negotiate the richest of all the merchants, and one moreover who is aggressively corrupt and inhumane, as evidenced by the parody of Hobbesian self-interest and commodification in "The Song of Merchandiser":

> What is a man actually?
> Do I know what a man is?
> God knows what a man is!
> I don't know what a man is
> I only know his price.
> (*M* 272)

In thus stylizing the moral stance of the merchant and in maximizing his corruption and cruelty, Brecht uses poetic license to give to a historically concrete state of affairs a narrative-dramatic-musical correlative. In thus transporting to theater much of what has already been recorded in public documents he is also giving a kind of generic status to the problem of having to make cruel decisions. In the present instance and on a collective level, this comes down to allying with a hated rival against an even more hated mutual enemy; individually, this comes down to deciding that it is strategically correct to ingratiate oneself with the very embodiment of Kuomintang corruption, since that is the only way to achieve the goal of arming the coolies against the British. In the event, a painful decision translates into the equally cruel problem of executing a "correct" plan of action. To assure the revolution that is the goal of the Party one must sacrifice one's feelings, even one's life.

This play, which raises so many other issues, including the nature of the Party, implicitly raises the issue of the role of the author as the transcendental authority who has already programmed the decisions that are necessary in order to alienate and reorient the experience of all participants. Given this, and given the preeminent role of the Party, one must reckon with that shadowing fact which is the concord between that role and the policy line of the Comintern under Stalin. The nexus made East German critics particularly nervous: "As an important communist artist, Brecht offers a special problem for these critics. His revolutionary commitment must be maintained, but not in any way that might prove awkward in the present. They do not want to speak of Brecht in connection with Stalin—the individual most prominently responsible for Brecht's specific experience of living revolutionary tradition."[33]

Not the least of the playwright's decisions is the destiny he determines for the Young Comrade, who is as it were subsumed into the final message of the piece, that changing the world requires, among other things, "COMPREHENSION OF THE SINGLE MAN AND OF THE WHOLE . . ." (*M* 283). On this question of the role of the individual in relation to the collectivity, Sartre's discussion of "The Constituted Dialectic," scrutinizing the function of just such an "organiser-agitator" as the Young Comrade, is suggestive:

> He is a medium and he knows it; and if he acts . . . it is through the group, and in secret. But since the orders of the people issue from his mouth, since the reorganisation has to be carried out through his individual *praxis*, and since his exhortations and gestures indicate the common objective, we have to conclude that popular *praxis* is essentially capable of being created, understood and organised *by an individual.*[34]

Given the dialectical nature of our subject, it seems only fitting that as a gloss on Brecht this statement can be read in contradictory ways. In the first place, it evidently departs from the Brechtian position, which loads the group with all the crucial actions and ultimate responsibilities. Moreover, in *The Measures Taken* the performers experience—perform and undergo—three scripted stories in which a critically positioned individual not only fails to forward the revolutionary cause but endangers the mission, the lives of his comrades, and himself. If this way of putting the matter does not convince, there can be no doubt that the playwright sharply disagrees with Sartre when the latter goes on to specify in the passage noted above "that the group can define its common action *only* through the mediation of the individual designation" (emphasis added).

But in the second place, Sartre's statement agrees with the playwright's conception of the individual organizer-agitator. On the grounds of *principium individuationis*, any plurality minimally consists in the individual members constitutive thereof. More concretely, the practice of the revolutionary group, such as the one Brecht presents, presupposes that each member *qua* individual accedes to the interests of all together. That the individual in question fails to perform his assigned task is not decisive. What is decisive is that he agrees with the fate determined for him in the interests of the group, even if this means his liquidation.

Sartre has been employed here merely to throw into relief what is already given in *The Measures Taken*: either the individual is *not* taken sufficiently into account, the proof being that he is sacrificed for the good of the party; or the individual *is* taken sufficiently into account, the proof being that he sacrificed himself, in effect, for the good of the party. In both cases, it is the same sublation through consent, which is to say the same subsumption, for the movement that cancels the limitations of the individual to recover his *gest* on the level of transcendence is the very same movement that renders the individual subordinate to that very level.

The polarity between sublation and subsumption, which can be translated into, respectively, revolutionary transcendence or revolutionary failure, is a correlate of the political space separating a wry and restless man of letters from an authority whose rule dictates strict adherence to transcendentally propounded doctrine.

But with Brecht, art sometimes believes before ideology remembers. His art believes that educative purposes are legitimately served in a mode of radical experiential immediacy, an immediacy otherwise reserved for ethnic rituals; although a similar claim can be made for the undertakings of Artaud's Theater of Cruelty, they remained largely visionary and theoretical. In its casting, the *Lehrstück* is democratic, providing every performer with the opportunity of getting "inside" everyone else's experience by assuming every role and telling every story, though there is no telling where such may lead. If we are to take the playwright at his word, his commitment to "the new social scientific method known as dialectical materialism," which he announced in

1948, means pragmatically that everyone is free to change. "There is a great deal to man, we say; so a great deal can be made out of him. He does not have to stay the way he is now, nor does he have to be seen only as he is now, but also as he might become" (*B* 93). In 1933 Brecht was already calling for a more open-ended esthetic in order to enable more dynamic experiences: "The new school of play-writing must systematically see to it that its form includes 'experiment.' It must be free to use connections on every side; it needs equilibrium and has a tension which governs its component parts and 'loads' them against one another" (*B* 46).

Brecht seems to have found no way, ultimately, of consistently controlling the loading of part against part; anyway, equilibrium is as much a dynamic phenomenon as a static one, and the experiential matrix of action in which the performers of the *Lehrstück* engage themselves is a *moving* matrix. I mean that through the changing of roles, through immersion in contradictory experiences and in their resolution, the performer undertakes what Brecht calls "self-production" (*B* 186). Each new role teaches what it is like to be made over, to make *oneself* over, in a process of redirective transformation that cannot, must not, achieve perfect closure. A recognition of this prospect may partly explain the tentativeness Brecht discloses as he feels his way, in the last year of his life, toward a more genuinely dialectical theater. He cannot have been unaware, at the same time, of the contradictions implicit in a creative praxis energized by a dedication to freedom but shadowed by the *Einverständnis* required to maintain political orthodoxy. To be thus aware is to recognize, if only imperfectly, that the cruelty and the danger are at the heart of the creative enterprise as conceived. For the sake of sublation it vows to remember ideology at the expense of forgetting art—at the possible expense, indeed, of sacrificing itself.

The creation of a drama on dialectical premises challenges the dramatist to believe his art before he remembers his ideology. This is not to say that the *Lehrstück* in general or *The Measures Taken* in particular have met the challenge with complete success. The latter, for example, is hardly open-ended. The stories being told eventually come to an end, with the Control Chorus sounding choral indeed, even hymnal. But this is fundamentally experimental theater, aiming at new powerful experiences, and its most revealing moments occur when its loadings and counterloadings are most dialectically intense and are thus, at least potentially, at their most contradictory and hence revolutionary stage. Such a moment occurs in the final scene when the Agitators narrate their last experiences:

> The time was short, we found no way out.
> As one animal will help another, we too
> Wished to help him

> Who had fought with us for our cause.
> With our pursuers on our heels
> For five minutes
> We pondered the possibility.
> Think of it again now.
> *You* think of it.
> *Pause.*
>
> (M 281)

The specification of five minutes is an important because concrete detail. It is a constraint not of their choosing that is absolutely crucial in what they *are* free to choose. Their position resembles that of the ship's officer who, after his vessel is sunk and the lifeboat is in danger of sinking as well, must decide which occupants to sacrifice to the waves in order to save the others. This is education at white heat: the Agitators are teaching the Chorus to experience what the Agitators experienced, to feel what it was like to face a fateful life-or-death choice. Like the faithful Party members they are, they want to raise the consciousness of the Chorus, to enable its members to know what the experience was like. Only in this way can their otherwise criminal act be canceled and through sublation be preserved in its positive intent. But when sublation comes, can subsumption be far behind?

The Agitators' story concludes with their killing of the Young Comrade and their justification for doing so:

> It is not granted to us, we said,
> Not to kill.
> At one with the will to change the world that will
> not be denied
> We formulated
> The measures to be taken.
>
> (M 281)

A theater that would "dialecticize" experience through alienation-effects in order to change the world is in danger when it subordinates itself to something so faceless as Will. This is not to tell Brecht anything he didn't know. Early in the play the Agitators blot out their faces so as to assume Chinese disguises: sublation requires such sacrifice. By a similar process the face of Stalin and Stalinism, the incarnation of the Party, not to mention cruelty, at the time Brecht was writing his instructional plays, is blotted out too.

Dialectical sublation, as it comes down from Hegelianism to Marxism, confronts the chronic danger of subordination to its subsumptive potentiality. When a Stalin is in power, the danger is the more acute, not least when his face is blotted out by the mask of Will. Arendt states the danger concisely: "Left to itself, man's Will 'would rather will Nothingness than not will,' as

Nietzsche remarked . . . in other words, the famous power of negation inherent in the Will and conceived as the motor of History (not only in Marx but, by implication, already in Hegel) is an annihilating force that could just as well result in a process of permanent annihilation as of Infinite Progress." [35] If it is the case that Brecht's ideology remembers before his art believes, then the theater of danger inclines to annihilation. If it is the case that his art believes before his ideology remembers, then the same art leads toward something like "progress." Brecht's struggle to go beyond epic theater, to do something unattempted yet in prose or rhyme by rendering experience productively dialectical, points to the possibility that he saw the danger.

Hölderlin already sees experience in dialectical terms:

> Wo aber Gefahr ist, wächst
> Das Rettende auch.[36]
>
> Where danger is, grows
> The saving power also.

Working from much the same assumptions, Hölderlin's friend Hegel did find, by his own measure, the saving power. Marx, as Hegel's heir, and with much the same qualification, found it too. Whether Brecht did as well remains a question. That his fate lies in the hands of posterity is not to say that as members of his audience we must play Control Chorus to his Agitator. It is to say that we have an opportunity to leave off deferring, an opportunity to "think about it *now*." The playwright should be credited, in my view, with courageously countering the political right at a time when many of his compatriots had yet to learn how dangerous it would finally be to do anything else. In response to the Wagnerian quest for a *Gesamtkunstwerk*, Brecht drew on both "high" and "popular" culture, on narrative, song, instrumental music, and visual documentation, to create a condition of possibility for transformative educational experience, and to a considerable extent actually *provided* that experience. He accomplished all this, however, at a price. Through all its experimenting with experience, the didactic cantata, instructional play, school opera, or *Lehrstück*—call it what you will—remains dangerously subordinated to what was most problematic in the playwright's concrete political engagement. And in doing so it is not merely endangered but is itself endangering.

8. Expense and Expression

In reconstructing experience through experimental theater Brecht engages head-on, as we have seen, the conflict between the interests of the group and the interest of the individual. The playwright speaks for the poor, bare, forked creature who is deemed to be, or at least made to seem, expendable; Brecht's conception is to this extent similar to the challenge posed by a suffering father figure such as Shakespeare's Lear, to whom Brecht makes explicit appeal, or to his complex counterparts in *The Good Woman of Szechwan*, *The Caucasian Chalk Circle*, or *Mother Courage*. For such figures experience is a hard thing, something you live through, if barely. The fateful discourse of existential economy that is "Lear" expresses the expense of experience through its synecdochic relation to the whole that is *King Lear*. "Expense" means: the human cost of experiencing the pathos of impairment, the loss of entitlement; even, in the forsaken wilds, of endowment in itself. In addressing such fateful matters this discussion draws upon Emerson's suggestion, in "Experience," that human life is after all not dialectical. One may well ask, If life is not a matter of dialectics, then what is it? To which one may respond that it is, for present purposes, the experience of expressing expense, the expense of expressing experience, the expressing of the expense of experience.

In addressing the issue Dewey defines experience as "primarily a process of undergoing: a process of standing something; of suffering and passion, of affection, in the literal sense of these words." The process is not in the least passive: "The most patient patient is more than a receptor. He is also an agent—a reactor, one trying experiments. . . . Even if we shut ourselves up in the most clam-like fashion, we are doing something; our passivity is an active attitude, not an extinction of response" (*MW* 10:8).

Such a process is in some sort private. In doing or undergoing there is a someone doing or undergoing, and to that someone we may safely ascribe a self. Individualism errs by *prescribing* that the role of social, political, economic or cultural phenomena be subordinated to the interests of the individual self. But it is only within the protective environment of individualist ideology that this rare bird has ever been sighted. The chimera of a purely inner self as the locus of experience, like the chimera of a purely private language to which Wittgenstein delivered an elegant quietus, would not have persisted as long as it did if political philosophy had turned more decisively from the quest for abstract certainty to the concrete question of what is really going on now, and why.

The requisite shift may be thought of as largely a shift from what is not concretely in evidence to what is. The search for the cause, the origin, is a search for something much more ulterior, more elusive and consequential, than the essentially Viconian investigation of what is and how it got to be that way. Here the phenomena are acts that are actually performed and the consequences of those acts, not some hypothetical *ur*-condition or origin.

The two main ways in which acts are consequential correspond respectively to the realm of the private and the realm of the public, the theme of the concluding pages of the present discussion. Acts that have direct consequences for individual participants in a transaction may be distinguished as primarily private, whereas acts that have consequences reaching beyond the individual participants may be distinguished as primarily public. Whatever the origin of the state may be, its existence is justified by the recognition that the latter mode of consequence warrants operations and institutions not required by the former; the very idea of social order or welfare, not to mention the fact of such order or welfare, would otherwise remain limited to immediate and individual interests.

The localization of private and public experience in the isolated individual turns the relation of the individual and the world inside out: the individual is no longer in the world, the world is in the individual; the actual concrete plenum of worldly experience disappears from the world. This is not to deny individuality; it just means that for Dewey as for Sartre an act is always at a minimum someone's *situated* act: neither salt nor legislation gets passed unless someone in a concrete social context behaves in such a way as to lead to passing. Overlooking this important qualification, theorists of causality and origin, under the sway of individualism, conclude that concepts of state and public merely mask the pursuit by private persons of private interests.

To say as Dewey does that experiencing is not only something you do but something you undergo is to say that it has its expense. Expense means, again, the human cost of experiencing, both as doing and undergoing. Few myths in Western tradition speak more directly and eloquently to such expense than the Romans' founding myth of Lucretia, who, after being raped by a political tyrant, takes her life, enabling the destruction of the Tarquins' tyranny and its replacement by republican liberty.

By insisting on the importance of her chastity, Lucretia underlines the central issue of the narrative so far as the experience of the male participants is concerned. From the first it is not the woman's beauty that is uppermost but her honorable condition. According to Livy, when Lucretia refuses the advances of Tarquinius Superbus's son Sextus Tarquinius, Sextus vows to murder her and a male servant and place their bodies in bed together to simulate adultery. Consequently, Lucretia submits.

As soon as Sextus departs, Lucretia relates her traumatic experience to her parents and to Brutus and Publius Valerius, and asks them to bring Sextus to justice. Although her parents find her still chaste in mind, Lucretia insists that she can remove the stain from her honor only by annihilating her violated flesh, and stabs herself to death. Brutus, who, according to Machiavelli, has been feigning idiocy until the opportune moment for seizing power, decides that this is that moment, grasps the bloody knife and—exploiting the spectacle of Lucretia's publicly displayed remains—swears to end the tyranny of the Tarquins. The violation experienced by Lucretia is rendered as something collateral to the central historical experience, which is the violation of male honor institutionalized in the patriarchal order. Though Lucretia is raped, it is Brutus who is memorialized with a statue portraying him, sword in hand, driving out the Tarquins, and it is Brutus, Stephanie Jed notes, who castigates his fellow Romans for weeping over the fate experienced by Lucretia:

> To castigate means to make chaste. In Livy's narrative, the passage from Lucretia's chastity to Tarquin's violation of this chastity to Brutus' castigation of the Romans for their tears forms a lexical chain which embodies a logic of chaste thinking: the rape of Lucretia is transformed into an injury against the honor of other male survivors by virtue of this chain; and Brutus takes over from Lucretia the function of preserving chastity by castigating the Romans for their tears.[37]

In reconstructing Lucretia's last words, the Florentine statesman Collucio Salutati creates the impression of getting closer to Lucretia's personal experience by letting her tell her story in her own words. More precisely, he offers a dialogue in which Lucretia's father and husband express their perspective on her experience and she then expresses hers. It is a fateful discourse indeed, this exchange of intensely intimate thoughts and feelings on one of the gravest of transgressions; all the more so because the process by which Lucretia discourses her way to suicide provides the condition, once the suicide is interpreted as sacrifice, for the constitution of a new Roman state. The reader of Salutati's text will recognize tensions and contradictions similar to those in Machiavelli's reflections on the same themes: "I feel that my appropriate desire of chastity did me an injury. The abominable adulterer wanted to assault not my beauty but my chastity. If I bore this fruit of continence, what awaits me as an adulteress, contaminated and raped?" In the first place, Salutati's Lucretia understands perfectly well the experience the rapist is after: by possessing her he will disendow her of natal chastity, which until then signifies that her husband is superior to him in honor. In the second place, Salutati has Lucretia broach the subject of mutual responsibility. While Sextus did her injury by violating her, she did an injury to herself by the very fact of being chaste: if her flesh had not been chaste, there would not have been anything for the attacker to attack—or so runs the author's tautological reasoning. In the third place, he employs a natal trope to express the fateful nature of that same chastity: if her continence could bear such a shameful fruit, what worse things would follow from contamination and rape? Here is the first suggestion of the crucial concept, to be exploited later in the declamation, of the bad beginning. Salutati continues:

Don't you think I will discover some pleasure in chastity of a corrupt body? Allow me not to harbor so much grief in my soul and not to recall so much the feeling of that embrace without the enticements of my disobedient members assaulting me, without remembering the traces of the marriage flame. That sad and unpleasing pleasure, of whatever sort it was, must be avenged by the sword. And it will be your responsibility, if there is anything in you of Roman spirit, to avenge such a crime. Let the feeling be extinguished; too great are the powers of Venus for anyone who has had some experience of pleasure. . . . If I spare adultery, soon adultery will be pleasing. A disgraceful thing has begun in me.

Here the overdetermination is such that a completely reliable interpretation is not easily achieved. The ambiguities, the dialectical interplay between chastity and contamination, the torsion in the manner of expression, combine to suggest the difficulty of shaping a narrative to the contours of the founding myth, which seeks to endow, entitle, and enable a radically new civil order. The author needs to show that the new beginning is the total negation of the old, disgraceful regime, which means that he needs in turn to show that in which the disgrace consists, the sacrifice undertaken to transcend it, and the spectacle that was staged to excite vengeance and vindication; the last requirement being arguably the decisive one in determining the necessity of the victim's death.

The disgraceful thing that the victim enables, just by being the type of person she is, is indissociable from her experience of pleasure, to which the author turns no less than three times. Until pleasure appears, emphasis falls on the experience of shame, infamy, and disgrace; now a sense of personal responsibility arises, with attendant feelings of guilt, to intensify the fear that her procreative endowment may have become contaminated in the rape: "What if his unpropitious seed adhered in my womb? Or shall I wait until I become a mother from adultery?" The disgraceful thing that has begun in Lucretia is more than this possible development, however; it is her significance as example: "If I spare adultery, soon adultery will be pleasing, and an adulterer will be welcome." The statement stresses the elevation appropriate to the political stakes: as Lucretia goes, so goes the morality of the society. So interwoven are the erotic and the political motives in this discourse that we find it equally appropriate that Lucretia's direct appeal to the Roman spirit of her father and husband should come between "unpleasing pleasure" and "the power of Venus," and that attention becomes increasingly focused on political compensation for the trauma she has experienced. In the process Salutati has Lucretia contradict herself:

You, earthly body, who produced the cause and occasion of adultery with your former beauty, give up your soul; pour forth this blood as an omen that from this point, the overthrow of the arrogant king and his unfortunate progeny may begin. You, my dearest husband, and you, my father, whose glances I flee with modesty, happily and willingly, and you, my friends, good-bye; carry out the revenge you promised not less courageously than I will perform my murder. Let not Lucretia be given as an example to Roman women, so that, on account of my life, they may convince themselves that life is lawful for the unchaste.

Salutati contradicts himself on the crucial issue of causality. Livy had indicated that the desire for Lucretia's chastity, rather than her beauty, was the goal of Sextus, and previously in the present text Salutati has had Lucretia state the same conclusion. It is a contradiction-without-sublation, of the kind that we will find in Machiavelli as well. Salutati is nearer the mark when he has Lucretia blame her beauty for providing the occasion of the adultery inasmuch as her beauty and her chastity were so united in her person that the former could serve as viaticum to the latter. But this is guilt by association, underscored by the fact that the impairment of her chastity entails the destruction of her beauty.

But if Salutati is contradictory in first deciding that Lucretia's chastity is central, then that her beauty is, this means that he is confused on the score of agency but not on the score of the agent. Whether chastity enticed or beauty did, the cause and occasion belong to the agent Lucretia, who needs their guilt by association to enable in turn, in the form of self-sacrifice, the cause and occasion by which Brutus can inflame the populace. With dead Lucretia exhibited as specular proof, the violation of chastity enables rallying *for* Lucretia to become rallying *against* Tarquinius Superbus. Not the least of the ironies here is the fact that in his own way the tyrant becomes a victim too. If each of the two objects of violence is thus to some extent a *pharmakos*, they arrive at this fate in different though related ways. Here the Girardian theory of mimesis and sacrifice comes into play.[38] In the first instance, husband Collatinus is oriented, as are his peers, toward the honored object, spousal chastity. When wife Lucretia comes to embody that virtue, Sextus imitates Collatinus, who thus serves both as model and rival. But the nature of this particular virtue creates a particular problem. If Sextus desired Lucretia's beauty, he could "out-rival" her husband by experiencing her sexually, leaving her beauty intact. But chastity cannot be experienced in this way, for in the adulterous act chastity ceases to be.

Chastity is a worldly thing, and, in the social, moral, and political framework of the Lucretian myth, a precious one, for it is the most conspicuous means by which the wife can express the honor of both masters, the husband and the father. With chastity destroyed, Lucretia's high status can be seen as sanctioning the imitation of her infamy if she should stop short of expiatory self-sacrifice. Lucretia and natality must be separated forever through the destruction of Lucretia, whose sacrifice becomes the liminal juncture from which a saving and creative counterpart can issue. The destruction of Lucretia will be answered by the rebirth of Brutus and the new birth of the republic it thus enables. It is critical, in these developments, that Lucretia be seen to take personal responsibility for her self-sacrifice. Though forced to submit to rape, she remains chaste in one absolutely crucial respect: the freedom of will with which she is natally endowed is unimpaired by her transgressive experience.

In his recension of the Lucretian myth, Machiavelli does not attempt to get close to the victim's experience even to the limited extent that Salutati does. Placing Brutus on center stage, Machiavelli reduces Lucretia to a piece of discursive scenery: "standing beside the dead Lucretia, he, among her father and her husband and her other relatives, was the leader in drawing the knife from her wound and making those present take an oath never in the future to allow anybody to be king in Rome."[39] Machiavelli's preoccupation with male experience informs the other passages as well, which hinge on the consequences confronting powerful men who do harm to women:

> First, it appears that women have caused much destruction, have done great harm to those who govern cities, and have occasioned many divisions in them; for, as we see in this *History* of ours [by Livy], the outrage to Lucrece took their position from the Tarquins. . . . So Aristotle gives among the first causes for the falls of tyrants some injury in a matter of women, either by whoring them, or raping them, or by breaking off marriages. (*M* 1:488)

The women begin as active agents responsible for destruction, harm, and division, thus falling under the same heading of cause and occurrence employed by Salutati in the case of Lucretia. Whereupon Machiavelli contradicts the premise by making the women into passive victims. He does not train his eye on women who are raped, or turned into prostitutes, or left waiting at the church; their experiences are not of interest. And while it is true that he judges the acts done against them to be morally objectionable, evil as such appears explicitly only, so to speak, at the point of impact. Thus princes and governors "ought to consider the evils that can result from an event, and find a remedy so early that the remedy will not bring injury and disgrace to the state of their republic" (*M* 1:489).

Viewed dialectically, Machiavelli has produced a flat contradiction, which is to say that no sublating stage follows from the manner in which one statement negates another. Viewed nondialectically, the problem is in the underlying disposition that accounts for the plausibility of the position he assumes in the third passage on Lucretia. Machiavelli is disposed to treat the woman now as cause and now as effect, now as victimizer and now as victim, because the difference is determined by expository opportunities. He adopts the explanation that serves his immediate purpose. In that third passage Machiavelli traces the fall of Tarquinius Superbus to his deviation from the line of conduct established by his predecessors:

> He was not, then, driven out because Sextus his son raped Lucretia, but because he broke the laws of the kingdom and governed tyrannically, for he took all authority away from the Senate and transferred it to himself. . . . So, by his unceasing acts of cruelty and pride, he had already prepared the spirits of all the Romans for rebellion, whenever they had opportunity for it. If the catastrophe of Lucretia had not occurred, as soon as some other came about it would have produced the same result. (*M* 1:427)

In the English literary tradition, several major texts rework Lucretia's experience in ways that the Italian humanists could only have found unsettling. In "The Legend of Lucrece," *The Rape of Lucrece*, and *Clarissa*, Chaucer, Shakespeare, and Richardson, respectively, begin to redefine the more public aspects of the myth in relatively private terms. The story that counts for Salutati and Machiavelli as an empirical resource for political reflection beckons the English authors into a hitherto hidden inner sanctum of intense emotional experience. This privileging of the private at the expense of the public suggests that, at least as early as the late fourteenth century (insofar as Chaucer is the key witness), English writers and readers are renegotiating social relations in ways that are unsettling to themselves as well. The antinomy of public and private begins to look less like an immutable polarity than a descriptive paradigm in need of modification. New concepts and terms were forged, capable of newly necessary discriminations. Authors of written discourse no longer found it adequate to confine the sense of "private" to the privative. In the early middle ages that which was private had meant, for persons, "not holding public office or official position." In fairly short order, as lexical innovation goes, speakers and writers proceed to distinguish the private as "kept or removed from public view of knowledge" (1472). The private soon becomes that which belongs to or is the property of such an individual (1502), a distinction obviously necessary to the constitution of any practice or theory of individualism.

By 1526 it has become clear that the private does not denote a single one over against a many; rather, what is "individual, personal" is thought of as "affecting a person, or a small group of persons apart from the general community." Such a group may then be thought of as constituting a kind of private public. Along the same lines, about a generation later, it comes to be recognized that "public" and "private" distinguish phenomena along a single continuum: "Not open to the public, or not publicly done or performed, dist.

from a thing of the same kind that is 'public' " (1560). Similarly, a conversation is private because it is "intended only for the person or persons directly concerned" (1560).

All these distinctions and changes of emphasis contribute to the experience of intensity remarked upon by Arendt:

> The presence of others who see what we see and hear what we hear assures us of the reality of the world and ourselves, and while the intimacy of a fully developed private life, such as had never been known before the rise of the modern age and the concomitant decline of the public realm, will always greatly intensify and enrich the whole scale of subjective emotions and private feelings, this intensification will always come to pass at the expense of the assurance of the reality of the world and men.[40]

Expense devolves, however, from a trope of exchange: to pay is to pay for something, which in this case is access to realms of experience previously constrained and devalued. Those realms are also promoted to full citizenship, as it were, in the representable realm of worldly things.

At the outset of "The Legend of Lucrece" Chaucer explicitly declines to follow the lead of Ovid and Livy, who tell of "the exilynge of kinges / Of Rome" (ll. 1680–81).[41] Implicitly distinguishing himself as well from Salutati, Chaucer prefers

> to preyse and drawe to memorye
> The verray wife, the verray trewe Lucresse,
> That, for hyre wifhod and hire stedefastnesse,
> Nat only that these payens hire comende,
> But that he that cleped is in oure legende
> The grete Austyn, hath gret compassioun
> Of this Lucresse, that starf at Rome toun
>
> (ll. 1685–91)

At no time does Chaucer even hint at those equivocal aspects of Lucretia's experience which Salutati directly engages. Chaucer's Lucrece is a living embodiment of the paradox of innocence-in-experience. Dropping in on her by surprise, to test her "trouthe in love," Tarquinius and Colatynes find her assiduously performing her domestic duties. When Tarquinius seizes her by the throat and points his sword to her breast, her innocence takes the form of extreme incapacity, as though the threat of trauma not only disenables her strategically but disendows her of native capacities: "No word she spak, she hath no myght thereto." / "What shal she seyn? hire wit is al ago" (ll. 1796–97). Chaucer does not indicate, however, that this incapacity is peculiar to Lucrece, as the following question might be taken to imply; rather, as the succeeding line makes clear, he sees the disendowment as an innate characteristic

of women: "What! shal she fyghte with an hardy knyght? / Well wot men that
a woman hath no myght" (ll. 1800-1801). The process of privation goes further: to keep the experience of violation at a remove Lucretia swoons, and so
"she feleth no thyng, neither foul ne fayr" (l. 1818).

If there is any equivocation in the poem about Lucrece's innocence, that
last somewhat problematic line may be the place to look for it. To say that
Lucretia swoons and feels no thing foul shelters her from the act she would
otherwise experience in all its horror. When she also feels no *fair* thing, it is
hard to see what could count as such except some aspect of the very process
simultaneously condemned as foul.

In Chaucer's version of the Lucretia legend, the truth in love that the
heroine embodies is preserved, as is largely the case in other versions, including those by Salutati, Shakespeare, and Richardson, through her sacrifice. It
is also the case that the other authors give the victim ample opportunity to
express her experience and the conclusions she draws from it; Chaucer does
not. In the presence of her family and friends Lucretia cannot for some time
express herself at all, either by means of words or by means of exchanging
looks: "A word, for shame, forth ne myght she brynge, / Ne upon hem she
durste nat beholde" (ll. 1835-36). She finally manages to be more forthcom-
ing: "But atte last of Tarquyny she hem tolde / This rewful cas and al thys thing
horryble" (ll. 1837-38). Far from descriptive, the statement is understandably
evasive, touching as it does on an experience incapable of adequate expression
at whatever expense: "The woo to tellen were an impossible, / That she and al
hir frendes made attones" (ll. 1839-40). Instead of invoking topoi of expres-
sibility regarding the experience as such, Chaucer shifts to the "woo" experienced by others in reaction to what Lucrece has told: if the mere hearing of
the victim's constrained expression is an impossible thing to tell, one can only
imagine—or rather, one can scarcely imagine—what the original act of violation was like. Neither the private experience of the rape nor the more public
experience of its discursive representation can finally be adequately expressed.

The gulf that separates Lucretia from family and friends corresponds both
to the division between them on the issue of her innocence and to the division between the private, hidden nature of her experience and the experience
of the gathered company, which is public in the general sense of the term that
I have been employing. On the one side we hear the minimalist expression of
Lucrece:

> She sayde that, for hir gylt ne for hir blame,
> Hir husbonde shulde nat have the foule name,
> That wold she nat suffre, by no wey.
>
> (ll. 1844-46)

To which there comes the hardly less terse reply:

> And they answerden alle, upon hir fey,
> That they forgave yt hyr, for yt was ryght;
> It was no gilt, it lay not in hir might;
> And seyden hir ensamples many oon.
>
> (ll. 1847–50)

Her involvement, in the first instance strictly private, becomes public once it becomes explicitly discursive. Her experience is no longer her own, and her shame or blame or guilt (which the poet speaks of interchangeably) are revealed to be the published cause of her husband's "foule name" and by implication of the dishonor to the family as a whole. From Ovid, Chaucer borrows the elements that compose the moment of his heroine's sacrifice.

> But pryvely she kaughte forth a knyf,
> And therwithal she rafte hirself hir lyf;
> And as she fel adoun, she kaste hir lok,
> And of hir clothes yet she hede tok.
> For in hir fallynge yet she had a care,
> Lest that hir fet or suche thyng lay bare;
> So wel she loved clennesse and eke trouthe.
>
> (ll. 1854–60)

In its emblematic way, this set-piece is every bit as expressive as Lucrece's own utterances. In particular it expresses her liminal position between the two counterpoised experiential realms: her suicide is the most private of acts, yet in the process of passing from the worldly scene she so conducts herself as to assure her assimilation into the remembered public experience that we call history—and she does so, moreover, precisely on her own terms. Chief among these is the assumption that her sacrifice serves the larger public interest; her regard for inadvertent personal display, as she is falling, looks to that interest from the angle of the individual person. On such terms the sacrificial victim can pass not only into the fateful discourse of worldly things in the general sense but into the more particular discourse in which Lucrece's experience is fateful for the Roman state:

> And Brutus by hir chaste blood hath swore
> That Tarquyn shulde ybanysshed be therfore,
> And al hys kyn; and let the people calle,
> And openly let cary her on a bere
> Thurgh al the toun, that men may see and here
> The horryble dede of hir oppressyoun
>
> (ll. 1862–68)

At the same time, the note on which Lucrece's emblematic fall concludes, with its closing reiteration of her embodiment of "trouthe," prepares the audience for the convergence of truth and will as Chaucer turns from the direct political consequences just described to the moral and social purport for which Lucretia paid the price of her very being:

> I telle hyt, for she was of love so trewe,
> Ne in hir wille she chaunged for no newe . . .
> For wel I wot that Crist himselve telleth
> That in Israel, as syd as is the lond,
> That so gret feyth in al that he ne fond
> As in a woman; and this is no lye.
> And as of men, loke ye which tirannye
> They doon alday; assay hem whoso lyste
> The trewest ys ful brotel for to triste.
>
> (ll. 1874–85)

This Christianizing of pagan experiences climaxes a poem that, though drawing on texts from antiquity, derives special authority from St. Augustine, whose discussion of Lucretia in *The City of God* helps to explain some otherwise enigmatic facts, such as Chaucer's deletion of her call for revenge, or the nonresentful resignation she exhibits in taking her life. In writing on the violation of Christian virgins Augustine already raises questions relevant to Lucrece; generalizing about the role of will any time that pain is inflicted or lust gratified "on the body of another," he observes that whenever anything of this latter kind takes place, shame invades even a thoroughly pure spirit from which modesty has not departed — shame, lest that act which could not be suffered without some sensual pleasure, should be believed to have been committed with some assent of the will.[42]

Here is the worry that Chaucer's Lucrece experiences along with her counterparts in other works. Actually it is two worries compounded: first, there is the possibility that Lucrece shares the stated belief, a possibility that is articulated in Livy and Salutati and left problematic in Chaucer. Second, there is the probability that the action, once brought before the public, will be believed by its members to imply the victim's shame. On either ground Chaucer could feel warranted in distancing his heroine from any direct experience of whatever fair thing could be imagined as accompanying the foul thing of sexual violation. The subtleties of the Augustinian inquiry are sacrificed in the interests of portraying what Lucrece undergoes.

Where Chaucer's interpretation of the relevant experiences is relatively simple, Augustine's is complex. Augustine posits two Lucretias, the innocent who experienced sexual violation and the woman who slew that innocent and is therefore guilty of murder. Through the forensic device of an appeal to the Roman judges and law, Augustine develops an insoluble dilemma. The more the case of murder is extenuated, the larger the adultery looms, and the more the adultery is extenuated, the graver the homicide. What finally interests the author of *The City of God* is the superiority of Christian over pagan experience, and in particular the experience of Christian women who are exemplary for their "true sanctity." Setting a pattern for his Renaissance successors, Augustine emphasizes Lucretia's shame; while he adduces evidence toward her exoneration, he raises questions about her innocence. Imagining Lucretia to be in the underworld, as depicted in the sixth book of the *Aeneid*, Augustine wonders if she is there "because she slew herself conscious of guilt, not of innocence? She herself alone knows her reason; but what if she was betrayed by the pleasure of the act, and gave some consent to Sextus, though so violently abusing her, and then was so affected with remorse, that she thought death alone could expiate her sin?" By associating Lucretia with qualities valued in Rome but not in the City of God, Augustine prepares for the contrast he will draw between her case and the case of Christian women who suffered rape without taking recourse to suicide: "and this Roman matron, with the Roman love of glory in her veins, was seized with a proud dread that, if she continued to live, it would be supposed she willingly did not resent the wrong that had been done her."

Lucretia's dilemma is compounded by perplexities of expression and interpretation. On the one hand, she cannot express what she thinks: "She could not exhibit to men her conscience." On the other hand, if she killed herself "she judged that her self-inflicted punishment would testify to her state of mind." When Augustine then refers to the shame she will feel if *mis*interpreted, he is reverting to her motivation for suicide, and not implying that she will necessarily be misinterpreted even if she does kill herself: "and she burned with shame at the thought that her patient endurance of the foul affront that another had done her, should be construed into complicity with him."

By contrast, true sanctity enables the martyred women to distance themselves from their experience to the point of wishing no ill against their attackers: "They declined to avenge upon themselves the guilt of others, and so add crimes of their own to those crimes in which they had no share." The Roman love of glory has been superseded by the glory of chastity to which the world may now bear witness, a still higher witness having already superseded that world as well: "Within their own souls, in the witness of their own conscience, they enjoy the glory of chastity. In the sight of God, too, they are esteemed pure, and this contents them; they ask no more: it suffices them to have opportunity of doing good, and they decline to evade the distress of human suspicion." The Christian women turn completely away from the more secular realm that is correlative with the Roman love of glory. As she faces the tribunal of her own free will and conscience, each woman experiences the gaze of God and conscience individually. But each does so even as every other does, as a member of a community bound by doctrine and discipline and by shared experience. It is this community of membership that enables Augustine to speak of the women in the plural and mostly uniform terms. Lucretia's experience, by contrast, as she is drawn one way by fear of public exposure and another way by the private appeals of family and friends, is singular and solitary.

In the version of Lucretia's experience ventured by Shakespeare, the animus of action falls to Tarquin, who says to Lucrece:

> Thus I forestall thee, if thou mean to chide:
> Thy beauty hath ensnared thee to this night,
> Where thou with patience must my will abide;
> My will that marks thee for my earth's delight[43]

On Tarquin's reading of male rivalry, one is entitled to increase one's competitive position at the expense of one's rival. Such motivation comes to be expressed "naturally," as a largely automatic function of the animal appetite thereby released—in a word, as lust. Thus the consistent analogy between the rapist and creatures of the "wilderness" (l. 545).

Sonnet 79 speaks powerfully to the relation of lust to expense. "The expense of spirit in a waste of shame / Is lust in action." "Spirit" here signifies soul or essence, that which makes a person selfsame and integral. Acting in lust is expense as expending, as dissipating that essential something that makes a Tarquin, for example, what he is. Shakespeare expresses an essence, one could argue, more than he describes an act; he states what it is in terms of loss and expenditure, as existing only in ceasing to exist. Its expression *is* its expense, its expense its expression. The same quality of contradiction without sublation appears in the will to violate any truth as a means to an end. Here a *locus classicus* is the moment of betrayal when Tarquin, speaking to himself, recalls,

> . . . She took me kindly by the hand,
> And gazed for tidings in my eager eyes,
> Fearing some hard news from the warlike band,
> Where her beloved Collatinus lies. . . .
> And how her hand, in my hand being lock'd,
> Forced it to tremble with her loyal fear!
> (ll. 253–61)

In the context of repeated references to chivalry and knighthood, this deceitful locking of hands parodies the feudal *immixio manum*, in which the lord grasps the hand of his vassal between his own hands as earnest of their mutual bond.[44] The relevance of the connection is further suggested by the fact that for Lucrece the mixing of hands is an expression of hospitality to Tarquin in virtue of a double obligation to him, first and explicitly as a guest to be honored as her husband's faithful friend, secondly and implicitly as the mighty leader who by his station commands the destiny of all Romans.

Looking at the poem as a whole, it could be said that Shakespeare's inclination toward inclusiveness combines with various shifts of discursive strategy and focus to create a certain disproportion between the degree of achieved expression and the potentialities over which it somewhat hungrily hovers. However articulate, Shakespeare's language shows the strain of trying to show what cannot be shown, of saying what cannot be said. The more attempts are made, the more the actual experience of Lucrece becomes unrepresentable.

If Shakespeare does not attempt to render the things that happen as Lucrece herself might have experienced them, he is consistent in his imaginative logic; for, if the victimizer is one who interrupts, and if this violation takes the form of interrupting the victim's discourse, the point to emphasize is the disenabling of the victim's capacity for expressing what she experiences:

> The wolf hath seized his prey, the poor lamb cries;
>   Till with her own white fleece her voice controll'd
>   Entombs her outcry in her lips' sweet fold:
>
> For with the nightly linen that she wears
> He pens her piteous clamours in her head
>
> (ll. 677–81)

This is abject disenabling, profound privation. The rapist deprives the victim of any articulate expression, a loss that is the more painful as all such expression, when she was capable of it, failed to deter the asssailant. The relation between pain and language, in Elaine Scarry's account, may be compared with the experience rendered in Shakespeare's text: "before destroying language," physical pain "first monopolizes language, becomes the only subject: complaint . . . becomes the exclusive mode of speech. Eventually the pain so deepens that the coherence of complaint is displaced by the sounds anterior to learned language." [45] In Lucrece we have both, the muffled cries and the articulate complaint: "To all the host of heaven I complain me, / Thou wrong'st his honour, wound'st his princely name" (ll. 598–99). After the rape Lucrece is ostensibly free to undertake the eloquent complaint that will extend for nearly forty uninterrupted stanzas before issuing in the long peroration on the painting of Troy. But Shakespeare may have felt that time needed to pass before she could manage to express her experience effectively. In any case the truism that he paraphrases just after the rape expresses the expense of her experience in general terms: "But she hath lost a dearer thing than life" (l. 687).

Paradoxically, Lucrece can be eloquent about the incapacity of words to accommodate the very experiences they are designed to express:

Out, idle words, servants to shallow fools!
Unprofitable sounds, weak arbitrators! . . .
To trembling clients be you mediators:
   For me, I force not argument a straw,
   Since that my case is past the help of law.
                (ll. 1016–22)

The alternative to the public redress, represented here by civil justice, "law," is an order of signification ostensibly beyond words:

This helpless smoke of words doth me no right.
   The remedy indeed to do me good
   Is to let forth my foul-defiled blood.
                (ll. 1027–29)

A physics of discourse lies behind the implied likeness between the smoke of words and (in the ensuing stanza) both the smoke of Aetna and the breath of Lucrece. The crucial issue is the similitude between language and *vox*, understood as vocal communication through the medium of air; the substance of speech, to paraphrase Chaucer in *The House of Fame*, is nothing if not air.[46] While words are expressive of presence—the aerial medium must be affected by some physical excitation—at the same time they exemplify ephemerality, even absence. By associating these qualities with Lucrece's desire to breathe her last, Shakespeare presents a woman all but disendowed of the capacity to express her experience:

But this no slaughterhouse no tool imparteth
To make more vent for passage of her breath;
Which, thronging through her lips, so vanisheth
   As smoke from Aetna, that in air consumes,
   Or that which from discharged cannon fumes.
                (ll. 1039–43)

In a variation of the paradox noted above, air, the medium of communication, here becomes the medium of dissolution; that the smoke consumes intransitively, not as the object of a consuming predicate, implies a parallel with Lucrece's impending self-dissolution. As a final enrichment, breath/smoke is sexualized by a further implied parallel between the fiery phallus of the rapist warrior and the smoke that fumes from discharging cannon.

Like her counterparts in the letter novel, Lucrece takes recourse to the pen, but her epistolary expression falls short of her experience.

Conceit and grief an eager combat fight;
What wit sets down is blotted straight with will;
This is too curious-good, this blunt and ill . . .
                (ll. 1298–1300)

The statement reflects a struggle to find a mode of expression adequate to the extreme experiences the author has chosen to depict. To some readers the result is a tension between the themes of evil and suffering, on the one hand, and Shakespeare's sheer virtuosity, reminiscent of an earlier taste for aureate embellishment, of which William Dunbar was a master, on the other. Such may be the price the poet is to pay if, as some evidence warrants, the primary animus of the poem is as much the display of its author's expressive powers as a commitment to represent a female experience of sexual violation.[47]

At the same time the poet sets a definite limit to what Lucrece's epistolary endeavor can achieve. It can express to her husband a sufficient sense of urgency to draw him home, but without sufficiently rendering her felt experience: "By this short schedule Collatine may know / Her grief, but not her grief's true quality" (ll. 1312–13). In a paradox perhaps more apparent than real, this experience becomes a resource and an animus; if it were not both, there would be nothing to sustain, for example, her engagement with the painting of Troy, a painting at once intensive and extensive, or her long perorations on its figures and themes (beginning at l. 1463). Lucrece holds back in her letter, believing that once Collatine is present, expression can occur on a more primal level of sounds anterior to learned language; only then can she afford the expense implied in her plan of expression: "Besides, the life and feeling of her passion / She hoards, to spend when he is by to hear her" (ll. 1317–18). "Spend" here means "to expend" (I.1.1175) as disposing of (in a sense, Lucrece desires nothing so much as getting *rid* of her experience) and "to expend or employ (speech or language)" (I.9.a.13). Sighs and groans and tears draw on some power subtending discourse as utterance, a primordial power that is yet a ready reservoir of expressive energy. At the close of the next stanza Shakespeare implies a parallel between Lucrece's experiential hoard, "the life and feeling of her passion," and a more general realm of oceanic *ur*-feeling that is like a natural resource:

> 'Tis but a part of sorrow that we hear:
>   Deep sounds make lesser noise than shallow fords,
>   And sorrow ebbs, being blown with wind of words.
>
>   (ll. 1328–30)

In her extended engagement with the painting of Troy, Lucrece resumes her role as reader, trying to make sense of what she is going through in relation to what the Trojans went through as rendered by the painter. Mediating his heroine's mediation of the painter's mediation, the poet renders an experience of her experience of the painter's experience of the Trojan experience. So much mediation makes for a density expressive in its own right; to the extent that the process of mediation can become more interesting than what is being mediated, it also has a distancing effect, which is to put in a slightly different way the problem of fit between Shakespeare's subject matter and his handling of it. In any case, the encounter with the painting is in a large measure the agon between the painter and Lucrece. While the painter has rendered the experience of the Trojan principals in such and such a way, Lucrece has a different interpretation, though not a fundamentally different experience; her way of expressing aims at what is similar between her situation and the painted situation, attempting compensations for deficiencies, especially in the case of Hecuba. On the plight of this sorrowing figure "Lucrece spends her eyes" (l. 1457), in the sense of shedding or allowing to flow (1602). Lucrece will express what Hecuba cannot: " 'Poor instrument,' quoth she, 'without a sound, / I'll tune thy woes with my lamenting tongue' " (ll. 1464–65).

Lucrece's memorial expressiveness, as sign and sacrifice for the Roman state, is postponed until Shakespeare can paint his picture-in-words, not of Lucrece's final moments but of her now emblematic blood. To discern that this is literary blood is to locate its provenance in an author such as Sir Philip Sidney, with whom the young Shakespeare is tacitly competing in showing his own poetic prowess. Book Three of the *Arcadia* describes the moment when Amphialus learns who the person he has slain in knightly combat was. In a new *aisthēsis* requiring female death as an enabling condition of male discursive power, Parthenia is beauty's epitome and integer.

Leading from episode to episode, before resulting in Parthenia's death in battle, the contestatory chain extends into Sidney's set-piece: there is "the whiteness striving by little and little to get upon the rosiness" of Parthenia's cheeks, then, as the troping turns "natural," a rivalry in expressive appearance between other components of the fleshly scene: "her neck, a neck indeed of alabaster, displaying the wound, which with most dainty blood laboured to drown his own beauties, so as here was a river of purest red, there an island of perfectest white, each giving lustre to the other; with the sweet countenance, God knows, full of an unaffected languishing." [48]

Like Sidney, Shakespeare is lavish in expending blood, and to that extent follows the new poetic fashion of the time. But that fashion is also a challenge for a knight of words competing to honor and be honored by patrons who, if they do not represent authentic chivalry, at least require, as part of what they do represent, some flavor of the chivalric. To meet such a challenge is to compete in the same general vein as the model author while nudging it in a different direction. Shakespeare first shows himself to be a qualified competitor:

> And bubbling from her breast, it doth divide
> In two slow rivers, that the crimson blood
> Circles her body in on every side,
> Who, like a late-sack'd island, vastly stood

Bare and unpeopled in this fearful flood.
  Some of her blood still pure and red remain'd,
  And some look'd black, and that false Tarquin stain'd.
                                        (ll. 1737–43)

Of this one can say what may also be said of Sidney's text, that it looks more like an experience of a poet's expression than an expression of a character's experience. Lucrece has paid the ultimate price: all that is left of her is this literal, incarnadine ex-pression in which her life's blood courses.

9. Opportunity and Occasion

We remember with Dewey that experience is both doing and undergoing and that doing and undergoing are forever shading into one another. Lucrece for a long time undergoes violation in a discursive mode before the overt attack, but in the same long time she does a great deal of doing. She is most effective, arguably, when, having undergone remorse and recrimination, she can express her suffering actively as a demand for revenge.

To say that the subsequent emergence of Brutus brings this doing to its consummation is to say that he takes advantage of the offered *opportunity*, signifying what is opportune, as adapted to some end or purpose, with reference to time or circumstance and possibly precipitated by chance (1325). The unpredictability of human action is always at issue when the question of opportunity—or occasion, as Machiavelli prefers to say—is seriously explored. "The distinctive characteristic of practical activity, one which is so inherent that it cannot be eliminated, is the uncertainty which attends it. Of it we are compelled to say: Act, but act at your peril" (*LW* 4:5–6).

Although Lucrece is traditional in associating opportunity with uncertainty, as exemplified by the wheel of Fortune, individual fortunes, and "mischance" (ll. 952, 934, 968), she personifies it, more negatively, as an "ill-annexed" and "vile" thing whose "guilt is great" (ll. 874, 895, 876). It is not surprising that Lucrece, still in trauma, further darkens this already dark picture. It is unsurprising that, in view of our previous discussion, she should frame it within the polarity of private and public:

'Thy secret pleasure turns to open shame,
  Thy private feasting to a public fast. . . .
  How comes it then, vile Opportunity,
  Being so bad, such numbers seek for thee?
                                        (ll. 890–96)

A fateful interventionist whose intent is as malevolent as its timing is exquisite, Opportunity would be a figure of paranoia if the paranoia were not, as here, entirely warranted: "My Collatine would also have come to me / When Tarquin did, but he was stay'd by thee" (ll. 916–17).

The criteria by which the opportunist is to be measured may be expressed in terms of our three offices as follows. He must possess the wherewithal to act effectively in public; it is of course the lack of this endowment that Brutus has feigned by living the life of the born fool. The opportunist must take advantage of whatever in the situation he has the capacity to enable. The occasion as such does not offer a clear choice among alternatives, but is co-created, as it were, by the way in which the agent acts. Finally, the opportunist must stand on some entitlement. Here it is the right of aggrieved parties to seek redress for hurt family honor.

These criteria are the same in Machiavelli as in Shakespeare, and Brutus meets them in essentially the same way. As we have seen, in the *Discourses* Machiavelli applauds Brutus for knowing when, where, and how to go public with his capacities and claims. More generally, Machiavelli says of founders and their occasions: "When we look into their actions and their lives, we will find that fortune provided nothing for them but an opportunity [*occasione*]; that gave them material, on which they would impose whatever form they chose. Without the opportunity their strength [*virtù*] of mind would have been vain, and without that strength [*virtù*] the opportunity would have been lost."[49]

As an endowment primarily associated with men, *virtù* is assertive and formative in contrast with opportunity, which, in parallel with traditional scenarios of the female response to male assertion, must receive whatever is imposed. Shakespeare speaks to the same issue when he observes:

> For men have marble, women waxen, minds,
> And therefore are they form'd as marble will; . . .
> Then call them not the authors of their ill,
>   No more than wax shall be accounted evil
>   Wherein is stamp'd the semblance of a devil.
>   (ll. 1240–46)

In Shakespeare and in Machiavelli alike, truly felicitous opportunity is rare; only briefly in the long stretches of worldly time does it offer at all. What occasions fateful founding, Machiavelli believes, is less luck or serendipity than something worthy of being overcome in the very process of seizing the opportunity. Speaking of Moses, Romulus, Cyrus, and Theseus, he observes that "specific occasions brought these happy men to power, and their unusual abilities [*virtù*] enabled them to seize the occasion and so to make their countries noble and very fortunate."[50] Occasion being a female with a forelock concealing her face and breast but otherwise bald, seizers who would be Caesars should consider how Machiavelli pictures her in verse:

Low on my brow before me spreads my hair,
So that it covers my breast and face;
Thus, no one knows me, coming, till I'm there.
Of hair behind my head there's not a trace.
Hence, one I've turned against, or hurried by,
Can never catch me: it's no good to try.[51]

To seize the occasion is to act quickly and decisively. Nor is speed any less a desideratum where, as in the case of a political founder like Brutus, the occasion is paradigmatically public and originary. On the contrary, the type of action appropriate to such an occasion is by definition prompt, since any delay or temporizing only increases the danger that long historical experience has shown to inhere in innovation: "Nothing is harder to manage, more risky in the undertaking, or more doubtful of success than to set up as the introducer of a new order . . . men don't really believe in anything new till they have had solid experience of it."[52]

Much is required of a founder. He must express the interests of those around him as his own, his own as theirs; he must tell them what they need to hear without their knowing that they need to hear it. What they need to hear is that they must act like real men, for, in expressing their expense as tearfully as Lucrece has expressed hers, they are, by their own standards, the less manly because the more feminine. Here is the leverage of Brutus's chastisement: "Courageous Roman, do not steep thy heart / In such relenting dew of lamentations" (ll. 1828–29). In one way this is to charge the political brethren with being *too much* like Lucrece—weak, emotional, private. But in another way it is to charge them with being *not enough* like Lucrece: for, by putting her private experience in a public perspective, this woman has embraced the consequences of her rape and suicide for posterity.

Ironically, the men must then emulate the woman, must do what she has already, heroically, done. But by a further irony this can happen only because the men have become the malleable matter that the individual virile founder seizes the opportunity of shaping. In the form-matter metaphysics of the epoch, it is because the male founders may be acted upon as women are acted upon, because they can be shaped by one mastering will, that they are reborn into the private identities through whom public order may itself be reborn.

In the figure of Lucretia, the author of *Pamela* and *Clarissa* finds an opportunity to explore experience not for breadth of public implication but for depth of intimacy. Like Sappho, Lucretia becomes a trope signifying an order of experience and discourse representative of a genre, the novel, and an age, the seventeenth and more especially the eighteenth century. Doing even partial justice to that genre, that age, and that order of discourse and experience requires a preliminary word about the interrelationship and interdependence of the social and the personal.

10. *Personal Experience and the Social*

More than differences in genre distinguish between, on the one hand, the founding in which the handling of Lucretian materials typically culminates, and on the other, the founding of the novel, and more particularly the letter novel, and what might be called novelistic experience. In the former, the fictional discourse reconstructs the constitution of a public order through the mediation of private persons acting in the interest of that order. In the latter, the discourse of origin, without for the most part directly engaging the public order, reconstructs an order of experience in which the dominant interests are immediately personal and mediately social. "The foundation of at least one domain in the literary order," the domain of the novel, in both its epistolary and historical varieties, "bears a striking resemblance to the scenarios that have been devised to account for the foundation of the cultural order." In the emerging novelistic genres of seventeenth-century France, a leading scenario expresses the expense of intimate female experience: "A multitude of aspiring literary figures came of age when they devised rules to govern not the exchange of women but the sharing of a fiction of female desire." [53] Like their counterparts in Richardson, say, or in Aphra Behn, these figures follow Ovid's lead into the realms of intimate feelings and desires, especially those of eros, and more especially those of female eros. The author of the *Heroides* had entitled himself to be, in the eyes of those whose discourse he most influenced, the representative voice of the female point of view. "On the basis of the *Heroides*, heroism was defined as a state of physical paralysis produced by a longing for love both lost and treacherous, limiting therefore its territory to tales of betrayal and abandonment. Because of Ovid's founding influence, a novelistic heroine, unlike her male counterpart, traditionally was almost always unhappy and unlucky in love." [54]

Emerging in the seventeenth century and flowering in the eighteenth, epistolary fiction was a proving ground in which to express, in all the registers of sensibility, these more intimate intensities of experience, and in particular the experience of love and desire. For both terms seem in order in a discursive field extending from the sisterly affection Clarissa feels for Anna Howe to the domestic bond she feels with her family; from the heterosexual desire that Lovelace demonstrably feels, to its transfiguration after Clarissa's death; from the possessive self-interest of Choderlos de Laclos's Valmont and Richardson's Lovelace to the connubial bond between Charlotte and her husband in *The Sorrows of Young Werther* to Werther's determination to replace him in her affections. Interwoven as it is with questions of power, interest, honor, sacrifice, and revenge, the intense and intimate interplay of incorporate love and desire falls within the purview of all that is sharably worldly, fateful, and thus, in various senses of the terms to be developed below, within the larger realm of social experience.

Arendt explores what she calls the social through Rousseau who, as the first to theorize the experience of intimacy, sets society in opposition to the individual. In contrast to the privacy of the household, which occupies an appointed place in an ordered social whole, the realm of the intimate is relatively placeless, hence Rousseau's desire to give it a local habitation and a name. To express intimate individual experience is to protest against the leveling tendencies of the social sphere, which is liable to disentitle the individual's claim to freedom:

> The decisive historical fact is that modern privacy in its most relevant function, to shelter the intimate, was discovered as the opposite not of the political sphere but of the social, to which it is therefore most closely and authentically related. . . . The astonishing flowering of poetry and music from the middle of the eighteenth century and until almost the last third of the nineteenth, accompanied by the rise of the novel, the only entirely social art form, coinciding with a no less striking decline of all the more public arts, especially architecture, is sufficient testimonial to a close relationship between the social and the intimate.[55]

It is a feature of such relations that what is distinctive in each may be inferred from the ways in which it differs from its counterpart. Which helps to explain the otherwise mysterious paradox we find in a confessional discourse like Rousseau's, or in letter writers who "speak from the heart": that the realm of the intimate, requiring shelter from the social realm, is exposed to the latter in the very act of expression. Perhaps believing that the best protection lies in self-justification, Rousseau is forever explaining himself to society even as he discloses what an erring egotist he truly is. In the case of letter writers, at least as they appear in epistolary fiction, the risk of exposure is countered by the fictional constructions themselves, which posit that the experiences the writers express are sharable because of the essential equality of writers and readers. Writers after all have their reading to do, even as readers have their writing to do.

The realm of the social may be defined negatively, in opposition to the private and the public:

> The distinction between a private and a public sphere of life corresponds to the household and the political realms, which have existed as distinct, separate entities at least since the rise of the ancient city-state; but the emergence of the social realm, which is neither private nor public, strictly speaking, is a relatively new phenomenon whose origin coincided with the emergence of the modern age and which found its political form in the nation-state.[56]

To say that the novel is the entirely social form is to say that the experiences it expresses can be identified neither with the hidden space of the household, where immediate needs and desires are ministered to, nor with the *polis*, where one's acts are exposed to the eyes of persons other than one's familiars or "inferiors." More positively, calling the novel entirely social signifies that the worldly things of which it discourses embrace all that is intimate and personal, as well as everything encompassed in our experience of society in all its complexity. But because the novel is, like other art forms, capable of contesting, altering, and transcending, it does not merely reflect the interplay of the intimate and the social. It problematizes that interplay, and indeed the polarity itself—for all the while the novel keeps open the channels implicitly connecting it with more traditional spheres of private and public experience. It weighs, to put the matter another way, the implications of such ponderable ratios as: the private is to the public as the intimate is to the social; or, the private is to the intimate as the public is to the social.

It may be said that the novel's *way* of being social encompasses not only everything that fills up the space between the private and public realms, but those extremes as well. Of the two extremes, the private, shading into the individual and the intimate, is what many readers seek in novels, and they can usually find it: modern novels are nothing if not explorations of individual experience. But there are enough exceptions to give pause. Novelists such as Tolstoy and Balzac, taking on subjects already belonging to, or concurrently becoming, part of the contemporary social record, make the activities of governments, armies, entrepreneurs, and functionaries a vital part of the reading experience that is ultimately a part of that record as well. Then there is the complex partial exception such as *Bleak House*, where Dickens's account of the interminable case of Jarndyce versus Jarndyce is in its own way an education in the law. In treating so public a matter, Dickens renders with special poignancy both the personal fates of a Volumnia or an Esther Summerson, and the more impersonal fate of the human/nonhuman environment embodied in Volumnia's blank domicile with its wilderness of passageways and labyrinths, or the no less labyrinthine confusion of manufactured iron things, perversely twisted, or the settling of iron-dust over everything in Rouncewell's factory. A miasma extending metonymically into the oppressive vapors of Krook's chambers experienced after his spontaneous combustion, the famous fog at the start of the novel is a bleakness of the social itself, seen through a glass very darkly: a realm where all experience is leveled in indifference, where destiny is decided by bureaucrats. What is left in the way of intimacy, the one thing you really experience when isolated in the nothingness of this terrible anti-womb, from which nothing new or good will ever come forth, is the close clutch of your self.

The letter novel privileges intimate experiences just at the point of their emergence, when they seem most spontaneous and pristine, as though liable to unmediated representation. Knowing perfectly well that only in theory does such representation exist, the epistolary novelist aims at a version of immediate register: if representation mediates, the closest thing to something fresh and unadulterated is the liminality of the experience, the very *process* of doing or being done to. The temporal unit of social intimacy or intimate sociality is thus the moment of expression. In this fateful moment experiencing *is*. Experiencing is also, and at the same time, reexperiencing. What the correspondent communicates is most often what has already happened, so that the representation of it in a letter means that the first experience is being experienced again and made available to reflection. I will return to this theme, exploring the relation of reexperiencing to consequences of actions, in the final section.

In this warm world of mine and yours and ours, correspondents luxuriate in such grand floods of experience as are enabled by their endowment of circumstance and sensibility. This use of "luxuriate" looks to Hume, who sees luxury not as a mode of excess but as an essential constituent of civilized life: "In general, it means a great refinement in the gratification of the senses; and any degree of it may be innocent or blameable, according to the age, or country, or condition of the person."[57] Without the opportunities for experience afforded by luxury, which Hume links with leisure, societies do not achieve refinement, let alone refinement in the arts. Those ages are most virtuous and happiest that enable their citizens' improvement through leisure by furnishing the necessary wherewithal: only an endowment much in excess of sustenance enables development in either industry or the arts, together with collateral improvement in manners.

Isolation of the correspondent is an enabling condition for the organization of personal and social experience favored by epistolary fiction.[58] Freely chosen or forced, the withdrawal of the correspondent from immediate contact with others enables the mediate contact with them that is both the origin and end of what Richardson calls the converse of the pen. Apart and alone, the letter-writer roams the world in a simulation of the freedom enjoyed by the author of the framing fiction, and is entitled, as if by delegation from the latter, to the authority of authorship and, with that authority, to the guarantee of authenticity. In the literature of the epistolary, nothing is more insisted on than the authenticity of what is written. This can be attested to by declaring that letters coming by chance into the possession of the editor are being published in their original form; the letters can also be discovered by accident, or offered as reliable testimonials by which to correct erroneous aspects of the public record. The strategy of soliciting letters from actual persons was adopted by Defoe, who worked some of the material he received into various texts of his own, while evidently reproducing others verbatim. And only reluctantly did Richardson give up his claim to have edited a correspondence actually composed by others. In any event, the novel in letters lays particular claim to the supposition of authentic representation: the experience that is most social in being most individual, intimate, and intense is the experience that happened just the way it is here and now said to have happened. This hardly alters the fact that a novel like *Clarissa* or *Les liaisons dangereuses* swarms with deceptions, for we are to suppose that the authorial account of those deceptions is itself authentic. Without such a supposition neither irony nor evil is liable to being meaningfully experienced.

While they overlap, isolation and solitude are not identical. The experience of pain, as noted above, is essentially personal and inexpressible; it literally isolates. In general, formal isolation from society may be directly punitive, as in the penal isolation cell, or reformative, as in Adams's penitential *boudoir*. But solitude is more frequently welcomed for its enabling capacity; it is a recurring theme in pastoral, where swains withdraw from the world to be worldly in a different way. Solitude and isolation are social phenomena. The solitary or isolated person is such temporarily, and in relation to one or another social formation to which that person otherwise belongs: thus the reference, above, to the others who are virtually or recollectively present. Solitude is an experience of society in a distanced, partly exclusionary mode. Ugo Foscolo's *The Last Letters of Jacopo Ortis* describes the experiences of those who have been forced outside of both family and nation, and in various ways Pamela and Clarissa and Werther, not to mention Aphra Behn's epistolary characters, experience the pain of separation and exclusion.

Solitude can draw upon the resources of society without succumbing to its seductions. A ready way to do this is to draw on those resources by citation. While often seen, rather narrowly, in terms of strictly "literary influence" and "literary tradition," the practice of quotation is socially significant as well. When Goethe's Werther incorporates in a letter a text from Ossian, a nexus of socially conditioned experiences and significations comes into play. When Werther and Charlotte are overcome with feeling on simultaneously recollecting an ode by Klopstock, their intimate shared experience is made available by a collectively determined sensibility. The irony is that Klopstock, the poet who endows solitary contemplation with a new legitimacy, becomes the enabler of experiential enlargement not only for these two individuals, but ultimately for a wide spectrum of the bourgeoisie that they represent.

Quoting inheres in the correspondent's own act of writing as a transcription of what this or that person has previously experienced and expressed. Its text is reportage; and it has in common with the newspaper the further fact that it cannot disguise its mediation of the past, as more traditional narrative techniques in the third person or the first person can arguably do. What makes this a different type of reporting from that practiced by, say, the mercurial Defoe is the type of experience that is made available to readers. For what is prized in letter novels comes largely to consist in the *experience of expression*, the news that is reported being inseparable from the feeling and thinking one undergoes in reporting it.

In epistolary fiction we often encounter not only the appropriation-by-quoting of a particular text, but the incorporating of something as large as another socially sanctioned literary *kind*. In *Werther*, Goethe interrupts what is essentially a romance to undertake, in Book 2, a depiction of his hero's experiences in court society that has elements of the novel of manners and of social satire, only to shift again when Werther experiences enough humiliation in high society to send him back to the relative intimacy of Wahlheim. Richardson will shift from breathless transcription to omnibus essayism, patterned on the conduct book and drawing on the argumentation of casuistry, to produce a secular homiletic. One justification is that correspondents, whose first allegiance is to the experience of expression, can, after all, say whatever they like. The claim of freedom is one that some letter novels make in an important way, especially those of Richardson, who stakes a great deal on his characters' specifically Christian freedom of will. But this same freedom leads also to the problem of impersonation, for if characters are free to say what they want to say, they are equally free to be who they want to be. To rely as extensively as the letter novel does on impersonation is to raise questions about the authenticity of the experience described. A letter asks to be believed, as it is supposed to be, in a basic sense, an authentic representation of an authentic experience. Even a letter written to deceive relies on this expectation. Like the feelings it tends to convey, the letter is to be experienced in its suddenness and intensity even as it is judged for its veracity.

What counts as authentic often depends on some form of authority more or less representative of society. Thus the intervention of a figure, commonly an editor, whose mediation provides perspective or assumes responsibility. Such an intervention occurs in *Pamela* following Letter 31: "Here it is necessary the reader should know, that the fair Pamela's trials were not yet over."[59] In *Werther* the intervention is based on the device of the fragment: because his friend's record of experience has been left behind in bits and pieces it is left to the editor to act in his behalf by providing a connecting narrative. Foscolo follows this lead by causing a friend of Jacopo's to intercede after the latter's death in order to complete his story, while in his *Hyperion* Hölderlin works a variation on the pattern by delegating the role to the protagonist, who becomes in effect the editor of letters from Diotima.

Let us look more closely at the first of these interventions. From the beginning of the story, Werther's lack of a home is experienced against a series of conjugal affiliations (those of the peasant woman whose husband is away, the vicar and his wife, and Mr. and Mrs. M), and against three pairs who are not shown to attain the marital state—Frederike and her suitor, the servant whose love for a widow is opposed by her brother, and a man named Heinrich, driven mad by unrequited love for Charlotte. The crisis that brings on the intervention of the social in the person of the editor follows Werther's encounter with the madman, his discovery that Charlotte is the woman in question, and an intensely intimate scene with Charlotte, who tries to make Werther understand he is unbalanced.

Now, all these man-woman relations gravitate around the family structure favored by market-society individualism, namely, the conjugal unit. The emphasis on romantic love associated with the rise of individualist ideology trains each prospective member of the unit to seek out that other person whose intrinsic qualities will be most likely to foster lasting, interdependent intimacy. From this it is clear that the intervention of the editor in *Werther* counterbalances the grave consequences of a failure to achieve the family solidarity on which the fortunes of this particular young man in this particular society ultimately depend. Shifting to a different order of narrative, the editor makes it possible for readers to avoid becoming too intimate with the character, and decreases the risk that he will appear in any way exemplary. Goethe has his editor favor an established form, the third-person omniscient narrative, just as he has his protagonist favor an established family: Charlotte's father is the district judge. Werther seeks not so much to venture forth into the social but to immerse himself in the intimate.

Another key social aspect emerges when we view the same process from the perspective of Werther's own felt experience and the need to restrain his antisocial tendencies. For Werther the world becomes a place of dangerous resemblance as he encounters versions of himself in the madman and in the homicidal servant. Realizing that the murder he has heard about was committed by a person he knows, Werther rushes to Wahlheim, speaks to the man, then defends him to the judge and to Albert. At issue throughout is the question of judgment and justice. Werther judges the murderer to be essentially innocent, and appeals to an actual judge who answers for society with the argument that, if Werther's defense of antisocial behavior were justified, law would give way and public security would be destroyed. Hearing this, Werther has yet sufficient judgment to recognize that he must capitulate to the claim of justice as socially institutionalized. Rather than screw the problem to a higher pitch, Goethe resolves it into a perspectivism: on the one hand, there is the slow-grown wisdom of social experience, and, on the other, the folly of the too spontaneous individual. The social definition of what is just is able to triumph not once but twice: first, when Werther capitulates; second, when, as a consequence of this, his sense of his own social being rapidly deteriorates. All his negative experiences parade before his memory, beginning with the humiliation he suffered at the ambassador's because of his low social status, a humiliation that heightens his sense of subsequent failures. Werther concludes that he has the right to be inactive—that he is justified as an artist in not producing art, and as a man in giving up the effort to find a place for himself in the greater social world.

The editor plays the role of a protecting presence; significantly, the first piece of action he describes turns on Werther's relation to a paternal power—to a man who is literally father and judge. The editor is himself such a power, a figure of authority but also of sympathy—again like a father and like a judge; but as one who enjoys an unquestioned power to constrain in order to protect, he is also like a noble patron. The function of this authority figure can thus be seen as the paternal-noble function estheticized. As Goethe fashions him, the editor perpetuates a vertical social structure, such as one finds in family and in court, but devises a different legitimation for it. The editor's power is neither legal nor filial; he acquires it neither by inheritance nor by heredity, but by experience. The basis of his social legitimacy is his worldly experience and profession, which is why his relation to readers is so important, for only readers can validate his judgment or certify his competence as a friend to truth.

Truth is attested by the word as bond, a venerable concept in Western tradition. But the particular bonding at issue here is between persons with shared experience, and is fraternal and spontaneous. It is a more or less improvised social construction along the lines that had begun to emerge in the thirteenth and fourteenth centuries, replacing more formal, inherited relations of a more rigidly hierarchical order. One sees a similar improvisation, a kind of spontaneous spinning off from immediate personal experience, in the proliferation in Chaucer's day of terms for various social formations. *Confederacy, brotherhood, fraternity, congregation, conventicle, assembly, alliance, conspiracy* give evidence of a general shift from the verticality of vassalage to horizontal relations of relatively equal actors composing what social scientists call affinity groups, the leading virtue of which "was, of course, flexibility: by escaping the rigidities of strict hierarchy . . . the affinity permitted a more flexible vocabulary of social relations, a widened array of rewards for specialized or temporary services." [60]

11. *Reexperiencing: Consequence and Reflection*

Such awareness of consequential change is a register of experience as well as of the need to revisit experience. It is thus a mode of what I referred to above as reexperiencing, which can be even more telling than the original experience. It is often in reflection, and sometimes only in reflection, that we comprehend consummations in themselves, as well as the acts and circumstances leading up to them.

In literary art, and in drama in particular, reexperiencing takes the form of recognition, *anagnorisis*, the moment wherein the tragic heroine or hero does not merely suffer but suffers anew. The story of Oedipus is in Western literature the paradigmatic instance of this, and in the pages that follow we will consider the fate of another tragic figure, Richardson's Clarissa. But for the moment let me draw on Arendt's comments on our subject:

> I deliberately mention tragedy because it more than the other literary forms represents a process of recognition. The tragic hero becomes knowledgeable by re-experiencing what has been done in the way of suffering, and in this *pathos*, in resuffering the past, the network of individual acts is transformed into an event, a significant whole. The dramatic climax of tragedy occurs when the actor turns into a sufferer; therein lies its peripeteia, the disclosure of the dénouement. But even non-tragic plots become genuine events only when they are experienced a second time in the form of suffering by memory operating retrospectively and perceptively.[61]

In the letter the process may go something like this. Chronologically, a correspondent has an experience A, which occurs prior to the space of time in the letter describing that experience. This description is then experience B, the original experience as reexperienced. The return letter experiences A through the mediation of B, and that experience can then become — if that is what she focusses on in her own letter — her own experience A, and so forth. Such a relation is important in the genre because it introduces a certain feel of experienced immediacy — not because there is no mediation, but on the contrary because the recipient's reexperiencing closely resembles that of the correspondent. This is to say nothing of such instances as Clarissa's formal meditations or Lovelace's acutely conscious sense of himself as theatrical performer. It is accurate to say that a crucial consequence of every experience in the texts at issue *is* the way it is reflected upon.

It is a consideration of which the authors are fully aware. When Goethe hears of young men dressing like Werther and killing themselves, he witnesses the kind of consequence that his creation of the editor as an intervention in his text is designed to preclude, or at least to limit. Goethe does not want his character to be thought of as somehow exemplary; this, however, is just what Richardson, if the moral and spiritual consequences of his heroines' actions are to be reflected upon, does want. To arrive at such reflection is to understand that example, consequence, and reflection itself each stands in relation to something else, usually an experience temporally or logically prior. More precisely, each follows from something else and, with its own consummation, opens the possibility that something further will follow from it in turn. Where Pamela, for example, is considered, the concatenation or chain begins neither when Pamela is shown to set an example nor when the ostensible auditor steps in to moralize her experience. To become an example, Pamela must relate to something prior, an example of the same basic kind. Exemplarity is thus a consequence of—which is to say, follows from—*imitatio*. Hence in an early encounter with Mr. B she takes recourse to published literary discourse: "I said, like as I had read in a book a night or two before, Angels and saints, and all the host of heaven, defend me" (*P* 25). The immediate consequence is a metadiscursive interplay in which one sphere of literary experience archly contests another, the shared point of reference being Lucretia:

> He by force kissed my neck and lips; and said, Whoever blamed *Lucretia*? All the blame lay on the ravisher only; and I am content to take all the blame upon me, as I have already borne too great a share for what I have not deserved. May I, said I, *Lucretia* like, justify myself with my death, if I am used barbarously! O my good girl! said he, tauntingly, you are well read, I see; and we shall make out between us, before we have done, a pretty story in romance, I warrant yet. (*P* 25–26)

Pamela's ability to counter so experienced a casuist is equally due to endowing and to enabling. Endowing, in that she has high native capacities, several times referred to as constituting genius; enabling, in that despite her inferior social status she has as the consequence of her schoolmaster father's efforts a good education. This connection enables us to see the extent to which Richardson's moral imagination departs from the Lucretian tradition in one respect while continuing it in another. He departs from tradition by concentrating on the intimacy and intensity of the experience expressed. Pamela's Lucretia meets Mr. B's Tarquin in isolation from society, and the fateful founding of a new civic order is scaled down to the founding of a new household. Richardson continues tradition, however, by attributing Pamela's triumph to a patriarchal nexus, the male endowing and enabling to which reference has already been made and which is revealed in terms of the masculine birth of time contemplated by Brutus.

> We walked on till we came to the coach, where was my dear father. Pamela, said my master, tell Mr. Williams who that good man is. O, Mr. Williams! said I, it is my dear father! and my master was pleased to say, One of the honestest men in England: Pamela owes every thing that she is to be, as well as her being, to him; for, I think, she would not have brought me to this, nor made so great resistance, but for the good lessons, and religious education, she had imbibed from him. (*P* 323–24)

This handling of Lucretian experiences seems almost casual in comparison with the intense energies to which comparable experiences give rise in *Clarissa*. In Letter 72 Belford reflects, for the edification of his friend Lovelace, on the fateful consequences in store for Clarissa:

> If thou proceedest, I have no doubt that this affair will end tragically, one way or other. It *must*. Such a woman must interest both gods and men in her cause. But what I most apprehend is, that with her own hand, in resentment of the perpetrated outrage, she (like another Lucretia) will assert the purity of her heart: or, if her piety preserve her from this violence, that wasting grief will soon put a period to her days.[62]

Clarissa herself recognizes the parallel between Lucretia's experience and her own, but the trauma she is undergoing makes expression difficult. She forgets her train of thought, then remembers it, then writes in a hurry for fear of losing it again, before trying to convince Lovelace that the price of possessing her is more than he will want to pay.

While it is Lovelace himself who can then speak of Clarissa and Lucretia in the same breath, he does so in order to deny any tragic consequences where Clarissa is concerned. The effect is made dramatically ironic by the fact that in the same statement Lovelace expresses an enlarged sense of the experience he is forcing Clarissa to undergo; he even understands that the inability to discourse articulately on that subject, due to intense emotion, is itself a crucial aspect of the experience:

> As I told them, I had prepared myself for high passions, raving, flying, tearing execration . . . But such a majestic composure—seeking me—whom yet, it is plain, by her attempt to get away, she would have avoided seeing—no Lucretia-like vengeance upon herself in her thought—yet swallowed up, her whole mind swallowed up, as I may say, by a grief so heavy, as, in her own words, to be beyond the power of speech to express—and to be able, discomposed as she was to the very morning, to put such a home question to me, as if she had penetrated my future view—how could I avoid looking like a fool, and answering, as before, in broken sentences, and confusion? (*C* 3:221)

Such reflective moments function, as in Shakespeare or Sidney, to test the limits of expression. Yet the very positing of a realm "beyond the power of speech to express" is in a measure to express that realm after all, and this can be enabling in two directions, both ending in extremes. For it leads not so much to the beautiful as to the grotesque or the sublime: a speaker "expressing" what is beyond the power of expression risks clownish splutter, at one extreme, or ventures upon high, even Longinian effects at another. Richardson gives us the first by recording how Lovelace, "looking like a fool," answers Clarissa's saintlike composure with "broken sentences, and confusion":

What—what-a—what has been done—I, I, I—cannot but say—must own—
must confess—hem—hem—is not right—is not what should have been—
but-a—but—but—I am truly—truly—sorry for it—upon my soul I am—
and—and—will do all—do everything—do what—whatever is incumbent
upon me—all that you—that you—that you shall require, to make you
amends! (*C* 3:221)

Clarissa counters transcendentally: "O thou truly despicable wretch! Then,
lifting up her eyes—Good Heaven! who shall pity the creature who could fall
by so base a mind!" (*C* 3:441).

Lovelace aims at the same high plane of expression when Clarissa, like
the Lucretias before her, suddenly gushes blood, evidently the consequence of
her having stabbed herself, just as Belford had predicted; whereupon Lovelace introduces into the novel an element of a threatened double suicide:
"Long will I not survive you! And I was upon the point of drawing my sword
to dispatch myself, when I discovered [what an unmanly blockhead does
this charming creature make me at her pleasure!] that all I apprehended was
but a bloody nose" (*C* 3:240). Whatever of sublimity this rendering might
otherwise have possessed has already, of course, been compromised, Lovelace
having exposed the true cause of the bleeding well before his histrionic response. Tragedy yields to farce, the sublime to the grotesque.

Far more fateful is the scene in which Clarissa confronts Lovelace and
his female confederates in her place of confinement. There is no expense of
blood; there is rather the threat that Clarissa will imitate the first Lucretia by
taking her life in order to save her honor.

To my astonishment, she held forth a penknife in her hand, the point to her
own bosom, grasping resolutely the whole handle, so that there was no offering to take it from her.

"I offer not mischief to anybody but myself. You, sir, and ye women, are
safe from every violence of mine. The LAW shall be all my resource: the LAW,"
and she spoke the word with emphasis, that to such people carries natural
terror with it, and now struck a panic into them. (*C* 3:288–89)

In this dramatic moment Clarissa expresses herself to rare effect: the specter
of society and its police powers suddenly looms in the imagination of her cap-
tors; the realm of legal officers with the authority to act against these wrong-
doers is not so far off after all. It is in order for Clarissa to accuse Lovelace
himself of lacking the authority to detain her. The problem, of course, is that
Lovelace is endowed with a social power, consisting of class, money, education, status, customs, but incorporated in personal demonic intensities. The
one thing that prevents the intimacy he seeks with Clarissa is her deeply felt
morality, the saintlike intensities of which enforce distance.

That this is a distance between two radically different realms of experience and reflection is dramatized as Clarissa, knife pointed at her heart, undergoes a spiritual struggle in which Lovelace and his women are spectators. In the spatial economy of Richardson's staging, Clarissa maintains a position to which Lovelace must accommodate his own. Advancing, Lovelace is turned back by her appeal to divine mercy for the suicide she is about to commit:

> "I dare — I dare — not rashly neither — my heart from principle abhors the act, which thou makest necessary! God in Thy mercy! [lifting up her eyes and hands] God, in Thy mercy!"
>   I threw myself to the further end of the room. An ejaculation, a silent ejaculation, employing her thoughts that moment; Polly says the whites of her lovely eyes were only visible: and, in the instant that she extended her hand, *assuredly* to strike the fatal blow [how the very recital terrifies me!], she cast her eye towards me, and saw me at the utmost distance the room would allow, and heard my broken voice — my voice was utterly broken; nor knew I what I said, or whether to the purpose or not — and her charming cheeks, that were all in a glow before, turned pale, as if terrified at her own purpose; and lifting up her eyes — "Thank God! — Thank God! said the angel — delivered *for the present*; for the *present* delivered — from myself! Keep, sir, keep that distance" [looking down towards me, who was prostrate on the floor, my heart pierced as with a hundred daggers!]. "That distance has saved a life; to what reserved the Almighty only knows!" (*C* 3:290)

"Ejaculation," coming from a libertine like Lovelace, obviously suggests the ex-pressing/expending of the sexual climax — expressive of "lust in action"; Richardson's texts are rich in such innuendoes, his ludic manipulations of "penetration" being a memorable case in point. In the thematics of the penknife, which is phallic and then some, the male organ is conflated with the fact that the knife, specifically designed to tool the type of quill pen then in use, is instrumental in the expressive process that is the essence of the entire genre, and with the fact that the knife may cause the fatal ejaculation of the heroine's own blood.

Ironically, Clarissa is more capable of realizing her will through this polysemous instrument than Lovelace is of realizing his will through his private (counter)part. Yet Lovelace's language improvises a bridge of sorts between the two contrasting realms of moral reflection and experience. For "ejaculation" also signifies the emission of rays by a luminary source, with overtones of the magical and the occult (1625); the usage reminds us of the derivation from *jaculari*, to dart, hence "javelin," and is pertinent here in relation to Clarissa's eyes. The sentence that begins with the ejaculation proceeds to describe her eyes, only the whites showing, as she sends her gaze upward, the final effect being the sort of *coup de théatre* that the magician Cagliostro aimed to produce; when Lovelace invokes the name of God, Clarissa cries, "God's eye is upon us! — His more *immediate* eye; and looked wildly. But the women looked up to the ceiling, as if *afraid* of God's eye, and trembled. And well they might; and *I* too, who so very lately had each of us the devil in our hearts" (C 3:290). Ejaculation further signifies, and here especially signifies, "The putting up of short earnest prayers in a moment of emergency; the hasty utterance of words expressing emotion" (1635c; cf. 4.b.1624). Clarissa, in other words, darts her eyes upward in prayerful expression to her God, who deems that her Lucretia-like experience will not end now in the expending of her life.

Clarissa's transcendence consists in the saving power of her experience of suffering, sacrifice, and expiation, an experience foreign to her would-be lover for as long as the novel aspires to be a revenge tragedy, which is a long time indeed. After reflecting on the proper disposition of Clarissa's remains, he writes to Belford: "Some exemplary mischief I must yet do. My revenge shall sweep away that devil, and all my opposers of the cruel Harlowe family, from the face of the earth. Whole hecatombs ought to be offered up to the manes of my Clarissa Lovelace" (C 4:377). This reckoning of the expense of experience stands in stark contrast to Clarissa's careful attempt to insure that all who survive her will receive as a consequence of her forgiveness and mercy everything to which they are entitled.

Lovelace's moral posture contrasts starkly with that of Belford, who desires nothing so much as the dying victim's blessing. At the boundary between existence and nonexistence, Clarissa finds herself also at the limits of expression:

> After a short silence, in a more broken and faint accent: And you, Mr. Belford, pressing my hand, may God preserve you, and make you sensible of all your errors — you see, in me, how all ends — may *you* be — And down sunk her head upon her pillow, she fainting away, and drawing from us her hands. . . .
>
> But soon showing signs of returning life, our attention was again engaged; and I besought her, when a little recovered, to complete in my favour her half-pronounced blessing. She waved her hand to us both, and bowed her head six several times, as we have since recollected, as if distinguishing every person present. . . . Bless — bless — bless-you all — and now — and now [holding up her almost lifeless hands for the last time] — come — O come — blessed Lord — JESUS! (C 4:347)

After this, Lovelace's lust for vengeance becomes even more regressive, futile, and blind. In vengeance some fateful eventuality is projected into a chain of consequential actions that might as well have been predestined: the energies of the revenge tragedy are powerful but inertial, with nowhere to go but into a vortex of redundancy. The originary event can be any trespass or transgression; that is, any action may impede or impair the action of someone else, for the web of worldly experience is not woven otherwise. But there must be provision for release, for interrupting the seriality that reigns if trespass is answered by trespass, transgression by transgression. The saving alternative, uniquely refusing to submit to expected consequences, is forgiveness:

> In contrast to revenge, which is the natural, automatic reaction to transgression and which because of the irreversibility of the action process can be expected and even calculated, the act of forgiving can never be predicted; it is the only reaction that acts in an unexpected way and thus regains, though being a reaction, something of the original character of action. Forgiving, in other words, is the only reaction which does not merely re-act but acts anew and unexpectedly, unconditioned by the act which provoked it and therefore freeing from its consequences both the one who forgives and the one who is forgiven.[63]

In his pseudo-moral debate with Lord M. and the Misses Montague, Lovelace is still being "natural" and "automatic." Where Clarissa's last words are interrupted by her failing condition, Lovelace, untransformed by forgiveness and unreflective, expresses himself only too well. He asks:

> But will you take upon you to say, supposing (as in the present case) a rape (saving your presence, Cousin Charlotte, saving your presence, Cousin Patty); is death the *natural* consequence of a rape? . . . And if not the *natural* consequence, and a lady will destroy herself, whether by a lingering death, as of grief; or by the dagger, as Lucretia did, is there more than one fault the *man's*? Is not the other *hers*? Were it not so, let me tell you, my dears, chucking each of my blushing cousins under the chin, we either have had no men so wicked as young Tarquin was, or no women so virtuous as Lucretia, in the space of— how many thousand years, my lord? And so Lucretia is recorded as a single wonder! (*C* 4:453)

Richardson heightens the intensity of his moral horror-show in several ways. In the first place, he positions the scene well after the apotheosis of Clarissa, and after the outpourings of grief for the forgiver who has spent her last reserves of time and energy in acts of blessing and benefaction. Lovelace, as if trapped in a moral and spiritual time warp, is the one actor who is so far unchanged by the acts of Clarissa. As a consequence his intolerable claim that he has been no more unjust to Clarissa than she has been to him discloses the depths to which the casuist can sink when loosed from all moral or spiritual moorings. In the second place, Richardson's handling of the scene problematizes the institution of patriarchy even more than the institution of casuistry. On the one hand, Lovelace's manner is a parody of the patriarchal:

he stands for the male interest whatever the issue, wielding authority with cavalier disdain, dominating the women even as he patronizes them. On the other hand, Lord M., whom Lovelace ridicules, stands for what is morally sound in the male-ruled management of contemporary social relations; he is the fair-minded peer, equally capable of reflection and action, who challenges the profligate when the latter pronounces himself guiltless of Clarissa's death. In the third place, Lovelace exhibits, in this last turn to Lucretia, the extent of his moral confusion. The gist of his argument is that the principle of shared responsibility tends to incriminate the rape victim as much as the rapist. Now, this may not be quite what he says; it *is* what he means. What he says is that the two parties are equally at fault—but where any equality worth the name is concerned, this is at best a tasteless parody. Forgiveness only goes so far. At some point the one who is forgiven must break the grip of consequence introduced by transgression. Only then may expiation occur.

In his last opportunity to express himself, Lovelace imitates Clarissa by uttering the word "blessed," first in an appeal to Clarissa as "Blessed Spirit," then twice more when he evidently imitates Clarissa in the act of ejaculation:

> *Blessed*—said he, addressing himself no doubt to Heaven; for his dying eyes were lifted up. A strong convulsion prevented him for a few moments saying more, but recovering, he again, with great fervour (lifting up his eyes and his spread hands), pronounced the word *blessed*. Then, in a seeming ejaculation, he spoke inwardly, so as not to be understood: at last, he distinctly pronounced these three words,
> LET THIS EXPIATE! (*C* 4:530)

As an account of what Lovelace himself experiences this is ambiguous indeed. The character F. J. De la Tour, author of the letter containing the account, proceeds from behaviorist description to interpretive probabilities that may be no more than possibilities. From the fact that Lovelace's eyes were lifted up it need not follow that he is addressing heaven, and "a seeming ejaculation" in which Lovelace is thought to speak inwardly is more speculative than reportorial. We are on firmer ground with the overtones that carry over into this scene from the scene of Clarissa's ejaculation and bring Lovelace into closer relation to Clarissa's exemplary moral and spiritual experience. It is Lovelace of course who identifies her ejaculation as such. What the reader does not know is whether Lovelace is himself offering a short prayer in a moment of emergency or merely making a hasty utterance of words expressing emotion; and a similar uncertainty attends his final words.

In his postscript Richardson is at pains to insure that, where the moral and social significance of Clarissa's life and example is concerned, the reader is well guided. Repeatedly he reverts to moments in the text that his readers will have experienced, the better to elucidate and reflect upon what the moral or spiritual consequences of that experience will properly have been. On the critical issue of whether Clarissa possesses more excellences than are probable or practicable, Richardson argues that she is entitled to his high claims for her because, as is largely the case with Pamela as well, of her educational enablement: "But the education of Clarissa from early childhood ought to be considered as some of her very great advantages; as, indeed, the foundation of all her excellencies" (*C* 4:564). And he reflects upon the fact that in contrast to Pamela's, Clarissa's education is represented as a predominantly maternal accomplishment:

> She had a pious, a well-read, a not meanly descended woman for her nurse, who with her milk, as Mrs. Harlowe says, gave her that nurture which no other nurse could give her. . . . Her mother was, upon the whole, a good woman, who did credit to her birth and fortune; and both delighted in her for those improvements and attainments, which gave her, and them in her, a distinction that caused it to be said, that when she was out of the family, it was considered but as a common family. (*C* 4:564)

The account plays around the conspicuously missing person, the heroine's father, who has given way to the great surrogate father, God; Clarissa's refrain-like allusions to her father's house erase the domicile of her secular father by the same stroke with which they inscribe Clarissa's final domicile in blessed immortality. Replacing father with Father is one of Richardson's ways of problematizing patriarchal rights and powers without contesting them directly. The nurture described enables in Clarissa the same nexus of ameliorative experiences that came to be understood in her century as development, or, in different vocabularies, and starting earlier, as history. His story of Clarissa is itself a history both of her intimate experiences and of the consequences she effects in others by the way in which she expresses her excellences.

To put the matter this way is to acknowledge the reciprocity, in Richardson's construction, between the private and the public, the individual and the social. Readers have properly associated Richardson's exploration of the intimacies of individual experience with English Puritanism. Conversely, his fascination with the figure of the libertine attests to his interest in and caution toward the consequences of a Cavalier interpretation of the world. How these two strains interweave, beginning in the late seventeenth century with Puritan introspection and peaking in the leading poet of the Restoration, has been suggested by Earl Miner, who calls attention to the Puritan preoccupation with providential evidences such as astrological auguries or the saints' experience in divine will, as exemplified in Cromwell's prayerful struggle to comprehend the necessitated destiny:

Moreover, the widespread Puritan habit of keeping diaries, and sometimes of writing spiritual autobiographies based on their journals, lent great importance to the intersection of individual personality, events of the time, and divine purpose. Such tendencies brought a result that no one could have anticipated and of which Dryden became the chief poetic exponent: the historical present, historical events, and historical process acquired an importance they had not held. Men had at last come to see that their own time was historically as real as the ages of Moses or David, of Alexander the Great or Augustus Caesar.[64]

The triumph of Clarissa's Puritan-like authorship over Lovelace's Cavalier-style bravado is a function of the lived experience of both characters insofar as the consequences are reflected upon. How that experience is represented changes as the book advances toward its conclusion. As Clarissa proceeds on the long path of dying she becomes less and less a character who experiences and more and more a character of whom others have an experience. In her acts of forgiveness, mercy, and charity, she becomes ever more Christ-like, and, as Arendt reminds us, the act of forgiveness is profoundly originary. In its way it changes the world, or at least a part of it; and at certain levels, to the extent that it radically redirects some person or persons, it can be said to make worlds. Lovelace's friend John Belton is a case in point: under the inspiration of Clarissa he is reformed into a virtuous husband; that is, his world begins anew.

If Clarissa becomes more and more a character of whom others have an experience, it is because she is becoming increasingly documentary, testimonial, archival. She is becoming, in short, a history of consequences recorded for reflection. Another reason why Richardson shifts toward the more or less public record may be that he is uneasy about exposing so much private, indeed intimate experience. Showing this exclusively from the "inside" could look, to a highly religious sensibility, too much like trespassing on sanctified terrain, an impropriety bordering upon impiety. The purer and more transcendental the heroine becomes, the more presumptuous it is to publicize her at her most intimate. In any case, it is more to the point, and also more dramatic, to represent not the provenance of her actions but their consequences. It is only in the form of consequences that actions consummate, and only as they consummate that they come within the purview of reflection.

Some may object that Richardson expects too much and relies too much on individual experience, to which one might reply that the individual in question is very far from being a common case. In any event, the model of social reconstruction underlying his reformative design is pragmatic, and in fact resembles one advanced by George Herbert Mead. At the center of the model stands the principle that individuals and society are interdependent and creatively interactive:

> Social reconstruction by the individual members of any organized human society entails self or personal reconstruction in some degree or other by each of the individuals, and vice versa, for, since their selves or personalities are constituted by their organized social relations to one another, they cannot reconstruct those selves or personalities without also reconstructing, to some extent, the given social order.[65]

Mead, like Richardson—or, for that matter, like Machiavelli—attaches great importance to the role of the leader. But for Mead this is because the individual endowment she or he brings to the reconstructive task derives from and expresses the community: "The great characters have been those who, by being what they were in the community, made that community a different one."[66] Clarissa Harlowe is a great character in this sense, and Pamela is a draft of one. Being women, neither is, of course, the type of leader Machiavelli has in mind. Yet we can see in both a strength like the strength of *virtù*, and in their circumstances are to be found the occasion on which that virtue is enabled to act. In a word: given the "matter" of opportunity, the exemplary person, drawing on what is available to her from enabling experience and endowed capacity, produces for other members of society examples to follow and consequences to reflect upon.

Returning for the last time to the myth of Lucretia, we see that Richardson reconstructs its meaning to a considerable degree. The female victim is no longer the specular object seen as an abstract other; she is a concrete human being who for the most part tells her own experience in her own words. In contrast to Lucretia, she enjoys a capacity understandably in favor these days: she is "in control." For finally it is Clarissa who sets the terms of the novel's consummation and of her own transcendence. On the other hand, her situation is as much a tragic paradox as Lucretia's. Lucretia's fate is that she is not a part of the new social order, which exists. Clarissa's fate is that she is a part of the new social order, which does not exist.

Clarissa does not survive but patriarchy does, and with patriarchy the ideology of individualism; and with individualism the nexus of worldly arrangements examined in the present study largely survive as well. Even if compensation for such expense awaits in an afterworld, it is in the fateful discourse of worldly things that genuine worldly experience is most genuinely expressed.

Concluding

To readers of the preceding attempt at concrete interpretation it will come as no surprise that this final portion takes its departure from the relation of concluding to consummating and other modes of culmination. To summarize, consummation is that process in which an interacting with environment realizes some purpose; and it is the entirety of this that is consummatory, consequential, conclusive.

As an expository form, the traditional conclusion — a summing up — has become as rare as the epilogue, coda, and afterword have become common. Some conclusions serve as thematic elaborations, as is the case with Edward Said's *The World, the Text, and the Critic*; here the modern prototype could be Pater's "Conclusion." More playful and experimental is the epilogue of Kenneth Burke's *Rhetoric of Religion*, which carries the subtitle "Prologue in Heaven." More playful still is Herbert S. Lindenberger's *Saul's Fall*, which concludes by parodying the editorial apparatus of scholarly studies that the entire book is concerned to demystify. The longest attempt in this mode may be Kierkegaard's *Concluding Unscientific Postscript*, which is not even a postscript but more a repository of ideas for the author's subsequent revision of Christian belief.[1] My own approach to concluding, the direction of which has already begun to unfold, will take a page or two from the more traditional conclusion, looking back and reflecting on some main points, but knowing full well that there is no obviously "right" way to conclude and that such reflection as I offer is only one mode, though I think a useful one, of reexperiencing.

An essential part of what we need to reexperience and reflect upon is the critical scene in which the present discussion is located, and this can begin with Emerson, asking the question that heads the next section.

Where Do We Find Ourselves?

To start the process of responding, I turn once more, and finally, to Arendt, who argues that a tradition, even when it is thought to have ended, sometimes has a way of living on, and can be a coercive force even when there is little or no living memory of how it started or what made it worth continuing. This is what happens, in her view, "after Kierkegaard, Marx, and Nietzsche had challenged the basic assumptions of traditional religion, traditional political thought, and traditional metaphysics by consciously inverting the hierarchy of concepts." The "twentieth-century aftermath of formalistic and compulsory thinking"[2] which then followed encompasses the aridities of logical positivism or other -isms, certainly including liberalism, which seem to survive by the inertial force of their orthodoxy.

As part of the same pattern, the Western tradition of political thought, according to Arendt, came to an end with Marx. Traditionally, political thought "began with the philosopher's turning away from politics and then returning in order to impose his standards on human affairs. The end came when a philosopher turned away from philosophy so as to 'realize' it in politics."[3] My concern here is neither with the accuracy of this account of Marx—the philosopher she has in mind—nor with the fact that Arendt is unwilling or unable to explain her own contribution to the "aftermath" of Marx and the others. My concern is with the ways in which political thought, broadly conceived, exists in a continuum with a politics of the human condition, which is the largest scene of all, as well as the true subject of Arendt's *The Human Condition*.

To illustrate worldliness in relation to time, Arendt adduces a parable by Kafka:

He has two antagonists: the first presses him from behind, from the origin. The second blocks the road ahead. He gives battle to both. To be sure, the first supports him in his fight with the second, for he wants to push him forward, and in the same way the second supports him in his fight with the first, since he drives him back. But it is only theoretically so. For it is not only the two antagonists who are there, but he himself as well, and who really knows his intentions? His dream, though, is that some time in an unguarded moment — and this would require a night darker than any night has ever been yet — he will jump out of the fighting line and be promoted, on account of his experience in fighting, to the position of umpire over his antagonists in their fight with each other.[4]

The parable suggests to Arendt that, "seen from the viewpoint of man, who always lives in the interval between past and future, time is not a continuum, a flow of uninterrupted succession; it is broken in the middle, at the point where 'he' stands; and 'his' standpoint is not the present as we usually understand it but rather a gap in time."[5] This reading anticipates the emphasis on discontinuity, disjunction, and the like that may have reached its apogee with the emergence of the postmodern. But it is a reading more in keeping with Arendt's own sense of being-between than it is with Kafka's. The problem in the parable is that time, in the period of the depicted struggle, is only *too* continuous; it goes on without interruption, with the sense of possible endlessness that is part of what makes us uneasy in reading Kafka. What "he" wants is not more continuity but less; he wants a *break*. After all, his dream is that by jumping out of the fighting zone he will finally escape the struggle, which of course must continue if he is to become its umpire. Arendt asks, "and what else is this dream and this region but the old dream which Western metaphysics has dreamed from Parmenides to Hegel of a timeless, spaceless, suprasensuous realm as the proper region of thought?"[6] Although there is something to be said for this rhetorical question, it misses the point of "his" (and Kafka's) worldliness, which is not the less worldly for containing otherworldly motives, including the perfectly normal desire to escape, sometimes, from the world. In the parable Kafka works a variation on his familiar plot in which a man is deemed guilty, and *then* is tried; the variation is that here a man is deemed trapped, then released. But in both there is the same movement of desire toward a solution, or an escape, involving some mode of the juridical. The man caught between past and future aspires to jump precisely into a judging role, so as to participate in the kinds of power structures that Kafka encountered in the bureaucracy that trapped him, and that exist in the streets and offices outside his building, as in all the streets and offices of the world.

The Emerson text from which this section takes its title is the much-discussed and difficult essay called "Experience." Looking back, in effect, to the subject matter of Part V, above, Emerson offers a paradigmatic instance of Kafkaesque strandedness, if you will, for which Peircean thinking about continuity will offer at least a partial reprieve.

Where do we find ourselves? In a series, of which we do not know the extremes, and believe that it has none. We wake and find ourselves on a stair: there are stairs below us, which we seem to have ascended; there are steps above us, many a one, which go upward and out of sight. But the Genius which, according to the old belief . . . gives us the lethe to drink, that we may tell no tales, mixed the cup too strongly, and we cannot shake off the lethargy now at noonday.[7]

As in the Kafka parable, we have a protagonist situated between two points of reference, but in contrast with the Kafka text, there is no impelling force, there isn't even a sense of what force might have operated previously or will operate in the future. The pathos of the text consists largely in the absence of normal felt relation. Facing the death of his son, Emerson can say, "The only thing grief has taught me, is to know how shallow it is. That, like all the rest, plays about the surface, and never introduces me into the reality, for contact with which, we would even pay the costly price of sons and lovers. Was it Boscovich who found out that bodies never come in contact? Well, souls never touch their objects" (EE 3:24). The inability to touch an object is like the inability of the soul in limbo to reach salvation.

What Emerson does reach, in the essay, is a series of conclusions about the nature of life; and yet as readers we rarely if ever get a sense of finality, and when we do it proves to be local and transient. Each segment in the series is so much its own little world that the overall effect of their successiveness is disjunctive. No cause for alarm: with Emerson, whenever this effect gets to be too much a kind of override switch releases current into new possibilities. To this extent one may speak after all of an impelling force moving toward not only a reconstructive vision but toward rebirth, and a very worldly rebirth at that; for the venue of new life is the nation in which Emerson now lives: "I feel a new heart beating with the love of the new beauty. I am ready to die out of nature, and be born again into this new yet unapproachable America I have found in the West" (EE 3:41).

In this inconclusive conclusion, in this consummation that is already a new beginning, Emerson traces yet one more of those circles dear to his thinking, and in the process anticipates the pragmatist vision of processes that "conclude" by engendering new processes, reaching consummations previously beyond reach and setting the terms by which further consummations may be realized.

The text at issue consists in a sequence of seven interconnecting themes, the last of which deals with what he calls subjectiveness. The sovereignty of the subject or self, as delimited by Emerson, is reminiscent of the sovereignty of the self in the tradition of individualism examined at length above. "I think, alone," it says, "and the only nature that exists for me exists through me, if not as nature's final purpose then as its mode of mediation." Subjectiveness thus conceived serves to locate the movement of moods, expressive of individual temperament, and adumbrating the role of moods in Heidegger. Presentment figures in the subjectivity as well, in that all the objects with which it deals exist as objects *for* this subjectivity. What is significantly missing in Emerson, and what keeps the process going, is the certainty so manifest in the Cartesian discourse of reason. Not only does Emerson not believe in the certainty of apperception, he associates the perceiving or presenting self with the imperfect technology of the optic lens:

> We have learned that we do not see directly, but mediately, and that we have no means of correcting these colored and distorting lenses which we are, or of computing the amount of their errors. Perhaps these subject-lenses have a creative power; perhaps there are no objects. Once we lived in what we saw; now, the rapaciousness of this new power, which threatens to absorb all things, engages us. Nature, art, persons, letters, religions, — objects, successively tumble in and God is but one of its ideas. Nature and literature are subjective phenomena; every evil and every good thing is a shadow which we cast. (EE 3:44)

Here is the loss of the public, discussed in Part V, as it feels from the "inside," a consequence, at least in part, of presentment, which makes worldly things that are not in the least human appear to be entirely so. Echoing Heidegger, Arendt concludes: "The modern age, with its growing world-alienation, has led to a situation where man, wherever he goes, encounters only himself."[8]

More than most authors, Emerson works one sentence at a time, shifting perspectives in a way that makes his traces difficult to track. This is particularly the case with the present text, which not only talks about successiveness but demonstrates it with a vengeance. Whatever succeeds something must differ from it and the difference must be finished enough for the reader to experience it *as* difference. Generally, the next thing does not necessarily subsume the previous thing; as Emerson says, "Life is not dialectics" (EE 3:34). What life is is a series of moods, of accesses of affect peculiar to the individual temperament, and as such are ordered to no subsuming purpose; and it could be argued that at times they are not ordered at all, as each mood reveals entirely and only what it discloses to itself in its transience.

Now, conclusive statements should be possible as long as causality guides and governs effects. But the phenomenon Emerson calls "surfaces," the theme of one of his seven sections, reflects the fact that causality, for him, deadends in a literal superficiality: "The teleological dynamic of causality moves away from cause and toward effect, and thus locates value solely in effects or surfaces."[9] By implication this fairly negates any initiative in the direction of even adequate intelligibility. Everything relies upon the accursed subject or "selfhood," which Peirce will call, in a passage to be discussed below, "the vulgarest delusion of vanity" (7.570). Factors making for continuity of experience and discourse are nonetheless much in evidence and ready to hand.

Continuities

To proceed further along these lines entails revisiting with Peirce the theme of Part V above, namely, experience, which he classifies into three types corresponding to the triadic model discussed in the main text above. These types are the simple or monadic experience, "which would be what it is if there were nothing else in all experience"; recurrences or dyadic experiences, "each a direct experience of an opposing pair of objects"; and comprehensions or triadic experiences, "each a direct experience which connects other possible experiences" (7.528). Simple experiences are of qualities, which are, as Firsts, what they are without relation to anything else. Recurrent experiences are experiences of opposition and reaction, and belong to the sphere of Seconds. Finally, comprehensive experiences, as Thirds, involve the continuities that make it possible to comprehend the connectedness of experience. On this type of experience Peirce observes that

> the idea [of] continuity is an extension of the idea of regularity. Regularity implies generality; and generality is an intellectual relation essentially the same as significance, as is shown by the contention of the nominalists that all generals are names. . . . Now that which brings another thing before the mind is a representation; so that generality and regularity are essentially the same as significance. . . . That this element is found in experience is shown by the fact that all experience involves time. Now the flow of time is conceived as continuous. (7.535)

Without the regularity that temporal continuity provides there would be no way to comprehend qualities, recurrences, or continuities because there would be no experience, which necessarily occurs in time. Whether Peirce arrived at this conclusion and then saw the connection between experience and learning, or vice versa, he sees them as finally inseparable, and the following remark on the topic brings us back to section 6 of Part I. "All flow of time involves learning; and all learning involves the flow of time. Now no continuum can be apprehended except by a mental generation of it, by thinking of something as moving through it. . . . For a mere dull staring at a superficies does not involve the positive apprehension of continuity" (7.536). The last remark sounds like a reply to Emerson (whose writings Peirce knew well) when the sage declares surfaces and superficies to be insuperable obstacles to genuine apprehension of reality. "All that is given in such staring," Peirce continues, "is a feeling which serves as a sign that the object might be apprehended as a continuum" (7.536), whereas it is actually the case that the feeling signifies that the object *must* be so apprehended; but this comes only with effort, a kind of upsurge in natal intellection, as Peirce's term "generation" makes clear.

For Peirce "continuity governs the whole domain of experience in every element of it" (7.566) and there is in experience much more connectedness than there is separateness. Thus his objection to Parmenides' claim that "being is, and not-being is nothing," which exemplifies for the pragmatist the philosophical habit of relying on binary opposition and artificially separating phenomena that exist holistically. On the contrary, says Peirce, "being is a matter of more or less" (7.569). In the following passage "synechist," from a Greek etymon for what is continuous, designates Peirce's way of being pragmatist:

> In particular, the synechist will not admit that physical and psychical phenomena are entirely distinct . . . but will insist that all phenomena are of one character, though some are more mental and spontaneous, others more material and regular. Still, all alike present that mixture of freedom and constraint, which allows them to be, nay, makes them to be teleological, or purposive. (7.570)

Even that sheltered realm of individual identity, which lies at the foundation of the individualist tradition, both political and philosophical, is a matter of more or less:

> Nor must any synechist say, "I am altogether myself, and not at all you." If you embrace synechism, you must abjure this metaphysics of wickedness. In the first place, your neighbors are, in a measure, yourself, and in far greater measure than, without deep studies in psychology, you would believe. Really, the selfhood you like to attribute to yourself is, for the most part, the vulgarest delusion of vanity. (7.571)

Given such continuity, oppositions come into question. Waking and sleeping is such an opposition, and it is not surprising that Diderot, in *D'Alembert's Dream*, should discover that these states can be differentiated only relatively; this is entirely consistent with his commitment to the continuity of all being. Since the same thinking necessarily applies to the temporality in which all experience of continuity occurs, it follows that temporal distinctions should also be regarded as a matter of more or less. To experience a past idea, say, is not to perceive it as belonging entirely to the past, for then it would be inaccessible to experience now; to experience the idea is rather to perceive it as "going, infinitesimally past, less past than any assignable past date" (6.109). For we could not have a continuous experience of this idea, or of anything else, if that idea or thing were not itself sufficiently continuous for us to be aware of it, feel it, comprehend it, perceive it, know it, *ipso facto*. "In fact, this infinitesimally spread-out consciousness is a direct feeling of its contents as spread out. In an infinitesimal interval we directly perceive the temporal sequence of its beginning, middle, and end" (6.111).

Given that the succession is temporal, and that it takes time to perceive the perceived even as it takes time for the perceived to *be* perceived, perception cannot be total and immediate, but is partial and mediate precisely insofar as it is successive. Some perceptions, however, are more equal than others, and what is more equal here is the consummatory moment, which is immediate and yet directly connected in a continuum with what is just passing and what is already past. "Let there be, not merely an indefinite succession, but a continuous flow of inference through a finite time, and the result will be a mediate objective consciousness of the whole time in the last moment. In this last moment, the whole series will be recognized" (6.111). The concluding moment, however, does not recognize itself; it recognizes immediately the moment just passing and mediately the moment before that. But what is to recognize the recognizer, so to say? Peirce hints at an answer: "Indeed, even this last moment will be recognized like the rest, or, at least, be just beginning to be so" (6.111). The final moment of the series becomes the initial moment of a new series, which, in reaching a conclusion, starts a new series. To put it another way, there is no stasis or strandedness in the process, there is only continuity, movement, and overlap, with relative interruptions of closure or consummation, and any such closure or consummation is already in the process of being apprehended by, assimilated to, being recognized by, some other apprehender, assimilator, or recognizer. To conclude is to be *more or less* conclusive, and it is with such a sense of qualification that this portion of the text aims at concluding, more than at conclusion.

Closing Reflections

It is now time to return to the previous, more limited focus in order to reflect upon the contribution the present study has tried to make in the context of the considerations just described. In such a context the most that one can reasonably hope for may be something like the measured goal envisaged by Michael Oakeshott in reflecting upon the modern European state:

> To consider the fortunes of reflection on the character of a state and the office of its government . . . gives a perspective to the inquiry which, of course, can be matched by others not less interesting, endowing its features with other shapes. But a historical inquiry which makes us capable of understanding and

criticizing *some* particular, coherent representation of a circumstantial situation has, perhaps, done all that may be expected of it.[10]

What Oakeshott means by "a circumstantial situation" encompasses more than most writers would indicate with the same phrase. In the present instance the situation is nothing less than the emergence, character, and fortunes of the modern European state. Oakeshott can be critical of such a state precisely because there is sufficient coherence in its representation to render it susceptible to an investigation that is itself coherent. Clearly such is not always the case with all situations, which can be incoherent and so various in representation as finally to become, or to seem, unrepresentable. This is one of the issues that arises in chaos theory:

> What in the present cultural moment has energized chaos as an important concept? Why does it appear as a pivotal concept for us here and now? I conjecture that disorder has become a focal point for contemporary theories because it offers the possibility of escaping from what are increasingly perceived as coercive strategies of order.[11]

I agree, but I would add the suggestion that part of the problem today is the existence of too many unexamined alternatives in every sphere of discourse — intellectual, esthetic, political, legal, religious, or what have you. It seems pertinent that William James attributed his "nervous breakdown," as we used to say, to the fact that in his affluent, education-oriented family he had an overwhelming number of alternatives from which to choose.

What Oakeshott calls "circumstantial situation" is an approximation, it seems to me, of what the early Sartre calls simply "situation." Or possibly it is an elaboration of the latter; for the ascription of "circumstantial" to "situation" looks like a redundancy and appears, one surmises, because the author wants to underline just how situated the situation is. The situation, that is to say, is not a static abstraction or an entity in a mental somewhere, but is rather, in a Deweyan way, a concrete nexus of specifiable features occurring in a definite place at a definite time. The purposes of concluding are better served if at this point I speak of *situated themes*, in relation to which I may then usefully restate what this study has endeavored to do.

I have explored the situated theme of *systems* because systems have attained relative dominance in a number of spheres, from politics to the economy, from technology to culture. Systems are constituted of units which, in the analytical manner still paramount today, can be broken down in such a way that the "stuff" being systematized becomes rationally comprehensible, calculable, and manageable. More interesting still is that "systematicity" becomes a philosophical cult dedicated to the equating of the rational and the logical, and to the proposition that purely logical principles suffice to explain conceptual change. Gradually, systems discourse, spreading its ideas, strategies, and terminologies, becomes a more or less autonomous agency not easily exposed to inquiry and criticism. It is not the case, however, that there exists no "other" in the sense of contesting voices. The problem is that these voices have yet to develop viable, alternative tropes and terminologies that systems discourse cannot assimilate. Still the possibility exists that voices on the margins of the cultural mainstream can perform this difficult task, and indeed they may be doing so even now.

I have explored the situated theme of *practice and theory* because if either term is to be considered the other must be too, for every statement, in whatever discursive context, is a practice already related to some theoretical position, however occulted it may be. The present study is nothing if not a series of such statements. In all theory there is a systematic tendency, as the theorist strives to account for a maximum number of confronted features with a minimum of explanatory effort. Although roughly the same goal is sought in hypothesis, Peirce brings out its implicit incorporate character by showing how hypothetical inference is signaled by nervous excitation or emotion. From a pragmatist point of view, all judging is practical: even the instance of walking entails judgment. Kant, for his part, by emphasizing the necessity that a judgment be stated publicly, reminds us that the political nature of judging has been a fact of life at least since it rose to prominence in ancient Athens. The communication of which Kant speaks, in whatever mode it occurs, serves always as a means to some end, a process of interacting toward a goal or consummation. The means-end relation may be generalized as *interacting is the way (means) that the doing to be done (end) gets done (consummation)*.

Dewey states somewhat hyperbolically that a thousand theories are worth less than a single experience. Of course he himself has much to say that is of theoretical interest. His substantive point, I take it, is that we need to recognize the limits of theory, the fact that it amounts to little or nothing if not tested in practice, and that the unwarranted overrating of theory, in the form I call theorism, goes hand in hand with the unwarranted overrating of consciousness, ideality, and specularity.

I have explored the situated theme of *presentment* that emerges in what Heidegger calls the age of the world picture. Representation in the general sense of display, showing, or exhibiting continues in the age of the world picture side by side, as it were, with this mode of representation unique to this age. Presentment occurs when a subject posits something, anything, as preeminently an object for that subject, and posits this relation as normative. To paraphrase Heidegger, the more objectivity appears the more subjectivity does, and since that subjectivity is human, the more the human dominates.

This contrasts with the ancient Greek orientation, where representation is apperception of what is, without appropriation by or assimilation to a representing subject. When this occurs, when something that was some thing becomes an instance of objectness for a subject, and in this sense equivalent to any other object, one senses a certain loss of being. In compensation for that loss, the transformation of the thing into an object is posited as a value in itself even as values themselves become an overall goal of human activity.

If the emergence of presentment is coeval with the emergence of humanism, it is with Descartes that it becomes normative. Galileo, in derealizing primary experience of things (odor or color, for instance), in order to establish the primacy of the calculable, complements the Cartesian enterprise of presentment. It is nonetheless the case that both men draw extensively, just as Hegel does, upon the wherewithal of everyday experience in support of their nontraditional experiments and research agendas.

I have explored the situated theme of *individualism*, and more particularly of the market model of possessive individualism, because of its ascent to dominance in the Western political, economic, social, and cultural scene. In the modern market society, as conceived by Hobbes and Locke, individuals are construed as possessing their own persons and labor as well as the freedom to alienate that labor at a price, which constitutes, in Hobbes's language, their "value." When large numbers of such individuals contract together to be represented by a superordinate authority, such as a monarch, the originary condition of society is supposed to have been met. With the enabling power of such authority justice emerges as the principle by which propriety, as the principle of owning or being owned, is legitimized as conforming with law or juridical rule. In Hobbes's words, "Justice is the constant Will of giving to every man his own. And therefore where there is no *own*, there is no Propriety, there is no Injustice."

Now, it appears that everything on this list of situated themes is something that the present study is for one reason or another "against," and this appearance is not without foundation. No student of Dewey can be anything but uneasy, for example, with the degree to which the sovereign individual has spread through social, political, and even metaphysical thought. And it seems impossible to defend modern society's exploitation of those least able to defend themselves against its sometimes disguised but only too efficient mechanisms. This society is indissociable from the state because state polities and strategies animate and inform market mechanisms. "State" here means, following Gramsci, civil society plus political society—that is, the realm of daily cultural practices in, say, education or religion, in combination with the operations and imperatives of the political arm of the state as such. Where the latter largely controls social life through institutional coercion, the former, in the parlance of Part I above, teaches and trains the members of civil society to consent to the operations and principles of the contemporary social, political, economic, and cultural order. What Gramsci calls hegemony is more the interplay of these and other worldly forces than it is any formal or monolithic dominance. And therein lies a difficulty. The obstacle to challenging the dominance of systems and systematicity, for example, is that it has already become, like the organization of society in market terms, second nature. It has been assimilated into hegemonic arrangements and dispositions, and indeed contributes to their equilibrium by increasing their "rationality" and efficiency. Such a hegemony is itself experienced as a second nature; it is not a visible dispenser of formal commands but the very social, cultural, political, and economic environment in which we live. The concept of hegemony in this sense of the term, says Raymond Williams,

> sees the relations of domination and subordination, in their forms as practical consciousness, as in effect a saturation of the whole process of living—not only of political and economic activity, nor only of manifest social activity, but of the whole substance of lived identities and relationships, to such a depth that the pressures and limits of what can ultimately be seen as a specific economic, political, and cultural system seem to most of us the pressures and limits of simple experience and common sense.[12]

To challenge such a complex status quo is for Williams to participate in a counter- or alternative hegemony. The "marginal" voices alluded to in Part I, in contesting systematicity, would be an example of what he means. There is then the danger, in using these overdetermined terms without examining closely the concrete situations in which they occur, of being reductive. More to the point, and more positive, is the fact that alternative hegemonies, as is the case with hegemony generally, are not only formative but transformative, works of art being in this respect exemplary.[13] And it may not be overreaching to add that works of interpretation and criticism, in some instances, may achieve a similar consequence. I suggest these points to underline both the possibility of working effectively against certain aspects of our cultural moment and the difficulty of actually doing so.

The context in which these considerations arise is that worldliness that has been the primary focus of the present inquiry. It is by virtue of keeping that focus in mind, whatever this or that section of this study might be dealing with "locally," that I have ventured not only to be "against" certain things but to suggest those aspects of worldly being that constitute their larger context and which are in themselves constitutive.

Near the end of his *Attitudes Toward History*, a book that has influenced me strongly over the years, Burke concludes by saying, "Might we, for envoi, put the main points together briefly . . ."[14] Here he takes his cue from the medieval gesture in which the poet addresses the reader; he then proceeds, more or less as I have done, to summarize; but, fudging, he supplies an afterword followed by an appendix. If asked, he would reply that he is just pontificating, building bridges, and he might admit that he would like the ending of his book to be the beginning of something else, both that ending and that beginning being stages in the kind of ongoing continuity championed by the pragmatists. I have been building bridges, too, and I could wish the same for my book as I have imagined Burke wishing for his. My envoi, then, is the hope of having provided passage to readers going in more or less the same direction that *The Fateful Discourse of Worldly Things* has endeavored to go.

Reference Matter

Notes

BEGINNING

1. Walter Pater, *The Renaissance: Studies in Art and Poetry: The 1893 Text*, ed. Donald L. Hill (Berkeley: University of California Press, 1990), 130; hereafter cited parenthetically in text as *R*.

2. Arthur O. Lovejoy, *The Thirteen Pragmatisms and Other Essays* (Baltimore: Johns Hopkins University Press, 1963).

3. William James, *Pragmatism: A New Name for Some Old Ways of Thinking* (1907; reprint: Cambridge, Mass.: Harvard University Press, 1975), 28, 32.

4. See Kenneth Burke, *Language as Symbolic Action: Essays on Life, Literature, and Method* (Berkeley and Los Angeles: University of California Press, 1968).

5. Giles Gunn, *Thinking Across the American Grain: Ideology, Intellect, and the New Pragmatism* (Chicago: University of Chicago Press, 1992).

6. Elizabeth Fox-Genovese, *Feminism without Illusions: A Critique of Individualism* (Chapel Hill and London: University of North Carolina Press, 1991); Gillian Brown, *Domestic Individualism: Imagining Self in Nineteenth-Century America* (Berkeley: University of California Press, 1990); Carole Pateman, " 'God Hath Ordained to Man a Helper': Hobbes, Patriarchy, and Conjugal Right," in *Feminist Interpretations and Political Theory*, ed. Mary Lyndon Shanley and Carole Pateman (University Park: Pennsylvania State University

Press, 1991), 53–73; Melissa A. Butler, "Early Liberal Roots of Feminism: John Locke and the Attack on Patriarchy," in *Feminist Interpretations and Political Theory* (see above); Steven Lukes, *Individualism* (New York: Harper & Row, 1973).

7. Definitions in quotation marks are from the *Oxford English Dictionary* (*OED*). Occasional definitions from the *Dictionary of American English* are identified as *DAE*. I draw on lexicography because it is a broadly valuable source of information on different periods and because the etymologies, derivations, shifts, and nuances it provides enhance our sense of the interplay between change and continuity. But even the imposingly learned teams directed by Sir James Murray and his successors stumble on occasion. Hence the discussions or definitions that appear in the pages that follow (see, for example, the early section of Part V).

8. Richard Rorty, *Philosophy and the Mirror of Nature* (Princeton: Princeton University Press, 1979), 368.

9. *Collected Papers of Charles Sanders Peirce*, ed. Arthur W. Burks (Cambridge, Mass.: Harvard University Press, 1966), 6.348. Subsequent citations follow the custom of indicating volume and paragraph number within parentheses.

PART I

1. John Dewey, *Reconstruction* (1894), in *Early Works, 1882–1898*, ed. Jo Ann Boydston, 5 vols. (Carbondale: Southern Illinois University Press, 1971), 497. All citations from Dewey are to this edition; hereafter cited parenthetically as follows: *EW = Early Works*, *MW = Middle Works*, *LW = Later Works*.

2. Giles Gunn, *Thinking Across the American Grain: Ideology, Intellect, and the New Pragmatism* (Chicago and London: University of Chicago Press, 1992), 213.

3. René Girard, *Things Hidden Since the Foundation of the World*, trans. Stephen Bann and Michael Metteer (Stanford: Stanford University Press, 1987), 287.

4. Jean-François Lyotard, *The Postmodern Condition: A Report on Knowledge*, trans. Geoff Bennington and Brian Massumi (Minneapolis: University of Minnesota Press, 1984), 89–90.

5. William James, *Pragmatism: A New Name for Some Old Ways of Thinking* (Cambridge, Mass. and London: Harvard University Press, 1975), 67.

6. Ibid., 32.

7. *Hegel's Logic*, trans. William Wallace (Oxford: Oxford University Press, 1975), 158 ff.

8. Hans-Georg Gadamer, *The Idea of the Good in Platonic-Aristotelian Philosophy*, trans. P. Christopher Smith (New Haven and London: Yale University Press, 1986), 172–73.

9. See Hannah Arendt, *Men in Dark Times* (New York: Harcourt Brace Jovanovich, 1968), 168.

10. Roland Barthes, *The Fashion System*, trans. Matthew Ward and Richard Howard (New York: Hill and Wang, 1983), 14, 282, 252.

11. Paul de Man, *Blindness and Insight: Essays in the Rhetoric of Contemporary Criticism* (New York: Oxford University Press, 1971), 140.

12. Jeffrey Barnouw, "Peirce and Derrida: 'Natural Signs' Empiricism versus 'Originary Trace' Deconstruction," *Poetics Today* 7: 1 (1986), 79.

13. Jacques Derrida, "The Principle of Reason: The University in the Eyes of Its Pupils," *Diacritics* 13 (1983), 17.

14. Ibid., 11.

15. Ibid., 12.

16. Thomas M. Alexander, "John Dewey's Theory of Art," in *Experience and Nature: The Horizons of Feeling* (Albany: State University of New York Press, 1987) demonstrates the centrality of esthetic experience in Dewey. Eugene Rochberg-Halton explains the relation between such experience and social theory in his *Meaning and Modernity: Social Theory in the Pragmatic Attitude* (Chicago: University of Chicago Press, 1986), 29–34, 37–40, 154–55, 238. Dewey's groundbreaking approach to technology is explored in Larry A. Hickman, *John Dewey's Pragmatic Technology* (Bloomington and Indianapolis: Indiana University Press, 1990). For recent perspectives on Dewey and education see Emily Robertson, "Is Dewey's Educational Vision Still Viable?" *Review of Research in Education*, ed. Gerald Grant (Washington, D.C.: American Educational Research Association, 1992), 335–81; and Robert H. Westbrook, *John Dewey and American Democracy* (Ithaca: Cornell University Press, 1991), 96–111, 161–82, 502–6. For an overall reassessment of Dewey see R. W. Sleeper, *The Necessity of Pragmatism: John Dewey's Concept of Philosophy* (New Haven and London: Yale University Press, 1986); and Alan Ryan, *John Dewey and the High Tide of American Liberalism* (New York: Norton, 1995).

17. J. E. Tiles, *Dewey* (London and New York: Routledge, 1988), 126.

18. Gadamer, *The Idea of the Good*, 172–73.

19. Ibid., 173 n.5.

20. Alexander, *John Dewey's Theory of Art*, 159–60.

21. G. P. Baker and P. M. S. Hacker, *Wittgenstein: Meaning and Understanding* (Chicago: University of Chicago Press, 1980), 32.

22. Kenneth Burke, *Attitudes Toward History* (1937); rev. 2nd ed. (Boston: Beacon, 1959), 361.

23. Jürgen Habermas,*The Theory of Communicative Action*, trans. Thomas McCarthy, 2 vols. (Boston: Beacon, 1987), 2: 325, 355. Cf. Niklas Luhmann, *The Differentiation of Society*, trans. Stephen Holmes and Charles Lamore (New York: Columbia, 1982), 315–30.

24. Stephen Toulmin, *Human Understanding: The Collective Use and Evolution of Concepts* (Princeton: Princeton University Press, 1972), 81.

25. Ibid., 82.

26. Georg Lukács, *History and Class Consciousness: Studies in Marxist Dialectics*, trans. Rodney Livingstone (Cambridge, Mass.: MIT Press, 1971), 88.

27. Ibid., 89.

28. Immanuel Kant, *The Critique of Judgment* (1928; reprint, Oxford: Oxford University Press, 1952), 111.

29. Justus Buchler, *Toward a General Theory of Human Judgment*, 2nd rev. ed. (1951; reprint, New York: Dover, 1979), 29–30; hereafter cited parenthetically in text by page number.

30. See the discussion in Hannah Arendt, *Lectures on Kant's Political Philosophy*, ed. Ronald Beiner (Chicago: University of Chicago Press, 1982), 40–41.

31. Ibid., 41.

32. Walter Pater, *Marius the Epicurean* (New York: Macmillan, 1926), 4–5; hereafter cited parenthetically as *ME*, followed by page number.

33. T. K. Seung, *Cultural Thematics: The Formation of the Faustian Ethos* (New Haven and London: Yale University Press, 1976), 207.

34. Caroline Walker Bynum, *Jesus as Mother: Studies in the Spirituality of the High Middle Ages* (Berkeley: University of California Press, 1982), 82ff.

35. The discussion that follows is greatly indebted to C. B. Macpherson, *The Political Theory of Possessive Individualism: Hobbes to Locke* (Oxford: Oxford University Press, 1962).

36. Macpherson, *Possessive Individualism*, 53.

37. Ibid., 3.

38. Ibid., 269.

39. Michel Foucault, *Language, Counter-Memory, Practice*, ed. Donald F. Souchard (Ithaca: Cornell University Press, 1977), 141.

40. Thomas Hobbes, *Leviathan*, ed. C. B. Macpherson (Harmondsworth: Penguin, 1968), 186; hereafter cited parenthetically as *L*, followed by page number.

41. *The Complete Essays of Montaigne*, trans. Donald M. Frame (Stanford: Stanford University Press, 1958), 610–11.

42. Kenneth Burke, *A Rhetoric of Motives* (1950; reprint, Cleveland and New York: World, 1962), 508.

43. Macpherson, *Possessive Individualism*, 140.

44. *Max Weber on Law in Economy and Society*, ed. Max Rheinstein, trans. Edward Shils and Max Rheinstein (1954; reprint, New York: Simon and Schuster, n.d.), 260–65.

45. *The Marx-Engels Reader*, ed. Robert C. Tucker (2nd ed.) (New York: Norton, 1978), 332–33.

46. Quoted in Macpherson, *Possessive Individualism*, 36.

47. On Hobbes in relation to nature, natural law, and related matters, see R. E. Ewin, *Virtues and Rights: The Moral Philosophy of Thomas Hobbes* (Boulder: Westview Press, 1991), 48.

48. Kenneth Burke, *A Grammar of Motives*, 32–33. Cf. Carole Kay, *Political Constructions: Defoe, Richardson, and Sterne in Relation to Hobbes, Hume, and Burke* (Ithaca: Cornell University Press, 1988), 31ff.

49. J. G. A. Pocock, *Politics, Language and Time: Essays on Political Thought and History* (1971; reprint, Chicago: University of Chicago Press, 1989), 172–73.

50. A. P. Martinich, *The Two Gods of "Leviathan": Thomas Hobbes on Religion and Politics* (Cambridge: Cambridge University Press, 1992), 290.

51. Pocock, *Politics, Language, and Time*, 188.

52. Ibid., 187.

53. Martinich, *The Two Gods of "Leviathan,"* 196.

54. Ibid., 197.

55. Carole Pateman, "'God Hath Ordained to Man a Helper': Hobbes, Patriarchy, and Conjugal Right," in *Feminist Interpretations and Political Theory*, ed. Mary Lyndon Shanley and Carole Pateman (University Park: Pennsylvania State University Press, 1991), 53–73.

56. Ibid., 62.

57. John Locke, *Two Treatises of Government*, ed. Peter Laslett (Cambridge: Cambridge University Press, 1960), 1: 46; hereafter cited parenthetically as L, followed by volume and paragraph number.

58. Melissa A. Butler, "Early Liberal Roots of Feminism: John Locke and the Attack on Patriarchy," in *Feminist Interpretations and Political Theory* (see n. 55 above), 91.

59. Elizabeth Fox-Genovese, *Feminism Without Illusions: A Critique of Individualism* (Chapel Hill and London: University of North Carolina Press, 1991), 177.

60. Hannah Fenichel Pitkin, *Fortune Is a Woman: Gender and Power in the Thought of Niccolò Machiavelli* (Berkeley: University of California Press, 1984), 147.

61. W. B. Yeats, *Essays and Introductions* (New York: Macmillan, 1963), 300–301; hereafter cited parenthetically as *E&I*, followed by page number. A. Norman Jeffares, *A Commentary on the Collected Poems of W. B. Yeats* (Stanford: Stanford University Press, 1968) first called my attention to this text; see 293. Yeats's *Explorations* (New York: Macmillan,

1962) is hereafter cited parenthetically as *E*, followed by page number. *Mythologies* (New York: Macmillan, 1959) is hereafter cited parenthetically as *M*, followed by page number. Citations to poems are to *The Collected Works of W. B. Yeats*, vol. 1: *The Poems*, ed. Richard J. Finneran (New York: Macmillan, 1983); hereafter cited parenthetically as *CWY*, followed by page number. *Purgatory*, in *Eleven Plays by William Butler Yeats*, ed. A. Norman Jeffares (New York: Macmillan, 1964) is hereafter cited parenthetically as *P*, followed by page number. *A Vision* (New York: Macmillan, 1983) is hereafter cited parenthetically as *V*, followed by page number.

62. Leo Spitzer, *Essays on English and American Literature*, ed. Anna Hatcher (Princeton: Princeton University Press, 1961), 8.

63. Jean-Paul Sartre, *Critique of Dialectical Reason*, trans. Alan Sheridan Smith, 2 vols. (London: New Left Books, 1976), 1: 71.

64. *A History of Technology*, ed. Charles Singer, E. J. Holmyard, A. R. Hall, and Trevor I. Williams (Oxford: Oxford University Press, 1958), 4: 277ff.

65. Northrop Frye, *Anatomy of Criticism: Four Essays* (Princeton: Princeton University Press, 1957), 158, 160.

66. See Jeffares, *A Commentary on the Collected Poems of W. B. Yeats*, 275.

67. Jacques Le Goff, *The Birth of Purgatory*, trans. Arthur Goldhammer (Chicago: University of Chicago Press, 1984), 233.

PART II

1. See Kenneth Burke, *A Grammar of Motives* (1945; reprint, Cleveland and New York: World), chap. 1.

2. Ibid., 21.

3. See Edmund Husserl, *Ideas: A General Introduction to Pure Phenomenology*, trans. R. Boyce Gibson (New York: Collier, 1962), 231.

4. For a fuller discussion see David Halliburton, "Endowment, Enablement, Entitlement: Towards a Theory of Constitution," in *Literature and the Question of Philosophy*, ed. Anthony J. Cascardi (Baltimore: Johns Hopkins University Press, 1987), 242–64.

5. Alfred North Whitehead, *Process and Reality*, ed. David Ray Griffin and Donald W. Sherburne, corrected edition (New York: Macmillan, 1978), 189.

6. Ibid., 21.

7. Burke, *A Grammar of Motives*, 31–32.

8. Martin Heidegger, *The Question Concerning Technology*, trans. William Lovitt (New York: Harper & Row, 1977), 20.

9. Ibid., 7.

10. Heidegger, *Poetry, Language, Thought*, trans. Albert Hofstadter (New York: Harper Colophon, 1975), 179–80.

11. Sir Thomas More, *Utopia*, trans. Paul Turner (Harmondsworth: Penguin, 1968), 96.

12. Alexis de Tocqueville, *Democracy in America*, trans. Henry Reeve, ed. Francis Bowen and Phillips Bradley, 2 vols. (New York: Knopf, 1954), 2:27.

13. Tocqueville, *Democracy in America*, 2: 27.

14. Ibid.

15. [Emile Chartier], *Alain on Happiness*, trans. Robert D. and Jane E. Cottrell (New York: Ungar, 1973), 61.

16. Georg Trakl, *Selected Poems*, ed. Christopher Middleton (London: Jonathan Cape, 1968), 59. I have taken the liberty of retranslating the final line of "Kaspar Hauser Lied."

17. Elaine Scarry, *The Body in Pain: The Making and Unmaking of the World* (New York: Oxford University Press, 1985), 213.

18. *The Complete Essays of Montaigne*, trans. Donald M. Frame (Stanford: Stanford University Press, 1958), 113.

19. Virginia Woolf, *The Moment and Other Essays* (London: Hogarth, 1964), 14; hereafter cited parenthetically as W, followed by page number.

20. Maurice Merleau-Ponty, *Consciousness and the Acquisition of Language*, trans. Hugh J. Silverman (Evanston: Northwestern University Press, 1973), 29.

21. Hans-Georg Gadamer, *Truth and Method*, trans. and ed. Garrett Burden and John Cumming from 2nd ed. (1965) (New York: Seabury, 1975), 33ff.

22. Thomas Jefferson, *Writings* (New York: Library of America, 1984), 19; hereafter cited as J, followed by page number.

23. Jay Fliegelman, *Declaring Independence: Jefferson, Natural Language, and the Culture of Performance* (Stanford: Stanford University Press, 1993), 45. The case for a syllogistic structure is made by Wilbur Samuel Howell; see 51.

24. Markley, "Sentimentality as Performance: Shaftesbury, Sterne, and the Theatrics of Virtue," in *The New Eighteenth Century*, ed. Felicity Nussbaum and Laura Brown (New York and London: Methuen, 1987), 218.

25. Bernard Bailyn, *The Ideological Origins of the American Revolution* (Cambridge, Mass.: Harvard University Press, 1967), 77.

26. John Locke, *An Essay Concerning Human Understanding*, ed. A. D. Woozley (New York: New American Library), 173–74.

27. *The Works of Francis Bacon*, ed. James Spedding and Robert Leslie Ellis (London: Longmans, 1870), 3: 424–25.

28. Tocqueville, *Democracy in America*, 1: 4 43.

29. J. G. A. Pocock, *The Machiavellian Moment: Florentine Political Thought and the Atlantic Republican Tradition* (Princeton: Princeton University Press, 1975), 440.

30. David Hume, *A Treatise of Human Nature*, ed. Ernest C. Mossner (Harmondsworth: Penguin 1969), 543.

31. See Dumas Malone, *Jefferson and His Time* (Boston: Little, Brown, 1951), 2:187ff.

32. Pocock, *The Machiavellian Moment*, 425.

33. It will be seen that "small is beautiful" merely recasts a theme with a long history, no slight portion of which embraces the eighteenth century. For discussion of the little, see David Halliburton, *The Color of the Sky: A Study of Stephen Crane* (Cambridge: Cambridge University Press, 1989), 15–37 *et passim*; cf. measure, 54–56 *et passim*, and scale, 15 *et passim*.

34. Fliegelman points out that in the eighteenth century communication was thought to rely less on the use of linguistic features than on the use of "the features of delivery and countenance, the body of the speaker and its attitudes." See *Declaring Independence*, 43.

35. Laurence Sterne, *A Sentimental Journey through France and Italy by Mr. Yorick*, ed. Ian Jack (Oxford: Oxford University Press, 1968), 76; hereafter cited parentehetically as S, followed by page number.

36. Carole Kay, *Political Constructions: Defoe, Richardson, and Sterne in Relation to Hobbes, Hume, and Burke* (Ithaca: Cornell University Press, 1988), 253.

37. Hannah Arendt, *On Revolution* (1965; reprint, Harmondsworth: Penguin, 1977), 252.

38. On Jefferson's moral struggle over slavery see Ronald Takaki, *Race and Culture in Nineteenth-Century America* (Oxford: Oxford University Press, 1979).

39. Quoted in Barbara McEwan, *Thomas Jefferson: Farmer* (Jefferson, N.C.: McFarland, 1991), 146.

40. Hannah Arendt, *The Human Condition* (Chicago: University of Chicago Press, 1958), 96–97.

41. Ibid., 97.

42. *The Literature of the United States*, ed. Walter Blair, Theodore Hornberger, and Randall Stewart, rev. ed., 2 vols. (Chicago: Scott, Foresman, 1953), 1: 416.

43. Henry Nash Smith, *Virgin Land: The American West as Symbol and Myth* (1950; reprint, New York: Random House, 1964), 10 ff.

44. John Locke, *Two Treatises of Government*, ed. Peter Laslett (1960; rev. ed. Cambridge: Cambridge University Press, 1963), 328.

45. Ibid., 332.

46. Ibid.

47. Bailyn, *The Ideological Origins of the American Revolution*, 198.

48. Walt Whitman, *Leaves of Grass*, ed. Sculley Bradley and Harold W. Blodgett (1965; reprint, New York: Norton, 1983), 2: 504, 17–19. Whitman citations are to this edition; hereafter cited parenthetically by volume, page number, and line number.

49. Betsy Erkilla, *Whitman, the Political Poet* (New York: Oxford University Press, 1989) is one of the very few critics who take note of the Whitman poems on Native Americans.

50. Roland Barthes, *Mythologies*, ed. Annette Lavers (New York: Hill and Wang, 1972), 116.

51. Erkilla, *Whitman, the Political Poet*, 242.

52. Walt Whitman, *Specimen Days*, in *Prose Works*, ed. Floyd Stovall (New York: New York University Press, 1963), 1: 282.

53. Francis Paul Prucha, *Americanizing the American Indians: Writings by the "Friends of the Indians," 1880–1900* (1973; reprint, Lincoln: University of Nebraska Press, 1978).

54. David Simpson, *The Politics of American English, 1776–1850* (New York and Oxford: Oxford University Press, 1986), 101 ff.

55. Loring Benson Priest, *Uncle Sam's Stepchildren: The Reform of United States Indian Policy, 1865–1887* (Lincoln: University of Nebraska Press, 1942), 180 ff.

56. E. M. Forster, *Aspects of the Novel* (London: Edward Arnold, 1927), 82.

57. The quoted remarks appear in Horace Traubel, *With Walt Whitman in Camden*, ed. Gertrude Traubel and William White (Carbondale and Edwardsville: Southern Illinois University Press, 1964), 5: 400.

58. The text is provided in Mary McNeer Ward, "The Disappearance of Osceola's Head," *Florida Historical Quarterly* 22 (Jan.–Apr. 1955), 197. For formatting purposes, Whitman's lineation has been altered.

59. Quoted in John Goggin, "Osceola: Portraits, Features, and Dress," *Florida Historical Quarterly* 33 (Jan.–Apr. 1955), 177–78.

60. A. Grove Day, *The Sky Clears: Poetry of the American Indians* (Lincoln: University of Nebraska Press, 1951), 116.

61. Justin Kaplan, *Walt Whitman: A Life* (New York: Simon and Schuster, 1980), 305.

62. Richard Sennett, *The Fall of Public Man: On the Social Psychology of Capitalism* (New York: Random House, 1977), 8.

63. Charles Baudelaire, *Oeuvres Completes* (Paris: Seuil, 1968), 91.

64. Jean-Paul Sartre, *Baudelaire* (Paris: Gallimard, 1962), 32.

65. Yehoshua Arieli, *Individualism and Nationalism in American Ideology* (Cambridge, Mass.: Harvard University Press, 1964), 318.

66. Erkilla, *Whitman, the Political Poet*, 178.

67. Citations to "For John F. Kennedy His Inauguration," with the pendant text "The

Gift Outright," are to *The Poetry of Robert Frost*, ed. Edward Connery Lathem (New York: Holt, Rinehart and Winston, 1969), 422–25.

68. Locke, *Two Treatises of Government*, 192.

69. Forrest McDonald, *Novus Ordo Seclorum: The Intellectual Origins of the Constitution* (Lawrence: University Press of Kansas, 1985), 28.

70. Ibid., 36.

71. Stuart Hampshire, *Innocence and Experience* (Cambridge, Mass.: Harvard University Press, 1989), 146–47.

72. Ibid., 148.

PART III

1. *El coloquio de los perros* (New York: Dell, 1963), 73.

2. Ibid., 74.

3. Ibid., 124.

4. René Descartes, *Philosophical Writings*, trans. John Cottingham, Robert Stathoff, and Dugald Murdoch, 2 vols. (Cambridge: Cambridge University Press, 1984), 1: 112; hereafter cited parenthetically as *PW*, followed by volume and page number. Citations from the original French are to *Oeuvres philosophiques*, ed. Ferdinand Alquié (Paris: Garnier, 1963); hereafter cited parenthetically as *OP*, followed by page number.

5. Denis Hollier, *A New History of French Literature* (Cambridge, Mass.: Harvard University Press, 1989), 327–28.

6. Martin Heidegger, "The Age of the World Picture," in *The Question Concerning Technology and Other Essays*, trans. William Lovitt (New York: Harper & Row, 1977), 130.

7. Heidegger, "The Age of the World Picture," 133.

8. Ibid.

9. Ibid., 142.

10. Ibid. My reasons for preferring "presentment" to the tranlator's "representing" will be taken up in section 3.

11. Antonio Manetti, *The Life of Filippo di Ser Brunellesco*, in *A Documentary History of Art*, vol. l, ed. Elizabeth G. Holt (Garden City, N.Y.: Doubleday, 1957), 172.

12. *The Complete Essays of Montaigne*, trans. Donald M. Frame (Stanford: Stanford University Press, 1958) 483–85; hereafter cited parenthetically as *CEM*, followed by page number.

13. The quotations and information on Dee are from Frances A. Yates, *Theatre of the World* (Chicago: University of Chicago Press, 1969), especially chapters 1 and 2. On *Monas* see Yates, *The Art of Memory* (Chicago: University of Chicago Press, 1966), 263.

14. Yates, *Theatre of the World*, 27.

15. Friedrich Nietzsche, *The Will to Power*, trans. Walter Kaufmann and R. J. Hollingdale (New York: Random House, 1966), 12.

16. Benedict de Spinoza, *Ethics*, trans. R. H. M. Elwes, in *The Rationalists* (New York: Doubleday, 1960), 263.

17. Arendt, *The Human Condition* (Chicago: University of Chicago Press, 1958), 225.

18. Lewis Mumford, *Technics and Civilization* (1934; reprint, New York: Harcourt, Brace & World, 1963), 124.

19. Ibid., 139.

20. George Santayana, *Scepticism and Animal Faith: Introduction to a System of Philosophy* (1923; reprint, New York: Dover, 1955), 289.

21. Ibid.

22. Ibid., 291.

23. Giambattista Vico, *On the Most Ancient Wisdom of the Italians*, trans. L. M. Palmer (Ithaca and London: Cornell University Press, 1988), 49.

24. Ernesto Grassi, *Rhetoric as Philosophy: The Humanist Tradition* (University Park and London: Pennsylvania State University Press, 1980), 44.

25. Vico, *On the Most Ancient Wisdom*, 102.

26. Ibid., 46.

27. John D. Schaeffer, *"Sensus Communis": Vico, Rhetoric, and the Limits of Relativism* (Durham and London: Duke University Press, 1990), 122.

28. Vico, *On the Most Ancient Wisdom*, 100.

29. *Twilight of the Idols* in *The Portable Nietzsche*, ed. Walter Kaufmann (New York: Viking, 1943), 49; hereafter cited parenthetically as *TI*, followed by page number.

30. Christopher Caudwell, *Illusion and Reality: A Study of the Sources of Poetry* (New York: International, 1927), 136.

31. *Basic Writings of Nietzsche*, ed. Walter Kaufmann (New York: Modern Library, 1963), 5.

32. Ibid., 5.

33. *The Complete Works of Ralph Waldo Emerson*, ed. Edward Waldo Emerson (Boston: Houghton-Mifflin, 1888), 3: 14.

34. Ibid., 24–25.

35. Martin Heidegger, *Being and Time*, trans. John Macquarrie and Edward Robinson (New York: Harper & Row, 1962), 205; hereafter cited parenthetically as *BT*, followed by page number.

36. Emmanuel Lévinas, "Intuition of Essences," in *Phenomenology: The Philosophy of Edmund Husserl and His Interpreters*, ed. Joseph J. Kockelmans (New York: Doubleday, 1967), 91.

37. Roman Ingarden, *The Literary Work of Art: An Investigation on the Borderlines of Ontology, Logic, and Theory of Literature*, trans. George G. Grabowicz (Evanston: Northwestern University Press, 1973), 262–64 *et passim*.

38. Martin Heidegger, *An Introduction to Metaphysics*, trans. Ralph Manheim (New Haven: Yale University Press, 1959), 191.

39. In his *Consequences of Pragmatism (Essays: 1972–1980)* (Minneapolis: University of Minnesota Press, 1982), 37–60, Richard Rorty suggestively discusses the similarities and differences of the two thinkers in their relation to Western philosophical discourse.

40. Martin Heidegger, *The End of Philosophy*, trans. Joan Stambaugh (New York: Harper & Row, 1973), 76.

41. Ibid.

42. "Noble discourse" is Michael Joyce's rendering of *logous kalous*, from Plato's *Charmides*, in contrast to W. R. M. Lamb's "beautiful converse"; Benjamin Jowett offers "fair words" as against the "noble discourses" proposed by T. M. Robinson. The Joyce translation is in *The Collective Dialogues of Plato*, ed. Edith Hamilton and Huntington Cairns (Princeton: Princeton University Press, 1961), 103. Lamb's translation is in his *Plato, with an English Translation* (London: Heinemann, 1924), 73–246. Robinson's rendering is in his *Plato's Psychology* (Toronto: University of Toronto Press, 1970), 7.

43. In *The Living Thoughts of Thomas Jefferson* (Greenwich, Conn.: Fawcett, 1940), Dewey makes much of Jefferson's idea that counties should be subdivided into wards to enable more active participation by citizens. Cf. Robert B. Westbrook, *John Dewey and American Democracy* (Ithaca and London: Cornell University Press, 1991), 454–55.

44. Lewis Mumford, *The City in History: Its Origins, Its Transformations and Its Prospects* (New York: Harcourt Brace & Jovanovich, 1961), 65.

45. Paul Friedlander, *Plato: An Introduction*, trans. Hans Meyerhof, 2nd ed. (Princeton: Princeton University Press, 1969), 1: 229.

46. Dumas Malone, *Jefferson and His Times* (6 vols.; Boston: Little, Brown, 1951), 2:91.

47. Hannah Arendt, *On Revolution* (1963; reprint, New York: Penguin, 1972); see chap. 6. On Gramsci and factory workers' councils see Anne Showstack Sassoon, *Gramsci's Politics*, 2nd ed. (London: Hutchinson, 1987), 31ff.

48. Arendt, *On Revolution*, 258.

49. Ibid., 259.

50. Robert H. Wiebe, *The Search for Order, 1822–1920* (New York: Hill & Wang, 1967), 67. Cf. Johann Huizinga, *America: A Dutch Historian's Vision from Afar and Near*, trans. Herbert H. Rowen (New York: Harper & Row, 1962), 61–118.

51. Arendt, *On Revolution*, 250.

52. Ibid., 280–81. Arendt goes on to echo Sophocles' view of the compensatory role of participation in the *polis*.

53. *The Early Lectures of Ralph Waldo Emerson*, 3 vols., ed. Robert E. Spiller and Wallace E. Williams (Cambridge, Mass.: Harvard University Press, 1971), 3: 348–49; hereafter cited parenthetically as E, followed by volume and page number.

54. Quoted in Yehoshua Arieli, *Individualism and Nationalism in American Ideology* (Cambridge, Mass.: Harvard University Press, 1961), 278.

55. Arendt, *The Human Condition*, 173.

56. Jean-Jacques Rousseau, *The Confessions*, trans. J. H. Cohen (Baltimore: Penguin, 1953), 218; hereafter cited parenthetically as C, followed by page number.

57. Hannah Arendt, *Men in Dark Times* (New York: Harcourt Brace & Jovanovich, 1965), 24–25.

58. Michael Oakeshott, *Experience and Its Modes* (Cambridge: Cambridge University Press, 1933), 62–63.

PART IV

1. Alfred North Whitehead, *Science and the Modern World* (New York: Macmillan, 1915), 55.

2. *Discoveries and Opinions of Galileo*, trans. Stillman Drake (New York: Doubleday, 1957), 275; hereafter cited parenthetically as G, followed by page number.

3. Aron Gurwitsch, "Galilean Physics, in the Light of Husserl's" in *Galileo: Man of Science*, ed. Ernan McMullin (New York: Basic Books, 1967), 397–38.

4. Heidegger, *Being and Time*, trans. John Macquarrie and Edward Robinson (Harper & Row, 1962), 189.

5. Stillman Drake, *Telescopes, Tides and Tactics: A Galilean Dialogue about the "Starry Messenger" and Systems of the World* (Chicago: University of Chicago Press, 1983), 27.

6. Ibid., 60–61.

7. Ibid.

8. Maurice Merleau-Ponty, *The Visible and the Invisible*, ed. Claude Lefort, trans. Alphonso Linguis (Evanston: Northwestern University Press, 1968), 149–50.

9. On the role of the material imagination of air in relation to the other traditional elements, see Gaston Bachelard, *L'Air et les songes: Essai sur l'imagination du mouvement* (Paris: Corti, 1943).

10. Octavio Paz, *The Bow and the Lyre*, trans. Ruth L. C. Simms (Austin and London: University of Texas Press, 1973), 89.

11. Henry Adams, "The Rule of Phase Applied to History," in *The Degradation of the Democratic Dogma* (New York: Macmillan, 1916), 276.

12. Walter Pater, *Miscellaneous Studies: A Series of Essays* (New York and London: Macmillan, 1896), 60–61.

13. *Pensées de Pascal* (Paris: Dezobry and Magdeleine, 1852), 13.

14. Ibid., 128.

15. *The Poetical Works of Gerard Manley Hopkins*, ed. Norman H. Mackenzie (Oxford: Clarendon, 1990), 144; hereafter cited parenthetically as H, followed by page number.

16. *Poems and Prose of Gerard Manley Hopkins*, ed. W. H. Gardner (Baltimore: Penguin, 1953), 141.

17. Ibid., 148.

18. Ibid., 145.

19. C. B. Macpherson, *Possessive Individualism*, 3.

20. *Poems and Prose of Gerard Manley Hopkins*, 148.

21. Ibid., 145.

22. Ibid., 149–50.

23. Paul Valéry, *Oeuvres*, ed. Jean Hytier (Paris: Gallimard-Pléiade, 1957–60), 2: 519.

24. *Paul Valéry: An Anthology*, ed. James R. Lawler (Princeton: Princeton University Press, 1956), 143.

25. Ibid., 151.

26. Jean-Paul Sartre, *Being and Nothingness: An Essay in Phenomenological Ontology*, ed. Hazel E. Barnes (New York: Philosophical Library, 1956), 627.

27. Jean-Paul Sartre, *La Nausée* (Paris: Gallimard, 1938), 141.

28. Ibid., 250.

29. Ibid.

30. Ibid., 246.

31. Ezra Pound, *The Cantos (1–95)* (New York: New Directions, 1956), Canto 51: 44.

32. George Santayana, *Reason in Art* (New York: Scribner's, 1905), 87–88.

33. Ibid., 90.

34. Ibid., 98.

35. Merleau-Ponty, *The Visible and the Invisible*, 144.

36. Ibid.

37. Denis Diderot, *Rameau's Nephew and Other Works*, trans. Jacques Barzun and Ralph H. Bowen (Indianapolis: Bobbs-Merrill, 1956), 82, translation modified.

38. Ibid., 39.

39. Ibid., 8.

40. Leo Spitzer, *Linguistics and Literary History: Essays in Stylistics* (Princeton: Princeton University Press, 1948), 153.

41. *Rameau's Nephew*, 72.

42. Ibid., 76.

43. Denis Diderot, *D'Alembert's Dream* in *Rameau's Nephew* (see n. 37).

44. Charles Baudelaire, *Oeuvres complètes* (Paris: Editions du Seuil, 1968), 561; hereafter cited parenthetically as B, followed by page number.

45. Rainer Maria Rilke, *Auguste Rodin*, in *Werke in drei Bänden* (Frankfurt: Insel, 1966), 3: 362; hereafter cited parenthetically as AR, followed by page reference.

46. Luis Cernuda, *Selected Poems*, ed. and trans. Reginald Gibbons (Berkeley: University of California Press, 1977), 57–59.

47. José Ortega y Gasset, *Man and People*, trans. Willard R. Trask (New York: Norton, 1947), 18.

48. Arendt, *The Human Condition* (Chicago: University of Chicago Press, 1958), 291–92.

49. George Santayana, *The Sense of Beauty: Being the Outline of Aesthetic Theory* (1906; reprint, New York: Dover, 1955), 39.

50. "Love," in *The Essays of Ralph Waldo Emerson*, ed. Alfred Kazin (Cambridge, Mass: Harvard University Press, 1987), 100.

51. Ibid., 105.

52. Ibid.

53. Gotthold Ephraim Lessing, *Laocoön*, in *Criticism: The Major Texts*, ed. Walter Jackson Bate (New York: Harcourt Brace & World, 1952), 245.

54. Ibid., 245–46.

55. M. C. Herder Norton, *Translations from the Poetry of Rainer Maria Rilke* (New York: Norton, 1938), 181.

56. "The Tragic Theatre," in W. B. Yeats, *Essays and Introductions* (London: Macmillan, 1924), 239.

57. *The Essential Plotinus*, trans. Elmer O'Brien (New York: New American Library, 1964), 36–37.

58. Ibid., 42. On Plotinus in relation to ecphrasis in particular and representation in general, see Stephen Bann's authoritative *The True Vine: On Visual Representation and Western Tradition* (Cambridge: Cambridge University Press, 1989), p. 118 *et passim*.

59. George Santayana, *Reason in Religion* (New York: Scribner's, 1905), 194–95.

60. Ibid., 196.

61. "Flesh" is the term employed by Michael Joyce. See Part I, n. 42.

62. James Milroy, *The Language of Gerard Manley Hopkins* (London: Deutsch, 1977), 90 *et passim*. On the relation of Hopkins's *bonfire* to Old English *ban-fyr, bone-fire*, and French *bon* to Scottish *bonnie*, see 232–48.

63. *The Poetical Works of Gerard Manley Hopkins*, 4.

64. César Vallejo, *Poesía Completa* (Puebla, Mexico: Premia, 1978), 310. All citations from Vallejo are to this edition; hereafter cited parenthetically as V, followed by page reference.

65. Christiane von Buelow, "Vallejo's *Venus de Milo* and the Ruins of Language," *PMLA* 104 (1989): 50. The English translation of this text, *Trilce* 36, is by von Buelow, whose reading of Vallejo has materially influenced my own. I have translated *por hai* as "there." Clayton Eshleman offers "that way." See his translation of *Trilce* (New York: Marsili, 1992), 93.

66. Von Buelow, "Vallejo's *Venus de Milo* and the Ruins of Language," 48.

67. Quoted in Jean Franco, *César Vallejo* (Cambridge: Cambridge University Press, 1976), 159, to which I am much indebted.

68. Octavio Paz, *The Bow and the Lyre*, trans. Ruth L. C. Simms (Austin: University of Texas Press, 1973), 82.

69. James Higgins, *César Vallejo: An Anthology of His Poetry* (Oxford: Pergamon, 1970), 180.

70. John Ruskin, *Unto This Last and Other Writings*, ed. Clive Wilmer (London: Penguin, 1985), 116.

71. Michel Serres, *Hermes: Literature, Science and Philosophy*, ed. Josué V. Harari and David F. Bell (Baltimore: Johns Hopkins University Press, 1982), 16.

72. Antonio Gramsci, *Selections from the Prison Notebooks*, trans. Quentin Hoare and Geoffrey Nowell Smith (New York: International, 1971), 9.

73. Franco, *César Vallejo*, 171.

74. Hermann Broch, *The Death of Virgil*, trans. Jean Starr Untermeyer (1945; reprint, New York: Grosset and Dunlap, 1965), 470–71.

75. Wallace Stevens, *The Palm at the End of the Mind: Selected Poems and a Play*, ed. Holly Stevens (New York: Knopf, 1971), 7.

PART V

1. Martin Heidegger, *Being and Time*, trans. John Macquarrie and Edward Robinson (New York: Harper & Row, 1962), 377.

2. Stephanie H. Jed, *Chaste Thinking: The Rape of Lucretia and the Birth of Humanism* (Bloomington: Indiana University Press, 1989), 115.

3. Friedrich Nietzsche, *Genealogy of Morals*, trans. and ed. Walter Kaufmann (New York: Modern Library, 1965), 481.

4. Henry James, *The Art of the Novel: Critical Prefaces* (New York: Scribners, 1934), 46.

5. Henry James, "The Art of Fiction," in *The Future of the Novel: Essays on the Art of Fiction*, ed. Leon Edel (New York: Vintage, 1956), 12.

6. *The Works of John Adams*, ed. Charles Francis Adams (Boston: Little Brown, 1855–56), 4: 469.

7. Douglas D. Adair, " 'Experience Must Be Our Only Guide': History, Democratic Theory, and the United States Constitution," in *The Reinterpretation of Early American History: Essays in Honor of John Edwin Pomfret*, ed. Ray Allen Billington (San Marino: Huntington, 1977), 131.

8. Michel Foucault, *Madness and Civilization: A History of Insanity in the Age of Reason*, trans. Richard Howard (New York: Random House, 1965), and *Discipline and Punish: The Birth of the Prison*, trans. Alan Sheridan (London: Allen Lane, 1977).

9. On confinement in the eighteenth century, see W. B. Carnochan, *Confinement and Flight: An Essay on English Literature of the Eighteenth Century* (Berkeley: University of California Press, 1977), and John Bender, *Imagining the Penitentiary: Fiction and the Architecture of Mind in Eighteenth-Century England* (Chicago: University of Chicago Press, 1987).

10. David Hume, *A Treatise of Human Nature*, ed. Ernest C. Mossner (Harmondsworth: Penguin, 1969), 350; all quotations from Hume in the present discussion are from this same passage.

11. *The Works of John Adams*, 4: 469.

12. Ibid.

13. Eric A. Havelock, *Preface to Plato* (Cambridge, Mass.: Harvard University Press, 1963), 209.

14. Alfred North Whitehead, *Process and Reality*, ed. David Ray Griffin and Donald W. Sherburne (New York: Macmillan, 1978), 21.

15. Ibid., 189.

16. Havelock, *Preface to Plato*, 45.

17. J. N. Findlay, *Hegel: A Re-examination* (New York: Collier, 1962), 18–19. I am much indebted to this study as well as to Hans-Georg Gadamer, *Truth and Method*, trans. Garrett Barden and John Cumming (New York: Seabury-Continuum) 1975, and Jean Hyppolite, *Studies on Marx and Hegel*, ed. and trans. John O'Neill (1969; reprint, New York: Harper & Row, 1973).

18. Martin Heidegger, *Hegel's Concept of Experience* (New York: Harper & Row, 1970), 13. Citations from Hegel in the present discussion are reprinted in Heidegger's text from the English translation of *Phenomenology of Spirit* by Kenley Royce Dove.

19. I draw not only on Hegel's exposition, which is abstract to a fault, but on the *Zusätze*, or appendices, of his students Leopold von Henning and Ludwig Boumann. Branching off from the main exposition, the appendices typically give examples of the large points Hegel is trying to make; the illustrative stories for their part tell of the concrete experiences the philosopher took into account in order to arrive at the generalities in the main text. Citations are to *Hegel's "Logic,"* trans. William Wallace (Oxford: Oxford University Press, 1975), and *Hegel's "Philosophy of Mind,"* trans. William Wallace and A. V. Miller (Oxford: Clarendon, 1971); hereafter referred to parenthetically as, respectively, *HL* and *PM*, followed by page number.

20. Wilhelm Dilthey, "The Hermeneutics of the Human Sciences," in *The Hermeneutics Reader: Texts of the German Tradition from the Enlightenment to the Present*, ed. Kurt Mueller-Vollmer (New York: Continuum, 1985), 152.

21. Findlay, *Hegel: A Reexamination*, 329.

22. Georg Lukács, *Goethe and His Age*, trans. Robert Anchor (New York: Grosset & Dunlap, 1969), 192.

23. Lukács, *Goethe and His Age*, 197.

24. *Brecht on Theatre: The Development of an Aesthetic*, ed. and trans. John Willett (New York: Hill & Wang, 1964), 15; hereafter cited parenthetically as *B*, followed by page number.

25. Alphonso Lingis, "The Elemental Background," in *New Essays in Phenomenology: Studies in the Philosophy of Experience*, ed. James M. Edie (Chicago: Quadrangle, 1969), 36.

26. Georg Lukács, *History and Class-Consciousness: Studies in Marxist Dialectics*, trans. Rodney Livingstone (Cambridge, Mass.: MIT Press, 1971), 299.

27. Hannah Arendt, *On Revolution* (1963; reprint, Harmondsworth: Penguin, 1973), 262ff.

28. Ronald Hayman, *Artaud and After* (Oxford: Oxford University Press, 1977), 106.

29. Heidegger, *Hegel's Concept of Experience*, 46–47.

30. *The Political Thought of Mao Tse Tung*, ed. Stuart R. Schram (New York: Praeger, 1969), 423.

31. Bertolt Brecht, *The Measures Taken*, in *The Modern Theatre*, ed. Eric Bentley (New York: Doubleday, 1960), 6: 277; hereafter cited parenthetically as *M*, followed by page number.

32. Sheila Delany, "The Politics of the Signified in Bertolt Brecht's 'The Measures Taken,'" in *Clio: A Journal of Literature, History and the Philosophy of History* 16 (1981), 70.

33. Delany, "The Politics of the Signified," 70.

34. Jean-Paul Sartre, *The Critique of Dialectical Reason: Theory of Practical Ensembles*, ed. Jonathan Ree, trans. Alan Sheridan-Smith (London: New Left, 1976), 1: 523.

35. Arendt, *The Life of the Mind*, 2 vols. (New York: Harcourt Brace & Jovanovich, 1978), 1: 50.

36. Cf. Martin Heidegger, *The Question Concerning Technology and Other Essays*, trans. William Lovitt (New York: Harper & Row, 1977), 28ff.

37. Jed, *Chaste Thinking*, 11. Jed provides an invaluable commentary as well as the English translation from which my citations are drawn (148–52). For a more general reading of the Lucretian myth see Ian Donaldson, *The Rapes of Lucretia: Myth and Its Transformations* (Oxford: Oxford University Press, 1982). On female sacrifice see Mihoko Suzuki, *Metamorphoses of Helen: Authority, Difference, and the Epic* (Ithaca: Cornell University Press, 1989), 3, 5–9, 16–17, 93–94, *et passim*.

38. See René Girard, *Violence and the Sacred* (Baltimore: Johns Hopkins University Press, 1977), *Things Hidden Since the Foundation of the World*, trans. Stephen Bann and

Michael Metteer (Stanford: Stanford University Press, 1987) and related publications identified in *Stanford French Review* 10 (1988), 3ff.

39. Niccolò Machiavelli, *The Chief Works and Others*, trans. Allan Gilbert (Durham and London: Duke University Press, 1989), 1: 423.

40. Arendt, *The Human Condition*, 50.

41. Citations from *The Legend of Good Women* are to *The Poems of Chaucer*, ed. F. N. Robinson (Boston: Houghton Mifflin, 1933), 565–611.

42. St. Augustine, *The City of God*, trans. Marcus Dods, George Wilson, J. J. Smith (New York: Random House, 1950), 24–25. Subsequent citations are to this text, 1.19: 23–25.

43. Citations from *The Rape of Lucrece* are to *The Complete Works of Shakespeare*, ed. Hardin Craig (Chicago: Scott, Foresman, 1951), 440–57. The lines here quoted are 484–87.

44. Paul Strohm, *Social Chaucer* (Cambridge, Mass.: Harvard University Press, 1989), 14.

45. Elaine Scarry, *The Body in Pain: The Making and Unmaking of the World* (Oxford and New York: Oxford University Press, 1985), 54.

46. Jane Donawerth, *Shakespeare and the Sixteenth-Century Study of Language* (Urbana and Chicago: University of Illinois Press, 1984), 16ff.

47. Nancy Vickers, " 'The blazon of sweet beauty's best': Shakespeare's *Lucrece*," in *Shakespeare and the Question of Theory*, ed. Patricia Parker and Geoffrey Hartman (New York and London: Methuen, 1985), 108–9.

48. Sir Philip Sidney, *The Countess of Pembroke's Arcadia*, ed. Maurice Evans (Harmondsworth: Penguin, 1977), 528.

49. *The Prince*, trans. and ed. Robert M. Adams (New York: Norton), 17.

50. *The Prince*, 17. Cf. Hanna Fenichel Pitkin, *Fortune Is a Woman: Gender and Politics in the Thought of Niccolò Machiavelli* (Berkeley: University of California Press, 1984), 56.

51. For the full text of Machiavelli's rather free translation from Ausonius, see *The Prince*, 138.

52. Ibid., 17.

53. Joan De Jean, *Fictions of Sappho, 1546–1937* (Chicago: Chicago University Press, 1989), 44.

54. Ibid.

55. Arendt, *The Human Condition*, 38.

56. Ibid., 28.

57. David Hume, *Writings on Economics*, ed. Eugene Rotwein (Madison: University of Wisconsin Press, 1970), 19.

58. Helpful discussions of this corpus include John J. Ricchetti, *Popular Fiction Before Richardson: Narrative Patterns, 1700–1739* (Oxford: Oxford University Press, 1969); Robert Martin Day, *Told in Letters: Epistolary Fiction before Richardson* (Ann Arbor: University of Michigan Press, 1966); Janet Altman, *Epistolarity: Approaches to a Form* (Columbus: Ohio University Press, 1981); Porter Abbott, "Letters to the Self: The Cloistered Writer in Non-retrospective Fiction," *PMLA* 95 (1980), 28–41; Charles E. Kaney, *The Epistolary Novel in France, Italy and Spain* (Berkeley: University of California Press, 1937); and G. F. Singer, *The Epistolary Novel* (Philadelphia: University of Pennsylvania Press, 1933).

59. Samuel Richardson, *Pamela or, Virtue Rewarded* (New York: Norton, 1958), 91; hereafter cited parenthetically as *P*, followed by page number.

60. This discussion draws heavily upon Strohm (see n. 44 above). It should be added that without such flexibility, and the increased social mobility it represents, neither individualism nor collectivism is easily imagined. For a group of affines is at once a *collectivity* of individuals and the *individuals* of that collectivity. It is, for example, the Richardian fac-

tion in the England of the late fourteenth century, and the person Geoffrey Chaucer, who benefits from his connections with that faction even as he benefits from his looser association with the Lancastrian affinity. Generally, alliances of affinity are strictly delimited quantitatively and qualitatively. There must not be too many people in them, and they must be the right kind of people. The membership defines itself apart from the "others," in one or another mode of interiorization. For example, it gathers in a place from which outsiders are excluded, as its members often seek that voluntary form of confinement known as retirement. True, one normally thinks of this in connection with an individual (like Pope), but retirement can be on a collective basis and can alternate with immersion in the larger social world. Exclusive or secret societies of the dilettanti or hellfire variety only throw the possibility into relief.

61. Arendt, *Men in Dark Times*, 20–21.

62. Samuel Richardson, *Clarissa or, The History of a Young Lady*, 4 vols. (London: Dent, 1932), 2: 483; hereafter cited parenthetically as *C*, followed by volume and page number.

63. Arendt, *The Human Condition*, 241.

64. Earl Miner, *The Restoration Mode from Milton to Dryden* (Princeton: Princeton University Press, 1974), 289–90.

65. George Herbert Mead, *Mind, Self and Society*, ed. Charles Morrison (1934; reprint, Chicago: Chicago University Press, 1974), 309.

66. Mead, *Mind, Self and Society*, 216.

CONCLUDING

1. Kenneth Burke, *The Rhetoric of Religion: Studies in Logology* (Boston: Beacon, 1961); Edward S. Said, *The World, the Text, and the Critic* (Cambridge, Mass.: Harvard University Press, 1987); Herbert S. Lindenberger, *Saul's Fall: A Critical Fiction* (Baltimore: Johns Hopkins University Press, 1979); *Kierkegaard's Concluding Unscientific Postscript*, trans. David F. Swenson and Walter Lowrie (Princeton: Princeton University Press, 1941).

2. Hannah Arendt, *Between Past and Future: Eight Exercises in Political Thought*, enlarged edition (Harmondsworth: Penguin, 1968), 26.

3. Arendt, *Between Past and Future*, 17–18.

4. Ibid., 7.

5. Ibid., 11.

6. Ibid.

7. *Essays: Second Series*, vol. 3, *The Collected Works of Ralph Waldo Emerson*, ed. Joseph Slater, Alfred R. Ferguson, and Jean Ferguson Carr (Cambridge, Mass., and London: Harvard University Press, 1983); hereafter cited parenthetically as *EE*, followed by volume and page numbers.

8. Arendt, *Between Past and Future*, 89.

9. David Jacobson, *Emerson's Pragmatic Vision: The Dance of the Eye* (University Park: Pennsylvania State University Press, 1993), 138.

10. Michael Oakeshott, *On Human Conduct* (Oxford: Oxford University Press, 1974), 199.

11. N. Katharine Hayles, *Chaos Bound: Orderly Disorder in Contemporary Literature and Science* (Ithaca: Cornell University Press, 1990), 265.

12. Raymond Williams, *Marxism and Literature* (Oxford: Oxford University Press, 1977), 110.

13. Ibid., 113–14.

14. Kenneth Burke, *Attitudes Toward History* (1937; reprint, Boston: Beacon, 1961), 339.

Index

In this index an "f" after a number indicates a separate reference on the next page, and an "ff" indicates separate references on the next two pages. A continuous discussion over two or more pages is indicated by a span of page numbers, e.g., "57–59." *Passim* is used for a cluster of references in close but not consecutive sequence.

Library of Congress Cataloging-in-Publication Data
Halliburton, David.
The fateful discourse of worldly things / by David Halliburton.
p.   cm.
ISBN 0-8047-2772-4 (v. 1 : alk. paper)
1. Literature—History and criticism—Theory, etc.   2. Literature—
Philosophy.   I. Title.
PN81.H24   1997
801′.95—dc21   96-37881
                                                                      CIP